No.

Verrier Elwin
Philanthropologist
SELECTED WRITINGS

Sanctuary in northern Siang

Verrier Elwin Philanthropologist

SELECTED WRITINGS

edited by

NARI RUSTOMJI

NORTH-EASTERN HILL UNIVERSITY PUBLICATIONS
SHILLONG

YMCA Library Building, Jai Singh Road, New Delhi 110 001

Oxford University Press is a department of the University of Oxford. It furthers the University's objective of excellence in research, scholarship, and education by publishing worldwide in

Oxford New York

Athens Auckland Bangkok Bogota Buenos Aires Cape Town Chennai Dar es Salaam Delhi Florence Hong Kong Istanbul Karachi Kolkata Kuala Lumpur Madrid Melbourne Mexico City Mumbai Nairobi Paris Sao Paulo Shanghai Singapore Taipei Tokyo Toronto Warsaw

with associated companies in Berlin Ibadan

Published in India
By Oxford University Press, New Delhi

First published 1989
Oxford India Paperbacks 2001

ISBN 019 565 8019

Printed by Sai Printo Pack Pvt. Ltd, New Delhi 110 020
Published by Manzar Khan, Oxford University Press
YMCA Library Building, Jai Singh Road, New Delhi 110 001

TO

VERRIER ELWIN

whose encouragement to me in his THE ART OF THE NORTH-EAST FRONTIER OF INDIA, has been an eternal inspiration. 'For Nari, pioneer and explorer in the worlds of men and ideas, whose desire that the whole of NEFA should be a work of art has been a great stimulant.'

22 September 1959. —Verrier Elwin

Preface

The idea of preparing this Anthology arose from a suggestion offered during the delivery of the Verrier Elwin Memorial Lectures before the North-Eastern Hill University at Shillong in 1985. While deploring the general neglect and lack of interest since his death in 1964 in Elwin's contribution to anthropological studies and his prodigious efforts to bring about a keener awareness of the need to do justice to the tribal people living in the remoteness of India's hills and forests, I had quoted Professor Christoph von Fürer-Haimendorf's assessment that 'no other anthropologist, neither British nor Indian, has made as massive a contribution to our knowledge of Indian tribal societies, and books such as *The Muria and Their Ghotul* and *The Religion of an Indian Tribe* are sure of a place among classics of anthropological literature. He was one of the greatest romantics of anthropology and the most inspired chronicler of India's tribal people'. I had pointed out that practically all Elwin's books including the two classics specifically referred to by Haimendorf, were out of print and, for all practical purposes, not available for the general reading public. The University thereupon took the decision to bring out Elwin's works in a uniform edition in its North-Eastern Studies Series. A decision was simultaneously taken to bring out an anthology to prepare the ground for the reprints. The University is to be congratulated for the initiative it is taking in this very worthwhile venture. Many of Elwin's books had been heavily subsidized and were seldom profitable. His wife, Leela Elwin, has been generous enough to place funds with the North-Eastern Hills University to be utilized at the University's discretion to prepetuate his memory. Elwin was, however, so remote and, if one may respectfully add, eccentric an individual that professional anthropologists have all but forgotten him within twenty years of his death. This Anthology and the reprint of his works will, it is hoped, revive interest in one of the most outstanding champions of tribal people.

On being invited to compile the anthology I sought the advice and assistance of Mr R. E. Hawkins who had been in charge of the Oxford University Press in India for the years 1937–70 and was publisher of so many of Elwin's books. Hawkins knew Elwin personally during the last thirty years of his life, and though he has very modestly declined to be named as co-author on the title-page of the book, he has, in fact, been its main architect and it has been on his advice that I have mostly depended in making the selections for this Anthology. This has not been easy as Elwin's output was not only enormous in quantity but of such a high quality that one is hesitant in deciding what can be omitted. It was on Mr Hawkin's suggestion that we decided to restrict our selections to pieces of more considerable length and significance rather than clutter the Anthology with a medley of comparatively irrelevant snippets. The bulk of the Anthology comprises Elwin's writings as an anthropologist and sociologist. But Elwin was a many-sided man and an attempt has been made to reflect also his many-sidedness, as a poet, essayist, art-connoisseur, photographer, scholar-administrator and political worker.

We feel a lengthy Preface is not called for. Elwin's writing is so personal—*le style est l'homme même*—that it is better to let the book be his story. For the reader who has not read Elwin's autobiography, *The Tribal World of Verrier Elwin*, the first two extracts of the Anthology, the Foreword to *Leaves from the Jungle* and Philanthropology, will give the broad details of Elwin's life and activities until 1955, when he was enlisted as Adviser for the tribal areas of India's North-Eastern Frontier. From 1955 until his death in 1964, Elwin was mainly preoccupied in helping to implement the policy of promoting deeper and wider respect for the culture and way of life of the tribes of India in general and of the North-Eastern Frontier in particular. Although he enjoyed no statutory powers, his influence and inspiration permeated the entire administrative fabric. The first step taken was to build up a Department of Tribal Research, to collect material and publish a series of monographs on NEFA's manifold tribes. A team of young research scholars was recruited and quickly put to work under Elwin's overall guidance. The objective was to make available to our Administrative Officers, in a compact and easily readable form, the basic data regarding the tribes amongst whom their work lay—their customs, beliefs and superstitions, their art, history and language. The more thoroughly our officers could be briefed about the tribal people, their traditional values, their aspirations, the less likely that they would cause offence through unintended indiscretions. But we also wanted the tribal people to know that their culture was important enough to be worth studying and telling the world about. For nothing is so damaging to a tribal's vitality and sense of well-being as loss of self-respect, as a devaluation in their own estimation of their own culture and heritage.

Had it not been for the inspiration of Elwin, his burning enthusiasm and his unflagging efforts, the battle for the tribes might well have taken a very different turn. Elwin's books on the art of NEFA, lavishly and beautifully illustrated by his own photographs, presented a fresh and exciting concept of the primitive tribal. The tribals' unerring instinct for colour combinations was confirmed in the reproduction of their lovely textile designs. Elwin's translations of tribal folk-poetry were also proof that their folklore was as rich in imagery as the literature of the most advanced societies.

This Anthology will, we hope, reflect something of Elwin's many-sided contribution to the tribal cause and will be a useful guide to the general reader for selecting works that may be of interest to him when the proposed uniform edition of Elwin's books is eventually published.

I can only close by expressing my deepest gratitude to Mr R. E. Hawkins for his invaluable assistance in compiling this work.

NARI RUSTOMJI

Contents

Plates

1

Leaves from the Jungle (1936)

Foreword to the Second Edition (1957)

It is over twenty years since this Diary of 'life in a Gond village' was first published, and exactly a quarter of a century since I became engrossed in the cause of tribal India. This is a long time and, reading the book on the eve of its republication, I find that there are a number of things which now require a word of explanation. There are, for example, mysterious references to some quarrel with the police, and with Bishops, for which no reason is given; there is a religious background to my adventures which would not be there if I were to write a similar book today. A little autobiography, therefore, is necessary to put the story in its proper setting, especially since (as I will show) it was not possible for me to tell it in its entirety in 1936, when the original edition was first published by John Murray.

I came to India in November 1927 and I have often been asked why. There were a number of reasons. At Oxford Indian friends had roused in me an enthusiasm for the non-violent idealism of Mahatma Gandhi, the internationalist culture of Tagore and the elevating symbolism of Indian mysticism. I knew that India was a poor country and, much as I looked forward to a donnish career at Oxford, I had begun to feel that the academic life was not enough. I was filled with a desire to do something to make reparation for what my country and my class had done to India. From childhood the ideal not only of a life of service, but a life of adventure had been held up before me. My father had been an explorer in the wilds of Africa. My mother had been nearly eaten in a cannibal village. I could hardly expect such privileges in India, yet even at this date, it was obvious that this was the country with which I was most akin and which would offer many adventures in the realm of the mind and spirit.

I did not want to be a 'missionary' in the ordinary sense of the word, but I was greatly interested in the monastic life. It so happened that about this time there was founded in Poona a monastic Ashram on liberal Christian lines which associated Indian and European members on terms of complete equality (a rather unusual thing in those days) and which was more interested in scholarship than in proselytizing. In joining it, my main interest was to study the relations between Christianity and Hinduism and to see how far Christianity in India could put on a more appropriate oriental garb. In Poona we lived in simple Indian style, wore khadi dress, went barefoot or in sandals, sat and slept on the floor, ate Indian food. We built a beautiful little Church in the style of a Hindu temple and its services followed the model of the Eastern Orthodox Church and had various oriental elements. I myself wrote a number of small books to illustrate the intimate relations between Eastern and Western mysticism: one of them, *Christian Dhyana*, compared the teachings of Yoga with those of the anonymous fourteenth-century mystic who wrote *The Cloud of Unknowing*; another expounded the ideas of Richard Rolle in terms of Indian Bhakti religion; a third tried to show how St Francis of Assisi fitted into the Indian scene. I was then a clergyman of the Church of England.

In January 1928 there occurred an event which was to disturb and change my whole life: I visited the Sabarmati Ashram and met Mahatma Gandhi.

At this time, the National Movement of India had risen to a pitch of sincerity and devotion that has rarely been equalled in the political upheavals of the world. The Ashram itself, standing on the tall banks of the Sabarmati River, was the home of some hundreds of people marked by that quiet and disciplined devotion to hard work and to the poor which has always been characteristic of the best type of Congressman. Among them Gandhiji walked in almost unearthly dignity and beauty. That was the first thing that struck me about him—his beauty, and the inner spiritual power that transformed his frail body and filled the entire place with kindliness and love.

From that moment I was doomed. Always a sympathetic fellow-traveller, I now became an ardent disciple. I took up spinning; I hoisted the Congress flag over the Poona Ashram; my sermons became a mixture of Christian and Gandhian ideals; I wrote a booklet called *Christ and Satyagraha* to show, contrary to the accepted ecclesiastical tradition of the day (that Christians were bound to accept the established order), that in fact they had more often been of the opposition and that there was no reason why they should not take part in a movement for freedom which was based on such essentially Christian ideals as Truth and Nonviolene. All this, somewhat naturally, was not regarded with any very great enthusiasm by the authorities of either State or Church.

Nothing brought home to me the subservience of the Church to the Government of the day more than the fact that when I invited Reginald Reynolds to give a lecture in the Ashram on the Gandhian philosophy, it was the Archdeacon and not the Commissioner of Police who put me on the carpet. It says much for the Christa Seva Sangh that it did not allow the constant pressure from the Church leaders and increasing irritations from the CID to turn it aside from what it felt to be right. With the full approval of the other members, for example, I entertained Mr Subhas Chandra Bose and at the end of 1929 I was allowed to accept an invitation from Sardar Vallabhbhai Patel to visit Gujarat and make an inquiry into police repression of the No-Tax Campaign that had been started there. This campaign was on a very wide scale, and the Government had taken strong measures to counter it, so strong indeed that in many places the whole population had migrated into the neighbouring Baroda State. I visited over sixty villages in five talukas—Anand, Nadiad, Borsad, Bardoli and Jalalpur—and wrote a report which appeared first in the *Bombay Chronicle* and later as a small booklet, *In the Deserted Villages of Gujarat*. In this I appealed to the 'Christian' Government to 'put all they know of the principles of Christ into the conduct of public affairs in Gujarat, so that whatever the issue of the present struggle may be, they will have preserved intact the authority of Law, the sanctity of Justice and left behind no heritage of bitter memories'.

I spent long periods in the Sabarmati Ashram, and during the following year it gradually became evident that I was drifting away from my friends in Poona and was an increasing embarrassment to them. I decided to leave the Christa Seva Sangh and start on my own.

But not entirely on my own. While I was at Poona, the Ashram attracted to its membership a number of remarkable Indians, among whom was one who was to be my lifelong friend and ally. This was Shamrao Hivale, whose name appears frequently in these pages, and who needs, therefore, a few words of introduction.

Shamrao was born in Madhe near Sholapur and when this Diary opens was about thirty years of age. He was educated at the Wilson High School in Bombay and at the Rajaram College, Kolhapur; his brother Dr B. P. Hivale is well known in western India as the founder of a flourishing College in Ahmednagar. Shamrao accompanied me on the Gujarat inquiry in 1929 and we have worked together ever since, except for a brief interlude in 1931 when he went to England to study at Mirfield for Holy Orders. This project he abandoned on hearing that I had left the Christa Seva Sangh, and when Gandhiji came to London for the Round Table Conference he joined his party and travelled back to India with him.

Shamrao has an extraordinary warmth and humanity about him, and within a very short time of our arrival in Karanjia he had established himself as the Chhota Bhai, the little brother of the people, and as their guide, philosopher and friend. It soon became the custom for any tribesman who was in trouble to 'go to Chhota Bhai' for help and he has brought comfort and reassurance into many thousands of lives. Once, when an old woman lay dying, she would not see any of her relations but called continually for Shamrao. One day a Gond friend said to him: 'Before you came here the moustaches of those who oppressed us turned up to the sky, but now they droop to the ground.' He has never been an outsider; he is never superior; never looks down on anyone or tries to 'uplift' him. To him every individual is a world and he accepts each child or growing youth or poor old woman, not as a 'case' but as a human personality, a sacred thing to be respected and loved, in whose sorrows and anxieties he himself must share. He is always accessible and in Karanjia used to be compared to a Hindu widow (old style) at the beck and call of everyone who wanted him, no task being too small, too humble or to unpleasant.

Some years ago he wrote a vidid monograph on a tribe allied to the Gonds, *The Pardhans of the Upper Narbada Valley*. For he has the advantage over many professional anthropologists in having the complete confidence of his people, in being able to live among them and watch their fortunes year after year, in speaking their language perfectly, and in having a great store of imaginative sympathy in his heart. If I have sometimes gently pulled his leg in the Diary that follows, that is the privilege of many years of friendship.

I was, of course, deprived of his advice during 1931 when I was trying to make up my mind what I should do. Some of my friends wanted me to follow in the footsteps of C. F. Andrews as a free-lance semi-political worker. I myself had an idea of going to live among the untouchables and trying to do something for them—it will be remembered that untouchability was a very live issue at that time. Then one day as I was driving through the streets of Ahmedabad with Sardar Vallabhbhai Patel and Seth Jamnalal Bajaj, I heard for the first time in my life—from the lips of Jamnalalji—the magic word 'Gond'. He urged me to go to the Central Provinces and take up the cause of the tribes who were then almost entirely neglected. We discussed the matter with Gandhiji and he approved.

In October, therefore. I set out on a long tour with Acharya Kripalani, partly to search for a suitable place for a settlement in the Gond area of Betul and Chhindwara, and partly to spread the message of khadi and the Gandhian ideal in general. We travelled widely in the Central and United Provinces, as they were then called, pursued everywhere by the police and reported, generally incorrectly, by the CID. In Betul and Chhindwara, official opposition was so strong that none of the local landlords, sympathetic as they were, dared to give us land. We completed the tour at the end of December and went down to Bombay to welcome Gandhiji—and Shamrao—on their return from England.

What happened then is still vivid in my memory and I will quote an account of it that I wrote at the time, for Gandhiji's arrest had a profound effect both on my own thinking and on my later fortunes.

Gandhiji was staying in a house called Mani Bhuvan and he invited Shamrao and myself to stay with him there. There was great excitement in the city; the Viceroy had finally rejected the Congress offer of peace, and the arrest of national leaders was expected at any moment.

But when we reached Mani Bhuvan and climbed to the roof, we found a great serenity in astonishing contrast to the crowds and turmoil outside. The roof is a charming place. Low tents have been erected, and there are palms and plants: at least 300 people can gather there. It is cool and you can see the stars. Bapu was sitting at the wheel, quietly spinning. He had already begun his weekly silence. I carried on a one-sided conversation with him, and he wrote down his questions and replies. Shamrao thanked him for his kindness to him on the voyage. Then Shamrao and I retired to the smaller tent and Bapu lay down about three yards from us, while some thirty others lay on the roof under the canvas shelter. Mrs Gandhi and Mirabehn gave us a delicious supper of dates, nuts and fruit. But I could not sleep. I felt I had to keep vigil, and for hours I was under those splendid stars that rose, tier upon tier above me, while beside me Bapu slept like a child committed to his Father's hands. I thought of Christ going up to Jerusalem, his eyes filled with determination and courage: and I seemed to see the Spirit of Christ travelling the centuries like a bright sword turned against all wrong and injustice. Among these sleeping friends so dear to us, brave, pure-hearted, sincere, the spirit of Love was manifest and unconquerable.

At last I lay down on a hastily improvised bed, and fell into a heavy sleep. It seemed as if I had slept all my life when suddenly like the coming of a dream there was a stir and a whisper: 'The police have come.' We started up and I saw what I will never forget—a fully uniformed Commissioner of Police at the foot of Bapu's bed, and Bapu just waking, a little bewildered, looking old, fragile and rather pathetic with the mists of sleep still on his face. 'Mr Gandhi, it is my duty to arrest you.' A beautiful smile of welcome broke out on Bapu's face and now he looked young, strong and confident. He made signs to show that he was keeping silence. The Commissioner smiled and with great courtesy said, "I should like you to be ready in half an hour's time.' It was five minutes past three. Bapu looked at his watch and the Commissioner said, 'Ah, the famous watch!' And they both laughed heartily. Bapu took a pencil and wrote, 'I will be ready to come with you in half an hour.' The Commissioner laid his hand on Bapu's shoulder with a gesture so full of affection that I thought it was an embrace, until I realized that it was the formal token of arrest. Bapu then cleaned his teeth and retired for a moment. The door was guarded, but all of us who were on the roof sat round in a circle. I looked out onto the road where some had been keeping all-night vigil and where a little crowd, very quiet and orderly, had collected, but there were no special police precautions. Bapu then sat in the midst of us for the prayers and we sang together the Song of the true Vaishnava. Then Bapu took pencil and paper and wrote a few messages, some last instructions to his followers and a letter to Sardar Vallabhbhai, which was as follows: 'Infinite is God's mercy' (these were the first words to be written after his arrest). 'Please tell the people never to swerve from truth and non-violence. Never to flinch, but to give their lives and all to win Swaraj.' He then wrote a short note and gave it to me:

My dear Elwyn,

I am so glad you have come. I would like you yourself to tell your countrymen that I love them even as I love my own countrymen. I have never done anything towards them in hatred or malice and God willing I shall never do anything in that manner in future. I am acting no differently towards them now from what I have done under similar circumstances towards my own kith and kin.

with love
yours
M. K. Gandhi

Then Bapu stood up to take farewell. It was a strange sight. The police at the door, Mirabehn and Devadas bustling to and fro with the baggage which was already packed, Bapu surrounded by his friends, many of them in tears. Mrs Gandhi with tears running down her cheeks said, 'Can't you take me with you?' Everyone in turn touched his feet, and when I said goodbye he pulled my ear with a beautiful smile and gave me quite a good slap on the side of my face. He was full of joy and laughter. Then, followed by the whole company, he went downstairs. But Shamrao and I watched from the roof. The tiny figure got into the car and the crowd surged round it. It was a wonderful tribute to India's non-violence that there were only a few policemen and they were able to be in the midst of the crowd without fear of danger. Just at that moment a message came to say that Sardar Vallabhbhai, the Congress President, was also arrested. And then the crowd scattered as the car bearing the very soul of India drove away through the dark and deserted streets.

Among the instructions scribbled for Mahadeo Desai after the arrest was one asking me to go to the North-West Frontier Province to discover what was really happening there. Disquieting reports had filtered down to Bombay about the severe repression of the 'Red Shirt' Movement and since no journalists were admitted and all press reports were strictly censored, there was great concern about the fate of the brave warlike Pathans who had so surprisingly adopted Gandhiji's non-violent technique. The following week, therefore, Shamrao and I left Bombay for Peshawar.

There is no room here to tell of our adventures, which were exciting, nor of our discoveries which were little to the credit of the local police and military. We visited Kohat and Utmanzai and a number of other villages, and on the last day went up the Khyber Pass. On our return, I was arrested, my things were searched, and we were deported from the Province under the escort of a dozen armed policemen.

One thing that gave me great satisfaction was that I managed to hide all my notes, as well as certain papers which would have brought some of the Peshawar people into trouble had they been found, in a packet of Force. This stood, like Poe's Purloined Letter, in full view on a table in our room, and though the police searchers went through everything else with humiliating attention, they ignored the innocent-looking packet of breakfast cereal. I carried it down in triumph to Bombay and was able to write and publish a report in consequence. This was immediately declared forfeit to His Majesty and, though it was reissued in London later, for many years even I myself was unable to get a copy.

Now in Bombay we had to face another problem. Shamrao had returned from England and sacrificed his higher education to work for the tribal people. My own inclination was in the same direction. But now, and specially since Gandhiji's arrest and my own deportation, a good deal of pressure was put on me to enter politics. For example, at this time the Congress was planning to appoint a series of Presidents which would include members of every community, and Jamnalalji asked me if I would be willing to become President when it was the turn of an Englishman to occupy that high office. It would not, he pointed out, mean a great deal of work, for I would certainly be arrested and imprisoned within a week. I told him that I was willing and I have sometimes wondered what would have happened if I had gone through with it.

But when Shamrao and I talked it over, we came to the conclusion that this was not really our line. I have always been a little doubtful of the value of the intervention of European political amateurs in matters at which they are not expert. And so we decided to keep to our original plan of going into the Gond country in the Central Provinces.

As I had been unable to get land in Betul and most of my friends were now in jail, I asked the Bishop of Nagpur (for it must be remembered I was still a loyal, if somewhat heretical, member of the Church of England) for his advice. This was Bishop Wood, a brave, strong man, with a sincere affection for the tribes and an equal devotion to the British Government. His biographer says of him: 'How fully he had won the confidence of Government is evident from the fact that in his third year in India he was awarded the Kaiser-i-Hind Medal.' In his dealings with us he fully justified that confidence.

The Bishop recommended Karanjia, a Gond village in the Maikal Hills, as particularly suitable for me. Of the last five Europeans to stay there, he pointed out with relish, four had died within a year. This sounded very much what we wanted, and so on the 28th of January 1932 Shamrao and I started out and I began the diary recorded in the following pages.

It is easy to find the position of the little village of Karanjia even on a map of the world. Trace the course of the great Narbada River from its mouth on the west coast to its sacred source amid the eastern spurs of the Satpura Hills. Go a hair's breadth from its tail and there is Karanjia.

As described in the Diary, we were fortunate to find a little hill overlooking the Pilgrim's Way that goes up to Amarkantak, eleven miles distant, where the Narbada River rises, and here we built the small huts of mud, wattle and thatch which constituted the 'Ashram'. In those early days all round us lay the vast mysterious forest, whose silence was broken at night only by the roar of the tiger or the high melancholy call of the deer.

The Ashram looked exactly like part of the village which lay around and below it, for it was our policy from the first to build everything in the Gond style. All the houses were of mud and thatch, the walls covered with Gond decorations, and there was no furniture which could not be matched in the village itself. At the same time, the Ashram was different, in that it attempted to demonstrate what a village might be like. The huts were clean and well-ventilated, everywhere there were flowers and fruit trees, proper houses for poultry and cattle, and many pits for refuse and manure. There was a good system of pit latrines. The Gond visitor therefore found himself perfectly at home, and yet at the same time, even without a word being spoken, had the chance to learn something that he could take back to his own village.

Entering the settlement by a long flight of steps, you came first to a tiny mud chapel of St Francis which was used by the Christian members of the Ashram. The Ashram was founded on a principle of complete religious equality and toleration; it was not of course a missionary society: its members were drawn from all communities: but no one was asked to surrender the tenets of his faith, or to cease its practice. We did not, in fact, aim at a syncretistic unifying of theologies, but rather at demonstrating that it was possible for believers in different religions to live and work together as one family. Our Mussalman was a good Mussalman; our Hindu members observed the tenets of their religion; and in the same way the Christian members tried to follow, however imperfectly, the ideals of St Francis of Assisi.

The Chapel of St Francis was a tiny building in the middle of a large court, in the front part of which was the library, office and sitting-rooms. The whole was surrounded by a high wall. In front of the chapel was a flagstaff (essential to any place of worship in the Gondwana) carrying the saffron flag of renunciation, and at its foot on a little cow-dunged platform grew the sacred *tulsi* tree. Round the chapel was the flower-garden, in memory of St Francis' wish that gardens should be made so that all who saw them should remember the Eternal Beauty. In front of the whole building was the place of the morning and evening prayer, on the edge of the hill, and from here there was a wonderful view of forest, valley and mountain.

You went along the hill, which was sheltered by trees, many of them laden with sweet-smelling flowers, and reached the dispensary—*Premayatna*, the House of Compassion. This was well equipped with medicines and villagers came to it from a radius of forty miles. It was the only dispensary along a main road of seventy-five miles, but there was a small Government dispensary across country twenty miles away.

Next came the Refectory for resident members which again, following the Gond style, was made up of three little huts—a kitchen, dining-room and store-house. Round the Refectory was a vegetable garden, and fruit trees were planted in the neighbourhood of all the buildings—mango, plantain, papaya, orange, fig, sour-lime, guava. Next door was the *Mitralaya*, House of Friendship, where in-patients, pilgrims and other visitors could stay, and opposite was a chicken-run and the House of the Bull, where an attempt was made to improve the breed of the village livestock. Farther along the hill was the *Ajib-khana*, or Place of Wonders, in other words the Museum, a very popular building, and then came the largest of our establishments, the *Vidyamandir*, literally Temple of Knowledge, or in plain English, the School. There was room for fifty boarders and a hundred others. The school was co-educational and a very fair proportion of girls attended. Here also was the carpenter's shop and the tailoring department. Beyond the school the hill became wild and thickly wooded, and the little path wound in and out of trees till it reached a gate beyond which no one might go without permission. This was the Leper Refuge, where fifteen or sixteen lepers lived and received treatment in a beautiful little home, with a garden in which they took great pride.

This was the centre. Round it, hidden away in remote valleys or in the midst of the forest, there were eight branch Ashrams within a radius of as many miles. Each of these had its resident worker, school, Hindi library and small dispensary, fitted with the simplest medicines. Once a week all the workers gathered at Karanjia for conference. Model classes were given, and the plan of work for the coming week decided. This was necessary because the workers were themselves villagers without any very advanced education, and in this way they not only took their part in the fight against illiteracy, but they also trained themselves to be leaders of their own people. There were between three and four hundred children in the schools, most of them belonging to the Gond and other tribes.

The prevention of disease is of primary importance in India. In every school we had regular courses of lectures about the human body, sanitation, and the common diseases. Anti-malarial measures are not very successful in a forest area, since short of cutting down the trees it is impossible to destory the breeding-places of mosquitoes, but we managed to sell a good many mosquito-nets (a real triumph) and of course the distribution of quinine never ceased. Water-borne diseases were also a constant menace, and we had a programme of well-making in villages where the water supply was bad. Another great enemy was venereal diseases, and simple sex-teaching was of great importance.

At this time, therefore, we saw things very simply: we had to work for the health of the community, we had to see that there was enough food and that it was properly cooked, then we had to help the people to get more money, and finally we had to give them sufficient knowledge and of the right kind to enable them to use their leisure properly. The first of these aims is secured by dispensaries, health propaganda, and the cleaning of villages; the second by the improvement of agriculture and the education of girls, specially if they can be given some training in the domestic arts and sciences. The third and fourth are to no small extent the fruits of education. The educated Gond is less likely to be swindled when he takes his goods to market; if he has learnt a little carpentry or tailoring he can make a few things for sale, or at least mend his clothes and so make them last longer; and he will not waste his money (if his education has been on proper lines) on weddings, funerals, litigation and caste-dinners. We found that one of the great difficulties in improving the lot of the villager was that as soon as we helped him to make a little money he poured it away on some tribal extravagance. Here caste had proved a great curse to the tribes, and large sums of money were wasted in expensive penalty dinners for every kind of fault.

My use of the word 'caste' will surprise those who in Assam, for example, have been accustomed to regard the tribes as altogether outside the caste-system. But the Gonds of the Mandla District were largely detribalized; they had lost their own language, worshipped Hindu gods, dressed like the ordinary peasants of the neighbourhood. It was taboo for them to weave. Their culture was concentrated in the dance and song, at which they were very good. And, as the reader will note, the Gond villages had a number of non-tribals living in them; there were Mussalmans, Hindu merchants, liquor-vendors, landlords, moneylenders and others. We could hardly have chosen a less favourable place for the preservation of 'museum specimens', had that really been our intention. When we went to Karanjia, I had never—so far as I remember—opened a book on anthropology: our interest was entirely humanitarian.

I have had to give the political, as I shall shortly give the religious, background of our history, for a special reason. It will be noted that there is a gap in the Diary between the 15th of June and the 1st of November 1932. During this period, I went to

Europe, partly for family reasons but mainly to do something to acquaint people in the West with what was happening in India. I contacted sympathizers with India in France and Italy, and in England gave lectures and met a number of those who we thought might be able to help towards a speedy solution, including Lord Irwin and Lord Sankey, then Lord Chancellor. The Secretary of State for India, Sir Samuel Hoare, however, refused to see me; it would be improper, he said, for him to do so, in view of my criticisms of his administration.

But Sir Samuel was not content with this, for when the time came for my return to India, I was informed by the Passport Office that 'in accordance with a request made by the Secretary of State for India' I could not be given passport facilities for my return to what I already regarded as my home. I was ultimately only allowed to return on condition that I would not take part in any kind of politics, would not associate (as far as possible) with persons engaged in political agitation, and would refrain from writing against the Government. I agreed to this because I felt that our work for the tribal people was, for us, more important than amateur interference in political affairs. Although some of my friends, notably C. F. Andrews, thought I was wrong, Gandhiji himself approved, and I remember Sir Francis Younghusband was good enough to say a few years later: 'I will always be grateful to Sam Hoare for one thing at least, that he forced Elwin from politics to poetry.'

But at the time these restrictions were irksome enough. When I wrote *Leaves from the Jungle*, I was still under police surveillance and living under the obligations imposed by my undertaking. This meant that I had to omit many curious and even exciting incidents, and readers of the first edition must sometimes have wondered what my occasional references to police raids and conflicts with the Church were about. Another result was that I had to give a rather inaccurate picture of those early days, which were much less peaceful than the reader would suppose.

For example, all that the Diary has to say of the first week of February 1932 is that we were settling into our goat-shed and fighting fleas. In fact, we were up against a more formidable enemy. I received a letter from the Deputy Commissioner which I have always regarded as a little masterpiece of official brevity. 'The Commissioner', he wrote, 'has asked me to inform you that in view of your political record we do not want you in this District.' I replied that we were doing nothing worthy of death or bonds and would remain until he removed us by force. We posted sentries to warn us of the approach of the police, but when they did actually come, on the 2nd of March, they decided to let us be.

The same week, however, on the day we opened the Dispensary, I got another letter, this time from the Bishop, telling me that the Commissioner had applied for my deportation from India and demanding that I should take an Oath of Allegiance to the King-Emperor and that I should 'separate myself absolutely' from the Congress Party. There is no hint in the Diary of the long discussions Shamrao and I had about this; I naturally refused both demands. And in the first edition, I considerably modified the manuscript account of an interview, on the 10th of May 1932, with some clerical visitors, but I have restored the original in this new version, for it is the kind of incident that reveals why it was we had to leave the Church.

Nor do I refer anywhere in the Diary to one of my preoccupations of the first months in Karanjia, when seated on the ground before my typewriter I tapped out with two fingers a book called *Truth about India*, which was published in London and helped to bring home to people there the justice of India's cause.

And towards the end of the Diary, in the entry for the 2nd of November 1935, which records the behaviour of our Rhode Islander cocks, there is no reference to the writing of what was for me a momentous letter to the Metropolitan in Calcutta, announcing to him 'my decision to be no longer a member of the Church of England either as a priest or a communicant'. To explain this I must say a little, not in any spirit of controversy but simply to make the story clear, about religion.

Looking back, I find it curious to recall that even when I was in the Christa Seva Sangh, I took the same attitude towards religious propaganda that I now, under the Prime Minister's inspiration, take towards any other interference in the life and culture of the tribal people. 'I am alarmed', the Prime Minister has said, 'when I see how anxious people are to shape others according to their own image or likeness, and to impose on them their particular way of living. We are welcome to our way of life, but why impose it on others? There would be more peace in the world if people were to desist from imposing their way of living on other people and countries.' This was the first and fundamental cause of conflict with the Church: that I refused to make converts.

At the same time, I was deeply, almost passionately religious and was specially attached to the mystical aspects of the Catholic religion and to that Christian Neo-Platonism which in its attachment to the Good, the True and the Beautiful, rises above communal and creedal restrictions. But a Neo-Platonic attitude is not easily reconcilable with Catholic orthodoxy, which claims absolute and exclusive truth for its teachings. My contact with Mahatma Gandhi and his followers, however, apart from anything else, made it impossible to believe that there was only one way to Heaven.

It is not surprising that these ideas did not commend themselves to the ecclesiastical authorities, and from the time I left the Christa Seva Sangh, we were in constant conflict with them. At the same time, my own ideas were changing. Long before, I had found it impossible to believe that salvation was confined to only one religion; gradually I came to question the very foundations of that religion. There is no doubt that the alliance of the Church of England with the British Imperialism of the day and the support it gave to the suppression of the National Movement did much to shake my confidence in it. The entire missionary enterprise became more and more distasteful to me. But the thing went deeper than that.

I once had a talk with the famous theologian Bishop Gore, who himself was at one time widely attacked for his liberal views. I expressed difficulty in accepting various miracles supposed to have been performed by the medieval saints and questioned certain passages in the Bible. 'All this, my dear boy', he said, 'is nothing. The real snag in the Christian, or any religion, is the belief in God. If you can swallow God, you can swallow anything.' I began to find it difficult to swallow all sorts of theological, mythological and so-called historical ideas and facts, and I came to the conclusion that it was no longer honest for me to remain in the Church. As early as December 1932 I wrote to the Bishop of Nagpur that I would not apply for a licence to function as a clergyman. Three years later I informed the Metropolitan that I did not regard myself as even an ordinary member of the Church. In 1936 I visited England and after consulting Archbishop Temple, who had always treated me with the greatest sympathy, I signed what is called a 'Deed of Relinquishment' under the Clerical Disabilities Act of 1870, whereby I relinquished 'all rights, privileges, advantages and exemptions of my office as by law belonging to it'.

I have given a very brief account of what was in fact a long, complicated and sometimes painful story, but I have never regretted this passage in my life's history. The act of relinquishment brought me a hitherto undreamt-of intellectual freedom; it adjusted many complexes and inhibitions; it was a kind of conversion in reverse, integrating me and filling me with new life. Now I was free to devote myself to the task of scientific inquiry and to the service of the tribal people in the spirit of science. No single act in my whole life has brought me greater happiness.

It has been necessary to refer to this, even at the risk of giving pain to some of my old friends, for otherwise the re-issue of this book, which has a certain religious background, might well give a wrong idea of my present position and outlook; indeed in the press I am still sometimes called a missionary, a circumstance which must be as embarrassing to the missionaries as to myself. It will now, however, be clear that for twenty years I have belonged to no religious body and in fact have held no religious faith of any kind.

And yet perhaps my attitude to life cannot be called altogether irreligious. I have a sincere respect for all true religion and I was deeply moved, for example, when I visited recently the Buddhist monastery at Tawang and found simple tribal people revealing in their daily lives the virtues of compassion, sympathy, gentleness and universal friendliness taught by the Lord Buddha. I have learnt much from a study of the sacred books of the Hindus. The true ideals of Christ are desperately needed in a world in danger of self-extermination through violence. Many of Mahatma Gandhi's teachings sank far into my heart and mind, and I have tried to practise some of them, though without much success, throughout my life. This is why I have agreed to this new edition of *Leaves from the Jungle*. I no longer hold the faith that inspired me during the four years it describes, yet those years were part of my life and represent something real and vital in it.

A final thing that strikes me as I re-read the pages of the Diary that follows is that I seem to have spent much of my time falling ill. I attribute this to the fact that in those days I was a non-smoker. Since I took to the cheroot, I have not had a single attack of malaria, and my health improved enormously in later years.

In 1936 we moved from Karanjia to another village. There was no chapel in our new settlement. We became interested in anthropology, or rather in what Haddon once called philanthropology. We changed the name of our little society to the Tribal Welfare and Research Unit and reconstituted it. I spent a lot of time in Bastar and later, in the lovely hills of Orissa. At the end of 1953 I was called to the urgent and fascinating task of acting as Adviser for Tribal Affairs to the North-East Frontier Agency, and at the same time I became legally what I had been so long in spirit, an Indian citizen.

Someday I may be able to tell the story of the twenty years since 1936. I hope so, for they have been happy, wonderful years, and they have never been happier than they are today.

Shillong V. E.

2

Philanthropology

The Tribal World of Verrier Elwin (1964)

His anthropology might be called Philanthropology. His great service to science was to lay the foundations and to build the framework of anthropology well and truly on sound scientific principles; his service to humanity was to show that 'the proper study of Mankind' is to discover Man as a human being, whatever the texture of his hair, the colour of his skin or the shape of his skull.

—A. H. Quiggin, *Haddon the Head-hunter*

I

I was once introduced at a cocktail party to the wife of a British Colonel as an anthropologist. We sat down together on a sofa but I noticed that the lady squeezed herself into a corner as far away as possible and kept shooting furtive glances at me. Presently, however, after she had strengthened herself with three pink gins, she leant over and in a confidential and slightly guilty whisper asked me, 'Tell me, Dr Elwin, is anthropology very prevalent in your district?'

I am essentially a scholar, a research man. There are few greater pleasures than getting a footnote just right or correcting the items in a bibliography, no dismay more upsetting than to find uncorrected misprints in your final, unalterable, copy. I have had to live far away from libraries, but old friends like B. S. Kesavan, who has transformed the National Library in Calcutta, and gentle, learned Saurin Roy at the National Archives have kept me in touch and made available almost unobtainable books.

Had I not gone to the forest, I might have developed into the typical pedant; even as it is, I take enormous pains over everything I write and, until I came to Shillong, I used to write or type everything over and over again myself. I took as my exemplar Addison hurrying all the way from his rooms at Magdalen to the Clarendon Press to correct a single letter in proof. I make mistakes, of course, but I try not to, and I check and recheck every item of information: I revised my book on Nagaland no fewer than thirteen times.

I have read a great deal of anthropology in the last thirty years. But unlike the professional anthropologists of today I did not begin with it. My interest in human beings began with literature and my first teachers were Jane Austen and Swift. What a wealth of sociological information and analysis can be found in *Pride and Prejudice* or *Gulliver's Travels*! And later, curiously enough, my studies in theology developed my interest in Man. The science of God led me to the science of human beings. I read a little history, philosophy and psychology: they too prepared the way.

My studies of Hinduism in Poona were also of great benefit. The majority of the tribal people outside Assam have been profoundly influenced by that great religion and it is not possible to understand them without knowing what it is about.

Anthropology is a very big subject, the science of man, man as a whole. We need different kinds of people to study it. We need the scholar trained in pre-history, archaeology, the exact measurement of physical characters, biology, statistics. But we also need some who come from a humanist background and I think it is unfortunate that nowadays what I may call the technical anthropologists look down on the humanist anthropologists though I must admit that the latter fully return the compliment.

From the very beginning I was attracted by the practical application of anthropology and encouraged by the life of A. C. Haddon of Cambridge, than whom there could not have been a more exact scientist. The extract which I have quoted at the head of this chapter suggests that there is nothing whatever hostile to scientific inquiry in having an intense and affectionate interest in the people one studies, in desiring their progress and welfare and in regarding them as human beings rather than as laboratory specimens.

The essence and art of anthropology is love. Without it, nothing is fertile, nothing is true.

For me anthropology did not mean 'field work': it meant my whole life. My method was to settle down among the people, live with them, share their life as far as an outsider could, and generally do several books together. My Baiga book took me seven years, *The Agaria* ten. I spent ten years on my first collection of folktales and fourteen on the *Folk-Songs of Chhattisgarh*. And they were all going on at the same time. This meant that I did not depend merely on asking questions, but knowledge of the people gradually sank in until it was part of me.

And with knowledge came the desire to help. It was my realization of the psychological and economic impoverishment of the Baigas that led me to question the entire forest policy about shifting cultivation, which I have now examined in many parts of tribal India. It was initially the study of the Agarias that impressed me with the urgent need of encouraging the small cottage industries which were at one time in danger of disappearing altogether. A study of the Santals and Uraons equally impressed on me the importance of encouraging the few existing arts of the people. Some administrators were disturbed at the suspicious and even hostile attitude of tribes like the Bondos and Saoras towards outsiders. It was only when I had studied them very fully that I realized that they were not being merely bloody-minded, but that their apprehension was due to deep-rooted religious and magical ideas. Even the study of folktales and myths, which some people regard as unworthy of the notice of a serious scholar, brought home to me the importance of the fears and anxieties of the people and the need to ensure that we did nothing that would intensify them.

There are, of course, some fields of investigation which can and should be entirely academic, but in India at the present time, where, as a result of the great Five-Year Plans, the tribal people are being very rapidly changed and merged into ordinary society, I believe that we should put every possible anthropologist and sociologist into the work of guiding development and training its agents. This need not mean any lowering of the standards of research, still less a bias towards any particular theory. For it is the glory of science to direct the radiance of truth into the dark places of human life and transform them.

II

One of the things that roused great suspicion among the pandits was that I came to anthropology through poetry. I still cannot see what was wrong with this. The chief problem of the student of man is to find his way underneath the surface; he has to 'dig' people. Poetry is the revealer, the unveiler; by heightening a man's own sensitivity, by opening to him the treasures of the imagination, it increases his powers of sympathy and understanding. And when his people are (as they were in the Maikal Hills) themselves poets by temperament, there is a link between him and them; they talk the same language, love the same things.

Ever since I left Oxford poetry has been my inseparable companion. It has brought me 'in hours of weariness sensations sweet'; comforted and restored me in stormy weather; filled times of loneliness and illuminated all that has been dull and dark. Like Keats, I cannot exist without Eternal Poetry to fill the day.

Now, feeling as I did, when I first went to live in the tribal hills of India, with my Wordsworth, my T. S. Eliot, my Blake and Shakespeare burning like torches in my little mud house, it was natural that I should look about me for poetry. And I soon found it, for among these gentle and romantic tribal people, poetry jumps out at you. It is there everywhere, in their eyes, on their lips, even in some of their actions. And so now poetry became, from something external to be admired, part of me, a personal possession, and whatever I have done in the name of poetry comes from the work I have done with my tribal poet-friends.

I found the people talking poetry. An old woman speaks of fire as a flower blossoming on a dry tree, of an umbrella as a peacock with one leg. Children playing round the fire at night ask each other riddles which are sometimes real poems. Chillies are red and green birds sitting on a bush; a lamp is a little sparrow that scatters its feathers about the house. A man, speaking of his pregnant wife, says to me, 'She must be treated as a flower, or the light may fade from her blossom.' Young lovers sing poems to each other across the fields, arranging an elopement in verse, discussing their love in poetic symbols. The grain in the fields is beautified: the smallest of the millets is sweet as a lotus; tiny as it is, when it is cooked with milk it swaggers about. The forest herbs are personified; one has a shaven head, another long tresses hanging to the ground, a third parts her hair. The poorest cot has legs of gold and a frame of jewels when a lovely girl is sleeping on it.

My very first 'tribal' book was a joint venture by Shamrao

and myself, called *Songs of the Forest*, which was published by Allen & Unwin with a kindly foreword by Sir Francis Younghusband. Although once I have finished a book I can rarely look at it again, I still read this one as well as my other translations with genuine pleasure, for many of the songs are beautiful by any standard. In the Mandla hills we had the immense advantage of talking a dialect of Hindi called Chhattisgarhi which proved very easy to learn and which we still talk at home. This meant that there was immediate and familiar contact with the people all the time.

Later, I published two other collections of folk-songs, one, (jointly with Shamrao)—*Folk-Songs of the Maikal Hills* in 1944, and another, *Folk-Songs of Chhattisgarh* two years later. Both were substantial volumes, one of 439 pages, the other of 527. I dedicated the first to W. G. Archer, and he wrote a long Comment for the second, which I regard as the finest statement about tribal poetry that has yet been made.

My method of translation was to be very simple and to be careful not to add any new images to the original. Arthur Waley says of his own method, 'Above all, considering images to be the soul of poetry, I have avoided either adding images of my own or suppressing those of the original.' A good example of the danger of breaking this rule may be seen in the work of Dryden, whose translations are really remarkable original poems suggested by classic models. In his famous stanza on Fortune occur the lines:

> I can enjoy her while she's kind;
> But when she dances in the wind,
> And shakes her wings and will not stay,
> I puff the prostitute away.

This is supposed to be a translation of the twenty-ninth Ode of the Third Book of Horace. But the excellent line which was so much admired by Thackeray—'I puff the prostitute away'—is represented in the original simply by the words *resigno quae dedit*. Thus a new image is added to the poem, for which there is no warrant. Caution in this matter is all the more important when we consider the essential place that symbolism holds in village poetry.

I followed as well as I could the example of Arthur Waley and worked on the principles laid down by W. G. Archer, that is to say, to avoid rhyme and make no attempt to reproduce the form of the original. I tried to represent the meaning as literally as possible, within the limits of the demands of poetry, and was scrupulous in introducing no new image.

Bill Archer, in his book on Uraon folk-poetry, *The Dove and the Leopard*, makes many comparisons with my translations of Baiga, Pardhan and Gond poems. He considers that the poetry of these different tribes is of the same general type but differs remarkably in technique. There is in Uraon poetry no two-lined verse such as is common among the Baigas, nor do we find the custom (which was also common in Hebrew poetry) of rhyming thought, in which one line parallels the next. If we define a love-poem as the expression of rapture, Baiga poems are as obviously love-songs as Uraon poems are not. 'It is the necessity of sex rather than the charm of love which dominates Uraon songs.'

It is a very great pity, and I entirely accept any criticisms that may be made of me on this account, that we have not been able to publish the originals of these poems. It would have made the books far too unwieldy had we done so immediately, but we had an enormous pile of papers containing the originals in Devanagari script, which Shamrao was preparing for the printer. Unfortunately, in one of our absences on tour a great storm destroyed many of our things and these precious originals were among them. The songs were not of any particular linguistic value, for none of them were translated from the obscure tribal languages but, at the same time, they would have been of artistic and literary interest and as a result of their disappearance I cannot claim too much for the volumes of translations, although they contain a great deal of commentary which is of some sociological value.

III

My first large work was *The Baiga* which John Murray published with the help of a subsidy from the Dorabji Tata Trust. Previously Dr and Mrs C. G. Seligman, to whom I look back as my real inspiration in this field, had helped me to publish an article on Baiga dreams in the *British Journal of Medical Psychology* and I later did a second article for the same journal on the Vagina Dentata.

It was rather thrilling writing *The Baiga* and it had a remarkably good press, indeed the praise it received now seems to me somewhat extravagant. But like all the work we did at that time there was a certain atmosphere of enthusiasm and excitement which was, I think, infectious.

To be among the Baigas was like living in the middle of a fairy story. Of all the tribes I know they are the most possessed by their mythology. And these myths were not just interesting tales tacked on to the fringe of their life. They were alive; every one of them was continually being put into action. When the Baiga was summoned to control a man-eating tiger, he faced this dangerous task with the more courage because he knew that the duty had been his from the beginning. When he performed magic on behalf of the Gond farmers, he recited the myth of the creation of the world and reminded his hearers of the unique share his tribe had in it. The myth breathed life into ancient custom; it made the unintelligible real; it turned the ancient heroes into contemporaries.

The founder of the tribe and its great hero was Nanga Baiga. Born on the Hill of Elephants, from the womb of Mother Earth, beneath a clump of bamboos, and nursed by the divine Bamboo Girl who gave him a golden axe to play with, Nanga Baiga appeared just when he was wanted. The Creator had made the world, spreading it on the face of the primeval ocean like an enormous, flat chapati; he had called the wind to harden its surface, but the wind is blind (that is why it is always knocking things over and banging against people) and did not finish the work. He called Bhimsen to put the mountains in place, but Bhimsen was always drunk and was so heavy that he kept on putting his foot through the thin surface. Nothing could make the earth firm and steady. It wobbled. It was like a broken spider's web.

So the Creator sent for Nanga Baiga. When he came and put his foot on the edge, the world tipped up—as they say the USA tipped up when Bernard Shaw landed in New York. But Nanga Baiga soon put things right. He got four great nails and drove them into the four corners of the earth and after that it was firm and steady. Then Nanga Baiga helped in the creation of the rest of mankind; it was through him that seed came to the world; he instituted magic; organized the social and economic life of man; established control over the wild animals. He was the first real man.

No wonder that the Baiga, tracing his descent from such distinguished ancestry, has an air about him. A king (or perhaps I should say an archbishop) is always peeping through his loop'd and window'd raggedness. And still today he is *the* magician and medicine-man, the classic type, who acts as intermediary between the other tribes and their gods. He is sent for by the Gonds to charm fertility into their reluctant seed; he is consulted even by Brahmins in time of sickness; it is believed that he can divert hail from a treasured field; he can detect with his divining-rod a stray bullock or a stolen goat far more efficiently than the police.

This tradition and pride of the Baigas brought them into conflict with Government in two ways. The first was that since they had been born from the womb of Mother Earth, they believed that it was a very wrong thing for them to lacerate her breast with the plough. The second was that, since they were the true Pashupati, lords of animals, they considered that they should have the freedom of the forest for their hunting. Nothing shows more clearly the evils of an administration ignorant of tribal mythology and indifferent to its custom than the way the old Government dealt with the Baigas on these two points.

From 1867 to the end of the century the unfortunate Baigas were pursued by zealous forest officers, determined to make them stop their axe-and-hoe cultivation and take to the plough. At the same time much of their hunting was stopped and some of them were even forced to make heaps of their precious bows and arrows and burn them.

Shifting-cultivation is a bad thing: unfortunately it is often the only possible thing. The Baigas used to cut down a track of forest, set fire to the wood when dry, and sow their seeds in the ashes. After repeating this for three years, they would move on to another patch of forest. Obviously, even where a tribe had a religious passion for this type of cultivation, it could not be permitted on a large scale and for ever. But where only a few tribesmen practised it—and the Baigas were a very small tribe—and where a regular rotation of at least twenty years was observed, the harm it did to the forest was greatly exaggerated. The Baigas have practised this form of cultivation for centuries in Mandla and Balaghat, yet nowhere is there better forest today.

But the Baigas were forced to the plough; many were reduced to poverty, for they hated the tabooed implement, and all suffered psychological disturbance deep in their souls. They have today sunk into the position of impoverished and inferior cultivators. Robbed of their bows and arrows, they are no longer lords of the forest, the great shikaris of former times. They have lost much of what used to make life so rich and enjoyable.

I had many Baiga friends and they were all pledged to inform me if anything interesting happened. So one day there would come news that someone thirty miles away had died, and we would be off within the hour to watch the funeral. Another day there would be a marriage; another we would have to climb a tall hill to see a Honey Festival, in honour of the bees, that occurs only once in nine years. Yet again the Baigas would come to my own village and protect it with a magic wall by driving nails along the boundaries.

It was in the very remote Bohi that I watched the strange and thrilling ceremonies designed to close the jaws of the man-eater and to frustrate the witch who had sent him. It was a desperately serious business; seven of the most powerful magicians came to do battle with the forces of evil. The Tiger Spirit came upon one of the spectators; he was transformed into a tiger and began to behave like one: there was an exciting tiger hunt; and in the end nails were driven into rocks and trees.

The next morning, I was standing in the forest when a large pig lumbered up to me with a leaf in its mouth which it dropped at my feet. I was rather moved by this—sort of Francis among the birds touch, I thought—and then forgot all about it. But no sooner had I returned home than I went down with a violent attack of fever. The local magicians waited on me, and soon diagnosed the cause—the witch of Bohi, annoyed at my presence in the village, had put magic in a leaf and sent it to me by her pig. They immediately took the necessary measures, and I recovered.

The Baigas are very fond of pigs. One day a man came to me complaining that his wife had run away with someone else. 'That', he said, 'I could have borne; but they took away my favourite pig.' A pleasant picture—the happy couple fleeing through the moonlit forest glades, and on the lover's shoulder is a pole bearing a protesting, squealing pig.

Once when we were driving through the forest beyond Kapildara we met a large tiger on the road. It was an open car and personally I was considerably alarmed. But an old Baiga sitting by me did not turn a hair; he began to mutter his charms and after a minute or two the tiger turned and went away quietly into the jungle. 'That is nothing,' the Baiga told me. 'There was a man called Dugru who used to be visited by three or four tigers at a time. They would lick his hands and feet and stroke him with their paws. Sometimes he got tired of them and would tell them to go away, and they always obeyed him.'

And he told another story of how once the Baigas, angry at some restriction of their forest rights, had warned all the tigers in their area that the Governor was coming for a hunt, and as a result His Excellency did not get a single animal!

It is very important that the anthropologist should come down from his perch and, as far as he possibly can, become what G. K. Chesterton once called 'the invisible man'. This was in one of the Father Brown detective stories where the murderer was the postman. All the witnesses declared that nobody had visited the house where the deed was done, but they forgot the postman who fitted into the picture so completely that he didn't count. It is not easy to reach this standard but I was always trying to, and one of the greatest compliments an ethnographer could be paid was once given me by a Baiga. I had visited his village and been received with great friendliness but none of the fuss and deference which the touring officer generally receives. One of my company was annoyed at this and said to the villagers: 'Here is a sahib: he must be somone important. Why don't you make proper arrangements for his reception?' The Baiga laughed at this. 'We know it's only Bara Bhai'—the usual name for me, by which I was distinguished from Shamrao, the Chhota Bhai: in fact we were often known by a portmanteau name, Bara Bhai-Chhota Bhai, Big Brother-Little Brother. 'He is such an ordinary man that when we see him coming we say, "Oh, it's only Bara Bhai, there's no need to bother!"'

IV

For my next book I turned to the Agarias, a small group of blacksmiths and iron-smelters, who are scattered all over the Mandla and Bilaspur Districts with cadet branches right across central India to Bihar. In this study I wanted to discipline myself and concentrated mainly on the techniques of craftsmanship with the mythology that vitalized them. I found it interesting enough and I felt it was good for me, but the Agarias are a dull people compared to the Baigas. Preparation of this book involved a great deal of travelling about and I kept on finding little groups of them in unexpected places.

Fifteen years later these early studies in iron resulted in my being invited to write *The Story of Tata Steel* for the jubilee celebrations of the Tata Iron and Steel Company, the only properly paid literary work I have ever done (they gave me ten thousand rupees for it) and the book was most handsomely produced.

All the time that I was working on these and other books I was collecting stories. I put some hundred and fifty of them in a book *Folk-Tales of Mahakoshal*, which was the first volume of my Specimens of the Oral Literature of Middle India. This included a fairly complete bibliography of the Indian folktale in English and was very fully edited with notes and comparative material. The second volume in this field was my *Myths of Middle India* which were not so good as stories, though of considerable significance for our knowledge of how tribal myths developed out of, and sometimes parallel to, the ancient Hindu traditions. Probably the most important section of this book was one, which some of my readers regarded as rather coarse, on the origin of the different parts of the human body and its natural functions. I was very pleased when the *American Anthropologist* described it as 'a landmark in the exploration of the intellectual history of mankind'.

Long afterwards I made two selections of folk-stories from my larger collections. The first was *Stories from India* in four small volumes published by the Oxford University Press; the other was called *When the World was Young*, and was a National Book Trust publication. The best thing about them was the illustrations. The gracious and beautiful Leela Shiveshwarkar did the first, the brilliant and delightful Amina Jayal the second.

Another book, the preparation of which gave me great pleasure, was my *Tribal Art of Middle India*, but unfortunately I was so excited about it that I published it too soon. Had I waited another year or two I could have made it much better, for I discovered many new things as time went by and made, for example, a superb collection of wood-carvings from the Santal Parganas. I also found many Jadupatua scrolls, tribal comic strips as I call them, which tell the ancient stories of the Santals in pictures. Even so this book revealed a good many unexpected treasures and stimulated designers elsewhere.

At this time I also wrote two novels, both of which were published by Murray. The first, *Phulmat of the Hills*, was the love-story of a Pardhan girl whose beauty was finally destroyed by leprosy. The second, *A Cloud that's Dragonish*, was a tribal crime-story in which the detectives were Gonds and Baigas. Both these books got very good notices in England, though they were little read in India, but they have been out of print for over twenty years and have not been republished. Later, I wrote another novel, *Traitor's Gain*, which turned on the iniquitous exploitation of the tribal people, but I was unable to find a publisher. Later still, I wrote two thrillers which suffered the same fate. One was about a master criminal in India, which Mr Gollancz nearly accepted. The second was based on a visit to French West Africa that Victor Sassoon and I made in 1949. The failure of these books depressed me a little for, while I was writing them, I saw myself as a best-seller and all my financial problems solved.

Yet another novel, which Victor liked very much, though I never dared submit it to a more exacting critic, was about a girl—it really was—who became a prostitute for twenty-four hours and sold her favours to four different men, one of whom gave her syphilis. She had it very badly, it affected her brain and she was sent to an asylum. She escaped and devoted herself to tracking down her former lovers and, as she did not know which of them was responsible for her disease, murdered them all one by one. The series of crimes was naturally baffling to the police, for there was no apparent motive for them and nothing to link them together.

The discovery of penicillin has taken most of the kick out of stories about syphilis, and in any case I have now lost the manuscript.

The Baiga brought me many new friends, chief of whom was W. G. (Bill) Archer. The popular notion in India about the Indian Civil Service, that its members were stiff and arrogant, is not altogether correct. It also included some of the most friendly, sensitive and intelligent people you could meet anywhere, people like Bill himself or N. R. Pillai, V. Viswanathan (now Home Secretary), J. H. Hutton, the present Governor of

Assam, and others whom I describe elsewhere in this book.*

Shortly after the *The Baiga* was published, Bill wrote inviting me to Bihar. He was then Census Superintendent for the Province and Shamrao and I went to stay with him and had the opportunity of touring in many Uraon, Munda, Ho and Asur villages. Later, when Bill was Deputy Commissioner of the Santal Parganas, I toured widely with him there and, later still, made a number of visits to the Santal and Uraon villages. These experiences enriched my book on the Murias and my first book on tribal art.

On this first visit I had the opportunity of meeting Sarat Chandra Roy, the veteran philanthropologist who not only wrote a whole series of books on the Bihar tribes but fought valiantly for the people both in the courts and outside. After his death Bill Archer and I, with the help of his son Romesh, took over the journal *Man in India*, which we edited for a number of years.

V

Lying to the south of what was then the Central Provinces was the State of Bastar, a territory the size of Belgium. The great plain of Chhattisgarh stretches down past Raipur and Dhamtari in hot and dusty monotony till it spends itself against the hills of Kanker. Thenceforward the journey is a never-failing delight; as the traveller moves towards the Bastar plateau the countryside breaks into song about him; he is greeted by hardy smiling woodmen singing at their work; the skyline is broken by fantastic piles of rock; l around is the evergreen sal forest. Presently he sees looming up before him a row of sharply-rising hills, the sentinels that stand on guard before the country of the Murias, and the long steep ascent of the Keskal Ghat has to be essayed. From the summit there is a magnificent view of the great sea of hill and forest below.

I was first attracted to Bastar by the late Sir W. V. Grigson, known to his friends as Frittles, one of the greatest men who has concerned himself with tribal problems in India, a witty, charming and faithful friend. From quite early days he had not allowed his attitude to me to be influenced by police reports. In the first place, I too had been to Oxford, and in the second, I

*Please refer to original edition, *The Tribal World of Verrier Elwin* (OUP, 1964).

shared his enthusiasm for all things tribal. He was Administrator of Bastar from 1927 to 1931 and wrote a book about it called *The Maria Gonds of Bastar*. I first read this book in Frittles' own house when I was laid up with fever and was so excited by it that my temperature rose appreciably. It was, however, a long time before I had the opportunity or money to make any serious study of the Bastar tribes. In the earlier years the local Administrator was not at all favourable to my paying a visit to the State for fear that I would start a Congress rebellion, but ultimately he was persuaded to allow Shamrao and myself to make a short visit, when we drove about the State and saw as much as we could from the roadside.

Later, I took the late Mrs Marguerite Milward the sculptress there—she has described her visit in her book *Artist in Tribal India*.

Marguerite had studied in Paris under Bourdelle and she worked with him for many years. Her first visit abroad was in his company to Ceylon where she began her studies in the sculpture of primitive peoples, to which she devoted the better part of her life. She visited Tibet, Burma, Java, north-west Africa, French Indo-China as well as India for this purpose and used sometimes to lecture on anthropology. One of her sayings was that 'art unites where politics divide'. The Indian Government bought a number of her heads and they may still be seen in the Indian Museum in Calcutta. One beautiful head, however, of a Gond girl, which she made during her visit to us and which formerly stood in the window of India House in London, she gave to me shortly before her death in her eightieth year.

Marguerite, who was a most engaging person but of enormous size, along with her cases of cement and clay, was altogether too much for our old car and as we were passing through Kanker everything fell out through the bottom and we had to send to Jagdalpur to be rescued.

Finally, in May 1940, I went to Bastar with the idea of doing something really serious, and I was actually given an official appointment, that of Census Officer, which paid a monthly salary of a hundred rupees. Even at that time I was hardly educated in the ways of the world and was not aware that both one's travelling allowance and the respect in which one was held in official India depended almost entirely on one's pay. When I got to Bastar, however, Norval Mitchell, a very good type, who had then taken charge and gave me all possible support, changed this extraordinary arrangement and paid me a lump sum of 1,500 rupees for my work on the Census. Of course, all I wanted was some kind of official status without which in those days it was difficult to do any work in an Indian State. Later we again changed the arrangement and I became Hon. Ethnographer to Bastar. A local paper, boggling at the word 'ethnographer', announced that I had been appointed Hon. Stenographer.

My idea was to follow my usual technique and settle down among the people. We built a lovely little house of stone (which cost only 200 rupees) opposite the stupendous and beautiful Falls of Chitrakot and made small huts, quite habitable, at 40 rupees each, in two Muria villages. Our main centre continued to be at Patangarh, where Shamrao held the fort while I was away.

At that time Bastar was entirely delightful. The tribal people were poor but they were free and happy. There was a quality of enthusiasm and zest in their lives. Their dances were amongst some of the finest in India and they had not been corrupted by Puritan workers into a belief that their beautiful bodies were something to be ashamed of.

I travelled all over the State and collected a lot of notes and photographs of the Hill Marias of the Abujhmar whom we visited on elephants, the Koyas, Bhattras, Dorlas and others. But my main interest was in two of the tribes—the Bison-Horn Marias of the south and the Murias of the north. I did a book on the Marias called *Maria Murder and Suicide*, trying to discover what it was that drove these simple people to homicide, and I also studied the conditions in the Jagdalpur jail which I tried to get improved.

Of all the tribes I have studied, I found the Marias the most attractive and field-work among them the most comfortable and pleasant. The Bison-Horn Maria area was even in 1941 accessible in the open season by car, and every village had a well-built rest-house for visitors. The people were friendly, the climate was excellent, and I enjoyed my years there enormously.

It was in Bastar that I first began to use the gramophone as a means of breaking down barriers and creating a friendly atmosphere. I got some excellent Hindi comic records and also used to play a little Mozart and Beethoven which, I am sorry to say, did not go down very well.

And then, in the middle of one of my tours, a young man suddenly arrived in camp with a very large box, which had been sent up from Jagdalpur by the police. When we opened it we found it full of superb mechanical toys sent by two friends in Bombay. These toys must have given more pleasure over a wider area than any collection of toys that was ever made. Some of them lasted for eight years and I took one or two, their well-worn mechanisms still ticking over, with me on expeditions in NEFA. They were certainly a great help in making contact with the Marias.

Yet normally, anything unusual was dangerous. The Marias were very suspicious, for example, of the Census. They recalled that after the 1931 Census many tigers had appeared in the forest. It is always risky to count and measure, for 'the sin of numbering the people' may reduce fertility. So after the 1941 Census, in most villages, the house number-boards were carried out and sacrifices of pigs were made before them.

The Marias were a tough and rather formidable tribe, with a very high incidence of homicide, six times that of the neighbouring Central Provinces. The jail at Jagdalpur was always crowded with Marias serving sentences for murder. The administration was worried about this, and I offered to try and discover why it was. I was given the freedom of the Record Room and here, after turning over a great number of dusty files, I found a hundred that gave me the sort of information I wanted. I also wanted suicide records, but these were not so easy to come by, for they were not kept at headquarters but in the local police-stations. But the Superintendent of Police called in all the suicide files, and I was able to find fifty about the Marias.

Having collected the records I mapped out the villages where anything had happened and visited as many as I could. I talked to the relatives of the murderers and of their victims, got the opinions of village elders, studied the attitude of the other villagers, and frequently met the actual individuals who had served their term (for the death sentence was very rarely imposed) and had now returned home.

This was an extraordinarily interesting job. In Aranpur I stood beside the still warm ashes of the ritually-cremated clothes of

Barse Chewa, who had recently been hanged in jail. At Khutepal, I watched Oyami's children playing on the very floor once stained by the blood of his murdered wife. In Rewali I was visited by a ferocious-looking youth, who had twice stood trial for his life and had twice preserved it.

Here too I talked with another youth who, in a fit of jealousy, had killed his wife and now—not unnaturally—found it hard to get another. In Doriras I saw the grave of the murdered Boti which had been desecrated by the Ghasias for the sake of the purse of money which had been buried to help the ghost on his journey to the other world. In the same village I visited the home of Kawasi Borga, then serving a life-sentence, and talked to his five sons and his sad pathetic wife.

An analysis of the reasons and motives for these murders was revealing. Quarrels over property accounted for 15 per cent; family quarrels for 16 per cent; jealousy, infidelity, sex motives in general, for 17 per cent. Nineteen per cent were more or less trivial crimes committed when drunk. Only five per cent were caused by the suspicion or accusation of witchcraft and sorcery. There were six murders committed for revenge, and nine out of resentment at abuse or 'word-magic'. This last is an important and curious motive: to use the wrong kind of words may be a very risky thing, being not only insulting to the feelings but dangerous (magically) to the person.

One of the things which was a revelation, not only to me, but also (I have been told) to more than one Sessions Judge, was the discovery of the part played by fatigue in promoting acts of violence. There can be a sort of fatigue-intoxication, not unlike that caused at a certain stage by alcohol. Fatigue can cause dejection and irritability, worry, desperation and a desire to escape from a situation which seems intolerable. And the Marias, like other peasants, often get very tired. They return home in the evening; supper is not ready, the child is crying, and in a flash there is a blow and a dearly-loved wife is dead and a home is ruined.

I spent many hours in the Jagdalpur jail, talking to Maria prisoners, and what struck me most was the remarkable innocence of many of them. They felt that an inexplicable destiny had overtaken them. They did not feel like criminals; in many cases their crimes were no more than tragic accidents. They were a very sad company.

I first became interested in prisons in the Satyagraha days when I made emphatic protest about the treatment of political prisoners. Then, later, my experiences with the police in Mandla gave me almost a horror of their methods and of the whole idea of punishment and retribution in the treatment of crime.

The descent of the police on a tribal village is a dreadful thing. For days the entire community is kept from its work and often has difficulty even in getting anything to eat. How often we watched it happen! The Sub-Inspector arrived and made his camp in the best house in the village. He and his constables had to be provided free of charge with food and drink of a kind that the people themselves could only afford at great festivals. Third-degree methods were often used before and, I am sorry to say, even after Independence to obtain evidence. No one felt safe. For days the shy and timid tribal people were distracted by anxiety. Large sums of money secretly changed hands and when the final arrest was made it was a heart-rending sight to watch the prisoner in his handcuffs escorted to the boundary of the village by a crowd of weeping relations.

I had the opportunity of visiting a number of prisons and seeing how the tribal people fared, and in Bastar my interest developed greatly. Dramatic incidents still further impressed on me the importance of revising our methods of investigation as well as our treatment of criminals. A girl in a village near Sanhrwachhapar was accused of poisoning her husband. The accepted routine was followed and though the villagers were convinced, as I was, that she was innocent—and villagers are seldom wrong about this sort of thing—she was arrested and sent to jail where she was capitally convicted. We did not think that there was any real danger of her being hanged, but one day I received a telegram from Frittles Grigson telling me that if nothing was done she would be hanged within a very short time. I have never driven a car so fast in my life as when I made the three-hundred-mile journey up to Pachmarhi, where the Government was having its summer session, in the hope of obtaining a reprieve. When I arrived I was told that it was too late. But I persevered and in the end succeeded in saving the girl's life, and she was reprieved to the terrible mercy of life-imprisonment.

On one of my visits to jail, I saw, and can still see, two young Gonds in handcuffs for murdering a Pathan moneylender who had driven them to the despair of hopeless poverty. With great eyes filled with bewilderment and fear, like frightened and beautiful deer of the forest, the two little Gonds were surrounded by enormous constables.

The tribesmen suffer out of all proportion in jail. 'If a Maria is sentenced to a long term of imprisonment', says Grigson, 'he will beg to be hanged rather than be confined within walls: and few of the wilder Bison-horn Marias survive long imprisonment.' The grim forbidding walls, the stone beds, the rule of silence, the unfamiliar food and language, the attitude of suppliant and obsequious deference before officials, the absence of recreations, the lack of religious comfort, the denial of human companionship, the appalling monotony oppress and crush them.

This is particularly true of the frontier areas. The NEFA tribesman, who is taken down from the mountains and sent to prison in the plains, suffers, in addition to the inevitable sense of isolation, the affront to human dignity, the loneliness and despair that afflict all prisoners, special deprivations. The heat of the plains is almost unbearable to a hillman. It is probable that no one knows his language. He himself may only have a few words of Hindi or Assamese. In some cases tribal prisoners have been in jail for years without hearing a word of their families and they are too far away from them for visits.

Some of us have been very keen to have a special jail for our tribal people, which will be a place of healing and restoration and where the whole idea of punishment and revenge will be banished. It is, however, extraordinary how even today many officials think in very different terms. 'They put on weight while they are with us,' a Jail Superintendent told me. 'They do not feel things as we do,' said another, and many people have urged that even in the worst jail a tribal convict has a better time than at home.

There was a theory about the threshold of pain which was supposed to be higher among 'savages' than the civilized. In other words, if you pricked a bishop and a Maria at the same moment, it would be the bishop who jumped first. He was more delicate: it would hurt him more. I don't believe a word of it.

I have always felt ashamed that I did not manage to go to jail as a Satyagrahi but, as I have explained earlier, the British Government would not have given me this privilege: they would simply have deported me. When I was in Jagdalpur I did discuss with the Administrator whether I could somehow go as an ordinary prisoner into the prison there, but he thought it would be difficult to ensure that the local magistrate would not give me a sentence rather too long for scientific purposes.

VI

The Marias

The most memorable thing about the Marias is their superb marriage-dance when the men, wearing great headdresses of bison-horns and carrying their long drums, move in a large circle, while a row of women thread their way among them. It is probably the finest dance in tribal India.

One day a young Maria called Alami Mata returned home from the forest to find that the splendid horns and feathers of his hereditary dance outfit had been stolen. This was something more than the loss of a precious possession. In a neighbouring village was a beautiful girl, unmarried and growing to love him; Alami was wooing her in the dance, and indeed in his magnificent headdress, shaking his horns and prancing before his love like a young bison, he must have been hard to resist. But now, like Samson shorn of his hair, there was no strength in him; how could he go to meet his girl in the mean and undistinguished attire that was left to him?

As he stood brooding on his tragedy, his father came in and abused him roughly for wasting time. It was too much for the boy; life without music, love or rhythm was not worth living, and he went out and hanged himself.

This incident illustrates the attachment of the Marias to their great dance and to the finery which adorns it. The headdress of bison-horns is the chief treasure of a Maria home. It is kept with the utmost care, dismantled, in closed bamboo baskets, and it takes nearly an hour to assemble.

This headdress, and the dance, is the sole expression of the Marias' aesthetic sensibility. They do not carve, or paint, or model images on their walls; they do not, like their neighbours, the Murias, make attractive combs and tobacco-holders. Everything they have to say goes into the dance.

And what a superb spectacle they created! The women were

less elaborately attired than the men, but they too were clothed in their own beauty, which was emphasized by the mass of bead and brass necklaces that almost covered the breasts, and the snoods and fillets of shining brass about their heads. I believe that officials have now taught them to put on white saris and cover themselves 'properly'.

The men, carrying their long drums, move in a great circle with a large variety of turns and changes; the 'bison' charge and fight each other, pick up leaves on the point of their horns, and chase the girl dancers.

The girls, each with a dancing-stick in her right hand, form a long line and go round and through the men dancers with many different movements and steps. They do not usually sing, and indeed the tune would be lost in the thunder of the drums. As they go, they beat the ground with their sticks, 'dum-dum-dum, di-dum, dum-dum'. Masked mummers, clowns dressed in straw, naked acrobats carrying clubs, wooden guns and nets, add to the gaiety of the scene.

To witness this dance was an unforgettable experience. 'Whosoever danceth not, knoweth not the way of life,' and conversely these people, for all their poverty, found in the supreme ecstatic rhythm of their dance a way of life that raised them above mediocrity into a kind of splendour.

VII

The Murias

But my most important work in Bastar was to study the *ghotul*, the unique dormitory-club of the Muria boys and girls. The Murias live to the north of the Marias, all over a very large wooded plateau, in substantial villages many of which could, even in my day, be reached by car. The climate was good, the people friendly and responsive, the country was easy—and the whole business was exciting and interesting and new.

At this time the Murias enjoyed almost entire freedom. Once I was off the main road and away from the few administrative centres, I hardly ever saw an official. The people lived their own life, unhampered if unimproved, and they lived it well. But what I shall say about them is a part of history now and I must write in the past tense.

The ghotul was the central focus of Muria life, coming down to modern times from Lingo, the heroic ancestor of the tribe, who founded it.

The first ghotul is described as beautiful as the horns of bison, beautiful as a horse's throat. Its central pillar was a python, its poles were cobras. The frame of the roof was made of kraits tied together with vipers and covered with the tails of peacocks. The roof of the veranda was made of bulbul feathers. The walls were of fish-bones, the door was fashioned of crimson flowers, the door-frames were the bones of ogres. The floor was plastered with pulse. The seats were crocodiles.

The lord of the house wore a turban like a white gourd-flower; his dhoti was coloured silk; his shirt shone in the sun; his clogs were made of sandalwood, his stockings of mongoose fur, his belt was a long thin snake; as he walked he sparkled. In his hand he carried the eighteen instruments of music, heavy with the charms of love.

Such is the legendary picture of Lingo and the first ghotul.

Similar institutions are widely distributed among communities of the Austro-Asiatic cultures, but it seems probable that the Muria ghotul was one of the most highly developed and carefully organized in the world. For what was a village guard-room for the Nagas, a boys' club among the Uraons, a refuge for temporary sexual association in Indonesia, was for the Murias the centre of social and religious life. For although the ghotul was an independent autonomous children's republic, it had an all-pervading influence on the grown-ups, who could not manage any social function without its help.

All the unmarried boys and girls of the tribe had to be members of the ghotul. This membership was elaborately organized: after a period of probation, boys and girls were initiated and given special titles which carried with them graded ranks and social duties. Leaders were appointed to lead and discipline the society; the boys' leader was often called the *Sirdar*: the girls' leader was the *Belosa*. Boy members were known as *cheliks* and girls as *motiaris*.

The cheliks and motiaris had important duties to perform on all social occasions. The boys acted as acolytes at festivals, the girls as bridesmaids at weddings. They danced together before the clan-gods and at great fairs. They formed a choir at the funerals of important people. Their games and dances enlivened and enriched village life and redeemed it from that crushing monotony which was its normal characteristic in other parts of India.

It was natural that the ghotul, 'dear nurse of arts', should foster every kind of art, for here the boys and girls were all the time on their toes to attract one another and to make life what they believed it should be, beautiful, lively and interesting. And so the boys made and decorated charming little combs for their girls, and elaborate tobacco-boxes for themselves; the girls made necklaces, pendants and belts of beads and cowries. The boys carved the pillars and doors of their ghotul building, which was often the finest house in a village. They made exciting toys and masks. And above all they danced.

But this is common to many other cultures. What gave the ghotul its unique interest was the approved and recognized relationship between the boys and girls.

There were two types of ghotul. In the first, and probably the oldest, which was sometimes called the 'yoking' ghotul, the rule was that of fidelity to a single partner during the whole of the pre-marital period. Each chelik was paired off with a motiari; he was formally 'married' to her and she took the feminine form of his title as her own. Divorce was allowed, though 'infidelity' was punished.

In the second type of ghotul, which was probably a later development of the classic model, any kind of lasting attachment between chelik and motiari was forbidden. No one could say that such and such a motiari was *his* girl; his attachment was rationed to three days at a time.

Although outwardly both types of ghotul were the same and often only the most careful investigation could distinguish them, the customs and atmosphere of the modern type were entirely distinct. Here everything was arranged to prevent long-drawn intense attachments, to eliminate jealousy and possessiveness, to deepen the sense of communal property and action. There was no ghotul marriage, there were no ghotul partners. 'Everyone belonged to everyone else' in the very spirit of *Brave New World*. A chelik and motiari might sleep together for three nights; after that they were warned; if they persisted they were punished. If a boy showed any signs of possessiveness for a particular girl, if his face fell when he saw her making love to someone else, if he got annoyed at her sleeping with another chelik, should he be offended if she refused to massage him and went to someone else, he was forcibly reminded by his fellows that she was not his wife, he had no right over her, she was the property of the whole ghotul, and if he looked like that he would be punished.

This was sometimes called the 'changing ring' ghotul; because in it you changed from girl to girl just as you changed your rings from finger to finger.

The ghotul was very literally a night-club; it was only in the evening that there was 'a noise in the belly of the elephant'; during the day, except on festivals, it was deserted. The real life of the ghotul was in the firelight.

At any time after supper, the cheliks began to assemble. They came one by one, carrying their sleeping-mats and perhaps their drums. The little boys brought their daily 'tribute' of wood, 'clocked in' by showing it to the official responsible and threw it in a corner. The elder boys gathered round the fire; one took a half-smoked leaf-pipe from his turban and ignited it by placing a bit of glowing wood in the cup, another played a few notes on his flute, a third spread his mat and lay down. The Kotwar inspected the buildings to see if the girls had done their work properly. Gradually all the boys assembled.

Then the girls came in, with a rush, all together, and gathered round their own fire. After a while they scattered, some sitting with the boys, others singing in a corner, some lying down.

The others occupied the time in pleasant harmony; sometimes they danced for an hour or two; the smaller children played rampageous games; sometimes they just sat round the fire and talked; in the hot weather on a moonlit night they scattered all about the compound. Often they sang lying down, two by two, chelik with motiari, or in little groups. A boy told a story; they asked riddles; they reported on the affairs of the day; there was sometimes a ghotul trial; they planned a dancing expedition or allotted duties at a wedding. I shall never forget the sight in some of the larger ghotuls of sixty or seventy youngsters thus engaged.

After an hour or two of dancing, singing, games or story-telling, certainly not much after ten o'clock, the serious business of the evening began. The little boys went round saluting their elders, a ritual then repeated by the girls. One of them distributed finely-powdered tobacco from the ghotul store, to which all the parents contributed. Then the girls each went to her partner of the day and sat down behind him. First of all, she shook out and arranged his hair and then combed it. When this was done, she massaged him, sometimes with oilseed, sometimes rubbing his back with her comb, and then she cracked his fingers one by one.

By then it was fairly late and the boys and girls prepared to sleep. The little boys and girls slept in long rows, while those who had permanent or temporary partners lay down with them in each other's arms on their sleeping-mats.

Every night, when everything had warmed up, there came a moment when I had to leave the ghotul. I would have given almost anything to have stayed on, to have traced (having watched the process of tumescence) the story to its end, even if only as an observer. But the rules were very definite and I knew that if I broke them even once my chances of obtaining information might be lost. So I always went away to my cold and comfortless camp, nostalgic for the happy, exciting world I left behind.

In the very early morning the Belosa got up and went round the ghotul rousing her girls. They had to be out of the building before dawn. 'They leave early', a boy told me, 'because they come laughing from the arms of the cheliks and feel shy about it.'

At least at the time I knew them, the Murias had a simple, innocent and natural attitude to sex. In the ghotul this was strengthened by the absence of any sense of guilt and the general freedom from external interference. The Murias believed that sexual congress was a good thing; it did you good; it was healthy and beautiful; when performed by the right people (such as a chelik and motiari who were not taboo to one another), at the right time (outside the menstrual period and avoiding forbidden days), and in the right place (within the ghotul walls where no 'sin' could be committed), it was the happiest and best thing in life.

This belief in sex as something good and normal gave the Murias a light touch. Their saying that the young lovers were *hassi ki nat*, in a 'joking relationship' to each other, expressed their attitude exactly. Sex was great fun; it was the best of ghotul games; it was the dance of enraptured bodies: it was an ecstatic swinging in the arms of the beloved. It ought not to be too intense: it must not be degraded by possessiveness or defiled by jealousy. It was believed that the best and most successful sex relations were to be had in the modern ghotul where partners often changed.

All this was, of course, very shocking to the conventionally minded. Yet there is much to be said on the Murias' side. In the first place the cheliks and motiaris were wonderfully happy. Their life was full, interesting, exciting, useful. The ghotul was, as they often said, 'a little school'. The cheliks were 'like Boy Scouts', as I was told in a village which had a troop in the local school. There was no comparison between these children and the sad-eyed, dirty ragamuffins of villages at a similar cultural level elsewhere. In the ghotul the children were taught lessons of cleanliness, discipline and hard work that remained with them throughout their lives. They were taught to take a pride in their appearance, to respect themselves and their elders; above all, they were taught the spirit of service. These boys and girls worked very hard indeed for the public good. They were immediately available for the service of State officials or for labour on the roads. They had to be ready to work at a wedding or a funeral. They had to attend to the drudgery of festivals. In most tribal villages of the Central Provinces the children were slack, dirty, undisciplined and with no sense of public spirit. The Murias were very different.

With all this the missionary or social reformer would be in agreement. 'But', they would say, 'that is not the point. Our complaint is that these boys and girls sleep together.' It was at least one point in their favour that this sleeping together did not seem to do them a great deal of harm. There were no signs of corruption or excess; these bright-eyed, merry-faced boys and girls did not give you the impression of being the victims of debasing lust. They were living a life of fulfilment and it seemed to do them good.

They did (perhaps they still do) sleep together, but under conditions of discipline and some restraint. Children in other tribal villages also have sexual congress but without discipline and restraint. The tribal and semi-tribal boys whom I knew for so many years in other parts of central India all too often began their sexual life before the age of twelve and indulged in it freely till they were married and after. It is notorious that venereal disease has long been rampant throughout tribal India, and some of the most pathetic sights I have seen have been cases of young boys and girls afflicted by it. I have no hesitation in saying that for the areas that I know intimately, there was more sexual excess among young people in ordinary villages than in ghotul villages.

Another interesting and curious point is that there were few people with a stronger sense of domestic morality and conjugal fidelity than the Muria. Adultery was very rare, and was visited with supernatural punishment when it did occur. You could not find happier or more united families. One of the reasons for this was that the ghotul system discouraged the custom of child-marriage which was then rapidly spreading through tribal India. Among romantically-minded tribal people, child-marriage means, inevitably, domestic infidelity. Boys or girls find themselves tied to partners in whom they have no interest and naturally leave them and seek others. Another reason for this remarkable fidelity among the Murias was that in many ghotuls boys and girls were 'married' and were taught the necessity of fidelity to their partners. In the other type of ghotul, they grew up from their earliest years to believe that, though change is the mark of the unmarried, stability must characterize the married. Once a girl was in your *haq* or 'right' she must stay there and you must stay with her.

Now one of the drawbacks of semi-tribal India is domestic infidelity. Divorce is universal, elopement common, adultery an everyday affair. The ghotul villages have a much higher standard in this respect. The incidence of divorce in Bastar was under 3 per cent. An examination of 50 marriages in Patangarh showed 23 divorces or 46 per cent.

We may also consider how the ghotul boys and girls were almost completely free from those furtive and unpleasant vices that so mar our modern civilization. There was hardly any masturbation; where it was practised, it was due to the mistaken efforts of reformers to improve the ghotul. Prostitution was unknown, unthinkable. No motiari would ever give her body for money.

The village dormitory is a symptom of a certain stage of cultural development. We ourselves consider that we have outgrown it; we may grow into it again. In the days when I shared the free and happy life of the Murias I used sometimes to wonder whether I was a hundred years behind the times or a hundred years ahead. I do not suggest that we should replace the Public

Schools by ghotuls and turn our own children into cheliks and motiaris, but I do suggest that there are elements in ghotul life and teaching which we should do well to ponder and that an infection of the Muria spirit would do few of us any harm.

The message of the ghotul—that youth must be served, that freedom and happiness are more to be treasured than any material gain, that friendliness and sympathy, hospitality and unity are of the first importance, and above all that human love—and its physical expression—is beautiful, clean and precious, is typically Indian. The ghotul is no Austro-Asiatic alien in the Indian scene. Here was the atmosphere of the best old India; here was something of the life (though on a humble scale) portrayed at Ajanta; here was something (though now altogether human) of the Krishna legend and its ultimate significance; this was the same life, the same tradition that inspired the Pahari paintings.

I wrote a big book of over 750 pages, *The Muria and their Ghotul*, about all this, studying first the whole life of the tribe and then going on to describe in great detail the life in the ghotul itself.

At the beginning of the book, I put three fine quotations. The first was from St Paul—'Unto the pure all things are pure; but unto them that are defiled and unbelieving is nothing pure; but even their mind and conscience is defiled.'

The second quotation was from Hirschfeld: 'For thousands of years human folly has overwhelmed love with debris, pelted love with filth. To liberate love from this is to restore that vital human value which among all human values stands supreme.'

And the third was from Westermarck: 'The concealment of truth is the only indecorum known to science; and to keep anything secret within its cold and passionless expanse would be as prudish as to throw a cloth round a naked statue.'

Even supported by this, I was not sure how the book would be received in India but in fact it was taken very well. A Bombay publisher tried hard to persuade me to put my discoveries of Baiga, Muria and other tribal intimate relations into *A Sexual Life of Tribal India*, but I resisted this, for my aim was never to titillate the reader's fancy, but to make a serious contribution to sexual knowledge, and this could only be done by regarding sex as a part of life as a whole: it could not be described in isolation, at least not by me.

My book was translated into French by Dr A. Bigot, a friend

with whom I have often corresponded but never met, as *Maisons des Jeunes chez les Muria* and published by Gallimard. By this time, the English version had been long out of print and when an Italian translation was proposed, we could not find a copy and had to supply the publishers in Rome with the French version. This was actually an advantage since Dr Bigot had abridged the original and made a much more serviceable book. Descriptions of the *comportement sexuel* of the Murias go better in French than in English.

VIII

In December 1942 I paid my first visit to Orissa. The Darbars of the Bonai, Keonjhar and Pal Lahara States, at the suggestion of Norval Mitchell who had by then moved on to take charge of the Eastern States Agency, invited me to tour in the tribal areas of these States, inquire into the life and habits of the people and make recommendations towards the solution of the problem of shifting-cultivation which was very widespread there at this time.

In view of the fact that it is frequently said that the British Government never took any interest in the tribal people, it is only fair to give my terms of reference, which incidentally give a programme for the philanthropologist.

Mr Elwin's task would be to show how best the people could be led away from shifting-cultivation into the settled life of the permanent cultivator after inquiring into their social, religious, economic, and physical conditions. In other words, the expert knowledge of an anthropologist would be added to the expert knowledge of Forest Officers. He would consider what elements of aboriginal life and culture should be preserved, and what should be regarded as anti-social. He should after his inquiry be in a position to advise what should be done to recompense and console aboriginals for the loss of their shifting-cultivation, with particular attention to arts and crafts, to see whether those could be preserved and developed in both the cultural and economic interest of the people. He would observe any other relevant features of aboriginal life, such as their need of medical services or education. The final result would be a full picture of the problem in all its aspects, which might be summed up as technical and humanitarian, against the background of which future policy and orders could be framed.

My charter of duties was once expressed more succinctly by another, very liberal, British official, who said, 'Your job is to make such a damned nuisance of yourself that we shall be forced to help your people.'

I found this tour, in the course of which I had some bad attacks of fever but was assisted by a couple of elephants, extremely interesting and I think my Report was useful. But this was the only time in all these years that I was met with opposition and for a very curious reason—that the villagers thought I had come to stop shifting-cultivation and rob them of their land whereas my Report actually made very different recommendations.

All sorts of rumours went about. An English official had gone with the Forest Adviser to the Bhuiya Pirh the previous year and the villagers believed that they were pursuing two European fugitives supposed to be hiding in the hills. Popular rumour had it that I myself was seeking to establish a place of refuge in the event of a Japanese invasion. In Bonai a belief that we were exporting girls 'for the war' meant that I hardly ever saw a woman who was not over military age. In the wilder Juang hills of Keonjhar, though some of the people remembered the former Administrator Macmillan (a popular, and then almost legendary, figure who married a Bhuiya girl), many had never seen a white face before and, believing me to be an evil spirit, fled into the jungle with shrill cries of horror and amazement.

But these suspicions soon disappeared and before long, specially in Pal Lahara and among the Juangs, there was a very friendly atmosphere—to which our elephants and Kumar, then a small baby, largely contributed. I soon found myself being called the 'Rusi Sahib'—Rusi being the name of the ancient cult-hero of the tribe. And once friendly, the Juangs were almost embarrassing in their attentions. They were full of interest about my way of life, invading the tent at all times, and even peeping into my bathroom (a very small leaf-hut) to study my techniques. Indeed, I often felt as if I was a museum specimen and the Juanga members of an ethnological committee investigating a creature of the absurdest habits!

One morning an aeroplane hummed distantly overhead. 'Do you see that?' said a Juang friend. 'It is Victoria Rani come for an inspection of her Raj, to see how it is getting on.' If she was really in the plane, I thought, and could see what was happening to her Empire today, she would probably fall out. But it started a discussion about aeroplanes. Somebody thought they ran on very thin wires stretched across the sky. Someone else suggested that there were men in them, special kind of men who did not eat ordinary food, but lived on air. The Saoras told us later that aeroplanes diffused a noxious vapour which gave fever to the children in the villages over which they passed.

This conversation illustrates how unusually out of touch with things were the Juangs, whom Dalton called 'the most primitive people I have ever met with or read of'.

At that time a visit to the Juang country was fascinating. The country was wild and beautiful. The journeys continually surprised us with the splendour of the landscape, and the palm-girt flat lands round darling Malyagiri, whose rocks caught the sun in ever-changing shades of colour, were unforgettable. In early December, the country had special charm, for all the hills were carpeted with fields of yellow sarson.

Two things about the Juangs stirred me very deeply. One was their poverty, the other their grace and beauty as displayed in their 'animal ballet'. To see a typical Juang village one had to go to the highest uplands of Keonjhar. Here were some of the most picturesque hamlets in peninsular India, comparable only to the enchanting Bondo villages of the Koraput Hills. Each village stood self-contained within a large fence in a site chosen not only for convenience but also for beauty. The houses, little huts of mud with red walls, were either in a huddle on top of one another or neatly arranged in narrow streets. Near by were well-kept sheds for goats and cattle. In the centre of the village was an open space used for a dancing-ground in front of the often imposing village dormitory or club, the Darbar, where the unmarried youths slept and the elders assembled on all important occasions. The people were comparatively prosperous.

The Juangs of Pal Lahara presented a melancholy contrast to those of Keonjhar. In the second decade of the present century, the forest round the slopes of Malyagiri was reserved and the Juangs suddenly found themselves cut off from their normal means of livelihood. They were given cattle and land in villages at the foot of the mountains, but they could not take to the unfamiliar plough, wild elephants destroyed the crops, and the cattle, 'which were old and decrepit', died in a year or two.

The Juangs swiftly fell into the position of landless serfs in economic bondage to their neighbours, got more and more into debt, lost their fields and, when I saw them, were making a miserable living by weaving baskets—one of the most pitifully unremunerative of India's village industries. A man could make one large basket a day and got half an anna for it. He paid eight annas a year, or the equivalent of sixteen days' work, for the privilege of taking bamboo from the forest he regarded as his.

The economic condition of these Juangs was deplorable. I shall not easily forget going by night into a Juang village and seeing old women, naked but for a single rag about the loins, lying on the bare ground and trying to get a little warmth from a flickering fire. The physique of the people was poor and they were very diseased; the fine hard struggle with wild Nature in Keonjhar developed muscle and strength—but in Pal Lahara basket-making was a sedentary craft.

Even worse than their economic decay was their complete religious and cultural collapse. Gone were the fine Darbar halls, with their often remarkable carvings, of the Keonjhar Hills. Gone were the stone pillars to the village goddess. Since they had lost their own land, the Juangs themselves were unable to offer worship or sacrifice to their gods; they had to call in (and pay for) outside priests and magicians to help them. The beautifully fashioned combs, the elaborate smoker's equipment, the gay necklaces, which were so marked a feature of Keonjhar Juang life, were hardly known here.

The Juangs of Pal Lahara were the worst possible advertisement for a policy of stopping axe-cultivation or of moving people down to the plains. They underlined everything that the most captious critics have said against the forest administration. They were a pitiful instance of what happens when highlanders are dislodged from their mountains.

The traditional dress of Juang women was a mass of bead ornaments round the neck and a skirt of leaves fastened about the waist by a girdle of bugles of baked earth. This dress was established in the tribe's mythology and hedged about with the sanctions of religion.

The year 1871 was a bad one for the tribal people. In central India British officials were forcing the Baigas to commit the sin of lacerating the breasts of Mother Earth with the plough, thus throwing them into a psychological confusion from which they have never fully recovered. In Orissa other officials were persuading the Juangs to change their costume. A meeting was held and some two thousand pieces of cloth were distributed, after which the leaves were gatherd in a heap and burnt. 'Persuasion' continued and a majority of Juangs took to putting on filthy rags instead of the beautiful and hygienic leaf-dress.

The futility of introducing the outward garb of civilization without doing anything to instil its spirit is seen in the effect this had on the Juangs, who still look back to the day when the sacred leaves were burnt as a conquered nation might recall the day of its defeat.

Since that time, the Juangs say, Sat—the spirit of truth and religion, the power to live safely in a world of hostile magic—has left the tribe. Tigers attack the cattle with impunity and the offended earth gives but a scanty crop.

This may seem odd today but to force improvement on very simple people without at the same time having an adequate programme of development to make their lives fuller, richer and happier can be disastrous and I was deeply disturbed by what I saw in the Juang hills and wrote strongly about it.

I have spoken of the extraordinary aesthetic experience of a genuine dance of the Juangs in the old style.

Long ago Dalton wrote splendidly about their 'animal ballet', and the dances which I saw again and again in 1943 were very like those he saw in 1866. Some of the women were still wearing their leaf-dress all the time, and they all put it on for ceremonial and special occasions. I do not know whether the custom still remains or how far they are maintaining their traditional ballet today, for one of the saddest things about the march of civilization into the forests is the way it kills so many forms of artistic expression. But when I saw it, the dancing was still adept and beautiful beyond words. The bright green leaves threw into relief the golden-brown bodies of the girls, whose beauty was so gracefully displayed. I specially remember the peacock and deer dances when the girls moved with the grace of the loveliest of all the creatures of the forest. They imitated the elephant and the vulture well too, and when they squatted on the ground like quails to peck up their food their movements were as characteristic as they were rhythmical.

At the end of my expedition, I wrote—among many other

things: 'Today the Juangs are a small and impoverished tribe; they demand great sympathy and knowledge for their administration. They live in forests capable of yielding great wealth; surely some portion of that wealth should be made available to them so that they can enjoy fuller and happier lives.' It is only now that this is being done and, even now, I hope it is being done properly.

Christoph von Fürer-Haimendorf, always a most successful explorer, had paid a visit to the Gadabas and Bondos while I was in Bastar and had written to me with enthusiasm of the beauty of the country and the attractiveness of the people. Once I had finished work on my book about the Muria dormitory, and encouraged by my experiences among the Juangs, I decided to extend my interest to the Ganjam and Koraput Districts of Orissa. On my first trip I was escorted by a large, friendly, generous-hearted timber-man, Val Blackburn, who lived in Raipur. He took me into the very wild and almost unexplored country of the Kuttia Konds. A little later, we climbed the Nimgiri mountain together and, later still, I made the first of several visits to the high Bondo plateau and at the same time made some study of the neighbouring Gadabas. Later, I moved across to the Saora country in Parlakimedi and Gunupur, quite the most lovely tribal area that I have ever seen anywhere. Here I found, in Gilbert Murray's phrase, 'the apple tree, the singing, and the gold'.

Touring, however, was already becoming more expensive, though not so ruinously so as it is today, and it became evident that to remain in the private sector would greatly hamper my work. I had made friends with some of the Orissa officials, who were very suspicious at first on account of my political opinions, but later evidently became convinced that I was not up to anything, and I was finally appointed Hon. Anthropologist to Orissa on an honorarium which covered my expenses. Long afterwards the late Mr S. Fazl Ali told me that when he was Governor of Orissa he had decided to invite me to be Adviser for Tribal Affairs for the State but, just as he was going to put the matter through, he heard that I had been sent by the Prime Minister to NEFA.

Out of my Orissa explorations came three books—*Bondo Highlander, The Religion of an Indian Tribe* (about the Saoras) and *Tribal Myths of Orissa*, as well as a special number of *Man in India* about the Juangs. I also wrote a number of reports for Government and made recommendations for the welfare of the tribal people. Had I been more energetic I could have done at least two more books, for I had a great many notes on the Gadabas and Konds and a large collection of photographs.

I will now give brief descriptions of three of the tribes I visited—the Kuttia Konds, the Bondos and the Saoras. They are not 'anthropological' descriptions and the reader who wants a detailed account must go elsewhere. It may perhaps be questioned whether what I say here and in chapter 9* on the NEFA tribes has a legitimate place in an autobiography. I think it has. The tribes were such an important part of my life and brought so much interest and pleasure into it that without them, without the Baigas and Murias, the Bondos, Konds and Saoras, my story would be incomplete. The Baigas introduced me to the wilder forests; the Kuttia Konds and Marias kindled and educated my sense of beauty. I thought about the Saoras, talked to and about them, loved them, was absorbed in them for years. I thought myself into the Murias, fascinated by not only the academic but also the human problems raised by their unusual social system. Only those who have some idea of them can really understand me. My entire attitude to life has been affected by the lovable NEFA folk. Apart from these tribes who, one by one, filled my life to the brim, there is not very much for me to talk about. Of the great events of my time I have only been a spectator; I have met very few important people. It is the tribes who have been my life and that is why I have had to put them in its record.

IX

The Kuttia Konds

First let me describe the wild, remote and devastatingly attractive Kuttia Konds.

The Konds are a large tribe, speaking a Dravidian language akin to Gondi, who are scattered all over Orissa, but the Kuttia Konds are confined to the desolate hills and forests in the north-western corner of the Ganjam District. These Kuttias were very poor, very timid, strikingly good-looking and, once you got to know them, charming and loyal friends.

*Refer to original edition, *The Tribal World of Verrier Elwin* (OUP, 1964).

They had a good deal of cause for their timidity. They were grossly oppressed by Dom moneylenders and Patro landlords; they had a hard time from the officials of the Forest Department; their simplicity made them fair game for any rascally merchant or black-marketeer who adventured into their hills; and they lived in an area where wild animals made frequent attacks on their lives and property.

During my first visit to their hills, a Kond, who was carrying my mail down to the railway, was killed by a tiger and next morning, when we went to the spot, all we could find was a pool of blood and my letters scattered about the jungle. Wild elephants also were a constant danger and did great damage to the crops. Sometimes on tour we moved as a sort of convoy, all sorts of people joining our party for protection through a dangerous tract.

The Konds were constantly shifting their villages, which they built in such inaccessible places that there was often no level spot for us to make a camp. Like the Baigas, they were passionately devoted to the practice of axe-cultivation, though they were much more careful than the Baigas in observing a rotation. so as not to ruin the forest permanently. Each village had perhaps a dozen traditional sites to which it shifted in turn when the available forest in the neighbourhood had been exhausted. Their houses were very small, often with tiny doors. Once when I was camping in one of their huts, the door was so low that I had to crawl in and out on my hands and knees.

The villages, however, were often very picturesque. They were usually laid out in two long rows of houses, each joined to its neighbour. In the middle, standing up impressively against the sky, was a forked pillar of sacrifice with buffalo horns placed on its points. The stone of Mother Earth stood in front of three other stones which served it as a protecting wall. Often there was an elaborately caved pillar of sacrifice, decorated with such relics as a buffalo's skull, the tail of a barking-deer, sambhar bones or a buffalo's hoof. The villages were usually kept spotlessly clean.

Even in 1944 the desire for human sacrifice was fundamental to Kond psychology. It will be remembered that, about a hundred years ago, the Government put an end to the savage Meriah sacrifices—human beings, who were offered to the Earth Goddess in order to fertilize the soil. It was hard to believe that these simple inoffensive folk could ever have practised so barbarous a rite or could even now long so greatly for its restoration. But it was so. In almost every village, hidden away in a priest's house, were the old implements of sacrifice—the knife, the chains, the bowl to catch the blood—and the priests told me how at certain seasons when the moon was full they could hear these horrid tools weeping for the human blood which was now denied them.

There were still carefully treasured a few human skulls, perhaps a hundred years old, or bits of human bone, which were brought out at special ceremonies or used as amulets. A great hunter, who had a bit of finger bone, told me that he attributed all his luck in the chase to his possession of it.

Long ago, when the Meriah sacrifice was put down by Government, the Konds began to sacrifice buffaloes in place of human victims. When this was done, an old human skull or mask was brought out and laid before the symbols of divinity. There was, when I was there, an attempt being made by well-meaning but not very intelligent persons to stop even the buffalo sacrifices in the interests of vegetarianism.

The Konds were devotedly attached to that 'vile weed' of which Charles Lamb used to speak so eloquently. The boys made excellent tobacco-tubes, decorated with patterns of lozenges and triangles. Their legend of the origin of tobacco is told all over tribal India, even in NEFA. There was once a very ugly girl whom no one would marry. She did her best to get a husband, but no one wanted her. In despair she went to the Creator and begged to be allowed to die, and to return in her next birth as something which all men would love. He granted her request and after her death caused a tobacco plant to grow out of her despised body. And so the girl whom nobody wanted is now the desire of all the world.

The Kuttia Konds had nothing—and everything. Long ago I wrote some verses about them which puts it better than anything I could say now.

The True Treasure

They have no treasure as the world counts gain.
Some starving cattle; a small bin of grain;
Torn scraps of dirty cloth; a string of beads;
A mat, a broken bed, a pot of seeds,

A basketful of roots, a little meat,
The bows and arrows and a wooden seat,
Is all their low-roofed hovels boast of store.
Such is the sad accounting of the poor.

They have no treasure? Let us look again.
See how their courage triumphs over pain;
How patiently they cast the annual seed;
How steadfastly they bear their daily need.

These riches of the spirit are their power.
And then—the beauty like a perfect flower
That blossoms as the lotus from the mud,
The glory of the children in the bud.

See the fine bodies, unimproved by art,
The plum-black hair that twines about the heart,
The eyes that with the grace of fireflies move,
The shining teeth, the breasts that foster love.

Regard the features ravishing and dark,
And the gay song-filled voices. Hark, O hark,
To the sweet koel-music of their words
That dance and wanton with the coloured birds.

The breathing loveliness of human clay,
Though transient, transforms the hardest day.
How can we call them poor, whose wealth unbought
By contrast turns the rich man's gold to naught?

X

The Bondos

Some years ago Michael Huxley asked me to do a piece for the *Geographical Magazine* on 'My Worst Journey', part of which I will reproduce here. I began by saying that I did not find it easy to describe my worst journey, for I had never made a journey that was entirely bad. And I went on to summarize my experiences in the period before I went to Assam.

On the whole [I wrote] my travels in tribal India have been exceedingly rewarding. They have indeed often been uncomfortable; the marching and climbing has been arduous enough; I have had my share of sharp fevers with their dreary sequels, far from medical assistance; supplies of food have raised complicated problems. But in general, as I look back, almost all my memories are pleasant: the beauty of the countryside, the charm and friendliness of the people, the excitement of scientific inquiry, the support of devoted assistants, the alliance of true friends—these things have made a quarter of a century, the greater part of which has been spent far from the imagined comforts of civilization and the supposed stimulus of educated conversation, a period of singular happiness.

But of course I have had my troubles. I have been bored by delays, irritated by tedious officials, exasperated by puritans, padres and police, disappointed, frustrated, wearied, as every traveller must be. But not a single tour or expedition has been without its great rewards.

First visits to any area are difficult: you do not know the country or the language; interpreters are hard to come by and, until they are trained, are usually worse than useless; you yourself are unfamiliar and the people are not sure what you are up to: all the minor irritations of life are magnified. And of these first tours, I think the most difficult was the one I made into the Bondo country of Orissa in December 1943.

The Bondos are a small tribe of the type now often called Austro-Asiatic which—at the time of the 1941 Census—numbered only 2,565 persons. Their country, elevated, beautiful and remote; lies north-west of the Machkund river. Notorious for their violent and inhospitable ways, they have preserved themselves comparatively unaffected by the march of civilization. Indeed by plainsmen and officials the Bondos are regarded as entirely savage, almost as the classic savage type: the strange dress and appearance of the women with their exiguous skirts and shaven heads, the passionate and homicidal temper of the men, their unfamiliar tongue, the inaccessibility of their abode, have long separated them from their mild and conventional neighbours. I do not know what has happened to them in recent years, but when I visited them for the last time in 1947, the only change I found was in their reaction to myself: by now suspicion had given way to an almost overwhelming friendliness.

The end of 1943 was, of course, a bad time to get about. All maps were, very properly, controlled by the military authorities, and so I had very little idea of where anything was. Food, with equal propriety, was strictly rationed, and for a traveller to obtain the necessary permits involved endless waiting about in dreary offices. Rations were issued by the week, but I needed supplies for several months. There was no regulation, the matter would have to be referred to Cuttack, what was the real purpose of my visit?

Many things were not available at all. The absence of tinned foods did not worry me, for I detest the stuff, but condensed milk was a necessity in a part of the world where milk was taboo. And of course there was no petrol.

To reach the Bondo country, if there was no petrol to drive your car, involved a train-journey from Calcutta to Vizianagram, and then a ninety-mile trip by country bus through lovely scenery to Koraput. The road winds steeply through the hills, and many of the passengers were sick. At Koraput the chief official had been a contemporary of mine at Oxford, but did not think it necessary to look after me, and I was accommodated in a sleazy dak-bungalow with broken windows. Sitting among the rats and fleas, I recollected with satisfaction that my fellow-collegian had taken a poor Third in History.

In the India of that time, unless you were an official, rich, or had unimpeachable or intimidating introductions, no one took very much notice of you. This was evident when we continued our journey for the further fourteen miles to Jeypore where a sumptuous guest-house was maintained by the Maharaja. Here everybody settled down to make my further progress as difficult as possible. In later years, I am glad to say, the local people were as helpful as they were then obstructive.

We first had to reach a place called Govindapalle, forty miles away. There was a bus, but it was not running that week: the proprietor's nephew was getting married. I waited several days and then put my stores and equipment on a couple of bullock-carts, a mode of travel which I have always rather enjoyed. Its one disadvantage is that it exposes you to interrogations: who was I, what was I doing, what was my aim in going to the Bondos?—everybody wanted to know. However, we reached our first Bondo village safely, but there discovered that no one was willing to go with us up into the hills. The Bondos were not used to carrying other people's loads—and who could blame them? It took a long time and much persuasion to get a dozen porters. But we did get them in the end, and one glorious morning climbed the steep hills to an enchantingly situated village, Dumiripada, on the top of the world.

It was beautiful, it was romantic, but it was not hospitable. There was no hostility: crowds of men, women and children thronged round as we put up a few leafy branches to make some sort of hut; they all beamed amiably, but no one would move a finger to help. Requests for wood and water, on extravagant payment, were met by charming smiles—but no action followed. The headman came, and he did his best, but Bondo headmen have little authority. At last, after tremendous argument and much shouting among themselves, a few boys brought just enough water for the kitchen.

The Bondos, in fact, are remarkably unwilling to oblige. They are prepared to sit round in the friendliest fashion, laughing, joking and chatting, so long as you do not ask them to do anything. They are always ready to give information. But they object very much to giving anything else. They have no apparent desire to earn money. At one village I offered some boys who had nothing whatever to do the equivalent of three days' earnings to catch some fish for me, but they refused. They dislike selling any of their possessions, and to live off the country here is a real problem. This was not a cause of irritation, for why *should* they do anything? But it was a practical difficulty.

Such help as we got came from an unexpected source. I have had the privilege of knowing a good many murderers, but hitherto most of these had been in jail. In the Bondo country, where the homicide rate is the highest in all India, murder is usually punished by a comparatively short sentence of five or seven years, and I found that the most affable and helpful people were those who had done time, even though I was sometimes apprehensive that one of them might feel the need of a little further practice. A further advantage was that these charming if ferocious ex-convicts usually knew some Hindi or Oriya, and we were therefore able to converse with them direct instead of through an interpreter.

Our next village, Bandapada, was very timid. As I went down the street, mothers seized their children and hurried them indoors, girls fled whimpering with fright, doors banged, fowls and pigs scurried to safety, one youth hastily got up a tree. Only a few old men, greatly daring, came to greet us. I can endure any hardship other than the realization that I look like a sort of ogre. Later I heard that it was supposed that I had come to take girls for the war, that I was going to send all the children to America to be baptized, and—most curious of all—that I was an Excise Officer who had come to introduce Prohibition. After a time, however, a delightful person, who had twice been to prison for successive murders and, as far as I could discover, was even then planning a third, turned up and with his help we got some kind of roof over our heads and a meagre supply of necessities.

I then brought out the gramophone, which is usually a great success. No sooner, however, had I put on a rather dreadful record entitled 'Fun with the Concertina', which I regret to say is everywhere in great demand, than one old woman fell down in a fit, several others flopped to the ground in an attitude of worship, and all the children ran screaming from the place. A deputation of elders quickly arrived to ask me to stop the music, if that is the correct word, as it was evident that there was something very dangerous inside the sound-box and they did not want to take any risks.

In the Bondo and Saora villages I departed from my usual custom of staying in someone's house and instead we made little huts for ourselves,

Under the bam
Under the boo
Under the bamboo tree.

These were of leafy branches with a deep layer of straw underfoot and a rough thatch above. They were surprisingly comfortable but unfortunately they were edible and almost every night cattle would come and start eating the walls, which was a constant disturbance.

On later visits I had a very pleasant time with the Bondos. On one of them Shamrao with his wife and two small children, Suresh and Ramula, accompanied me and on my last trip I had Victor Sassoon, who enjoyed himself thoroughly and took a large number of first-class photographs, some of which I reproduced in my book, *Bondo Highlander*.

And the Bondos were well worth photographing, for on the whole they are a good-looking people. Boys and young men are often most attractive. Their fine carriage, magnificent physique, free and open countenance, delightful smile, are captivating. The way they do their hair is specially charming. As they grow older, however, they degenerate a little; the face coarsens, the body is dirtier, the hair is done in a different, and less pleasing, fashion. Like most tribesmen above a certain age, the Bondos let themselves go. In jail, they look terrible.

At first sight a visitor may exclaim that Bondo women are the ugliest he has ever seen. But in a few days, after he has got over the first shock of their rather unconventional appearance, he may revise his opinion. The illusion of ugliness is largely created by the shaven head. But a young girl with something covering her head—a fish-basket or a sickle-curved bundle of bark—often shows the world a face of character and charm. Little girls, ten or twelve years old, are sometimes very pretty, especially when they decorate their head-bands with sprigs of greenery and white, mauve or scarlet flowers. The chief fault of the older girls (apart, of course, from the lack of hair) is that there is perhaps a little too much of them. They are apt to be plump, rather sleek and smooth, big-lipped, bagpipe-breasted, with large thighs, thick calves, 'thick as plantain stalks'. Older women are often very charming with good features and an indefinable attraction that speedily made one forget the oddity of their appearance.

Bondo boys have very definite views about feminine beauty and one day a group of them used some rather poetical expressions while attempting to explain the meaning of a love-song. The phrases are probably traditional or at least based on the highly condensed song-technique. They described a girl's body as 'beautiful as a white cloud', her arms and legs 'round and shapely as a bamboo', her breasts 'sparkling as two fishes'; her shadow 'broad and healthy as a buffalo'. Above all, the beautiful girl is 'useful as the leaf of a giant creeper'—from which leaf-cups and plates are made.

The Bondo sexual tradition was very different from the Muria. To the Bondos sexual experience was difficult, dangerous and expensive; while the Gond or Baiga often thought of intercourse as little more than a pleasant experience, the Bondo regarded it as a very serious matter. There were several reasons for this. The Bondo youth was bound by the most rigorous taboos from having anything to do with the girls of his own village; when he met the girls of other villages, he did so in public and under conditions of the strictest conventionality. This placed an effective brake on those casual everyday affairs which were the normal recreation of village boys in other parts of India.

Then again sexual intercourse was a risky matter; it involved the introduction of the most precious of life's possessions into an unknown and alien world. This was something fundamental in the psychology of the tribe; the Bondo could not bear going abroad. That was his real torment in jail; that was why he was so unwilling to carry our baggage to another village—I once saw a group of women weeping in utter despair because a member of the household was carrying some of my things to a place only four miles away. Like other tribesmen, the Bondos had the strange and sinister legend of the Vagina Dentata, which is closely connected with the fear of castration. These legends, which I have found among many Indian tribes and which have also been recorded in North America and from the Ainus, were entirely serious. They were not just dirty stories calculated to raise a hiccoughing chuckle in the dormitory; they were the attempt of Bondo fiction to suggest the risk of sexual congress.

But the most potent influence against promiscuity was that the girls would not have it. It is generally admitted in other tribal societies—and I believe it is largely true—that it is the girls who lead men on. But this was not true of the Bondo girls. To them sexual intercourse in the pre-marital period implied a serious intention; it was almost equivalent to a betrothal. The Saora youth drove an arrow between breasts carved in wood on the pillar of the house where his beloved lived; after that she was his. But if the Bondo youth translated this symbolism into actuality, he was caught: he was hers.

All this was characteristic of the eastern group of tribes, who were remarkable for their sexual reticence. The Saoras had the same outlook, so did the Juangs, Gadabas and Marias. But the Gond group had a very different tradition. The Gonds, Pardhans, Konds and other allied tribes regarded the expression of sexual passion, however delightful it might be, as a comparatively trivial affair, to be indulged as a passing entertainment, unimportant (provided certain conventions were observed) in its effects. This does not mean that they do not fall in love; they do, deeply and disastrously; but they found it possible at the same time and in a different compartment, as it were, to enjoy sex without getting too much involved.

I came to like the Bondos immensely and made many personal friends among them. They were not only very lovable but unusually exciting. This was due mainly to their bad tempers, which meant that you never knew what was going to happen next. The Bondos were aware of this defect and had devised a curious and unique rite of mutual castigation, for the express purpose of teaching themselves to keep their tempers. Conducted with a mixture of ferocity and hilarity, it began with little boys. To the excited beating of drums they armed themselves with long switches, stood up two by two, and beat each other as hard as they could. It was no pretence; soon backs were covered with weals, and the little fellows bit their lips as they went for each other with all their strength. When a couple had had enough they saluted one another with mutual respect, clasped each other in a warm embrace and retired in favour of another pair. When all the boys had completed this piquant exercise, the priest gave them a special kind of cake 'to stop their quarrels' and delivered a little lecture: 'Never beat anyone in anger. Let everyone treat his fellow as a brother. Never make other people angry.'

This was all right. The anxiety came when young men, perhaps jealous rivals for the same girl, or old toughs hardened by years in jail, began to beat each other: then there was a real sense of tension. I think that this unusual rite does to some extent succeed in its aim of training the Bondos to keep their tempers under the sudden stimulus of pain, and serves as a surrogate for the grosser emotions.

In spite of this there were a great many Bondo rows, some of which I was privileged to watch. I was once present at a violent quarrel when a Bondo attacked a Gadaba, who was supposed to have insulted him by exposing his private parts. The contrast between the ferocious Bondo, screaming abuse in three languages (including bits of English), and the meek Gadaba bowing before the storm with folded hands, was striking. Another day I saw a group of Bondo boys invade a Gadaba village, and rob its favourite sago palm of its juice. The Gadabas chattered with rage and anguish as they watched their precious wine slipping down the ample Bondo throats, but not one of them dared to interfere. When they had drunk their fill, the Bondo boys paraded the village with an electric insolence and charm. In spite of her rage, every Gadaba girl came out of her house and stood gazing fascinated. After executing a particularly obscene little dance just to put everyone in his place, the Bondos finally departed, leaving the village exhausted as a person through whose body has passed a powerful, but not quite fatal, shock.

It is indeed an extraordinary experience to witness a Bondo quarrel. There is first an exchange of words. Hints about a wife's chastity, allusions to a sister's virtue flicker to and fro. Then the Bondo suddenly comes to the boil; the waters rise and topple over. He twirls his moustache. He spits at his adversary. He pulls out a few hairs and throws them at him. He chatters and bubbles with temper. And then he draws his knife or jumps for his bow and arrows.

Yet this is not the last word. Bondo life was marked by courage, freedom, equality, independence and industry. The defects of these qualities were equally evident; courage became an indifference to human life, freedom and independence degenerated into ill-mannered aggressiveness, too strong a sense of equality could become bad citizenship. The Bondo drank too much; he was often lazy and drove his womenfolk too hard; he was not very clean; he wasted a lot of time in the exact, and rather fussy, performance and repetition of ceremonial. But otherwise there was a great deal to be said for him. If he was a savage, he was at least a noble savage. If he was poor, he was at least patient and courageous in his poverty. If he was outside, and perhaps behind, the main stream of civilization, he was at least free of many of its debasing vices.

In a hotel where I stayed at Chiengmai in northern Thailand there was a notice announcing that young ladies and 'excessive persons' were not admitted into the rooms at night. The Bondos attracted me because they were excessive persons, and after all Blake once said that 'the road of excess leads to the palace of wisdom'.

XI

The Saoras

My study of the Saoras extended over seven years. I concentrated on one section of this very large tribe, the Hill Saoras of Ganjam and Koraput, and particularly of the villages in the hills above Gunupur, which at that time were almost completely untouched by missionary or other external influence and where it was possible to see the old life as it must have continued for hundreds of years.

To these I went from Patangarh to stay long periods and often made my camp in one village for two or three weeks at a time. I took my books and papers with me and settled down as though I were at home. In fact, I wrote a good deal of my book about the Saoras on the spot, and was able to correct or verify things as I went along. The people were very good to me and used to make me charming little two-roomed huts of branches and leaves, with good verandas. The quickest way to their hearts was by gifts of country-cigars called *pikas*. For these they had, and I hope still have, a passionate attachment. They were also very fond of tea and were constantly dropping in for a cup or two. I often had half a dozen people round my bed soon after dawn anxious to share my morning tea.

Yet in my day at least, the Saoras did not really want to have visitors. After any outsider had been to the village they made special sacrifices to purify the place from any possible magical defilement. In one area I found a regular tariff: for a Forest Officer they sacrificed a goat, for a Sub-Inspector of Police a fowl, and for an anthropologist a large black pig.

They had a god called Sahibosum, who was propitiated for the express purpose of keeping touring officials away. A sahib, of course, is anything in a hat and a pair of trousers. Wooden images were made and erected outside the village. There was also an image of the 'Memsahib' goddess, usually just a little larger and more formidable than her husband. She was always represented as wearing a sola topi.

There was nothing personal about this. Even your best friends would make these sacrifices and erect these images. It was simply that if you came from the outside world you might bring, clinging invisibly to you, some sort of spiritual infection; a spirit or demon might use you as a vehicle to get inside the charmed village boundaries.

In spite of this, I managed to visit almost all the hill Saora villages and in some of them I felt like an explorer, for those in the remoter parts of the hills had not been visited in living memory by any outsider, and for months at a time I did not meet any official: Sahibosum had clearly been effective. I was there in the cold and also when it was very hot, indeed at all times of the year except the height of the rains.

The beauty of the country was almost overwhelming. When I

was younger I had a feeling for Nature akin to that of the young Wordsworth. Natural beauty haunted me like a passion. It was 'an appetite; a feeling and a love' that had no need for any interest 'unborrowed from the eye'.

But I think that from the very beginning of my time in tribal India I moved on to Wordsworth's further stage of hearing oftentimes 'the still, sad music of humanity' against the background of Nature. This was particularly true of my years in Bastar.

Later, in NEFA among the northern mountains, their mystery and grandeur disturbed me with the sense of the universal presence, 'the joy of elevated thoughts', of which Wordsworth writes again.

But in the Saora hills the appeal of Nature was largely sensuous. It was, it is true, always a setting for human beings and yet its impact was almost physical. I ached for it and when I had to leave it, it was always with a very heavy heart.

The Hill Saoras had large substantial villages; they erected menhirs and sacrificed buffaloes for their dead; their religious needs were served by male and female shamans; they engaged in both terraced and shifting cultivation; their men put on a long brightly-coloured loin-cloth and their women wore a handwoven brown-bordered skirt and did not usually wear anything else; the women also greatly enlarged the lobes of their ears and had a characteristic tattoo mark down the middle of the forehead. They retained their own language and very few of them spoke any other.

Saora houses were well-built and in long streets, and some Saora chieftains were comparatively wealthy. Indeed, they might all have been fairly well-to-do, so laborious and careful were they, had it not been for the shocking exploitation to which they were subjected by their landlords and moneylenders.

It was a heart-breaking sight to stand by a Saora's threshing-floor and watch his creditors and parasites remove in payment of their dues so much of the grain which he had laboured so hard to produce.

The great achievement of the Saoras is their terracing. They build up the hillsides for a thousand feet, terrace rising above terrace, perfectly aligned, so carefully done that not a drop of water escapes uselessly and all erosion is checked. Sometimes a great stone wall, fifteen feet high, will hold up a ridge of cultivable soil only three feet wide. These terraces have been rightly praised as works of great engineering skill.

The main subject of my study was Saora religion, for the Saoras are quite the most religious people I have ever met. Happily, they did not resent my inquiries but were rather flattered by them. Where other tribes postpone a festival or ceremony if a visitor comes to the village, the Saoras used to insist on my presence at everything. They took me into their houses, made me sit on the floor near the officiating priest and explained it all in great detail as the long ceremonies took their course.

In fact we used to have a saying that there was never a holiday for the anthropologist in the Saora country. Every day something happened. You were just settling down to a quiet siesta when you would hear the roar of gunfire echoing in a neighbouring valley, and you knew there was a funeral which you simply must attend. Or someone would arrive at dawn with news of a most exciting ceremony in a village five miles away and due to start in half an hour.

I was rather often ill in the Saora country, for malaria was a dangerous scourge there and I had some very bad bouts of toothache. Even this worked out well, for the priests and even the priestesses used to crowd in to my little hut, sit by my bedside and attempt to cure me by their own techniques. And cure or relieve me they often did, for their methods were extremely soothing and their affection and interest was reviving. I also learnt by personal experience a great deal about their ideas that I might otherwise have missed.

During this happy period I found that my old Oxford studies in theology, which at one time I had written off as wasted, were of unexpected value. Heiler's monumental book on prayer, for example, William James on the varieties of religious experience, Otto on the numinous element in religion as well as many other books helped me to understand the Saoras better.

Saora life was completely dominated by their religion. Beyond and around this life and this visible world is an unseen realm of vital reality, peopled by a host of spirits whose activities impinge on normal existence at every turn.

The ghosts live in an Underworld, which is something like this world of our own, but everything is on a Lilliputian scale. The houses are very small; the clouds lie low upon the land; it is always twilight under the infernal moon. The ghosts live a sad half-life, ill-fed and poorly clad, until they themselves die again and, if they are cremated in proper form, vanish from the misery of existence forever.

But the rulers of the Underworld, the tutelary spirits, do themselves well. They have large houses, the best of food and clothing and many servants. They keep tigers and leopards (as men keep dogs) as pets. The bear is the priest and the porcupine the medicine-man of this strange world.

It is the great desire of the tutelary spirits, both male and female, to find partners among the living. They come to them in dreams and beg them to marry them. There is a special class of girls who at the age of puberty have dreamt of these unearthly lovers and after a turbulent period of wooing have agreed to marry them.

The marriage is an elaborate affair, quite as elaborate and expensive as an ordinary marriage, and when it is over, the girl is a Kuranboi, a priestess who henceforth will be able to do the work of divination and healing with the aid of her unseen husband. The Saoras believe that the girls can have children from these husbands, and I met many Saora women who had families both in this and in the other world. Sometimes, listening to the way they talked, I used to wonder which was the more real to them.

But in spite of the realm of fantasy in which they lived, these women were practical and devoted servants of their tribe. They were always ready to hasten to minister to the sick and console the sorrowful. Men also were subject to these experiences, and they became, as a result, the all-important medicine-men of the tribe.

The work of these simple 'doctors' had great survival value. It gave the patient the sense that someone cared about him. It made him believe that he was going to get well. It settled his conscience and gave him the will to recover. And the medicine-men took their profession seriously and worked very hard at it.

To the research man there is no greater happiness, no deeper love, no more thrilling excitement than to work in such a field as this. I have found not only among the Saoras but other tribes too that there comes a moment when everything falls into place and you suddenly see the life of a people as a harmonious whole and understand how it works. This decisive moment, which can only be achieved after arduous study, is one of the greatest experiences that a scholar can have.

But it always took a long time. A friend of mine who read this book in manuscript, unlike my other friends who wanted me to put in more about my vices, told me I should say something about my virtues. 'That would be very nice,' I said, 'but what virtues have I?' He was a little stumped by this but after some thought he said, 'I think your greatest virtue is patience.' There may be something in this, for I have always been content to go forward without reward or recognition and in my search for the truth to take any trouble and to spend any amount of time in finding it. Things take me a long time, and I have always been content to wait.

Sometimes people wrote about the sacrifice I made in going into tribal India. But that is certainly not a virtue I can claim. What sacrifice could there possibly be in living in the beauty of the Saora hills or in the heart-warming atmosphere of Patangarh? There has never been a moment of sacrifice in my life; for everything I have given I have been repaid tenfold, and of myself I can say:

Love had he found in huts where poor men lie;
His daily teachers had been woods and rills,
The silence that is in the starry sky,
The sleep that is among the lonely hills.

My memories of life in Bastar and Orissa are, like my memories of Oxford, inconsolable. I shall never see, no one will ever see, the Muria ghotul as I saw it, or the Saoras as I saw them. It may be that I myself helped by my very presence to destroy what I so much admired. But all over tribal India the old freedom is disappearing and with it something of the old happiness. Change is inevitable and I have no doubt that the great schemes of village welfare have brought some profit to some of the people already and in time will bring new life to them all. How far this will in the long run result in their happiness is a problem that vexes all those who think seriously on the subject.

But however this may be, one thing is clear. The old romantic exciting days, the beauty and the zest have gone for ever. I would not recall them if it meant loss to even a single child, yet it is hard not to feel nostalgic for what used to be.

I heard a voice that cried,
Balder the beautiful
Is dead, is dead.

XII

A special, and very important, aspect of research is photography: this led me into many adventures, especially in the early days and the remoter regions, where it was by no means easy.

The camera to many tribal people is an object not only of embarrassment, but of fear. That mysterious aperture which points in their direction in so sinister a manner, the almost inevitable fuss and preparation that precedes the taking of even the simplest photographs, the fixing of the tripod, the manoeuvring for position, cannot fail to alarm them. In a bazaar in Mandla District I saw a rather photogenic blacksmith—it was when I was writing my book about the Agarias—but when I pointed my camera at him I was startled to see a wave of fear pass over everybody within sight. The local constable came up to me, saluted smartly, and said, 'I can get you a much better man than that,' but before I realized what he meant the whole bazaar was on the move. People leapt to their feet upsetting the stalls, throwing baskets of vegetables to the ground, trampling on bales of cloth, and in a few moments they were all streaming away into the jungle. I later discovered that even the constable supposed that my camera was a sort of anthropometric instrument by which I could measure the stature of likely recruits for the Army. Another time in the Raipur District, people trembled with fear while I was photographing them and afterwards one of them said, 'You have taken all my strength and shut it up in that little box.' In another place I found that the people supposed the camera to be a sort of X-ray instrument with which I could see right through their clothes and bodies down to their livers. Everybody knows, of course, that the liver is a very important thing in black magic. You try to affect the person's liver as a preliminary to murdering him by witchcraft. If you can get hold of a bit of the liver of a dead man or even a picture of it, it is a very potent source of supernatural power.

In Bastar, when I was making a documentary film of the Murias and Marias, I found, on the whole, that they were very good about letting me photograph them and I was often astonished at the willingness of even the children to come before the camera. But sometimes the luck was bad. I once went to photograph a Muria wedding; in fact, I was invited to go by the father of the bride, who was an old friend. For the first day everything went swimmingly. We exchanged presents: we were allowed to see everything that went on: I have seldom been in a more friendly company of people, I was able to get a number of excellent pictures. Then, on the morning of the second day, the bridegroom had a fit. I was standing nearby with my ubiquitous camera in my hand. My heart sank. I knew what would happen. Gradually, inevitably, the eyes of the entire company turned to me. I knew what they were thinking: that queer little box had brought the wrath of the gods on the bridegroom. After a few minutes the boy's mother, a very forceful woman with a mass of false hair curled up and up on the top of her head (she was said to be an incarnation of the god Mahadeo), declared to my face that it was the camera that had troubled her son. There was nothing to be done. The atmosphere was ruined. After that, even though I put the camera away, whenever people saw me they looked embarrassed and awkward. I felt as though I had indeed a black monkey sitting on my back.

Once when I was touring among the Bison-Horn Marias in the beautiful mountains of south Bastar I had with infinite trouble arranged to take a photograph of boys and girls fishing in a river. As always, of course, the people had first of all declared that they did not know what fish were. Then, when they had gone so far as to admit that there were fish, they said they never actually caught any of them (they probably thought that I was making an inquiry to take their fishing rights from them—a thing which has been done in some parts of India). Then they said they had no fish-traps and we had to go and search for them in the village. When at last we got the boys and girls carrying their traps down to the river bank, a sinister-looking old man appeared and said something in a loud voice. Immediately, before you could count ten, the place was deserted. Everybody disappeared into the jungle, leaving the traps and fishing-tackle on the ground. I then discovered that the old gentleman was the village priest and had announced that it had been revealed to him by the gods that anyone who allowed himself to be photographed would die forthwith.

I dealt with this by making the priest himself pose for his photograph. At first he presented a large and obstinate back, but I ultimately made him face me, and so was able to declare that if anybody was going to die he would be the first. I then showed the villagers photographs of the Maharaja and my own wife and myself and pointed out that we were all alive and happy in spite of the way our 'souls' were plastered on these bits of paper. On this occasion it was possible to make a certain impression and I shortly afterwards got an excellent picture of a cock-fight, the villagers presumably supposing that even if my lethal weapon did slaughter the cocks they could always eat them; but I was unable, with all our persuading, to recapture the same happy natural atmosphere which we had had before and which is, of course, essential to the making of a successful film.

Sometimes local subordinates or helpful friends can be equally embarrassing. Once in Sarangarh I had succeeded, with a lot of trouble, in getting a group of villagers natural and at ease, just ready for a good picture, when a zealous chaprasi rushed up exclaiming 'How dare you sit in that casual manner in front of the Sahib!'

I had similar experiences in NEFA, and among such highly photogenic people as the Boris and Wanchos I had to put my camera away entirely when I visited most of their villages. I never had any difficulty, however, among the Buddhist tribes along the frontier.

XIII

Composing books is one thing. Typing them out and getting them printed is quite another. Until I came to Shillong, except for a brief period, I never had a stenographer or typist and I myself typed out all my larger books. My practice was to type out a rough draft, then retype it again filling in the gaps and finally to make a fair copy. This involved an enormous amount of work but it was worth it, for I am convinced that you can do much better when you write yourself than when you dictate.

Then there is the business of proof-reading. My publisher, Roy Hawkins of the Oxford University Press, who undertook the profitless task of producing a whole series of my books during the war-years when paper was hard to obtain and printers were overburdened, used to tell me the way to read a proof before you sent your typescript to the printer. The Oxford Press impressed on me, among many other things, how careful you must be if you are going into print. What used to happen was that soon after I sent them a manuscript I would get a letter with a long list of queries. I have never been very good at spelling and the Press usually discovered that I had spelt words in different ways on different pages. Sometimes there were mistakes in grammar, sometimes in punctuation. When I began publishing I had the idea, so common among young authors, that somehow or other the printers would 'put it right'. I now learnt that, particularly in India, the printers would reproduce exactly what they saw in the text. Many compositors, in fact, do not know English but are simply trained to follow their copy exactly.

Then proofs would come and go; I would read them two or three times; the office of the Press would also read them; and finally Hawkins himself reads, I believe, every book he publishes at the final stage before it is struck off.

Sometimes we had amusing problems, particularly when I wrote about more intimate matters. There was one compositor, clearly suffering from a little complex about it, who, whenever the word 'sex' came in my manuscript, set it upside down. Nearly all compositors, I found, set up the expression 'public hairs', which is one of the curious things anthropologists sometimes write about, but this is, of course, exactly what they are not. When my book on the Murias was half ready there was a crisis because the Mission Press which was doing it suddenly realized what it was about and wrote to say that they could not possibly print such a shocking work. Hawkins, however, was firm and told them that they should have read the typescript before accepting the contract. Fortunately, the manager of the press was an exceptionally liberal Baptist and he himself thought the whole business rather funny. I estimated that by the time we finished, the Oxford Press and I between us read the proofs of this book no fewer than eight times, with the gratifying result that in three-quarters of a million words only three misprints have been found, an achievement to which the Baptist Mission Press of Calcutta notably contributed.

3

Organization of the Tribe

The Muria and their Ghotul (1947)

I. The Clan System

An elaborate discussion of the clan system of the Muria would be out of place and not very profitable, for it is impossible to bring any kind of order out of the confusion into which that system has fallen in modern times. But some account of the clans and their rules must be given, for they are of real importance to the children in the ghotul and a breach of the clan-rules may merit not only the vengeance of the Departed but severe punishment from the leaders of the ghotul and of the tribe. The clans regulate the absorbing question of marriage and the still more absorbing relationships of chelik and motiari. Their distribution directs to some extent the annual dancing expeditions. The clan festivals are among the most exciting and colourful incidents in the ghotul's life.

I will therefore briefly outline the clan system—though it must be remembered that it is not really a system—and I will then give a few stories about the origin of these clans and finally an account of the rules and customs that are observed.

The clan system of the Muria is now greatly confused. In the old days it seems probable that the inhabited territory of north Bastar was divided up among the different clans of Maria and Muria, and each had its own particular *bhum* or clan area. In each *bhum* there was a spiritual capital called the *pen-rawar* or *pen-kara*. Here lived the clan-god or Anga with the clan-priest to tend him and mediate between him and his kinsmen. Here they came for the chief festivals of the Anga; here they brought their dead and erected their menhirs; here they gathered for the special panchayat that discussed offences against the clan laws.

Traces of this organization exist, but the increase of population, the occupation of vast new tracts of land, the scattering of the clansmen in all directions has destroyed the clear pattern of former days. Many Muria have never visited their *pen-rawar*, many are living in *bhum* that really belong to other clans, most clans have *bhum* rights in villages that are widely apart. There are no longer compact clan areas, and in every village—though each is regarded as the *bhum* of some special clan—there live members of several other clans.

It was this fact, of course, that made the ghotul, in its Muria form, possible. Among the Hill Maria, where the old one-clan-to-one-village system still survives,[1] girls are not allowed to share the dormitory with the boys because of the obvious danger of clan incest.

The Muria, then, preserve the old traditions but in a confused and disorderly way. Many clans have more than one *pen-rawar* and several gods. The Naitami clan, for example, has spiritual headquarters at Kharkagaon, Kabonga, Chingnar and Sirpur; the Poyami clan worships Samrath Dokara—an Anga—at Sirsi, as well as Budha Pen at Lanjora and Chingnar. The Dhurwa clan has a clan-god, Son Kuar, at Metawand and another, Budha Dokara—an Anga—at Kharkagaon. The Sori clan worships Budha Pen at Chingnar, Kara Hurra at Garanji and Lalit Kuar at Gorma.

In each case, however, there is one ancient *pen-rawar* to which the more orthodox elders of the tribe go when they can and where they will have their menhirs erected. This belief in the clan-*bhum*, whether original or adopted as a result of immigration and settlement, is still sufficiently alive to excite serious quarrels. It was a dispute over the rights to a clan-*bhum* that began the deadly feud between the sorcerer Singlu and the people of Almer.[2] Most of the inhabitants of Almer belong to the Kaudo clan (which has its *pen-rawar* at Kharkagaon) and they consider that the place is Kaudo-*bhum* since they first settled there. But Singlu is a Karanga. One day he said to the Kaudo priest, 'Let me erect memorial stones in your village; then my ancestors will live here and will help me and my family'. But the priest

[1] See W. V. Grigson, *The Maria Gonds of Bastar* (Oxford, 1938).

[2] See p. 204 of original edition, *The Muria and their Ghotul* (OUP, 1947).

pointed out that the headquarters of the Karanga clan was at Kokori. 'If you bring your ancestors to this village, our gods will be neglected,' he said and refused to give him any *bhum*.

There was a similar conflict at Bandopal. The *bhum* here also belongs to the Kaudo clan which has erected a number of menhirs. Members of the Gaude clan, which stands in the *akomāma* relationship to the Kaudo, demanded a share of the *bhum*, probably because it was more convenient for them than to go to Kharkagaon. After many quarrels and a long dispute, the Kaudo people agreed to let the Gaude clan erect its menhirs within their *bhum* territory, and they even made a Gaude Gaita assistant to the chief Kaudo Bhum-Gaita (priest of the soil). But many of the Kaudo clansmen objected to this and stopped erecting menhirs at Bandopal, going instead to Kharkagaon (where indeed they ought always to have gone). In the end the Gaude people decided to give up erecting menhirs at all because of the expense, and gave back the land to the Kaudo clan.

The clans fall roughly into five phratries, which are generally called by the Hindi word for 'race', *vans*. There is the Nagvans or Serpent Race, which includes a number of brother-clans, most of which have the cobra as their totem and cannot marry among themselves; the Kachhimvans or the Tortoise Race, the Bakravans or the Goat Race, the Baghvans or the Tiger Race and the Bodminkvans or the Fish Race.

All the clans within one phratry are *dādābhai*, or brothers, to one another, and all the members of each clan are *dādābhai* to each other. The word used to describe the relation of a clan into which you can marry your daughter is *akomāma*, a combination of the words *ako*, which means a man's mother's father, daughter's son and daughter's daughter (all of whom will belong to a different clan in a different phratry) and *māma*, which means a man's mother's brother, his father-in-law and his wife's brother's son (who will again, of course, be members of different clans).

A chelik or motiari, therefore, who is seeking either amorous adventure or permanent domestic relationship, has to turn to members of the *akomāma* clans. Fortunately, owing to the wide distribution of the population, there are nearly always members of such clans in one's own ghotul or near at hand.

Before going on to describe the origin of the clans and the special rules that govern them, I will give in tabulated form a list of clans with their totems. It is not worth while adding to this an account of the *bhum* territory as this is too scattered and disorganized; the same is true of the clan-gods and *pen-rawar*.

It will be noticed that in addition to the phratry totem each clan has its own totem which is sometimes different. The Sori clan has three different totems.

CLAN	TOTEM	CLAN	TOTEM
	The Nag (Cobra) Phratry		
Buyi	Bullock	Maravi	Goat
Dhurwa	Goat	Kassi Maravi	Kassi tree
Duga	Cobra	Etikal Maravi	She-goat
Kalo	Cobra	Nei Nuroti	Dog
Karanga	Wild buffalo	Nuroti	Cobra
Kaudo	Goat and horse	Partabi	Goat
	The Kachhim (Tortoise) Phratry		
Kawachi	Tortoise	Parchapi	Tortoise
Komra	Tortoise	Poyami	Tortoise
Markami	Tortoise	Tekami	Tortoise
Naitami	Tortoise and dog		
	The Bakra (Goat) Phratry		
Gaude	Goat	Ori	Goat
Karhami	Goat	Uika	Kassi tree
Komra	Goat	Wadde	Goat and kassi tree
Kunjami	Goat		
	The Bagh (Tiger) Phratry		
Sori	Tiger, buffalo and bod fish		
Wadder	Buffalo		
	The Bodmink (Fish) Phratry		
Halami	Bod fish	Kuhrami	Kassi tree
Hurpundi	Bod fish	Kumoti	Kumot bird
Kachlami	Kassi tree	Usendi[3]	Usi bird

[3] Russell and Hiralal put the Usendi clan in the Kachhimvans. R. V. Russell and R. B. Hira'al, '*The Tribes and Castes of the Central Provinces* (Nagpur, 1866) Vol. III, p. 65.

I have somewhat arbitrarily divided the clans into these five phratries, though we must not suppose that this is how the Muria usually thinks of them. In each area he is only concerned with the relatively small number of clans in his own neighbourhood. When Dhanuram, my Usendi assistant from north-west Narayanpur, went to Kondagaon Tahsil, the Kuhrami and other related clans did not recognize him as one of themselves, for they had never heard of the Usendi—which is a great clan of the Abujhmar and north-west Bastar.

There are other clans which I have not been able to fit into the scheme of phratries—the Hurra clan with its clan-god Lingo Mudial at Semurgaon, the Karati with its *bhum* at Phunder, the Vetti which has the lizard as its totem and the Kodovetti which has the mongoose. These, of course, fit into the scheme of *ako-māma* and *dādābhai* relationships of their own neighbourhood.

There are not many songs about the clans. I give one Jhoria Pata from Sirpuri.

Those who kindle fire in the field
  are boys of the Uika clan.
    How strong the Uika boys are!
Those who make a hearth with brinjals
  from the Panara's house are
  boys of the Maravi clan.
Those who sit on a gate and call it a horse
  are boys of the Maravi clan.
    How strong the Maravi boys are!
Those who build a hearth of pig's droppings are
  boys of the Halami clan.
Those who sit to clean their teeth
  with a twig are boys of the Halami clan.
    How strong the Halami boys are!
Those who blow the buffalo horn are
  boys of the Halami clan.
Those who throw fine rice on the road are
  boys of the Halami clan.
    How strong the Halami boys are!

II. The Origin of the Clans

Many of the clans derive their origin from some historic journey in the course of which a river had to be crossed. Others have local and special reasons for their origin.

FIG. 1. Decorated Muria knife
Length 1′ 5″

This legend of crossing a river is known throughout central India. Many Gond, Baiga and Agaria trace their clans and the attachment of those clans to certain totems from this.[4] In Muria mythology we are sometimes told that this first great journey was the coming of Lingo with his brothers to the earth. This is the Alor version of the tale.

At the beginning of the world, after Lingo and his brothers had put the earth in order, heaping up a mountain here and hollowing out a river there, the earth began to weep crying, 'There is no one to serve or worship me.' But Lingo and his brothers said, 'Do not distress yourself, we will go to find a priest for you.'

Then Lingo took his brothers to Lanjhi and Dhamda. In Lanjhi Raja Naitam was living. He had seven sons and seven daughters. Lingo came to them and said, 'The earth is ready in the Middle World and we have come to take you there.' When they heard that, Raja Naitam and Raja Markam with their sons and daughters and their subjects, Sori, Kawachi, Poyami, Kuhrami and Kaudo, set out with Lingo and his brothers to the Middle World. Raja Naitam and Raja Markam had many possessions and they travelled more slowly, lagging behind the others.

After a time they came to a great river. Lingo and his brothers said to themselves, 'We are gods and can cross without difficulty, but how are these human beings to get over?' On the bank tall grass was grow-

[4] Compare, for such tales in the Central Provinces alone, Russell and Hiralal, op.cit., Vol. III, pp. 61ff.; Grigson, op. cit., P. 241; C.G.C. Trench, *Grammar of Gondi* (Madras, 1919), Vol. II, pp. 8ff.; Elwin, *The Agaria*, p. 75; M.P. Buradkar, 'Totemism among the Gonds', *Man in India*, Vol. XX (1940), pp. 120 and 277f.; *Census of India, 1931,* Vol. 1, Part III B, p. 77 (the Gond emigrating from Phuljhar cross the Gondki river in flood).

ing and Lingo and his brothers made it into a rope and stretched it across the river. The subjects clung to the rope and got across, but they were jealous of the two Rajas who were coming behind and, once they were safely on the far bank, they cut the rope. Then Raja Markam and Raja Naitam not knowing that the grass was cut began to cross, but under their weight the rope went down and they sank up to their necks in the middle of the river and stood there weeping. The *dandai* fish, who is the king of all the creatures that live in water, heard the sound and sent a tortoise to save them, and since then the Markami and Naitami honour the tortoise as their god.

At last the whole party reached the Middle World. Raja Naitam and Raja Markam had brought their cattle with them, and they offered a black calf to Mother Earth and pleased her greatly. These are the old priests of the Earth. All the gods have come from Lanjhi-Dhamda except Danteshwari and Maoli, who came from Warangal.

There are endless versions of this tale. In Lanjora a member of the Naitami clan said that

At the beginning of the world a brother and sister on their way to a certain village came to a great river. The sister went ahead and reached the other side. Then a flood came down and the boy was left behind. Each wept on opposite sides of the stream. Then came a tortoise and asked the boy why he was weeping. When he told his story, it took him on its back and began to swim across. Half way across, the tortoise sank, but as the boy was drowning a dog came from the far bank where the sister was standing and swam out to him. He caught the dog's tail and was dragged to safety.

This story obviously attempts to explain how it is that the Naitami clan, which is named after the dog (*nei* is the Gondi word for dog) yet honours the tortoise as its totem. Many Naitami, however, have a special reverence for the dog as well.

Another very common variation of the legend is that told by the Hirko clan:

When the first twelve brothers came to Bastar from Warangal, they came to a great river and decided to have their midday meal before crossing. Six of the brothers said, 'The river may flood; let us eat our food quickly' and they mixed their rice with water, ate it and went ahead. The other six mixed ghee in the rice instead of water and it took a long time to cook. As they were waiting for it to be ready the river came down in flood and, unable to cross, they sat on the bank and wept. Then came a tortoise and asked them what was the matter. When they told their story, the tortoise said, 'Will you worship me and never eat my people if I take you over?' They swore to do so and the tortoise carried them across on its back, and ever since these six brothers honour it as Bara Pen. In Dongar, Bara Pen used to go from place to place in the form of a tortoise.

Other clans are connected with the bod fish.[5] Members of the Halami clan at Gorma described how.

There was a great tank in the jungle and below it was a village. The people of that village thought that if the banks were to break they would all be drowned and they decided to make a channel to carry the water away in another direction. Hearing this Kana Pen came to the place and camped below the tank. 'I will break the bank,' he said to himself. By his magic he put all the Muria to sleep and then broke the banks and the water poured out. Kana Pen saved himself by clinging to the root of a tree, but as the water poured over him the bod fish came, angry and saying, 'I will eat one of the eyes of whoever has dried up my tank.' It caught Kana Pen and ate one of his eyes and since then Kana Pen has been one-eyed. Since that day we worship him and with him we worship the bod fish in order to stop it eating his other eye.

Another clan which in certain places honours the bod fish is the Sori. At Masora members of this clan had a slightly different version of the story. Here they regarded Kana Bod as a man.

The people of the village went to a nearby river to make a bridge. They had iron spades, but Kana made a wooden one. When the others began to dig out the stones, Kana sat idly on the bank. The others got tired, but the bridge was not yet ready and they shouted to Kana, 'Now come and work yourself'. So he took his wooden spade and began to dig. As they watched him the others said to themselves, 'If we kill this man and throw him in the river, then the bridge will soon be ready'. When he heard them Kana jumped into the river and was carried away by the water. A great fish caught him and ate one eye. After that Kana Bod turned into a fish and we have worshipped him as a god.

The Sori clan is actually the tiger clan (*sori* means tiger in Gondi), but it is connected with bees and buffaloes as well as with tigers and bod fish. In Karikhodra, a member of this clan described how his ancestors were born from a tigress:

Two children were born: one brother was a tiger, one was a human

[5] The bod fish is regarded as specially sluggish in Chhattisgarh and is often compared to a drunken Kalar. See R. B. Hiralal, 'Why Kewat Women are Black', *The Indian Antiquary*, Vol. LX (1931), p. 35.

being. When the boy grew up, one day he was going to the fields with eleven other men. A tiger came by and asked each in turn, 'Who are you?' Each of them, knowing that the tiger would not kill its own child, said, 'I am Sori' and it spared them. When it came to the real Sori boy it was angry and said, 'You can't all be Sori' and ate him. Ever since we have been angry with the tiger that betrayed us, and when a tiger is killed we put an egg and a pice in its mouth.

In Sidhawand I recorded yet another story of the origin of the Sori clan.

The twelve Sori brothers went to get honey in the forest. The tree where bees lived stood beside a stream and the shadow of the hive could be seen in the water. Eleven of the brothers seeing the shadow in the water tried to reach it, but they fell in and were drowned. The twelfth brother looked up and saw the hive; so he climbed the tree and got the honey. In this way the Sori clan came into being.

In Cheribera the Maravi clan trace their origin to an incident in Chingnar.

In Chingnar a Marar dug a well but could not reach water. Presently a tortoise came out of the well and everyone said, 'It must be a god'. Then the tortoise came to the Marar in a dream saying, 'I am Bara Pen, I will give you water in your well and a son to your wife if you worship me'. The next day the Marar took a goat to offer to the tortoise but it refused the sacrifice saying 'I must have a cow.' This the Marar refused to give. So the tortoise said, 'I will stay no more with you, I will go to the Muria.' The Muria gave the tortoise a cow and thus became Maravi (for Bara Pen came to them from the house of the Marar), but because the Marar offered a goat, the Maravi do not eat goat.

Other stories throw light on the way in which some clans possibly did originate—through dreams and the divisions of families as well as by migration. In Silati village, the Naitami told us that

Long ago an old Muria widow lived with her son. When the boy was old enough he was married, but the next day he died and they broke the girl's bangles. The girl and her mother-in-law were weeping bitterly, but at last the husband came to the girl in a dream saying, 'Worship me as Dulha Deo, and I will go on being your husband.' The next day she made offerings to Dulha Deo and from that time he used to come daily to her by night till a son was conceived and born. The elders of the village came to the girl and asked whose child it was. 'I have been to no one,' said the girl, 'It is the child of Dulha Deo.' They were all laughing at her when the dead boy came out of the house and they realized that it really was Dulha Deo who had given the child. So we Naitami call ourselves *rāndike vans* (born of a widow) and our women do not wear bangles.

From the same place I recorded a story explaining why the Naitami and the Poyami, though both having the tortoise as their totem and both being descended from the same parents, can yet intermarry in some villages:

During a great famine, a Poyami was dying of hunger and went to a Naitami's house to beg for food. The Naitami said, 'There is no food here, I can give you nothing.' But the Poyami said, 'At least keep my daughter to work in your house and give me a little food.' So the Naitami fed him and kept the daughter in payment. When the time came for redeeming the girl the Poyami had no money, so the Naitami kept the girl and married her. From that girl there was born a daughter who was Naitami and from her brother there was a son who was Poyami. These two married, for the girl was *dudh-bahini* to the boy.

III. Clan Rules

Every clan has its own distinctive regulations based often on some incident in the story of its origin, often, too, on something that has happened, probably really happened, to a member of the clan.

The first rule is, of course, the obvious one; that no one may marry within the clan or a member of a clan that is related as *dādābhai*. Marriages can only take place between clans that stand in the *akomāṃa* relationship to one another.

The second rule is that members of a clan must avoid injury to the totem animal, tree or plant, must not eat it, and must usually give it some special honour to worship. In many clans, when the totem animal dies, the members observe mourning just as they would if a human being of their own clan had died.

Thirdly, there are a number of special rules such as that forbidding the members of the Naitami clan to wear bangles.

Among the food rules, some are clear enough. None of the members of the Bakravans or Goat phratry may eat goat's meat. We have seen that there is an added reason for this among the Maravi because, in the story of their origin, the Marar from whose house the tortoise emigrated offered it a goat. When a goat dies the Maravi perform funerary rites for it; they will not even touch the water from which a goat has drunk. This rule is taken very seriously. Twenty years ago in Palari one Bhaira Maravi ate goat's flesh by mistake and died of it, his throat swelling and choking him. Raghunath Maravi also ate it by accident, but he sacrificed a pig to Mati Pen and a buffalo to Bara Pen and was saved, though his brother died. In Kondagaon a man of the Partabi sect ate a goat and was very ill. He was excommunicated and only readmitted to the tribe after paying a heavy fine.

The members of the Kachhimvans or Tortoise phratry avoid eating the tortoise and worship it. The Naitami clan in addition to honouring the tortoise revere the dog, which they regard as their elder brother. Members of the Sori or Tiger phratry, however, have a buffalo totem, since members of the clan consider that they were betrayed by the tiger who ate the original member of their clan. But they still refuse to kill a tiger, and when one is killed they perform funerary rites for it.

Members of the Nagvans or Serpent phratry are supposed to be immune to the bite of the cobra, but some of the members of this phratry also honour other animals. For example, the Karanga has the wild buffalo as its totem and the Nei Nuroti has the dog.

Members of the Usendi clan which, being a Hill Maria clan, does not fit easily into any of the Muria phratries, do not eat the *usi* bird. The Kaudo sect has to avoid the horse: its members may not ride a horse or touch it. If a horse is tide in front of a Kaudo house, it goes mad or dies. The Komra sect never cut down a kassi tree, nor do they eat its leaves as vegetables. They must not cook roti with oil, and at the New Eating ceremonies they must not themselves cook at all but must get their food from others. If they do cook in their houses a tiger will kill their cattle.

A similar rule applies to members of the Poyami clan, who have been forbidden by their clan-god to cook in their own houses at Diwali. Once an old man broke the rule and his cattle died. The Poyami sect also must not eat carrion, though a cadet branch, the Busar Poyami, may. Long ago a Poyami ate a dead cock and died of it. Randa Pen, who is the same as Dulha Deo, has forbidden it. The Poyami are so particular about this avoidance of carrion that they must not use even grain or fruit that has fallen of its own accord to the ground or they will lose their eyesight; if a gourd falls down or if rice falls from a basket or bin, they must not use it but must give it away to someone else. The grandfather of the Pujari of Karanji broke this rule and was supernaturally blinded as a punishment.

The Kuhrami clan must not eat cocks and they are said to place a small image of a cock on the forehead of a bridegroom at a marriage.

I have already noted the fact that Naitami women cannot wear bangles. If they do, it is believed that a snake will wind round the wrist or that the arm will swell until the bangle is broken, and both husband and wife will die. So when members of this sect go to perform the betrothal ceremony they do not give bangles, as is usual, to the future bride. The Naitami frequently marry the Poyami, and after a Poyami girl is engaged to a Naitami boy she also gives up wearing bangles even before she is married.

This custom derives from the story that has already been given. It was said in Silati that many years ago when a boy and girl were shut up together in the house on the last night of their wedding and the boy took his wife to bed for the first time, a snake coiled itself round her wrist. The boy hastily promised to break the bangles in its honour and the snake went away.

A wife, of course, changes her clan to that of her husband after marriage and even, in many cases, after betrothal. Once the ring-cowrie has been placed in the Pot of the Departed of her father's house,[6] a girl is regarded as having made compensation to her own ancestors for her desertion of their clan, and is now a member of her husband's clan. Sometimes she even goes for festivals, especially those of the clan-god, to her future husband's house instead of remaining with her own family. She is now free to eat her old totem animal and generally some opportunity is taken after the marriage to enable her to do this. Before she does so a few drops of liquor or a coconut are offered to her own ancestors to ensure that they will not be offended.

Adoption is uncommon among the Muria, but it exists. Where a baby is adopted from a family belonging to another clan, the child's clan and totem is changed—unless it is a sister's son. There is a small ceremony for the changing of the clan: offerings are made to the clan-god and the Departed and a feast

[6] See p. 127 of original edition, *The Muria and their Ghotul* (OUP, 1947).

of pork and liquor is given to the village. After this the child takes his new father's clan and ancestors as his own.

IV. The Family

Such, very briefly, is the system into which the chelik and motiari must adjust their lives. But can a chelik marry any girl of the tribe provided she belongs to an *akomāma* clan? As in the rest of India, the Muria regard certain relations as standing in a forbidden relationship; with others there is the fullest freedom to joke and even to intrigue; with yet others marriage is almost obligatory.

A boy obviously cannot marry relatives of the inner circle or any of his classificatory 'aunts' or 'nieces'. He is strictly forbidden to marry his wife's elder sister, his mother-in-law, his younger brother's wife or widow and any other woman in a parallel relation to them. There is no objection to his marrying his grandmother or granddaughter even when they are in the direct line of relationship. A few cases are known of men marrying their great-aunts or grand-nieces.

As we shall see presently, the great majority of Muria marriages are of the cross-cousin type and are celebrated between a boy and his mother's brother's daughter or his father's sister's daughter, or with girls in the same classificatory relationship to him as these.

Throughout India certain relations are regarded as standing in a privileged position to each other. They have licence to laugh and joke with each other, generally in a rather vulgar manner, and in some cases sexual relations between them are not very severely condemned.

The Muria have their own system of joking relationships. As a result of the common cross-cousin marriages, a chelik has special licence to joke and flirt with his mother's brother's daughter or his father's sister's daughter (both *mandāri* in Gondi). A motiari can be equally free with her father's sister's son or her mother's brother's son (both *manriyo* in Gondi). This freedom, however, only lasts so long as they are not engaged to be married. Should such an arrangement be made the joking relationship changes into one of avoidance, for a girl must never have anything to do with her betrothed.

So long as these cousins are not engaged, however, they have many jokes together. A boy is at liberty to catch hold of the girl's breasts and he may have intercourse with her. If he sees her going to the river to wash her clothes at the end of her catamenial period, he is free to shout to her, 'Are you off to polish it and take off the rust? What are your plans for tonight?' Or again 'How long was the bank of the lake broken?' The girl in turn often teases her boy-cousin by accusing him of having relations with his own sister: 'I saw you with her; you'll have to pay a fine, or if you don't you'll have to marry her.'

An uncle stands in a joking relationship to all his nieces except the daughters of his own sister. For example, a man and his uncle's daughter's daughter are in this relationship.

As elsewhere in India, a woman and her husband's younger brothers or a man and his wife's younger sisters are specially privileged. So are grandmother and grandson or grandfather and granddaughter. A boy may say to his grandmother, 'Once you are dead I will eat beef in your honour; I will go dancing in front of you with a drum; why don't you die quickly so that I can get a good feast?' And she replies, 'If I die you will have to spend a lot of money, you will have to get rice, you will have to bring several tins of liquor, so what good will it be?' A grandfather always flirts and jokes with his granddaughter. Sometimes he says to her husband, 'How dare you sleep with my wife? You will have to give me the bride-price for her', and so on.

The connexion between a man (*dewar*) and his elder brother's wife (*ange*) is the central theme of the Lingo legend. This kinship is more than a mere joking relation; it is often one of deep romance. A Ghotul Pata illustrates the kind of humour that passes between them.

Dewar : O Ange, the gruel is made of broken rice.
Ange : O my Dewar, where are you going today?
Dewar : Today I am not going anywhere
For I have to load my bullocks.
Tomorrow I go to another land to trade.
Ange : I too will go with you to drive the laden bullocks.
Dewar : Don't come with me, for all know how we stand to one another.
Those who do not know us will call us brother and sister.
And when they call us that we shall be ashamed.

The relations between *samdhi* and *samdhin* are generally of an amiable, coarse and humorous nature. For men this is a drinking rather than a joking relationship, and all their lives whenever they meet they regard it as an excuse for a bottle. The women, specially as they get older, are more obscene in their conversation. They catch hold of each other's breasts, stick feathers into the private parts and exchange the coarsest jokes.

The place where this joking and fun most commonly occurs is at a marriage. 'There is no purdah in a house of marriage.' Everybody feels free to fool about; no one is going to be offended; everyone is slightly drunk.

V. Summary

The clan and the family dominate and control Muria social life. Nothing reveals more clearly the extent of this domination than the fact that out of 2000 marriages examined no fewer than 1799 were of the cross-cousin type and, in spite of every temptation to the contrary, 1884 out of 2000 boys married according to their parents' wishes. This could only happen in a society which had a strong regard for its own organization and laws.

The clan system retains its vitality both as an exogamous unit and as a means of organizing its members round the clan-god and the memory of the Departed. Clan festivals remain great and notable occasions. The clan system, as a study of marriage statistics will show, continues to regulate betrothal and marriage. The *samdhi* relationship, as may be seen in every song and story, continues to be of the first importance. Clan traditions still regulate funerary rites and memorial customs. Totemism is less important, but is still far from moribund. The whole complex of ideas and customs is greatly confused, but the very confusion is perhaps a sign of its vitality.

THE GHOTUL BUILDINGS

The position and architecture of the ghotul is largely determined by one simple fact. In every village in Bastar, as we have seen, the people have to build and maintain a hut for the use of travellers and touring officials. This is an excellent arrangement: it prevents the invasion of aboriginal homes by outsiders, and it means that in every village there is some clean and roomy place where disputes can be settled and official business transacted. This Paik-ghotul or Thana-gudi, as it is called, is supposed to be separate from the Koitur-ghotul or Ghotul-gudi, the club of the boys and girls, and in some Muria villages it is. But in many others the elders of the village seem to have decided that it would save them a great deal of trouble if they combined the Paik-ghotul and the Koitur-ghotul in one compound. It would take up less room, means less building, and the young men would be always there to do the work. I have already quoted some Muria elders as saying that this was actually how the ghotul originated. If the young men were kept together in one place they would always be ready to serve visitors and could hand over their house to them for the night. This situation is of course comparatively modern. Old Muria like Yogi and Bindo remember the day when there was no revenue staff and they never saw a touring officer.

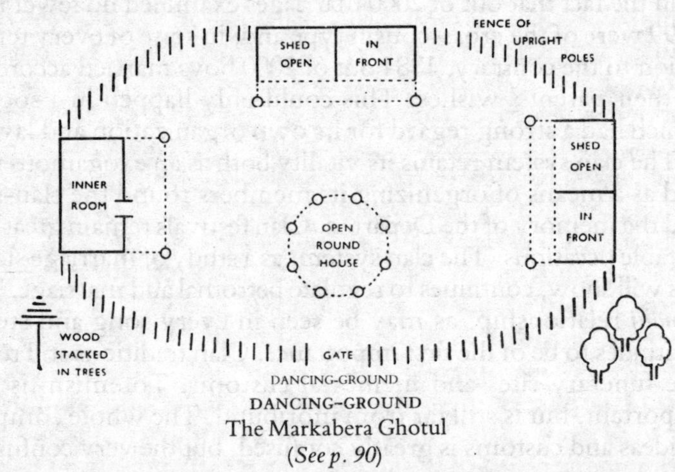

DANCING-GROUND

The Markabera Ghotul

(*See p. 90*)

The original ghotul, then, was probably a small building on the outskirts of the village, among trees, perhaps originally in some sacred grove, aloof from the public eye, with a small secret door. You may still see this kind of ghotul in predominantly Hindu villages and in parts of Kondagaon, at Esalnar and Sonawal, for example, in the south, and Kerawahi, Majhiboran, Lihagaon in the north. But there is no rule. Near the eastern boundary, there was a small ghotul at Baghbera, and a combined Thana-gudi and Koitur-ghotul at the neighbouring Ulera. Where a village consists, administratively, of several hamlets, there will probably be a large ghotul in the main village (where officials usually halt) and small ones in the hamlets.

In all such villages there is a separate building in the middle of the village for officials. In Masora, for example, there was a large Thana-gudi inside the village, and away on the outskirts, among trees, is a small hut with a fenced compound in front. This is the home of the chelik and motiari. In Baniagaon, a predominantly Hindu village with a school, the ghotul is similarly separated from the officials' halting-place, and is a single building with a small door facing away from the village towards the forest. In Kachora, near by, you may see the same type of ghotul, even further removed from the ordinary dwelling-places of the village, beyond the shrine of the Village Mother, perhaps because an aggressive Brahmin lives there and tries to dominate the Muria. I obviously cannot give a list of all such villages, though there are not very many of them. In the Chalka Pargana, I think of Kajen, Naria and Maranar as places where the Thana-gudi was separate from the ghotul. In such villages there is sometimes not even a fence to isolate the compound; that is not necessary, forest and field keep the children separate from the world. But in all there is a small secret door, a hatch which you have to bend down to and climb over—not unlike the door by which Alice entered Wonderland.

But, as I have said, in the majority of Muria villages the Thana-gudi is combined with the Koitur-ghotul, and this influences both its plan and its location. Officials will not want to camp outside the village in the jungle; they will need a hut for their horses, and accommodation for servants. And so we get the large ghotul with its spacious compound, standing in the very heart of the village, which is familiar to every touring officer in the north of Bastar. This arrangement is unsatisfactory and was never contemplated by the Administration. Into the very heart of Muria life is injected the all-too-often poisonous contact of every casual wanderer. There is a type of touring subordinate who makes a point of halting in ghotul where it is known that there are pretty motiari and pesters the chelik to pimp for them—which to their honour, be it said, they never do. Contractors for myrabolams or tendu leaves camp for days in the ghotul, making it impossible for the boys and girls to live their normal lives. I once found an opium-seller permanently established in a ghotul with his wife, thus outraging the fundamental Muria rule that the presence of a married woman there is an offence to Lingo Pen. He was removed at once by the Administrator, but Bastar is a big place and it is impossible to say in how many other places the integrity of the ghotul is thus destroyed. This is, of course, the Muria's own fault. It is due to the slackness and selfishness of the older men who want the youngsters to do all the work. It is thus difficult to do anything about it.

Let us examine some of the villages which have ghotul of this type. Often, so long as there are no visitors, the enlarged ghotul is all to the advantage of the boys and girls. In Markabera, for example, chelik and motiari have in all five different sleeping-places and a spacious compound. The house with the very deep verandah is, of course, the original ghotul and the other buildings have developed from it to meet the pressure of outside visitations. But the extra room thus provided and the open sheds available as dormitories are a boon to the children's health. The one-room ghotul with its tiny door and no windows and its crowded floor, its stuffy smoky atmosphere, cannot be good for anyone.

Fortunately—from this point of view—the larger type of ghotul is far the most common. This model with its central house with deep verandah, spacious inner room, large door, open hut for conference or sleep in the hot weather, and several small sheds, the whole surrounded by a fence, may be seen in scores of Muria villages. There is the same arrangement at Bandopal, at Ulera, at Amgaòn, at Jhakri, at Almer, at More Berma. This is the plan of the ghotul at Almer in the Bara Dongar Pargana:

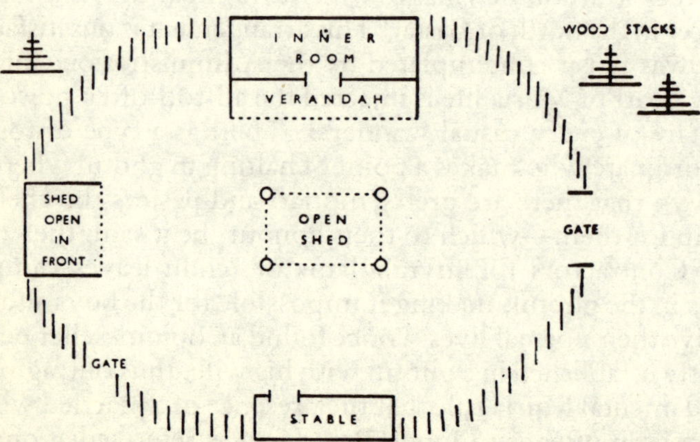

This ghotul stands in the middle of the village, in a grove of tamarind trees.

In a third type of ghotul, its position in the middle of the village is possibly due to Maria influence. The traditional Maria ghotul is the centre of the male life of the village. The men assemble there in the evenings, and talk, smoke, drink and sleep. But girls do not normally attend. In villages like Palli Barkot, Watia, Phulpar, Koilibera, on the fringe of the Abujhmar Maria country, the ghotul is in the heart of the village; it is generally (except at Koilibera) not so spacious as those we have been considering. The plan below of the ghotul at Palli Barkot is typical.

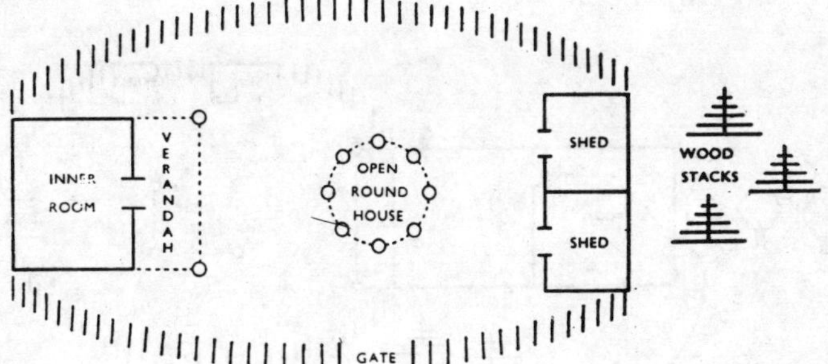

These ghotul are often beautifully kept. At Khutgaon, there is a spotlessly clean compound forty paces square; in it are three open sheds, one with a finely-constructed round roof, and two large houses with thick mud walls. One of these is the Thanagudi, the other has an inner and an outer room for the boys and girls. The Telenga, Temrugaon and Chureng ghotul are of the same pattern, like Palli Barkot; a big house with a small or deep verandah, a central open hut with often a rounded roof and two small open sheds, the whole surrounded by a high wooden fence.

In the north of the State, on the Amabera plateau and generally to the north of the forest road from Berma to Antagarh and up to the Kanker border are to be found the least attractive ghotul—and ghotul members—in Bastar. The buildings are mean, dilapidated and draughty. The dormitory actually used by the boys and girls rarely has a door and thus loses its intimacy and cosiness. My memories of Pupgaon, Chikhli, even Penjori, are not happy.

It remains to mention a few special dormitories. Semurgaon is traditionally the site of the first ghotul, built there by Lingo himself. He could hardly have chosen a lonelier or more charming spot. But the ghotul today is small and almost unique in having unplastered walls made of bare logs. On a pillar in the centre are carvings of chelik and motiari, horses and combs. From the door you look out over a wild expanse of forest and *dippa* clearings.

No visitor to Nayanar can ever forget the ghotul there—the long building with its little windows and two doors, at one end like a hatch, at the other large and dignified, its carved pillars, its charming site at the edge of the village among great trees. This is its general plan—

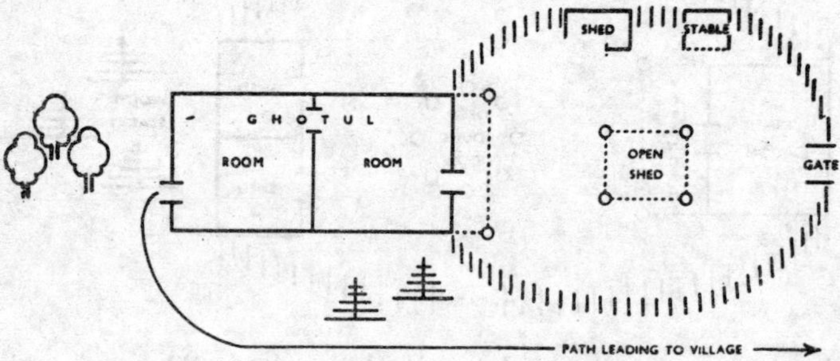

One of the most delightful and original of all the ghotul is at the Budakasa Para of Malakot. Here outside the village, in the woods, shadowed by tall sago-palms, is a house lifted well above the ground on pillars eight feet high. Above the wooden floor is a low wall two feet high all round, then an open space to the roof. This platform is reached by a ladder. Both the upper room and the space below it are used; there are fires kept burning in each.

The ghotul is built by the chelik themselves, though the boys often get the help of the older men by promising to help in their fields at sowing-time or harvest. The motiari bring grass for the roof, stones and earth for the floor and, when the walls are ready, plaster them with mud. Before they begin the work, the boys mark out on the ground the proposed plan of the building and put there a little pile of rice covered with a leaf-cup. They leave it all night and in the morning go to examine it, sometimes only for one day, sometimes for three days running.

Should the rice be scattered, it is taken as a bad omen and they build the ghotul elsewhere. But if the rice remains just as it was under its leaf-cup, they proceed to dig holes to take the four corner pillars of the house. If, as they dig, they come across white ants they move the site. They put four pillars into the holes and tie a garland of mango leaves round them. After this they proceed to build in the usual way.

At Phunder the boys put a grass 'top-knot' on the roof and a small flag, the *chelik-bairag* or Palo Pen, so that 'all might know it was a ghotul'.

Such are the main types of building; what of the decorations and the furniture? These vary greatly from place to place. They are least ornate to the north and east, most carefully imagined and executed in the west central parganas, in the typical Jhoria area.

Doors are sometimes very small, sometimes large and heavy, occasionally of light bamboo, sometimes carved as at Bandopal; sometimes there is no door at all. Often there is an arrangement for shutting the door from inside—a latch falls into a wooden hook attached to the door. But it is interesting that there is no means of shutting the house from outside: the ghotul is never locked up. It is a shrine and no one would steal from it.

As you move west across the centre of the Muria country you find more, and more elaborate carving. The ghotul has stimulated artistic creation, not only in the realm of personal adornment but also in wall-painting and wood-carving. The chelik desire that their ghotul really should be 'lovely as a bison's horns'. In many of the Jhoria ghotul there are excellently carved pillars. These may be seen at Almer, Nayanar, Remawand, Amgaon, Bandopal, Malinar, Koher and elsewhere. At Almer, one of the pillars has kiddari birds at the top, another has tortoises. On the body of the pillars are carvings of the moon, boys and girls dancing the Hulki, elephants. Down the pillar there are three *pidha*, the seats that are supposed to hold it up. At Amgaon also, each of the pillars has four of these *pidha* 'for the roof to sit on'. At Nayanar, one of the pillars is decorated with tortoises and another has hooded snakes projecting from all four corners. In Malinar, there are carvings on all the pillars—combs beautifully fashioned, a boy with a large phallus, a realistic bow and arrow, a snake. Outside, as at Remawand, there are pillars in the fence with remarkable designs clearly illustrated in Plates 2 and 3 (Section V). At Jhakri I saw a fine pillar ingeniously carved to make a wooden ball inside with no way of putting it in or taking it out. At Binjhe too the Sirdar had carved some good pillars and had made windows in the ghotul with serrated bars.

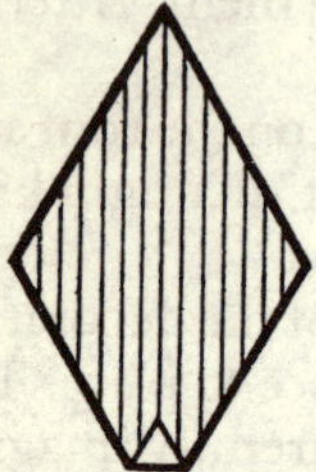
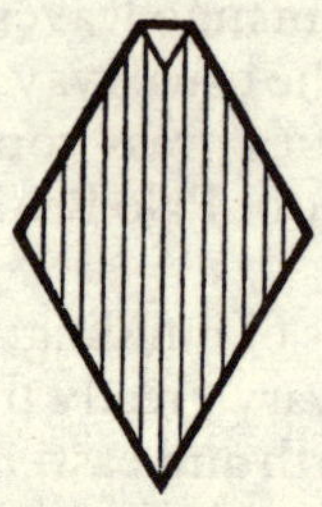
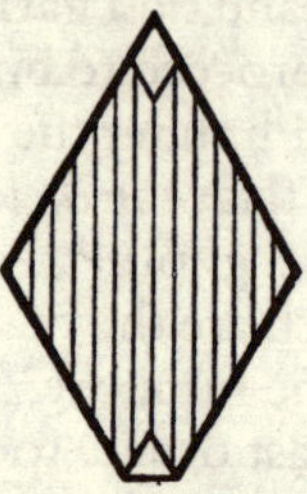

Phallic symbols are very common.[7] In nearly every ghotul there is somewhere the representation of the vagina, often about two feet from the ground on the central pillar. In the small Kolur ghotul there is one slender pillar covered with carvings of the vagina, as always showing the clitoris, but here there was a double clitoris and a clitoris upside down.

At Markabera there were similar carvings of the vagina with the clitoris.

Often a chelik may be seen with an enormous penis, a motiari in his arms. The boys say that these carvings are very useful as an approach to girls. It may be that the vagina in the central pillar is the relic of a custom now forgotten of initiating smaller boys by pressing them against it.[8]

The walls of the ghotul are often decorated with drawings and paintings. In 1940 there was a fine display in the Remawand

[7] Similar phallic symbols occur in the Juang and Bhuiya and in some Uraon dormitories. The Juang often make a row of breasts right across the main beam of the roof. So do the Kond. Hutton describes carvings of men and women 'in a condition of sexual excitement' in Naga *morung*—J. H. Hutton, *Diaries of Two Tours in the Unadministered Areas east of the Naga Hills* (Calcutta, 1929), p. 48.

[8] A remarkable parallel from an English Public School (Repton) is provided in Denton Welch's *Maiden Voyage* (London, 1943), p. 48. The author is describing the House dormitory. 'Two lips had been painted on one of the beams and all new boys had to pull themselves up by their arms, to kiss them. I remember straining up, and at last reaching the yellow pitch pine and the two crimson lips. They looked indecent, for some reason; as if they were the drawing of another part of the body.' If the boys were not quick or could not reach the lips, they were flicked with wet towels as an encouragement.

ghotul. The following year I saw a frieze of fantastic paintings (illustrated in Plate I, Section V) at More Berma. At Netagaon there were models of motiari, tigers and a monkey. In Urdabera there was a model of a chelik with his motiari, and over the door a mud model of a horse. In Deogaon, there were modellings of a chelik and motiari riding on a horse. At Kuntpadar, one wall was well decorated with drawings of a boy, a vagina, a girl, a bow and arrow and the sun and moon. At Palki there was the representation of a bird trap.

But this might equally well be a sexual symbol, similar to the design of the phallus within the vagina that I noted at Metawand:

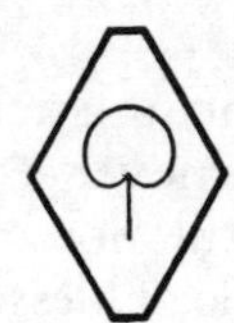

The day-time visitor to a ghotul will find little enough there by way of furniture. Cots are never used; everyone sleeps on the ground. Seats and stools are rare, but in many ghotul are to be found long narrow pieces of wood raised some two inches from the ground. These are the *kutul* which may be used either as seats or pillows. Some are very long and suggest the custom of several boys and girls sleeping together. They are often carved with geometric designs, figures of boys and girls, crude representations of the vagina. I have one with four breasts carved on its under-side. Occasionally you may see a *kutul* with a little drawer hollowed out below for storing necklaces or other ornaments during the night. As far as I know these head-rests are the corporate property of the

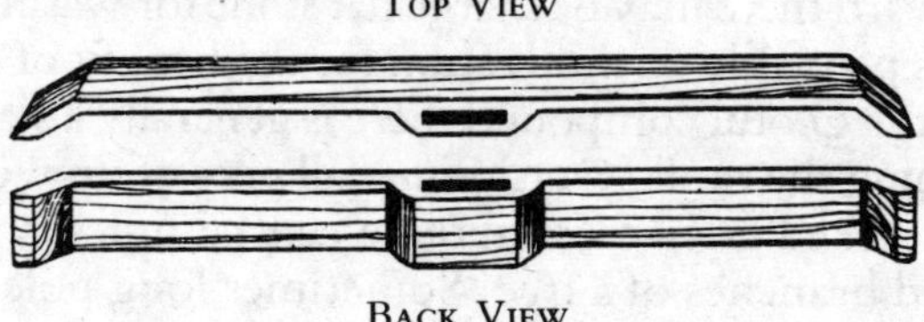

Fig. 2. *Kutul* from Talabera showing small drawer for keeping ornaments
Length 2′ 7″

ghotul, though they are usually appropriated by particular boys for the period of their membership.

In eastern Kondagaon drums are usually kept in the ghotul; at Masora a dhol-drum hangs under the verandah roof—it is the

FIG. 3. Carved head-rest from Markabera
Length 3′ 6″

local habitation of Lingo Pen. At Dongrigura and other villages in this area, the whole ceiling is of drums, a fine and impressive sight. Special officers are appointed to provide rope for hanging them up and to see that they are kept in good order.

FIG. 4. Carved underside of wooden head-rest from Kumli
Length 4′

Flutes are often pushed into the thatch, but dancing-sticks are kept in the shrine of the Village Mother. I have never seen the emblem of a god, a flag or a 'horse' in the ghotul, nor any village symbol, but in Palli Barkot there was a bundle of blessed seed hanging from the roof.

There are often little holes in the wall for keeping tobacco and other small treasures. Sometimes too there are holes in the floor—for husking the rice that is brought home from the Pus Kolang and other expeditions. In one or two ghotul I have seen holes low down in the wall to serve as urinals. Outside in the courtyard there may be a large flat stone for washing clothes, but this is probably an innovation for the benefit of outsiders.

Inside the ghotul compound there is generally a stack of grass for thatching the roofs. Outside are tall piles of firewood, which may be stacked criss-cross about a central pole or piled up in the forked branches of a tree. Sometimes long poles are stood upright against and round a tree. In Jhakri I saw near the ghotul four different ways of storing the chelik's wood—it was stacked horizontally criss-cross round a tree; it was laid in parallel rows between two trees; it was criss-crossed between two upright poles tied together at the top by a rope; and it was stacked upright against a tree.

These stores of wood play an important part in the consciousness of every Muria boy, for his earliest ghotul memories are of his duty to add one or two pieces to them every evening, failure to do so earning dreaded punishments.

Ghotul Discipline

I

'We obey our ghotul laws more faithfully than the laws of Government; for we ourselves made the ghotul laws, and so we love them.'

—Common Muria saying

The life of the chelik and motiari is strictly regulated, and when a leader is appointed one of the powers with which he is entrusted is that of judging and punishing offenders against the ghotul code. It is surprising how important a place these punishments hold in the minds of the children. When they are initiated, the little boys are told—'You must come every day, or you'll be punished'. The girls are likewise told—'You must come every day, or you'll be punished. You must massage the chelik, or you'll be punished'. And when a girl leaves the ghotul at marriage, her most tender memories, as revealed in the farewell songs, seem to be connected with punishments. '*Dudhār gai ke lāt mithai*—The cow that gives milk: even her kicks are sweet'. A study of ghotul offences and the type of punish-

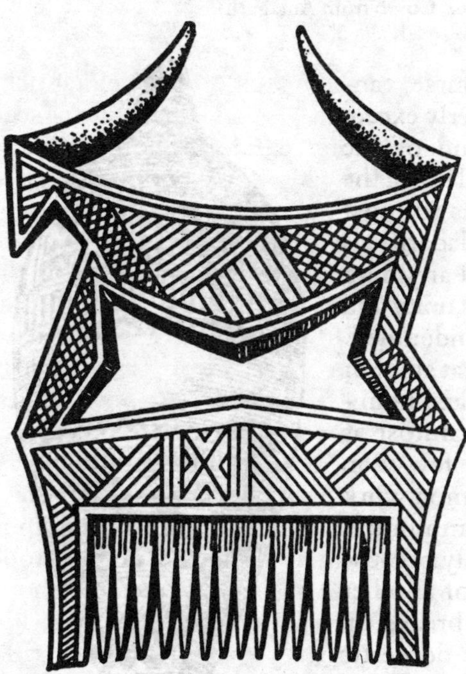

Fig. 5. Comb from Palari. The two horns are of bees-wax *Width 2½"*

ment awarded, therefore, may be expected to throw some light on Muria notions of morality and the inner life of chelik and motiari.

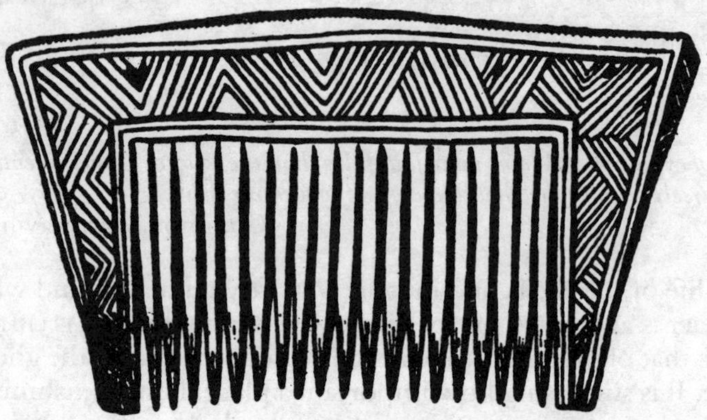

FIG. 6. Comb from Antagarh
Width 5″

Their offences, of course, cannot be understood properly except against the background of the general moral and social life of the tribe. To the Muria, as to most aborginals, tribal solidadarity is the supreme good, and anything that breaks this precious unity and fellowship must be condemned. Individualism is the great sin. For this reason, quarrelling and homicide are rare, theft is almost as uncommon. There are few who refuse to share the common work and interests of the community. Adultery is bad, not only because it infringes the rights of another Muria, but because it breaks up the carefully regulated domestic system of the people, and threatens to disrupt it by jealousy and hatred.

FIG. 7. The *Pude-gota*
Actual size

We have already seen the stress

laid by the Muria on work. Slackness and laziness are very severely regarded, and are the commonest sources of friction between wife and husband. Cleanliness, decency, decorum and modesty are virtues much prized. A quiet and kindly attitude is expected of the tribal leaders; the bully and the coward are equally disliked.

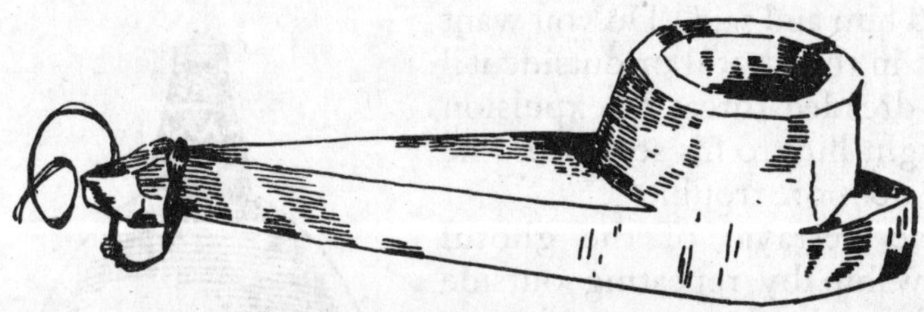

FIG. 8. Tobacco pounder
Length 12″

Against this background, what sort of actions are condemned by ghotul opinion and punishable in ghotul law? Let us first consider those actions that are held to betray the common interest. They are doubly important, for in the highly specialized and concentrated fellowship of the ghotul, the general tribal instinct for unity becomes intensified.

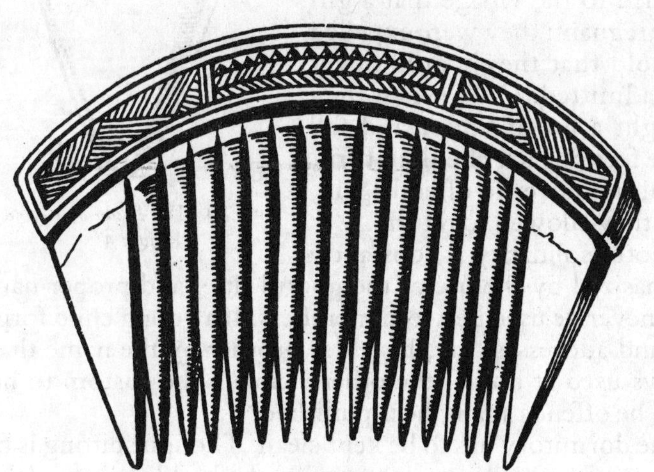

FIG. 9. A Jhoria comb from Markabera
Width 3¾″

II

Quarrles in the dormitory are strongly condemned. They are disturbing to the peace of ghotul life and specially offensive to so gentle and uncontentious a people. Children are fined for this, and may even be expelled. In Khutgaon there was once a very quarrelsome chelik. After a time, the leaders of the ghotul called him and said, 'Do you want to be in the ghotul or outside it?' The dreaded threat of expulsion brought him to his senses and he gave no more trouble.

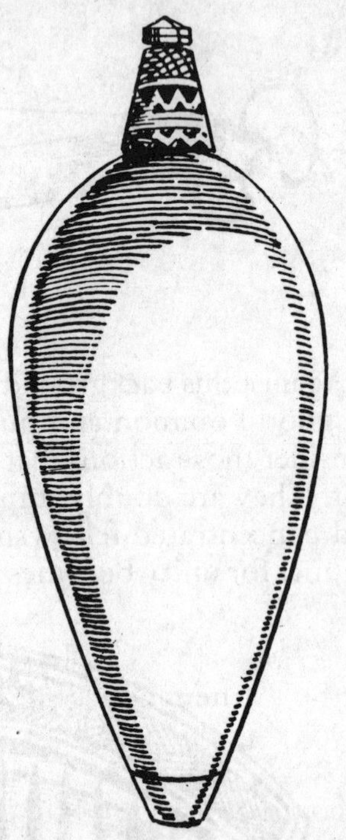

FIG. 10. The *Dudo-muri-gota*
Height 4″

The betrayal of the ghotul fellowship by repeating outside anything that happens within its walls, especially any stories of the intimate relations of chelik and motiari or some scandal about a pregnancy, is one of the greatest of ghotul crimes, for 'that which comes from the mouth bears fruit throughout the world'. Once at Gorma, the Kotwar and Belosa revealed to the village that a girl was pregnant; they were expelled and told that they would never be readmitted. Only when they brought a lot of liquor and fell at the feet of each chelik in turn, promising never to offend again, were they allowed to return.

Ghotul solidarity is constantly emphasized by the use of the ghotul title, and proper names may never be used between members. If a young child forgets this and addresses, say, his elder brother by the name that is always used at home, the others explain the custom to him; but if he offends again, he is punished.

The dormitory has to be kept clean. Though spitting is permitted, anyone who urinates inside the building is punished. This prohibition extends, in some places, to the court outside. To break wind is not a very serious offence; the children laugh

FIG. 11. A brass tobacco-box made by the local Ghasia *Actual size*

at the offenders and call them *padra* or *padri*. Only a light punishment is imposed. At Esalnar the culprit had to salute every boy in turn saying, 'Johar, *mahārāj*, I have farted.' An interesting rule prohibits the other boys and girls from laughing at the offender too much. The name *padra* may be used three times but not more; anyone who carries the joke too far is fined.

A bed-wetter is punished with the *khotla-pahara* described below; if incurable, he may be expelled.

Most ghotuls are actually kept beautifully clean; occasional lapses are severely penalized. It is the special duty of the girls to sweep and cow-dung the building, but often the Kotwar in charge of them is punished instead. At Kabonga, when the Diwan found that the ashes of the previous day's fires had not been cleared away, he reported the matter to the Inspector who called the Kotwar and threw ash all over him. The Kotwar insisted that it was the girls' fault, not his, and so the girls were called and ash was thrown over them and pushed into their private parts. At Kokori also, two girls were tied to the roof by their feet and ashes put into their vaginae. 'As you've let the ghotul be dirty, we are making your privates dirty', said the boys.

It is generally the chelik who have to see to the surroundings of the ghotul. At Palari in 1941, the Munshi, Sipahi and Likandar were told to clear a space in front of the building for a dance, but they failed to do so. They were hung together from the roof until they begged forgiveness and promised to do the work at once. The younger boys are often punished for failing to bring their daily tribute of wood—a task they all dislike. In the Jamkot ghotul there was a boy called Antar (from a hunter-whip) who had the duty of 'whipping' boys who failed in this task.

Chelik and motiari are insistent that everyone must take an equal share (though not always the same share) in the common labour and common recreations. Failure to attend the ghotul regularly is punished; an absence of two or three days, unless there is a very good excuse, means a fine. It is specially bad for the motiari to absent themselves. This is regarded as a really serious offence, an infringement of the chelik's rights, a breach of ghotul fellowship; it raises the suspicion that the girl is having an affair with a married man or a member of another caste. On the other hand, if a girl enters the ghotul during her menstrual period she must provide liquor and perhaps a more substantial sacrifice to appease Lingo Pen whom she has offended.

A girl's conduct is controlled when she visits another village. She may go to the ghotul to dance and even perhaps massage and comb the boys but she is expected to return home before bedtime. If she does not, and the boys of her own ghotul discover that she has betrayed them, they punish her with a heavy fine.

The motiari are often obstinate and troublesome—at least in male opinion—and have to be disciplined. Sometimes they get sulky and refuse to join the games and dances; the Jularo of Sarandi was fined an anna for failing to attend a dance. Sometimes they refuse 'to let a boy play with them on the ground'; sometimes they fail to comb or massage properly. At Kajen the ghotul Kotwar reports every Tuesday whether any of the girls have lost their combs, or have refused to do the chelik's hair.

It is regarded as very offensive for a chelik to force a girl against her will: in Markabera a chelik once forced the Alosa, who was the ghotul-wife of another boy, and was fined as much as two rupees. But if a girl refuses—once she is mature—to have intercourse with at least one of the cheliks, there is consternation, and if she persists, both boys and girls may refuse to attend her wedding.

Boys also may be punished for failing to fulfil their social obligations. At Palari, the Baidar and Dafedar refused, on account of some private spite, to attend the Captain's marriage and each was fined four annas. At Gorma the headman's son, who went to school and learnt there to despise the ghotul and its ways, found when the day of his marriage approached that the boys and girls would not attend it. 'All these years', they said, 'you have despised us. You have not joined our dances or helped us in our work. Now you can get married without us.' The boy had to dress in all the Muria ornaments, change his little cap for a turban, and sleep in the ghotul for a week before he was forgiven.

III

Ghotul officers who fail to perform their duties are punished. No one is privileged and no one is exempt. This is an important point. Were an older man, like the Diwan of Masora who still holds office at the age of forty, to try to protect his own son or daughter, he would himself be fined even though he was the leader and a final court of appeal in all disputes. If the head of the chelik tried to protect his own special motiari or his ghotul-wife, he might be turned out of office. Bindo had no hesitation in punishing the Dulosa, who was his lover, for failing to clean the ghotul.

Mangru of Masora told us how when he was Pahardar it was his duty to punish people. But he could never bring himself to do it, so he himself was punished. His legs were tied to the roof and he had to hang there while boys and girls sang one Relo song. A former Chalki of the Jamkot ghotul was similarly punished for failing in his duty to make the chelik and motiari work at a wedding. As a boy Bindo punished the ghotul Kotwar for disobeying his orders to fetch the motiari in the evening; fifty years afterwards he still remembers the incident with satisfaction.

When the head of the ghotul is penalized, it is a convention in some ghotul that the motiari should beg to be punished in his stead. This happened at Chandabera when I was there, and the Sirdar was fined for not making proper arrangements for his visitors. The girls implored to be allowed to suffer for him.

Should the head of the ghotul turn out a bully or a slacker, the chelik and motiari take the help of the village headman and remove him. This does not happen very often because there is plenty of time to test a boy before he is appointed. But it is not always possible to judge how far power is likely to corrupt character, and scandals do occur. I have recorded a number of cases from the history of the last few years. In Mannegaon, the Leyur-Gaita was removed for bullying and abusing the children. The Malik of Esalnar was once degraded for bullying. The Kotwar of the Berma ghotul a few years ago got very much above himself and used 'to punish for four hours instead of one' until the members rebelled. They fined him a rupee, deprived him of office, made him a 'subject' with the name of Silledar, and appointed the Kandki in his place. Recently in Kehalakot the Kotwar gave so much trouble to the girls that he was fined eight annas and removed.

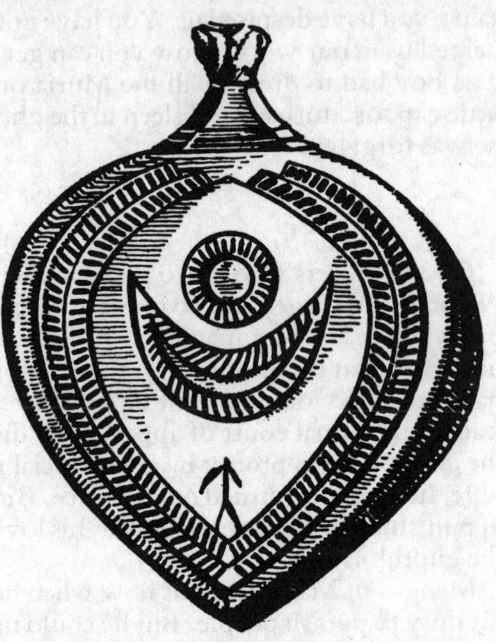

FIG. 12. A sun and moon tobacco-box
Height 2¾"

Laziness also disqualifies a boy from holding high office. In Atargaon the Manjhi was dismissed 'for not working properly'. The Kokori Chalki was degraded to the rank of Kotwar for laziness and the Kotwar was appointed in his place. The Belosa of Berma was removed because she was too slack to control the girls.

I have only once heard of a boy being removed from office for abusing his sexual privileges. In Sonawal the Diwan seduced another chelik's 'wife'. The others fined him, but he refused to pay, saying, 'I am your master, I am not going to pay a fine to my "subjects".' He and his own wife, the Diwanin, or head of the girls, were both degraded and made 'subjects'.

IV

We now turn to breaches of the sexual conventions of the ghotul. Here, according to the type of ghotul, two opposite types of offence are recognized.

In those ghotul where there is a rule against 'pairing off', boys and girls are punished if they sleep together too often. The Subedar and Silo of the Binjhli ghotul were fined four annas each for sleeping together every day. In these ghotul too it is considered very bad form for a boy to be 'possessive' about a girl, to be jealous over her and claim her as his. 'We must change every two or four days, or we are fined.'

FIG. 13. Boy's necklace, from Kajen, of cowries strung together with red and 'silver' beads

But in the other type of ghotul, boys and girls are fined for committing what may be called 'ghotul adultery'. If a chelik sleeps with another boy's motiari during her 'husband's' absence, he is fined. If the Kotwar 'finds the cloth of a girl' who is not the boy's 'mate' on his mat, he reports the matter and the boy is punished.

In villages where there are separate ghotul for boys and girls, they may be fined for visiting one another on days when this is taboo. In Lihagaon, where there were separate dormitories for boys and girls, some years ago the Likhen of the boys was Lamhada to the Mularo of the girls. One night she came to the boys' ghotul and slept with him—a double impropriety since engaged couples are not supposed to sleep together in the ghotul. He was fined a rupee by the chelik, but refused to pay, and on the third day ran away with the girl whom he had already made pregnant. They were brought back and fined two rupees. This time they paid up, and the ghotul members agreed to the marriage and said they would attend it.

With all the freedom of the ghotul, there is a strict insistence of decorum and modesty. It is remarkable that at weddings when the older women and men behave with a complete lack of restraint, abusing each other and catching hold of each other in the most obscene manner, the motiari are never molested. The chelik are sometimes punished for showing an indecent interest in the girls even in the ghotul. Once at Palari the girls were dancing the Durpa Dandi, or Lotus Stalk Dance, when each girl rests one leg on her neighbour's waist. It is considered a rather risky dance and the girls rarely perform it in public. The Kandki of the ghotul sat down near the dancers and tried to peep up in a rather unpleasant manner. The girls stopped dancing and took him inside the ghotul. 'What were you sitting down for?' 'Nothing.' 'You wanted to look at us, you dirty little beast, so we're going to punish you.' They tied his hands together and bound them to the roof for fifteen minutes. When he was released, he had to salute each of the girls in turn and beg forgiveness.

V

How does the machinery of ghotul justice work? How are its punishments inflicted? I will give one or two actual examples before proceeding to tabulate the penalties.

In the first week of November, 1940, the older boys of the Masora ghotul were away watching the field-crops and the Chalan was in charge. For several days five of the girls—Belosa, Tiloka, Piosa, Janka and Alosa—had reported to him that they too were going to watch the crops. Actually, however, they went to sleep at home. Probably they found the ghotul dull without the bigger boys; possibly they simply wanted a rest. On 4 November the Kamdar who, in the absence of the older boys, was attending to the girls' behaviour, reported to the Sipahi (ghotul 'policeman') his suspicion that the girls were deceiving them. That night they watched and found their belief well founded. They returned to the ghotul and told the Chalan. The Chalan issued orders that when the girls next came to report, they should be arrested and given the stick-punishment.

The next evening, when the Janka and Piosa came to say they were very sorry but they must go to watch in their fields, the Kamdar and Sipahi stopped them. But the girls abused them violently—'You can drink our urine, but you won't punish us, *mailotia*'—and ran away. When this was reported to the Chalan, he went to consult the Diwan, an older married man who exercised general supervision over this ghotul. The Diwan said, 'Call all the girls tomorrow night, and certainly punish them.'

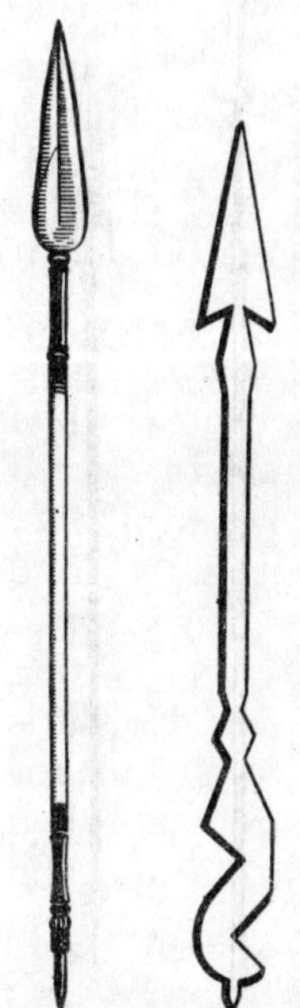

FIG. 14. The ghotul Kotwar's wooden spears
Lengths 6′ *and* 5′ 1″

On the afternoon of the 6th, therefore, the Kamdar went round the village telling all the boys and girls that they must attend, for 'tonight there will be a judgement in the ghotul'. But when the time came, Belosa, Tiloka and Piosa refused to come. The Chalan sent the Kamdar and Sipahi to bring them by force.

When they were at last assembled inside the ghotul—and it is noteworthy that neither the Diwan nor the older boys thought it necessary to attend: they were content to leave it to the juniors—the Chalan asked the Belosa whether it was true that she had been sleeping in her house, and why. She replied, 'There was no wood for the ghotul fire; it was cold; so I slept one night at home.' This retort, which implied that the boys had been failing in their duty of providing wood, and was probably true, was hardly tactful. The Chalan became abusive and pointed out that there was plenty of wood. 'You slept at home every night; you are all sleeping with married men.' Then he examined the other girls, but they refused to answer. At last the the Alosa cried, 'It was only one night; all the other nights we were sleeping in the fields.'

No witnesses were called; everyone knew the girls were guilty. The Chalan said, 'What punishment will you have? Choose!' The motiari made no reply, so the Sipahi said, 'Why not make them get up and down a hundred times holding their ears?' 'No', said the Chalan. 'The stick-punishment would be better.' Hearing this, the Belosa broke out, 'Why should you punish us at all? We haven't done anything.' The Chalan replied, 'Well, why didn't you come to the ghotul? Why don't you answer our questions? We'll certainly punish you if you don't speak properly.'

But the girls were still silent, so the boys pushed them out of the ghotul and shut the door. The girls were now really frightened and did not dare to run away. They crouched against the wall in the cold, while the boys discussed their fate round the fire. At last the Chalan said to the Sipahi, 'Bring in those *bāploti*, and give them the stick-punishment.'

So the door was opened and five very subdued girls were brought in. The Chalan asked if they were ready for punishment and they said they were. The Kamdar brought in five thick logs, and put them between their legs, making them squat on the ground, away from the wall, their arms folded. They were sentenced to 'two Relo'. This meant they were to sit like this, and very uncomfortable it is, while the boys sang through two Relo songs. During the second song the Alosa touched the ground with her hand and was immediately slapped and pushed over by one of the boys. The Janka began to cry, and the boys roared with laughter. When the Relo songs were finished, the Chalan asked the girls one by one if they would offend again. When each promised to be good in future, he let her get up. The girl who wept was forgiven last. Each girl had to go round the circle of boys and salute them with a smile. Then said the Chalan, 'That's finished. Now comb our hair and massage us, and we'll go to sleep.'

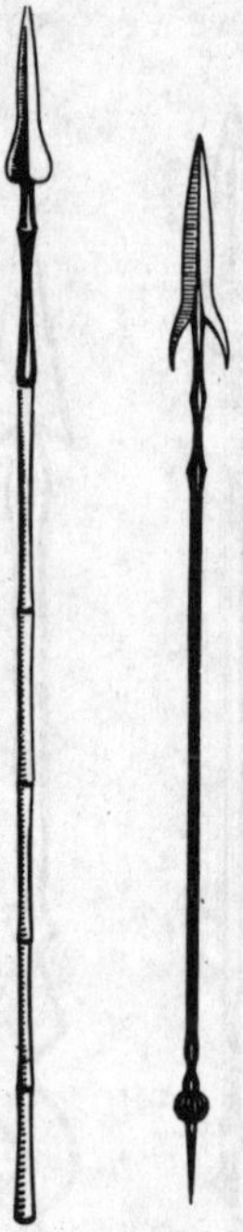

FIG. 15. Iron spears used by the chelik in hunting
Lengths 6′ 6″ and 5′ 5″

Less severe treatment was given to the girls at Bandopal, when I was sleeping in the ghotul on 25 April 1941. At about 10 o'clock at night, as the dancing and games came to an end, I was surprised to see all the girls filing out of the courtyard and sitting by the gate. The Manjhi had discovered that the verandah of the main building, where he and the other leaders slept, had not been properly cleaned. He sent for the Belosa and Dulosa and ordered them to take their girls out of the compound. They did so, no one took any notice of them, the boys lay down and slept as usual, and for a time the girls sat quietly outside the gate. Presently a subdued and penitent voice called, 'Silledar, let us come in.' There was no reply. Then very seductively and sweetly, 'Kotwar, do let us come in.' Still no reply. There was a pause, and then two or three girls at once cried, 'Manjhi, let us in and we'll do anything you want.' This went on for half an hour, and then the Manjhi sent the Kotwar with four other boys to interview the girls. The panchayat squatted down on the near side of the gate and there was a long consultation. At last, the girls promised never to neglect their work again and the Kotwar went to report to the Manjhi who was sleeping on the verandah with a few of the senior boys. He told him to bring the girls in. They filed in and went to the Manjhi. He again made them promise to keep the ghotul clean, then forgave them and told them to massage him and the other senior boys as a penance before they went to sleep.

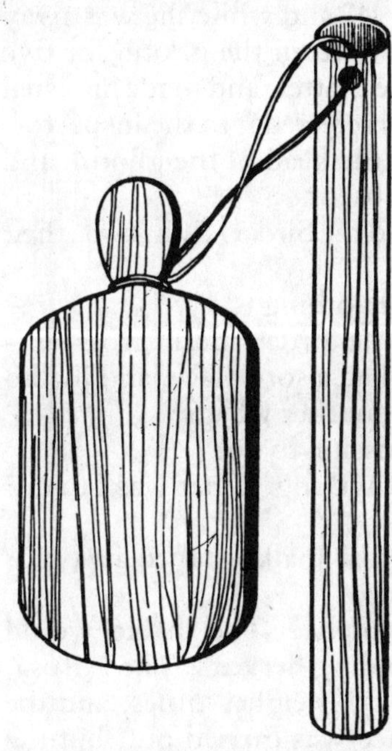

FIG. 16. Toy wooden records used by the Kotwar of the Naria ghotul
Length of upright cylinder 1′

In the Chalka Pargana, in such villages as Kajen, Chimri and Temrugaon, the chelik imitate very closely the ordinary police procedure of the State. The ghotul Kotwar has a wooden spear (Fig. 14) in imitation of the State Kotwar's spear, and a wooden tablet (Fig. 16) which corresponds to the village report-book. It is his duty to report once a week (just as in fact the village watchman reports once a week) to the Inspector of Police, who records the information and if necessary takes it to the Diwan. Fines are paid in pieces of wood or siari seeds, a piece of wood representing a rupee. The thing has the semblance of a game but it is taken very seriously, and a fine of fifty 'rupees' means quite a lot of work.

The following incident is typical. At Palari the Jhalko went to Banjora for a week in January 1942 and while she was away the Nirosa and Jhankai stayed away from the ghotul for five days. The Kotwar inquired into the matter, and made his usual report to the Havaldar who in turn referred it to the Inspector. The Inspector went to the Sirdar, the head of the ghotul, and reported that three girls had been absent.

'Have you examined them?' asked the Sirdar. 'What was their excuse?'

'I questioned them, but they had nothing to say.'

The girls were brought before the Sirdar and in cross-examination it came out that Jhankai had a sore place, and Jhalko claimed that she had been away in another village.

'Did you get the Kotwar's permission to go?'

'I asked him, but he didn't say anything. What was I to do? My parents told me to go.'

Witnesses were called to show that Jhalko stayed away for two days more after she had returned.

The Sirdar then pronounced sentence. The Jhalko would get up and down twenty times holding her ears. The Nirosa, who had no excuse at all, would do it eighty times, and the Jhankai fifteen times. This sentence was carried out, but the Nirosa managed to get hers reduced in appeal to ten. 'But I will count very carefully', said the Sirdar.

Afterwards the Sirdar asked the girls, 'Now you've been punished. Was it fair or are you angry with us?' Each of the girls in turn said, 'No, it was perfectly fair; I was guilty.'

On 25 March 1941, one of the boys at Chimri pretended to be a visiting official; he came into the ghotul and complained that it was dirty, there was no wood or fire. He sent for the Kotwar and Manjhi, who came with folded hands, and he abused them, fining them ten 'rupees' each. Another day the Kajen Kotwar reported to the Inspector that he had noticed on a boy's mat a cloth which belonged to a girl who was not his ghotul-wife. The Inspector pretended to write this down in his 'book', and sent the Constable who handcuffed the two lovers with lengths of siari twine and brought them to the Tahsildar. He lectured them and fined them five 'rupees' each. They appealed to the Diwan who enhanced the sentence to twenty-five 'rupees' or bits of green wood.

VI

These examples will be sufficient to show how the machinery of ghotul justice works and which officials are involved. It sounds like a game, but is taken very seriously. We have seen how the Kotwar or other boy with similar duties first discovers and reports an offence. It is investigated by the Thanedar or Inspector, who in turn brings the culprits before the Tahsildar. Finally the leader of the ghotul considers the case, pronounces judgement and inflicts punishment. In those ghotul which have some older man still holding office an appeal may lie to him. There is often a boy whose special duty it is to carry out the sentence.

The punishments inflicted are of some variety. We have already seen the *khotla pahara*, or stick-punishment, in operation. Sometimes the stick is put through both legs and arms and the hands are tied in front. In Kajen it was the Tahsildar's special duty to see that the victims did not support themselves against the wall or ground.

The *porokal werana* or *pahara orator* is more severe. Hands and feet are tied and the victim is slung from the roof by his feet, remaining topsy-turvy while the others sing one, two or three Relo songs.

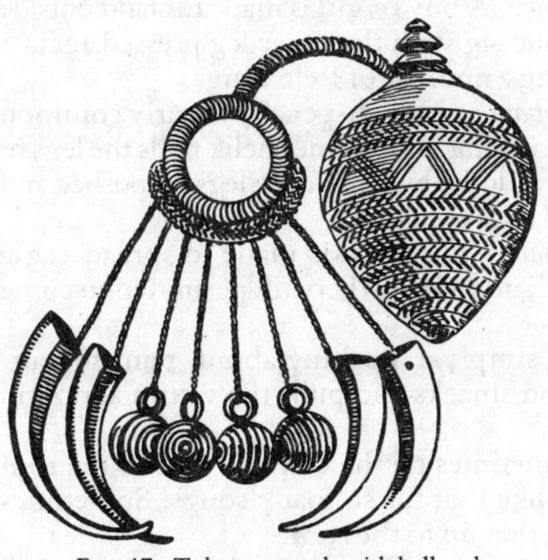

FIG. 17. Tobacco pouch with bell and tusk ornaments *Height of pouch 3½″*

Kawing taliyana is the very common Indian punishment of making someone squat down on the ground and get up and down holding his ears with his hands. It is difficult, exhausting and undignified. But it is not very painful and it leaves no trace, which probably accounts for its popularity among subordinate officials. In Lihagaon, pebbles were held to the ears while the culprit was pushed up and down twenty-five to fifty times. This was how the Manjhi punished Dursal Rani in the song recorded at p. 608.*

An Nanipodar, the chelik connected this punishment with a story of a Raja and a dancing girl of the Mirdangiya caste—whose girls are famous for their wit and beauty.

There was a Mirdangiya. She danced before a Raja. He was so pleased that he said, 'Ask what you will and I'll give it to you.' She said, 'Spit on the floor and then lick up the mess'. The Raja said, 'How can a Raja do such a thing?' Then the Mirdangiya said, 'Very well then, give me the turban from your head.' He did so and she wore it herself and went away well pleased.

The movements of a girl jumping up and down holding her ears are supposed to resemble the Mirdangiya dancing before the Raja, and the chelik taunt the girls saying, 'Ho re Mirdangiya! Today you've become Mirdangiya.' To which the girls reply, 'We are Kanchnin [good and beautiful] girls. If we were Mirdangiya we would be dancing and you'd have to give us your turbans.' The boys laugh and say, 'Then it was the Raja who was punished, now it is the Mirdangiya.'

Nit mandana or *kal nitana pahara* is a simple punishment of expulsion and endurance. A boy or girl is made to stand outside the ghotul fence on one leg with the other leg pressed against it, while the others sing a number of Relo songs.

The *nagil puhana pahara* or plough-penalty is fairly common as a punishment for breaking wind. One chelik pulls the legs of the victim and two push down his shoulders; legs are pushed and shoulders pulled until he is exhausted.

In the *porokal karhana* the culprit is made to spread-eagle himself from the roof and to hang there till permitted to come down.

The *korit pahara* is simply a 'pushing about' punishment. Everybody pushes and smacks and pulls the victim about till he cries for mercy.

In Masora they sometimes tie the culprit's hair to the roof and make him stand like that for so many songs. Sometimes his hands are tied together up to the roof.

It will be noted that these punishments can be described, shall we say, as chronic rather than acute. The sharp, abrupt sting or

* Refer to original edition, *The Muria and their Ghotul* (OUP, 1947).

corporal punishments, so familiar to the European schoolboy is unknown. The punishments, in so far as these are physical at all, involve the endurance of discomfort and distributed pain, and above all the loss of dignity. This is perhaps what we would expect of so gentle a people to whom the catastropic decisiveness of a flogging would appear intolerable. Even the punishments must be associated with something beautiful; they are endured to the sound of music, the rhythmic movement of the Relo songs.

A fine is a very common form of penalty. In the ghotul the fines are almost always interpreted in terms of bits of wood or siari seeds. A fine of ten rupees probably means ten bits of green wood (dry wood is brought by the younger boys in the daily routine), a fine of a hundred means a hundred siari seeds. This type of substitution is not confined to the ghotul. In Bandopal I once saw a root sacrificed instead of the pig the villagers could not afford, and elsewhere I have seen sticks given in place of chickens—sacrificed and treated exactly as if they really were chickens.

The seed-fines are collected until there is enough to invite the whole village to a party. Any monetary fines are usually put in charge of the village headman for safety, and used to buy liquor. The seeds are fried as a relish; liquor is distributed; and it is said that during this party the chelik and motiari recount the history of the fines and penalties of the past year to the amusement and benefit of all.

The most dreaded punishment is expulsion from the ghotul. A foretaste of this is given to very small boys who fail to bring their daily wood, when their elders refuse to accept their Johar in the evening. The little boy goes round the circle saying Johar, but each chelik looks through him and refuses to answer. This soon reduces the child to penitence and he promises never to offend again. If he does, or if the little girls fail to clean the building, they may be sent to sit outside the door for two or three hours. This is regarded as equivalent to excommunication. It is a rather pathetic sight to see a little boy or girl, in the cold winter or the rains, crouching lonely by the door while the others enjoy the warmth and company inside. Occasionally a boy or girl is forbidden to join the ghotul expeditions or go to a marriage. Sometimes members are actually expelled—incurable laziness, obstinate refusal to submit to ghotul discipline, a quarrelsome temperament, the breach of clan and relationship rules may lead to this extreme penalty. It is indeed extreme, for it means the death of youth, the loss of company and the shame of a wedding without dancers.

That is, in fact, the final sanction of the ghotul rules—the fear that the chelik and motiari will refuse to attend one's wedding. It is no idle threat; it has been done; it has been still more often threatened, and the parents have had to pay a fine. Once at Jhakri the Piosa failed to do her share of bringing leaves at someone's marriage, and the boys said, 'This girl is too great for us. She evidently likes to be alone. Well, she shall marry alone'. When her marriage day arrived there was a great disturbance and the elders of several villages had to pacify the offended boys. But at last, after her parents had given a gift of liquor, they agreed to assist.

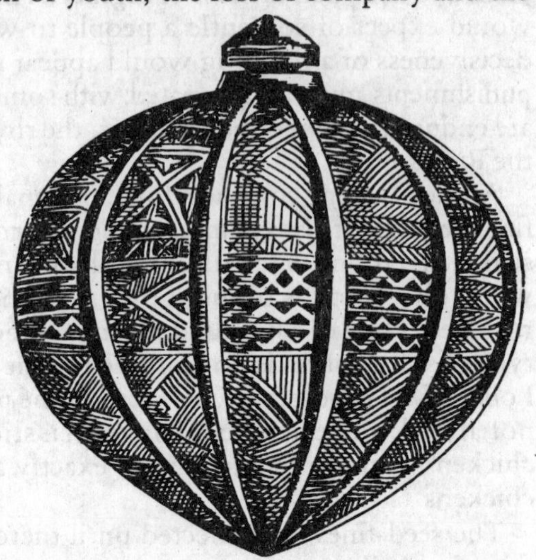

FIG. 18. Carved tobacco-box from Nayanar
Actual size

No reader of chapter V* can fail to see the importance of this threat. No wedding can proceed without chelik and motiari. Their absence would mean that on the greatest day of one's life there was drabness, mockery and disgrace. So long as this ultimate sanction remains, the youngsters submit cheerfully to all the penalties, harsh as they may sometimes seem, that the leaders of the ghotul may inflict.[9]

* Refer to original edition, *The Muria and their Ghotul* (OUP, 1947).

[9] Anyone who thinks the ghotul discipline too hard should read a curious paper by Thurston on 'Corporal Punishment in Vernacular Schools' in India, in which forty-two different manifestations of pedagogic sadism are listed. *Ethnographic Notes*, pp. 433–40.

VII

It may be of interest to compare these penalties with the disciplinary measures taken in other village dormitories. There is a curious account in an old book on the Chittagong Hill Tract by Captain Lewin, who was Deputy Commissioner of this area and seems to have been a man of considerable sympathy and knowledge.

In the village communities, even as the adults have a recognized head, so also is there a head boy appointed to control the boys of the village. This head of the juvenile community is called the *goung*. I shall give here, as illustration of their village customs, a recital which I heard told at the camp fire one night in the jungles, by one of our policemen of the Palaingtsa clan. He said: 'I was formerly *goung* over the unmarried lads of Hmraphroo village; this was when I was about seventeen years old. At night all who were unmarried, and weaned from their mothers, used to sleep in the *khiong*. One night Ougjyn, and Reyphaw, and Chaindra, came to me and got leave to go and sleep with their sweethearts. The girls were named Aduhbyn, Hlapyn, and Aduhsheay. I remember their names quite well; they are married now, and two of them have children. Our lads went by stealth, of course: if the parents had known it there would have been a row. Next day a little girl told me that Pynhla, another of our lads, who had not got leave to sleep out, had passed the night with her sister. This was quite contrary to rule, and it was therefore determined to punish him. Next day we all went to the Raja's *joom* to help to build his house, and in the evening, when we returned, we made a big fire on the bank of the stream that runs through the village; and I sent and called Pynhla, but he was afraid, and would not come; he stayed in his father's house, and said he had fever. I knew this was only an excuse; so I sent three lads to bring him forcibly, and they went and brought him, although his mother abused them much; but the father and mother could not hurt them, as they were acting by the *goung*'s order. When he came, I called upon him to say why he had slept away from the *khiong* without leave. At first he denied all about it, and then I brought forward the little girl, and he asked her, 'How did you know it was I? It was dark'; and she said, 'The moon shone on your face in the early morning when you opened the door to go away.' When he heard this he saw there was no escape, and he fell at my feet and asked forgiveness; but I fined him three rupees on the spot for the sake of discipline.[10]

[10] T. H. Lewin, *Wild Races of South-Eastern India* (London, 1870), pp. 118ff.

In the Uraon *dhumkuria*, as in Bastar, many different punishments are inflicted. In Mandar the boys described the penalty for not keeping the dormitory clean; if any animal or bird dirtied the place they had to make the excrement into little balls with their own hands and throw it away. If a boy wet his bed, they said, the others stuck a pin into the ground and spat on it; the offender had to pick it up with his own teeth. In the middle of the ruined dormitory at Agru I saw a fine stone pillar. Boys who failed to attend the dances were forced to hop round this five times with two bits of bamboo tied tightly to their legs. Fines were also inflicted.

FIG. 19. A tortoise tobacco-box
Height 4¼″

Roy has described the 'slit' in the central pillar of 'some of the *dhumkuria*' and connects it with a fertility ceremony in which the boys insert their 'penile organs' into a slit in a sal sapling.[11] In *Oraon Religion*[12] he says that this is to be found 'in most *dhumkuria* houses'. He only mentions the name of one village, however, Borhambey. We saw the slit there, but did not find it in any of the other dormitories we visited, nor has W. G. Archer been able to find any trace of the custom elswhere.

It is probable that the 'dormitory slit' was chiefly used for punishing refractory boys. According to the *dhangār* who talked to Shamrao Hivale at Mandar, it was used as a punishment for boys who were shy or sulky and refused to join in the communal games and dances. 'A lump of red earth is put on the pillar, and the Mahato stands by with a stick, and hits us on the legs and

[11] Roy, *The Oraons*, p. 243.
[12] p. 53.

tells us to push our penis into the earth, and then he pushes us against it again and again till we become red. If a boy is sulky, we bring him at night to the *dubri* (mistress) and we push his penis into the slit until he cries and promises not to offend again. We all hit him and push him to and fro against the pillar till his penis hurts and he cries.'

Discipline in the Naga morung is, as we might expect, more rigorous and the punishments more drastic. 'Among the boys of the village', says Mills,

FIG. 20. *Marka-batta-gota* or mango tobacco-box
Height 2¼"

there is a certain amount of rough play, and a bumptious or obnoxious youngster is taught his place exactly as he is in an English Public School. He may sit down in the dark and find stinging leaves have been put ready for him. Or a more elaborate punishment may be inflicted which many a mother in England would not approve of for her darling. A plank is laid like a see-saw over a log. One end is weighted down with a wooden pillow. The boy has to jump on the other end and the wooden pillow flies up and hits him on the back of the neck.[13]

There is nothing in Bastar to compare with the Naga bullying, a process by which young boys are hardened to face every kind of danger and difficulty. 'Men who are now middle-aged say that when they first entered the *morung* they were very severely disciplined, not to say bullied. They were, for instance, held over the fire and compelled to endure the heat without a cry. Or they were made to show their pluck by being sent alone on a dark night to fetch a bamboo from a certain clump. The boy

[13] Mills, *The Rengma Nagas*, p. 52.

sent was allowed no torch or weapon, and had to gnaw the bamboo through with his teeth or hack it off with a sharp stone. Or, again, a boy would be sent to leave a torch at some particular spot far away in the jungle and come back alone in the dark without a light. In the morning the older boys would go and see if the burnt remains of the torch were in the proper place. Nowadays boys have an easier time, but a considerable number of duties falls to their lot, and for the first three years a boy's life is very like that of a fag at an English Public School. Boys of the lowest class must keep a supply of torches in the *morung* for travellers passing through the village late in the evening; they have to massage the bigger boys' legs when they come in tired from the fields; they are responsible for the wood and water needed for cooking; they must make pipes and sharpen *daos* for their seniors. In fact, for three years they have to do what they are told, and do it quickly—a most excellent system.[14]

VIII

Hitherto we have considered only the trivialities of ghotul discipline. The sexual relationships of chelik and motiari give rise to far more serious problems. I discuss the large question of ghotul pregnancies in a separate chapter: here we must consider how far life in the dormitories encourages breach of the clan-laws or leads to incest between near kin.

There are the strictest rules against clan-incest. Do they work? It is not easy to give an answer. That clan-incest is possibly not uncommon may be gathered from such sayings as 'When the door is shut there are no clans, we are only chelik and motiari'; 'Once the door is shut and the fire dies down, all relationships are levelled out'; 'Our tribal rules extend to the border of the sleeping-mat; we watch the youngsters as far as that; what happens inside that country no one knows.' It was the opinion of an educated Muria that the chief danger of the ghotul was that it promoted intimacy between members of the same clan and even exposed near relatives to unnecessary temptation.

It is impossible to say. Even if I filled pages with village gossip it would prove nothing. Only an exact statistical inquiry could answer the question whether the Muria chelik was prone to

[14] Mills, *The Ao Nagas*, pp. 179f.

incest or no. And that could never be obtained. But certain things may be affirmed.

At first sight, considerable freedom appears to be allowed. A motiari may comb the hair of a boy of her own clan, and may massage him. Even a close relation like an 'own sister' may do this. In Kabonga the Muria said that girls and boys of the same clan might sleep together, but must not have sexual intercourse. At Kajen in 1940, all the boys and girls were of the Halami sect, except one girl who was a Kuhrami. Yet they went daily to the ghotul and slept together there. They denied that they had sexual intercourse. This may be true, but no reliance can ever be put on a denial in Bastar. In the Metawand ghotul I found the following pairs 'married' to each other—Partabi and Maravi, Wadder and Maravi, Maravi and Maravi, Maravi and Katlami, Maravi and Wadder, Maravi and Maravi, Kuhrami and Maravi. In Dongrigura, in 1940, nearly all the ghotul members were Sori, save one or two Naitami and Kuhrami. The Pahardar and Pahardarin were 'married': both were Sori. So were the Beldar and Beldrain, the Sirdar and Sirdarin and the Supedar and Supedarin. If members of the same sect could be 'married' to each other, the feeling against clan-incest *inside the ghotul* cannot be very strong. So long as the relation does not result in pregnancy it does not seem to matter greatly. No one knows except the chelik and motiari—and they never tell.

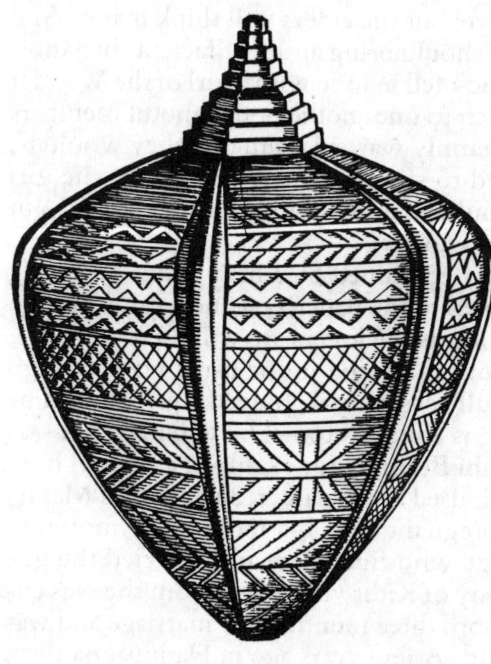

FIG. 21. Carved tobacco-box from Markabera
Height 2¾″

But if there is a pregnancy it is a serious matter. In such a case,

I was told at Kabonga, the members of the ghotul assemble and pass judgement. 'Look, brother, look, sister, you are both of the same clan; you are brother-sister to each other, yet you have done this evil. If the elders hear of it, we can give them no answer. We ourselves do not think it sin; it was the lust of youth, you were mad with love; but the elders will think it sin.' And they insist that the boy should bring an abortifacient. In Munjmeta when a Katlami boy fell in love with a girl of the Wadder clan—these are forbidden to one another—the ghotul members held a meeting and solemnly warned them that they would be fined if they continued to sleep together and that if the girl became pregnant it would be most serious for them both. But I heard that they took no notice.

The offence is usually condoned by a heavy fine, anything from six to twelve rupees to the panchayat and a calf or pig to the clan-god. But so long as the lovers are willing to separate, they are not barred from marrying in the usual way, though not always with the full ceremonial. Indeed a girl should be married to the boy she is engaged to—if he will have her—as soon as possible. At Kibi Belanga, for example, a Maravi boy, the Panda of the ghotul, used to have intercourse with a Maravi girl, and she became pregnant. The matter became known to the elders of the village who fined him and married the girl quickly to a Naitami boy of Kidir village to whom she was engaged. The child was born three months after marriage and was accepted by the husband. A few years ago in Hathipakna there was a scandal when the Malko, 'a daughter of Naitami', was made pregnant by the Jamadar, also a Naitami. They attempted an abortion, without success, but after the boy's father had paid twelve rupees, the Malko was married, by the reduced ceremonies, to a boy at Sodma.

The kindly, gentle Muria makes things as easy as possible for the young. 'Even an elephant with four legs sometimes stumbles'. 'What can you do to one who has missed the road?' But if the girl refuses to leave her lover, the matter becomes very serious, and both are outcasted. In Metawand, I was told that such people were never re-admitted into the tribe, and after death only the chelik would touch their bodies and take them to the pyre. If a *kutukal* was erected it would have to be apart from the others.

A few years ago, at Alor, a member of the Kuhrami clan

eloped with a Kuhrami girl. They were condemned by the panchayat, but took no notice. For 'the mouth that desires its fill and the genitalia that are excited never listen to advice'. They are now living together at Hirri. No Muria will eat with them, and at festivals of the clan-god they get no share of the consecrated meat. If a son is born, he will be called Bhula Huwa, but he will not be regarded as outcaste. He will have all the tribal privileges denied his parents. 'For he was tied up in the bundle; he knew nothing of what was done.'

This rigorist attitude is not so much one of moral condemnation as due to a fear of the supernatural vengeance that may descend upon the whole clan. In some cases, the guilty pair are forgiven if they perform an elaborate ceremony and pay sufficient fines. For two years they have to wait. Then if the Gaita approves he takes them to a tank or stream. Near the bank they make a ring of stakes and build a little bamboo wall, covering it with grass and thatch, inside which the boy and girl are made to stand together. The grass is set on fire and as it blazes up they jump through the flames into the water. After bathing, they put on new clothes and throw the old ones into the water. They make suitable offerings to the gods and are henceforth free of their guilt.

The general atmosphere of kindly tolerance probably accounts for the fact that so few tragedies have occurred. In the police records of the last ten years there are only two cases of suicide which arose out of clan-incest. The first was in January 1932. Chime and Kule of the Timri ghotul were of the same clan and in love with one another. The girl's parents married her to a boy called Jhola, from Supbeda, who had a wife already. She left him and it is said that she returned to the Timri ghotul and began to sleep there again. If this is true, it is remarkable in view of the normally strict taboo on married girls entering the ghotul. But all such rules are broken sometimes. After a time she was found to be pregnant but only after several months did the matter come to the ears of the village elders. When they questioned Chime about it, she took the hand of Kule and named him as the father of the unborn child. This was too much for him and on the night of 18 January, though he went to the ghotul as usual, when all were asleep he went quietly out and hanged himself.

For months everyone must have known all about it. Before

the girl's marriage Kule's breach of the clan laws was complete and open; it must constantly have been discussed in the ghotul, and the elders must have known of it. Yet until the day of the 'trial' it had never been openly proclaimed in the village that he had offended against the laws of the tribe. That was too much for him, he saw his girl lost to him, a lifelong shame, and heavy penalties. So he killed himself.

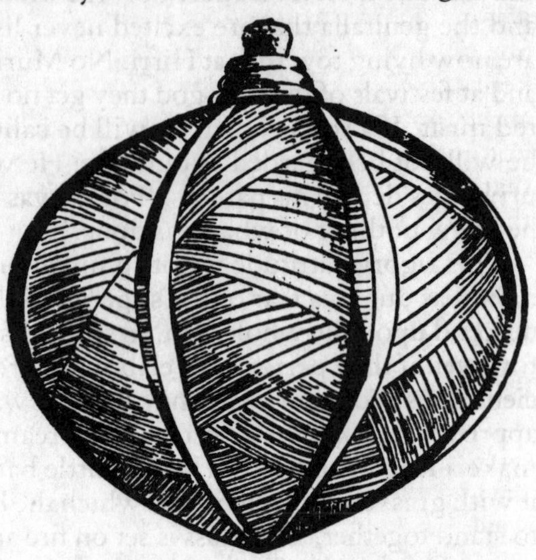

FIG. 22. Carved tobacco-box from Metawand
Height 2½″

There was another case in 1936 in Kerawahi when a chelik and motiari[15] who belonged to the same clan fell in love with one another. They often used to slip outside the ghotul at night and sleep together. After a time the girl found herself pregnant. When the matter became known, there was a great scandal and the elders announced that they would hold a panchayat. The boy was so ashamed and so afraid of paying the fine that was certain to be inflicted, that he hanged himself. The girl was afterwards married to another boy, but was punished—the people said—by excessive menorrhagia. She grew thinner and thinner, and after a year her husband left her and married someone else.

IX

I have heard of very few cases of incest between near relatives. In spite of all the joking, in spite also of the close proximity in which near relatives grow up together in the ghotul, I think that

[15] According to the police report, the chelik was Lati, son of Dhanaji, and the motiari was Koli, daughter of Bhimram. Lati was Koli's paternal uncle. I do not know their ghotul titles.

the rules are kept. On the rare occasions that they are broken, the act is regarded with severe censure. At Sahimunda a girl was made pregnant by her own *māma*, her mother's brother. She publicly accused him and he was fined. In Adenga, a Muria kept his own father's junior wife. He was excommunicated and banned from all tribal privileges. He and the woman were not even allowed to get water from the usual place. I am told that he is never to be admitted into the tribe. In the same village the Gaita kept his mother's sister, and was excommunicated.

A tale of incest from Kapsi is obviously satirical and hardly suggests approval of what was done.

Long ago there lived an old man who married his son to a very lovely girl. When she came to his house the father at once fell in love with her. He sent his old wife and son to another village to get rice, and that evening he himself pretended to get high fever and lay groaning on his bed. The poor daughter-in-law came to him and said, 'What can I do for you?' He said, 'Ask the Departed in the granary what they want you to do.' She went to them and asked, 'What can I do for my father-in-law?' The old man crept out of bed and stood behind the wall. When the girl asked the question, he replied in a loud, strange voice, 'Your father-in-law is going to die; there is only one way to save him; lie with him and his fever will be cured.' At this the girl was frightened and said to the Departed, 'But the marriage haldi is still on my body, how can I do such wickedness? The marriage booth is yet green, how can I betray my husband?' But the old man replied, 'If you want your father-in-law to live, do as we say; the sin will not be yours, but that of the Dead.' Then the poor daughter-in-law went back to the old man and told him what the Departed had said, and he asked her what she thought of it. She said she was willing to do what they ordered and she lay with him. When all was over, she asked whether his fever had left him, and he told her that it had, and praised her devotion to the Departed.

4

Preface

Maria Murder and Suicide

This book is a contribution to social anthropology rather than to the study of crime. For many of the tragedies here are not crimes in any intelligible sense, though in our present state of dealing with such matters we treat them as if they were. Moreover, I have naturally approached the subject from the angle that was most familiar to me. I am neither an administrator, a lawyer nor a policeman. In dealing with crime this is a great disadvantage. It is specially so in India where these simple village crimes offer few problems of detection, and where it is impossible to study the general reaction of society through the columns of the daily press or in such revealing impulses of compassion as petitions for reprieve. It is only rarely that anything like a detective problem with clues and counter-clues is set for the police. It is equally rare for interesting points of law to arise during a trial. In the great majority of cases the accused confesses. But this does not mean that these aboriginal crimes have no importance. It is of absorbing sociological and psychological interest to study the reasons that drive unsophisticated primitive men to kill and wound their fellows; and their behaviour afterwards, as well as the conduct of everyone concerned, is of almost equal importance.

While I was collecting material for my book *The Muria and their Ghotul*, I was greatly struck by the difference in the incidence of crime between the Muria and the great Maria tribe to the south. For homicide the annual incidence to the million is only 21 among the Muria, while it is 69 among the Bison-horn

Maria; for suicide it is 22 against 53. In the last 10 years [illegible] only been 21 Muria murders, and a large number of these [illegible] occurred either on the boundaries of the State or in the Mardapal Pargana in the extreme south of the Muria area, bordering on the Maria territory. The Muria differ from the Maria in the quite extraordinary absence of jealousy among them, in their lack of attachment to property and personal possessions, in their very strong civic and social instincts, in their gentleness and kindness. I believe that this difference is largely due to the existence among the Muria of the Ghotul or village dormitory,[1] in which the boys and girls of the tribe grow up from childhood under a high degree of discipline and are trained in the tribal virtues. A system of what is practically pre-nuptial sexual communism teaches them from an early age the impropriety of jealousy. The habit of sharing everything all through childhood and youth in the dormitory weakens their individualistic attachment to personal property. The result is that several of the main causes of murder only lightly press upon them. The Bison-horn Maria probably had a similar dormitory club at one period and traces of it may still be found today. But it no longer exists as a social force, and the result is that the Maria—compared to their northern neighbours—grow up passionate and jealous, strongly attached to individual goods, undisciplined and revengeful. The Muria do not seem to consume any less alcohol than the Maria. Indeed the consumption of mahua spirit per head in the Muria area is higher than in the south. The Maria, however, drink more rice-beer, and there are many more cases of illicit distillation detected among them.

When my friend Mr A. N. Mitchell was Administrator of Bastar, he was troubled by this problem, and one day in conversation about it, one of us—I forget which—suggested that I might make some sort of survey of Maria homicides from my own independent angle. Mr Mitchell, with his unique zeal for everything affecting the life and welfare of aboriginals, gave me all possible facilities for my inquiry, and I was thus able not only to study official documents but also to visit the jail and discuss matters with many criminals.

The first task in my inquiry was to get at the records. I decided

[1] For a detailed account of this institution, see my *The Muria and their Ghotul* (Bombay, 1947).

usive study of the Bison-horn mediately faced by our first difficulty who were to be included under this ome to be used in Bastar and in anthro- Mr W.V. Grigson's memorable book, *The* ...*tar*. But it is not, of course, a word that is used of themselves. Many of them now do not call Maria at all. At the 1941 Census, thousands of Maria hemselves as Muria, because they thought it sounded spectable. Many others in the south have for some time past taken the title of Dorla. Others again are known as Koya, and a few call themselves Gond. When I was in Konta, the very wild Maria there said, 'We are not Maria. That is the name of the uncivilized fellows in Dantewara'. When I was in Dantewara, the equally wild Maria there indignantly rejected the old name which, they said, was only properly given to the savages of Konta. The expression 'Bison-horn Maria' is an obvious linguistic makeshift. Another name for the tribe is Dandami Maria. But I have never heard this used by the people themselves, and many do not know what it means. The name 'Bison-horn Maria' is derived from the tribe's custom of using a magnificent head-dress of bison-horns for their marriage dances, and possibly 'Tallaguda Maria' or even 'Sing Maria' (an expression in actual use) would preserve both the descriptiveness of the title and linguistic propriety. But for the time being I have continued to use the very convenient term, Bison-horn Maria, and throughout this book it will be understood that, wherever the word 'Maria' is used without qualification, it is to the Bison-horn and not the Hill variety of the tribe that I refer.

It will be evident, however, that official records, which are not concerned with scientific classification, were not likely to preserve these nice distinctions between one tribe and another, and I was at first provided with a very large number of files, many of which had nothing to do with the Bison-horn Maria at all. I think it is not unlikely that the bad reputation of this tribe for violence is, to some extent, due to the fact that a number of people who do not belong to it are included when statistics are compiled. However, at last, after much sifting and sorting, I found that I had a collection of 103 records of Bison-horn Maria homicides covering the years 1921 to 1941. During this period there must have been nearly 250 such cases altogether, but some of the files had been eliminated and others for one reason or another were not available. However, 103 was a very fair sample. For convenience I omitted the last 3 cases, and was thus left with a set of 100 taken entirely at random, distributed throughout the period under review and taken from every part of the area.

It was rather more difficult to get records of suicide, for these were not kept at the headquarters of the State, but distributed in the police stations and many of them had been eliminated. But the State Superintendent of Police called in as many aboriginal files as could be found; these were not above three-score in number, and I took the first 50 which were extracted. These extended over a period of 10 years.

Between 1935 and 1942 I made many tours in this enchanting land among these enchanting people. On the earlier tours I was accompanied by my friend Mr Shamrao Hivale whose amazing sympathy and insight helped me to catch my first vision of Maria culture. Later I had the support of my wife who, being herself a Gond, was able to get quickly in touch with the people and immediately established a friendly atmosphere. Particularly in the later tours I tried to see as many scenes of violence as possible, to talk to released convicts and to discover the general attitude of a village towards any crime that had been committed within its boundaries. In Aranpur I stood beside the still warm ashes of the ritually-cremated clothes of Barse Chewa who had recently been hanged in jail. At Khutepal, I watched Oyami Masa's children playing on the very floor once stained by the blood of his murdered wife. In the forest near Jabeli I had a clearing made so that I could photograph the carved pillar erected in memory of a famous murderer. In Rewali I was visited by a ferocious-looking youth who had twice stood on trial for his life and had twice preserved it. Here too I talked with Hemla Bakka who killed his wife for infidelity and was now unable to get another. In Doriras I saw the grave of the murdered Boti which had been desecrated by Ghasia for the sake of the purse of money which had been buried to help the dead man on his journey to the other world. In the same village I visited the home of Kawasi Borga then serving a life sentence, and talked to his fine sons and his sad pathetic wife.

Later I spent many hours in the Jagdalpur Jail talking to Maria who were serving terms of life-imprisonment for homicide.

Some of them were as informative as the limits of their psychology allowed, for it must always be remembered that aboriginals are not accustomed to discussing those matters which are of special interest to anthropologists. Other prisoners clearly suspected some trick and told me very little. On the whole I was impressed by the great sadness of their life, even though in the jail they are well and kindly treated. Most of them, I think, felt that an inexplicable tragedy had befallen them. They did not feel like criminals. Their lives had been destroyed by a capricious destiny.

It was naturally more difficult to get information about the suicides, for, in the nature of the case, the person of most interest could not be present to tell his story. Relatives also and the villagers were more reticent, I thought, in discussing this subject, possibly because they feared that any revelations might lead to further police investigation. But even so I was able to get a certain amount of information about the Maria's attitude to self-murder.

But inquiries among the Maria are never easy. The people say that, as a result of Mr Grigson's investigations when he was writing his book on the tribe, their villages have suffered an invasion of man-eating tigers. In one village where I myself took photographs it was declared afterwards that I had made all the women barren. The Maria are friendly people, and I was able to make many friends among them. But particularly on matters which have a police reference they are naturally inclined to be secretive and prefer to claim ignorance rather than expose themselves to possible later difficulties by confiding in the investigator. Moreover, there is undoubtedly throughout aboriginal India a belief that talking about tribal affairs may anger the ancestors of the clan or disturb some godling's peace of mind. It is said of Korava children, members of a criminal tribe in Mysore, that they are taught from infancy to say 'I do not know' in reply to questions put to them.[2] Many Maria adopt the same attitude.

I do not suggest that in this book I have discovered anything new. But the transition from a social order where everything was settled by the tribe to a state of affairs where everything is

[2] L. K. Ananthakrishna Iyer, *The Mysore Tribes and Castes* (Mysore, 1930), Vol. III, p. 612.

settled by outsiders and nothing at all by the tribe, is of obvious interest. The tragedies described here throw light on many aspects of tribal life, and are specially valuable as indicating what things are emotionally disturbing to the Maria mind. When we read a monograph on a tribe, its whole life is laid out before us. Some things are interesting and exciting to the reader, but it is not always easy to discover what is interesting to the people themselves. Supplementary studies like this help us to appreciate the actual realities of, for example, a polygamous household or the real difficulties of the serving-marriage. The impact of witchcraft on the minds of the people, the extent of their attachment to property, their jealousy and desire for revenge are vividly illustrated here.

The value of such a study as this is not, however, only for the student. As the tribal areas are opened up, and as the aboriginals come more and more into touch with the outside world, it will become ever more essential for administrators and magistrates to understand tribal mentality. It is hard enough sometimes to understand any kind of aboriginal action. There is nothing more baffling than aboriginal crime. The Courts are all too ready to save time and energy by accepting a plea of drunkenness as an explanation of what seems incomprehensible. Undoubtedly a proportion of aboriginal crime, like the crime of civilized people, is due to alcohol. But I do not believe the proportion is large and there is reason to suppose that the plea of drunkenness so frequently put forward is often suggested to the accused by his legal adviser.

The importance of anthropological knowledge for the proper evaluation of aboriginal crime hardly needs illustration. One of the most difficult things that a Court has to decide in a case of homicide is whether the deed that it is evaluating comes under any of the Exceptions to Section 300 of the I.P.C. Was the crime premeditated? Was it provoked by a serious and unbearable insult? The difficulty here, which every Sessions Judge admits, is that what seems an extreme provocation to him or the Assessors may hardly be noticed by the aboriginal, and incidents that seem quite trifling to the 'civilized' mind may rouse the Maria or Naga to a fit of homicidal rage. The matter is complicated by the fact that the tribes vary greatly from one to another. The Bison-horn Maria, for example, are passionately concerned about female chastity, and a wife's infidelity is constantly a cause of murder. But in this their Gond and Baiga neighbours to the north have a much lower standard. Love is comparatively free. Divorce is easy and a wife's betrayal is readily compensated by the payment of a small fine. It is obvious, therefore, that a Gond or Baiga who suspects his wife of infidelity is not put to anything like the same degree of provocation as that suffered by a Bison-horn Maria under similar circumstances.

Premeditation may be indicated by tribal customs. The Bison-horn Maria express the spirit of implacable revenge by certain dramatic symbols. They pull out their pubic hairs; they remove a few handfuls of grass from an enemy's roof; they whistle loudly the dreaded *sui* whistle. In any case where an accused is proved to have indulged in one or other of these acts, it may be assumed that his crime was premeditated.

A Bastar tragedy, the murder of Tati Hirme by her deceased husband's younger brother Doga, provides an interesting example of how a knowledge of local custom can explain an otherwise meaningless crime. According to tribal practice a younger brother has a right over his elder brother's widow, a right which extends not only to her person, but to her property. This right Tati Hirme refused to Doga, and there is evidence that for a long time the youth bitterly resented her behaviour. On the day of the tragedy he went to her house and asked her for some tobacco. She refused, and he murdered her.

At first sight here is precisely one of those motiveless crimes which have so often puzzled outside observers. It is true that there was hostility between the parties, but the refusal of a small gift of tobacco was hardly sufficient for so disastrous a result. But in Maria practice to ask a woman for tobacco is a symbolic way of inviting her to sexual intercouse, and when the boy asked his elder brother's widow to have congress with him, he was only demanding his right and when she refused it, he found the provocation, both to his pride and his desire, so great that he killed her.

Research, both by medical science and by anthropology, may in time reveal how far the apparently motiveless homicides of aboriginals can be explained as crimes of exhaustion and fatigue. Again and again a man kills his loved wife in a sudden explosion of temper and for no apparent cause. It is probable that in many cases the real reason is not alcoholic intoxication, but extreme fatigue.

A point that often troubles the Courts is the time-element in cases where provocation is pleaded as an excuse. It is often found that there is a lapse of some hours between the actual incident that gave provocation and the subsequent act of violence. It has too often been held that this lapse of time should deprive the accused of gaining the benefit from Exception 1 of Section 300 of the Indian Penal Code. But there can be little doubt that an aboriginal's intelligence does not work so quickly as that of a more sophisticated person, and even in matters of everyday life it often takes an appreciable time for an idea to take root and effect a result in his mind. Laubscher's analysis of the psychology of the Tembu Negroes of South Africa is of some importance here. The Tembu, he says,

> Is not by nature blood-thirsty, but his aggressive instinctive or pugnacious propensities are excitable, easily roused and explosive. His aggressive libido flows outwards, becomes readily externalized, and sudden impulsive assaults, often fatal, are not uncommon. Careful study of the emotional reactions of the participants in stick fights, of course initially playfully performed for my benefit, has shown me how quickly and explosively the native loses his temper and retaliates with death-dealing blows at his opponent. Fatal blows are only avoided by the defensive skill of the opponent. Aggressive impulses are quickly evoked, although there is no apparent bad feeling after such a stick fight. I came to the conclusion that once an emotional impulse is aroused and the stimulus continues to be present, the native just drifts along with the impulse and exercises little or any inhibitory power, unless this inhibition is brought about by the evocation of another impulse, opposite in aim to the first, such as a fear of consequences, but it must be a fear stimulated by something present at the moment. Resultingly, the intellectual mechanisms of foresight, judgement and self-control are readily submerged by the instinctive impulse.[3]

I have not burdened these pages with many cross-references. The two Summaries at the end of the book give the names of the murderers and suicides in alphabetical order, the clan-name in each case coming first. The Summary of homicides enables the reader to trace the sentence and subsequent history of each of the main characters in the book and also to see at a glance the entire outline of Maria crime.

[3] B. J. F. Laubscher, *Sex, Custom and Psychopathology* (London, 1937), p. 302.

My first friend in Bastar was Mr E. S. Hyde, I.C.S., a lifelong champion of the aboriginals. The assistance given by him and Mr A. N. Mitchell was continued by their successor, Mr K. Radhakrishnan, I.C.S. At every stage of my inquiries I had the sympathetic interest of Dr W. P. S. Mitchell, M.B.E. Dr Mitchell was for many years the Superintendent of the Jail at Jagdalpur and was extremely popular among the prisoners. Every ex-convict with whom I talked praised him, and indeed he reminded me of what Dostoevsky said about the good-natured Russian Prison Governor who treated his men as equals. 'They did not love him, they adored him. I do not remember that they ever permitted themselves to be disrespectful or familiar. On the contrary when he met the Governor the convict's face suddenly lighted up; he smiled largely, cap in hand, even to see him appraoch.' Another popular figure in the Bastar Jail was Dr Satyanarayan who is believed by the Maria to perform some medical magic to free them from erotic desires. The late Rai Saheb Niranjan Singh, Assistant Administrator, who himself had tried and sentenced a large number of Maria criminals, threw much light on the social conditions that give rise to crimes in Bastar. To the police I must give a special word of thanks. Instead of resenting the intrusion of an amateur, Mr A. C. Mayberry, M.B.E., State Superintendent, and his staff gave me every possible assistance. Thakur Manbahal Singh particularly gave me information about the psychology of the homicide which revealed his very deep knowledge of the people. To many other policemen, Circle-Inspectors, Sub-Inspectors and Constables, who aided me in my tours and inquiries, I must express my gratitude. Mr Qudratulla Khan gave me valuable information on Excise matters. Mr Janardhan Joshi and Mr Ramakrishna took great trouble to find records for me, and helped me in every way. Mr S. M. Ishaque's experience of the Maria is unique. He accompanied me on one important tour, and even when lying in great pain in hospital gave me guidance and advice. Mr Q. Huq and Mr M. M. Khirey, who were at the time Tahsildars of Jagdalpur and Dantewara respectively, exerted themselves in every way to assist me in my tours, and greatly encouraged me by their support.

Mr Sampat Singh acted as my interpreter and teacher in Gondi on most of the later tours. His help was quite invaluable. He himself had been present as a clerk at many murder trials, and was often able to expose the real points at issue. I am very grateful for his company and for the intelligence and energy which he put into a difficult and exacting task. Gulabdas, my assistant, who has been under training for many years and can now be regarded as an expert in his particular sphere of inquiry, did excellent exploratory work, and by his affable and insinuating address won the confidence of many Maria and persuaded them to reveal their secrets.

Part of the expenses of research were covered by a research grant from Merton College: I owe a heavy debt of gratitude to the Warden and Fellows for their assistance. The actual publication of the book was made possible by the enthusiasm and practical assistance of my friend Mr Jehangir P. Patel. The deeper realities of friendship and alliance are not matters for public acknowledgement: this book is itself a token and a proof of them. Mr Patel's share in it has been complete.

Mr Justice C. R. Hemeon, I.C.S., and Mrs Hemeon read the manuscript and made important comments and suggestions. Mr Hemeon adds to an extensive legal and judicial experience an ardent interest in criminology and Mrs Hemeon's unique gifts of understanding and insight make her the kind of critic that an author prays for.

Mrs Maeve Scott made two beautiful drawings (the Anga Pen and the Bison-horn head-dress) and gave much help in the preparation of the maps and half-tones. Mr R. D. Motafram's ready and expert hand was responsible for the other line-drawings. The picture of the Meriah sacrifices was discovered for me by Mr Evelyn Wood.

To Mr C. R. Gerrard I am specially indebted for the dust-cover which takes the book out into the world with beauty and significance.

The late Sir W. V. Grigson first inspired me to visit Bastar and then helped to make it possible for me to stay there. A Foreword from him is peculiarly appropriate: his knowledge and love of Bastar is unprecedented and he himself handled with understanding and justice many of the incidents in this book.

Sir W. V. Grigson was succeeded in Bastar by Mr D. R. Rutnam, I.C.S., who established administrative principles which have been of the utmost advantage to the aboriginals and from whom I have learnt much about the mentality of the Maria criminal.

Patangarh, V. E.
Mandla District, India
1 July 1943, revised *1 May 1949*

5

The Religion of an Indian Tribe (1955)

The Art of the Ikon

I

An important and characteristic feature of Saora religion is the custom of making drawings on the walls of houses in honour of the dead, to avert disease, to promote fertility and on the occasion of certain festivals.

These drawings, which are called *ittalan*,[1] a word I translate as ikon, may be made by 'anyone who knows how'; he need not be a priest, but the artist who becomes adept achieves a sort of dedicated position and is known as the Ittalmaran, 'wall-writing-man' or, in fact, artist. Many of the shamans also combine this art with their regular professional duties.

The routine procedure, which is almost standardized, is for the shaman to recommend the painting of an ikon as one of the means of satisfying a god or ancestor who has brought trouble on a home. The making of the ikon may be the pivotal point of a ceremony, or may be auxiliary to its main business, but it is always associated with some sort of sacrifice. As the regular festivals come round, the renewal of the old paintings, especially

[1] Probably derived from the Saora root *id-* which means 'to write' and *tālan*, a contracted form of *kitālan*, a wall—*ittalan* thus meaning 'the writing on the wall'. Ramamurti gives the word as *jotālan*. In some villages the drawings are called *sedatal*, and the person who draws them is the Sedatalmaran. *Sedá-* is a verb meaning to select, and Sedasum is a tutelary who selects a shaman.

those for improving the fertility of the crops, is accepted as a normal religious obligation.

When an ikon is to be made, the householder may either paint it himself, following the inspiration of his dreams, or he may send for a shaman or Ittalmaran and tell him what has to be done. In this case the artist comes to the house and spends a night there before beginning work. In the evening the householder places a small basket of rice and a pot of palm wine on the ground before the wall on which the picture is to be made. If necessary his wife washes the wall with fresh red earth and water to provide a good background. The artist offers the rice and wine to the god or ancestor concerned and says, 'I am an ignorant fellow; I know nothing; but I have been told to make you a house. If I make any mistakes, do not punish me, for it will not be my fault.'

The reference to the 'house' is significant. The ikons are the one-dimensional homes of the spirits. 'A spirit', I was once told, 'sits in his picture as a fly settles on a wall.' The same idea is emphasized in a story which I recorded at Kinteda.

> Before ikons were made the ancestors used to give people a great deal of trouble. One day an ancestor came to Bojai the shaman in a dream and said, 'I have nowhere to live; I want to stay with you.' The shaman said that there was nowhere for a ghost to stay in his house. The ancestor was angry and made him very ill with fever. Bojai sent for another shaman and when the ghost came upon him, he said, 'Sacrifice a goat and make me a house on your wall.' The poor shaman, who had no idea what to do, tried to build a house with bamboo against the wall, but the ghost came and laughed at him. At last Bojai went to Kittung and asked him what to do. Kittung mixed rice-flour with water and showed him how to paint a house on the wall and furnish it. In this way the custom of making ikons began, and as a result the spirits were pleased and did not trouble people quite so much.

Another story, from Sogeda, gives a highly charged magical significance to the ikons, though I doubt if the ordinary Saora of today regards them in quite this way.

> After the world was made, Kittung built a house for himself. On the wall he made drawings of a man and woman with white earth. At that time, all creatures, except men and women, had been made; Kittung wanted to make them, but he had no notion of how to do it. He went to Uyungsum and asked what he should do. Uyungsum said,

Cover your drawings of the man and woman with leaves. After seven days cut your little finger and let the blood fall on the drawings, two drops on the man, three on the woman.

Kittung covered his drawings with leaves and let his blood fall on them, as Uyungsum had said. Nine days later from the woman's picture came a girl: she at once began to cry. Next day a boy came out of the man's picture. Kittung looked after them, and when they grew up, he asked Uyungsum to marry them to one another. From them came all mankind.

The artist sleeps on the floor beside the dedicated rice and expects to have a dream telling him exactly what to do. Sometimes, however, the householder or a shaman has the dream instead, and then the artist works under his guidance. But invariably, I think, the ikons are directed by dreams.

In the morning the artist gets up and has a wash, but he must not eat—though he may drink palm wine—until he has finished. He again makes offerings of rice and wine before the wall, and then settles down to work.

He uses a twig slightly splayed at the end, and his canvas is, of course, the red-washed wall of the house. For paint he has rice-flour and water mixed in a small bowl, or sometimes ashes and water, a mixture which looks a dirty grey at first but dries a sharp white. Occasionally he gives emphasis to his figures with a little lamp-black or red ochre. Unlike other tribesmen who make their pictures in red or black on a white background, the Saoras nearly always paint in white on a red background.

Most of the ikons are built up round the idea of a 'house'—a square, circle or rectangle, which is filled in and surrounded with the figures of men and animals. The artist makes the outline of the house first, for this determines the approximate size of the picture, and then proceeds to decorate and fill it in. He draws the frame with multiple straight lines, with lines elaborately enhanced or with rows of dots or stars. But he always follows the same technique, whether he is making a house, a human figure or an animal. He first makes the outline and then fills it in. In drawing a human figure, for example, he first makes an outline of the whole body with two opposed isosceles triangles which meet at the tips. He adds the arms, then the legs, then the head, and finally fills in the two triangles to make a solid body with a sharply accentuated waist.

For an elephant, the artist first makes the outline of a rough rectangle, adds the legs, tail, head and trunk in that order, whites in the body and finally draws the rider. He makes a horse with two triangles similar to those for the human figure, but turned on their side. He then adds legs, head and rider, taking great care to suggest the hair by fine strokes along the neck and tail. Similarly in making a bear, after he has filled in the body, he draws hair all round it. Equal attention is paid to a peacock's tail, a deer's horns or a porcupine's quills.

When the artist has finished the preliminary draft of the picture, he sends for a shaman who at once proceeds to complicate the course of true art with fussy religious inspirations. He offers rice and wine before the ikon, and calls on the spirit for whom it has been made to come and inspect it. He falls into trance, takes his sacred lamp in his hand, and inspects the drawing by its light; he criticizes it and suggests improvements. 'You have not given me a comb,' he may say, or 'There are not enough chaprassis sitting at my gate' or 'When I was alive I once sat on a bicycle; why haven't you put it in?' This is one of the ways whereby the pictures get so overcrowded; the spirits do not seem to like blank spaces; every inch of wall must be filled with symbols of honour; their greed abhors a vacuum. I once watched the symmetry of an admirably balanced picture being destroyed by this kind of supernatural interference.

I attended the dedication of an ikon at Abbasingi on 5 May 1948, when Gurpanu, a shaman, made a new painting of his tutelary. On a mud platform in front of the picture, he put two pots of rice, a small mirror, the bowl of rice-flour used by the artist, many little leaf-cups for the tutelary and her relatives, and on either side bunches of green plantains. He offered rice and wine while an assistant rang a bell, and called on the gods and ancestors and particularly on his own tutelary.

I have made a house for you. Here are your elephants and horses. Come riding on them. Here is your tiger and your bear. Here are your birds. Come and see what a fine house I have made for you. Tutelaries of the sky, come and see the house. Tutelaries of the hills, come and see the house. All is ready. Come and feast with us and examine your new house. Bring your clerk and your chaprassis. We are watching the road for you. Come quickly, for here is your house and door. Your elephants and horses are ready. Come quickly.

The shaman passed into trance and his tutelary came upon him. There was a long argument about the quality of the entertainment provided and it was only after the shaman had offered rice, plantains and wine and had promised a fowl at the next Harvest Festival that the tutelary condescended to examine his new house. The shaman lit a lamp and looked it over carefully. The tutelary said, 'Yes, that's all right. But where's my lizard? I always have one as a pet in my house. I must have my lizard.'

The shaman hastily promised to add a lizard to the picture, and the tutelary at last declared himself satisfied and went away. The shaman concluded the ceremony by dedicating a new pot into which he put some rice and a copper coin; he hung it up with a branch of plantains above the ikon.

Once it has been accepted and dedicated, after sacrifice has been offered and a pot or gourd hung up above it, the ikon is regarded as a little temple within the house. Offerings are made before it on every ceremonial occasion, and bunches of fruit or ears of grain are hung round its pot at the Harvest Festivals. In certain cases the ikon is repainted every year, often with variations, so that in some houses there is a sort of palimpsest effect, old designs showing dimply behind the bright outlines of the latest drawing.

The ikons are so important, as an element in the cure of disease, for the fertility of the crops, in the marriage of a shaman with his tutelary, and for the light they throw on Saora theology, that it will be necessary to consider them in detail. I propose to examine, and illustrate, fifty of these pictures under various headings according to the purpose for which they were made.

II

I. IKONS[2] DESIGNED TO PROMOTE OR PRESERVE THE FERTILITY OF THE CROPS

Ikons are painted at the Jammolpur, the ceremonial removal of the seed from store for sowing, when a sacrifice is offered to guard it and improve its fertility. Such ikons often depict agri-

[2] The ikons illustrating Nos. 1, 4, 11, 13, 19, 20, 22, 27, 29 and 30 which were pictured, sometimes in larger size, in my *The Tribal Art of Middle India*, are reproduced here for convenience.

cultural operations such as ploughing or hoeing and include fertility symbols. They may, for example, show a man ploughing, a pregnant woman, a woman carrying seed, a potter laden with pots, gods seated on an elephant. These are friendly and auspicious symbols, and each kind of seed is offered before them with a prayer that the gods and ancestors will be favourable.

FIG. 1

Such ikons are made as a matter of routine every year, and others are painted for the Harvest Festivals and retouched annually. Other ikons for the protection of the crops are made in emergency, and may then be of a rather different pattern.

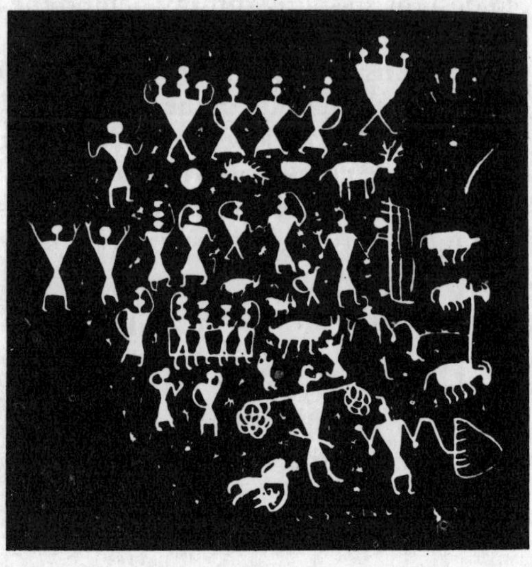

FIG. 2

The fertility ikons are made either for Labosum, the earth-god, or for the ancestors, whose interest in the harvests is thus emphasized.

1. *In the priest's house at Karanjaju*
Length, 34″ (No. 1)

For Labosum. Painted at the Jammolpur, this ikon shows a ploughman with a characteristic (and auspicious) pipe in his mouth, with his son, engaged in ploughing. The cow is followed by its calf. There is a pregnant woman carrying seed on her head. A potter and his wife bring loads of pots to cook the bumper crop which is expected. On an elephant sit Jemra Kittung and Sidibiradi (see pp. 316ff.[3]), who are specially placated at this time. This ikon, with its fertility symbols, may be taken as a sort of standard picture, for in various forms it is reproduced all over the Saora country.

2. *In the house of Saronti, the eunuch, at Sogeda*
Height, 23″ (No. 2)

This ikon, also made for Labosum at the Jammolpur, though it lacks the simple dignity of the preceding picture, displays a scene of great exuberance. While the ploughmen and men with harrows continue with their work, a party of merry-makers dance round them, some waving their arms in the air, some

FIG. 3

[3] Please refer to original edition, published in 1955 by Oxford University Press.

carrying pots on their heads, some holding them on their shoulders. A few people carry two pots to suggest that the harvest will be twice as good as usual. The sun and moon look down as witnesses. Birds, deer and a porcupine are painted in the belief that if they are honoured here, they will not go into the fields and damage the growing plants.

3. *In the Chief's house at Gunduruba*
Height, 28″ (No. 3)

This ikon was painted at the Jammolpur for the ancestors by an Idaimaran, priest of the dead, as this was considered to be specially his concern. The main building is the palace of the ancestors. Monkeys frolic on the roof and attendants and guards surround the building as they do the bungalow of any very important person on earth. Below to the left is a house for three tutelaries and beside it is their armoury. The tutelaries themselves are seated on an elephant, carrying umbrellas in their hands; their clerk rides on a horse before them.

FIG. 4

This picture illustrates the Saora doctrine of the second death; there are three dead men here, and it was explained to me that the two groups, one on each side of the house in which two men are shown carrying a third (rather incongruously drawn as sitting upright with an umbrella), are in fact bearers taking corpses to the pyre. A potter carries a load of pots for the funeral ceremony.

There is nothing here about agriculture, but it was supposed that the ancestors would be so flattered by the ikon that they would do their best to help. Speaking of this picture the Chief said, 'So long as this is on the wall, there will be no fear of thieves. The ikon is the watchman of the home.'

4. *In the priest's house at Pandiguda*
Height, 46″ (No. 4)

Another Jammolpur ikon for Labosum. It shows one man ploughing, another with his hoe, a row of women going to weed, potters with their pots. At the bottom Labosum sits on his elephant. Sun and moon witness to the bargain that if the picture is made there will be a good harvest.

5. *In Singraju's house at Arangulu*
Height, 32″ (No. 5)

Singraju painted the usual ikon for Labosum at the Jammolpur. He sacrificed a fowl before it, dedicated his seed, and planned to go the following day, a Friday, to sow it. That night, however, he dreamt that as he was carrying his seed to his clearing a tiger tried to kill him. He fled and, as he was running away, he saw his mother and father—both long dead—and they drove the tiger away. The next morning he sent for a shaman and the father's ghost came upon him and said, 'Don't take your seed to the clearing today, for your picture is all wrong. Rub it out and make a new one and take out your seed next Monday. Unless you do this, your harvest will be a failure.'

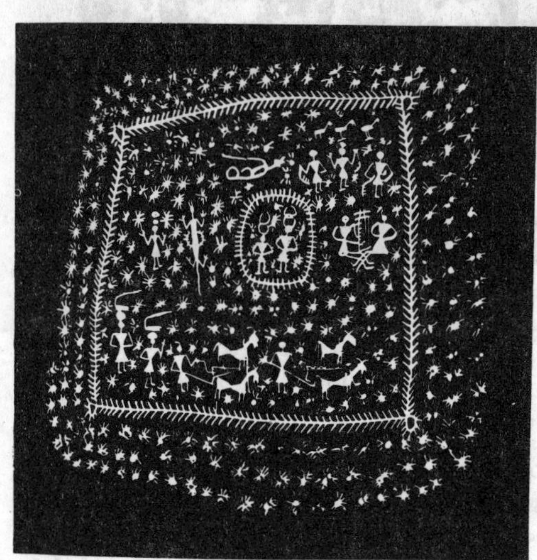

FIG. 5

Singraju was now in a quandary, for he had no idea what kind of picture was required. But that night he had a dream, and his father showed him just what he had to do. On the Sunday, therefore, he fasted and painted the new ikon. He sacrificed another fowl, and on the following morning sowed the first seed of the year and in due time reaped a fine harvest.

The picture shows, within an unusually elaborate border of stars, the forest-clearing, in the middle of which is a house for Singraju's parents. One man is ploughing, and another breaking up the soil with a harrow. There are two women with hoes on their heads and three with sickles. Another woman is bringing food for the workers, with pots of rice and gruel on her head. Singraju is drawn consulting the shaman, who is playing his *Kurānrājan*. There is a very old snake which is trying to swallow the sun: this motif is included to avert any possible danger from eclipses.

FIG. 6

6. *In the Chief's house at Mannemgolu*
   Height, 18″ (No. 6)

The Chief's younger brother Dampo died in 1942, and his Guar and Karja ceremonies were duly performed. Two years went by and the family was not once troubled by the ghost. But in 1944, at the time of the Osanadur, the Harvest Festival of the millet *Eleusine corocana*, Dampo's ghost came to his brother in a dream and showed him a pattern on the wall. 'Make a painting for me like that', he said. 'Then your millet crop will always be very good.' The Chief at once drew the picture and Dampo's ghost came in another dream and said that he was very pleased and that he would personally see to it that the millet crop was good. This ikon is in the same simple style as No. 1, and shows the usual agricultural operations in progress.

II. IKONS DEDICATED TO GODS TO AVERT DISEASE

In some, but by no means in all, of the sacrifices offered to the gods in an attempt to avert disease, the shaman prescribes the painting of an ikon. Such pictures usually aim at flattering the god by showing what a splendid palace he has and how many servants and pets, and what important people come to call on him. But occasionally, as in the case of some of the ikons for Uyungsum, the picture may be very simple, consisting of nothing more than a rude symbol of the god.

I have noticed that comparatively few of the gods in the Saora pantheon are honoured in this way. Although I have seen a great many ikons, in all parts of the Saora country, I have never seen them made for any of the smallpox deities, or for Dorisum, Ajorasum, Ramma-Bimma, Tuttumsum, Kannisum or Kinnasum, among the more important gods, or for a great many of the less distinguished ones. This does not mean that such ikons are never made, but it does suggest that they are uncommon.

Gods of local cult, Kittungs and hill-gods of the neighbourhood seem to be honoured more frequently with ikons than the great popular gods, for whom the more expensive sacrifices are made.

7. *In Karika's house at arbum*
Length, 62" (No. 7)

Addia and Karika were two brothers who for some years lived together with their father, but after the old man's death set up separate establishments. Addia had made an ikon for Gadalsum, Karnosum and Madisingsum in his house, and when Karika built his new home they came to him in a dream and said, 'We have already got a house with your brother, but we want to live with you also.' Karika forgot about his dream, and this made the gods angry; one night when he was coming home drunk in the dark, Karnosum gave him a vigorous push in the back and knocked him down. Then Gadalsum and Mandisingsum beat him as he lay on the ground, and he reached home a very sick man. He summoned a shaman and the three gods declared through him that, 'This man's father used to worship us, and so did his brother. So long as he lived with them he joined in the worship, but now he has separated from them, he neglects us. If he wishes to recover he must honour us in his house also.' Karika, therefore, begged the shaman to paint an ikon without delay, and one evening after dark a goat was sacrificed before it, and the gods were apparently satisfied, for Karika recovered.

FIG. 7

The ikon shows the houses of the three gods. Each is crowded with servants, and one has a party of dancers with feathers in their hair. The gods, with their clerks, are riding on elephants and horses. A man carries a bundle of grass for Gadalsum, and potters bring pots for a feast.

8. *In Addia's house at Arbun*
Length, 22″ (No. 8)

This rather poor ikon is for Gadalsum, the god of grass-cutters. Addia's father, Poraila, once went to Gunupur and on the way met Gadalsum and the god followed him home. On his return Poraila fell ill and Gadalsum told the shaman who came to treat

1. Laju: A Nocte village on the Patkoi Range in the map of Frontier Division

2. Kaman Mishmis in a forest clearing

3. A Kaman Mishmi girl of the Khamlang valley

4. A girl weaving at Bomdo on the right bank of the upper Siang river

5. Phom dancers with shields at Longleng in 1954

6. A Monpa girl of Dirang-Dzong carrying a water pot with its cane cover

7. A Tagin priest of northern Subansiri

8. A Monpa wood-carver of Dirang-Dzong with a mask which he has nearly completed

9. Bugun children at Senchong village in western Kameng

1. Apa Tanis at work in their fields on the Ziro plateau

2. A Pailibo in the extreme north of Siang

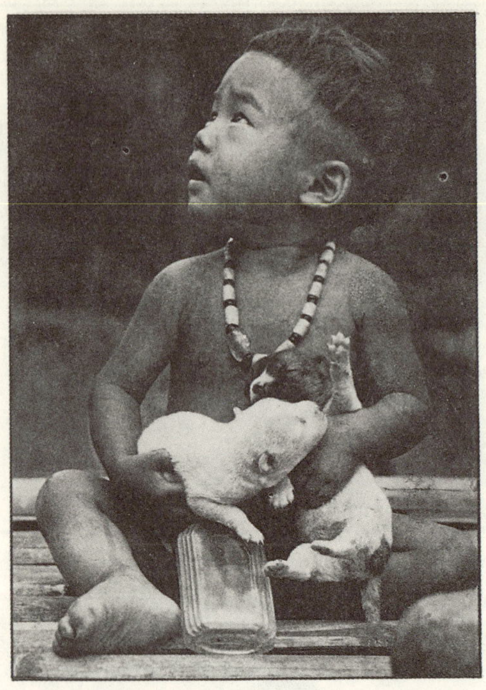

3. A Minyong child

4. Acculturation! A former head-hunter of Tirap decorates his basket with a plastic doll instead of the traditional carved wooden head

1. Muria Cheliks of Bastar

2. Bondo girl picking castor-seeds

1. The daughter of a Konyak chief, photographed in 1947

1. The ghotul at Masora

2. Carved pillar at Chandabera

3. Carved pillar at Remawand

him, 'I was looking after my grass, and since I was all alone and hungry I followed this man home. I want a house and some food.' The shaman therefore painted this ikon and offered a fowl.

FIG. 8

The picture shows Gadalsum's houses, in each of which the sun stands as witness. The human figures represent grass-cutters; Gadalsum himself stands on the left with a bundle of grass, protected by two snakes which will bite anyone who comes to cut grass before the proper time.

9. *In Budda's house at Dantara*
Length, 43″ (No. 9)

At the time of the Harvest Festival of red gram, the Saoras celebrate the Gadalpur, at which sacrifice is made to Gadalsum. It is strictly taboo to cut grass before this. The custom is for the priest to cut the grass first, and when he has finished for the villagers to follow his example.

Long ago there was a very famous priest who broke this taboo. Retribution came upon him swiftly. As he returned home with his load of grass, a tiger (sent by the offended god) came out of the forest and stood in his way. The tiger was invisible and the priest advanced confidently towards it, and the tiger said to itself, 'This is such an important person that he is afraid of nothing; how can I eat him?' But Barusum, who with Gadalsum watched over the affairs of the hillside, said, 'How do you mean he is important? I am much more important than he is, and yet he carries away my grass and gives me nothing for it.' In a temper he went up behind the priest and knocked him down. The tiger, relieved of its doubts, sprang on the unfortunate man and devoured him. Back in the village, the priest's relations watched the road for him and when he did not come by nightfall sent for a shaman. Barusum came upon him and described what had happened. Then the unhappy shade of the priest himself came and said that he would become Gadalsum (not Kinnasum, as is usually the case when a man is eaten by a tiger) and warned the people never to cut grass before the Gadalpur. The shaman sacrificed a goat and drew this ikon for Gadalsum and Barusum; it appears to be a traditional subject which has been redrawn many times.

FIG. 9

In the picture we see the priest with his load of grass, his 'long-tailed' loin-cloth hanging from his waist. A substantial tiger prepares to spring upon him. The houses are for Gadalsum and Barusum; the people in them are grass-cutters. The priest's tutelary sits in an easy chair, Gadalsum and Barusum ride on their elephants, and other gods and tutelaries ride and stand about. There are three little birds, which usually give warning when a snake or a tiger is in the neighbourhood, and it is said that these birds tried to warn the priest, but he was so conceited that he took no notice of them.

10. *In Sonia's house at Talasingi*
Height, 44″ (No. 10)

The ancestors of Karbu, a Saora of Munisingi, a village in the valley below Talasingi, used to live in the Kond country to the north. After migrating to his new home, Karbu kept up the worship of Kondasum to protect himself from the malice of any Kond sorcerer who might send his magic after him. Some years afterwards Karbu's daughter, a young woman named Lobari, went to Assam and while she was there married Sonia. A year later Sonia and Lobari returned and settled in Talasingi. One day they went down the hill to Karbu's house to attend a sacrifice offered to Kondasum. When Lobari came home she fell ill. When the shaman came to make his diagnosis, Kondasum came upon him and said, 'You came to my feast and I have come home with you. You were drunk and danced wantonly, but I too was dancing and saw everything that you did. Now I am going to live in your house, you in one room and I in the other.'

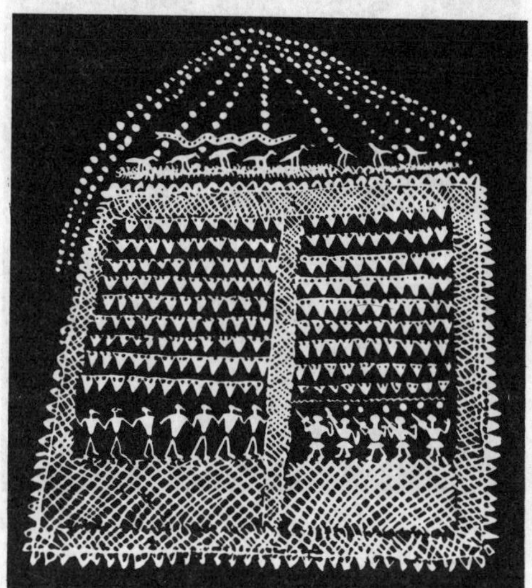

Fig. 10

Sonia had an ikon painted at once, but Kondasum said, 'That is all very well, but I am a drinker of human blood.' The Saoras replied, 'We are not Konds; it is not our custom to kill human beings.' They gave the thirsty god pig's blood to drink instead, and he declared himself satisfied.

The ikon shows the two-roomed house which Kondasum

demanded; in one the people are dancing at his feast, in the other are his armed retainers.

11. *In the Chief's house at Kattumeru*
Height, 62″ (No. 11)

In 1943 the wife of the Chief of Kattumeru fell ill, so ill that she was practically insane. The shaman diagnosed the case as the result of the hostility of Jaliyasum. 'Make an ikon in his name,' he said, 'and sacrifice a fowl, and she will be all right.' That night the Chief dreamt that he was to make a picture representing the marriage of the gods.

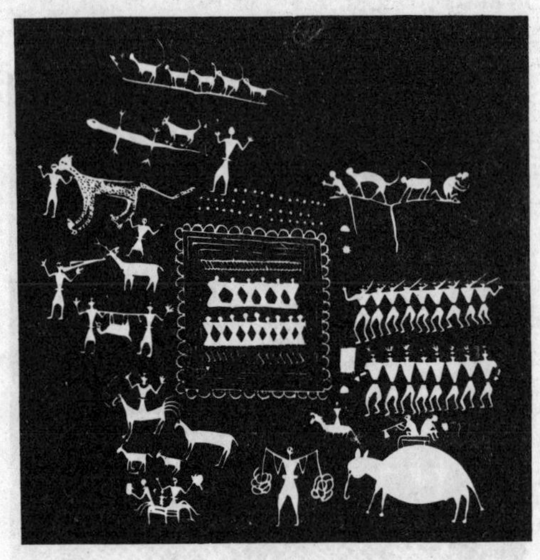

Fig. 11.

The picture, therefore, shows us Jaliyasum's own marriage. In the centre is the palace; people are dancing in it, led by the god himself; on a tree outside, monkeys too are dancing for joy. Approaching the building are Jaliyasum's mother, sister and daughters dancing in a row. There is a comb, obviously inserted as an afterthought, for Jaliyasum's mother. Sun, moon and stars shine down on the scene. Sahibosum comes to the wedding on an elephant. The potter of the gods brings pots for rice-beer. The local landlord comes on a mare followed by its foal; he brings two she-goats for the feast. Two men bring in a sambhar killed by the god's servants. The Range Officer also attends and sits with his family on chairs. An unwanted guest is caught by Jaliyasum's dog—a tiger—and another dog attacks a lizard while a man shoots at it with his bow and arrow.

The obvious intention of all this is to show what an important person Jaliyasum is, how many servants he has, what powerful friends he can command, what an expensive wedding he can afford. And in fact, since the Chief's wife recovered, the neighbours believed that Jaliyasum was sufficiently flattered by this attention.

12. *In the house of Sondan the shamanin at Bungding*
Length, 24″ (No. 12)

This ikon was drawn for Karnosum, and it was redrawn every year at the Harvest Festival for the red gram. At any time when Karnosum made people ill sacrifices were made before it. In the street before the house there was formerly a small shrine where Karnosum's horse and elephant could be stabled when he visited the village.

The picture shows men carrying Karnosum and his relatives in a litter. He has a potter with him, for this god is regarded as a Hindu and he cooks every meal in a new pot. There are two knives, one to cut up Karnosum's meat and the other to cut his hair.

FIG. 12

13. *In the house of Sartino at Angda*
Length, 58″ (No. 13)

Sartino fell ill, and the shaman advised the painting of an ikon with three 'houses', one for Karnosum (who had caused the sickness), one for Jammolsum (so that fertility-sacrifices could be made before it) and a third for Sardasum.

We see in this not very distinguished picture the three 'houses' filled to capacity with relations of the three gods—it is one of the embarrassments of godhead to have as many relatives as there are leaves on the tamarind. Below there is a procession, led by Sardasum's clerk on a horse and followed by the servants of the other gods on elephants and horses. Potters and their wives bring up the rear, for (as we have just seen) Karnosum needs a great many pots since he uses a new one at every meal.

FIG. 13.

14. *In the Chief's house at Bodo Okhra*
Length, 19″ (No. 14)

I include this ikon as a contrast to the elaborate and delicate work done by some of the Saora artists. At the Festival of red gram, the Chief of Bodo Okhra got very drunk and lay down to sleep it off in his clearing in the forest. All the other villagers brought branches of fresh pulse for the festival, but there was no sign of the Chief. After some time his wife went to fetch him and brought him home. But when he neared his house, he got high fever and collapsed on the veranda. There was a shrine in front of the house at which a shaman was sacrificing at the time. He went into trance and Karnosum came upon him and said, 'You have got fever because you neglected the festival. But if you make an ikon and sacrifice a fowl you will recover.' The Chief himself painted the ikon on the wall of the veranda just where he was resting. It had, I was told, no special meaning: 'it was his own work; the work of a drunken man, a man with fever.' That is what it looks like.

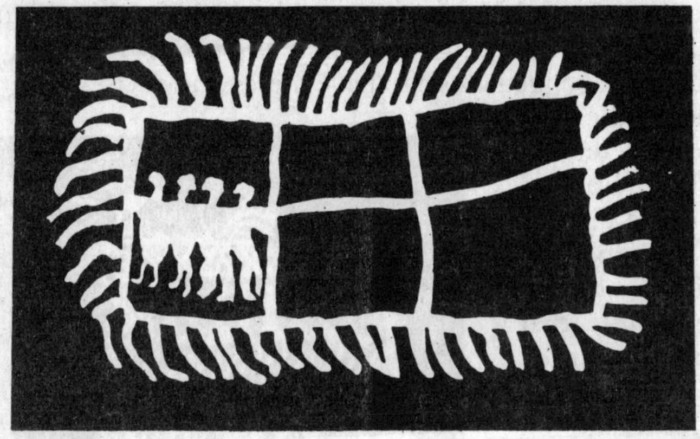

FIG. 14

15. *In Kutano's house at Dantara*
Height, 26″ (No. 15)

One day Kutano fell very ill with fever, and the shaman prescribed the sacrifice of a fowl to Tangorbasum. But this was a mistake, for Kutano got no better and after a day or two a god whom the local Saoras called Orissa-Manjorsum, the god of Puri, came upon the shaman and said, 'I havĕ not come with the desire to cause you trouble. I want to be friends with you. As a usual thing Rajas, great landlords and rich peasants come to me but as a special sign of my favour I have come to you. Now make a house for me and sacrifice a goat so that the people may know that I am the greatest of all the gods.'

The significant thing about this ikon is the representation of Orissa-Manjorsum as two men with a woman in the middle, shown seated on an elephant at the bottom of the picture, an obvious echo of Jagannatha.

16. *In the Chief's house at Barasingi*
Height, 38″ (No. 16)

In 1945 the Chief's son Sukta went to Gumma for a festival for Gosai Mahaprabhusum. He returned home the same night and four days later developed high fever with acute pain in all his bones. Gosai Mahaprabhu came upon the shaman and said, 'This boy came to my festival. I saw him and wanted to go with him, but he returned home without asking my permission. Had he asked me I would have come and looked after him. But he took no notice of me and now I am going to take him away.'

The people begged Gosai to have mercy and at last she agreed to release the boy provided a temple was built in her honour and she was given a goat in sacrifice. The ikon is the temple that was made. Inside there is growing a tulsi plant and on the top is the peacock watchman of the Saora shrines.

This ikon is interesting as showing how the Saoras believe that even the Hindu gods can attack them and behave for the time being exactly like the Saora gods.

FIG. 15

17. *In Buab's house at Barasingi*
Height, 40″ (No. 17)

Buab had a daughter, a beautiful dark girl named Legamiboi. One day Kittung Mahaprabhu attacked her with fever and made her temporarily dumb. When the god came on the shaman he declared, 'I am going to take this girl away; I shall not allow her to live here. For I have no maidservant in my house and she will do very well to look after my kitchen and garden.' But when the shaman promised to sacrifice a goat and make Kittung an ikon, he relented, and soon after the painting was completed, the girl recovered.

The ikon shows the usual overcrowded establishment of a Saora deity. The house, with its peacock watchman on the roof, stands in the middle of a compound. There is a tree with monkeys clambering over it, deer, a pet tiger, a shaman divining with his fan, two rows of retainers. Two chaprassis carry the shades of the newly dead in a litter. At the bottom is Mahaprabhu himself on an elephant, followed by servants armed with guns and two clerks on horseback. Sun, moon and stars look down from above.

18. *In the house of a shaman at Liabo*
Height, 22″ (No. 18)

A Kittung was passing by Liabo and got tired. He gave the Chief's son fever as a sign that he wanted to stay in his house. The shaman advised the painting of a 'house' in which the Kittung could stay and this ikon is the result. It illustrates the crude and simple style of the painting in this area.

FIG. 16

We see Kittung's house and Kittung himself sitting on his horse. A servant brings his bicycle and his wife comes with a comb in her hand. Another servant has a snake which has coiled round his leg—this is probably a half-forgotten eclipse motif: the snake is swallowing Uyungsum the Sun in human form. In a kitchen to the left are three Brahmins who are engaged to cook Kittung's food.

19. *In Hargu's house at Arangulu*
Height, 24″ (No. 19)

One day Hargu went to Boramsingi and got very drunk. He staggered home across the hills and the next day felt extremely

FIG. 17

ill. The shaman told him that 'Benasum came with you from Jopsir Hill and it is he who has made you ill. If you are not careful, he will give you a lot of trouble.' He called on Benasum and the god came upon him and said, 'Hargu was very drunk, rolling along the path, when he met me. I was hungry, but he was rude to me and would not even give me a scrap of tobacco. So I followed him home. Now if he gives me somewhere to live and plenty to eat, I'll let him alone.' That night Hargu dreamt of the sort of picture he must make, and the next day he made an ikon showing the Jopsir Hill—the wavy lines, he explained, represented his tracks as he walked across it.

20. *In a deserted house at Angda*
Height, 36″ (No. 20)

This ikon is for Sahibosum. 'Long ago', said the Saoras of Angda, 'our ancestors warned us that the sahibs would come and give us a great deal of trouble. But they said that if we made ikons for Sahibosum and his wife, things would not be so bad.'

The ikon shows a row of men, who represent Sahibosum and his friends. Below Mehamsahibosum or Sahibosumboi stands in a row with her friends. The crisscross lines in the middle represent a cot for Sahibosum to sit on.

21. *In Bopna's house at Sogeda*
Height, 12″ (No. 21)

This and the following pictures illustrate the very simple ikons that are sometimes made. In Bopna's house, there were two such ikons, almost identical in size and pattern, on the same

FIG. 18

wall. One of these was for Tutiyumsum, who is the god of a mother's nipple. This god made Bopna's wife, who was nursing her baby, ill with a swollen breast and painful nipple. The other was for Uraljungsum, who had attacked Bopna's son-in-law, Suddo, with toothache so acute that his face swelled up and he sweated with the pain. Suddo's own wife, the shamanin Sinaki, diagnosed the trouble and declared that unless a suitable ikon was made and sacrifice offered her husband might get an attack of epilepsy.

22. *In the house of Jigri, the shamanin, at Boramsingi*
Width, 27″ (No. 22)

This is a conventional symbol for Uyungboi or Uyungsum, the Sun, and may be drawn for the relief of anyone suffering from fever caused by the god.

23. *In Japno's house at Kerubai*
Height, 14″ (No. 23)

This is another conventional symbol for Uyungsum. In this case it was made on behalf of Japno's two-year-old son who had been afflicted with diarrhoea by him.

FIG. 19

FIG. 19. Saora picture of the hill-abode of Benasum. Another drawing in Hargu's house. *Height* 24″

24. *In Sida's house at Barasingi*
Length, 17″ (No. 24)

It often happens that, after a large central ikon has been painted on the wall of a house, some other god or ancestor may demand attention. In such cases a single figure may be added near the main ikon, or perhaps an elephant or a tree or a little shrine. In this ikon at Barasingi a row of dancers was added for Karnosum above an older ikon previously made for the ancestors.

FIG. 20 An ittal-drawing representing in the top row Sahibosum and his friends, and in the lower Mehmsahibosum and her friends; in between is a bed for them to sleep on. In a Saora house at Angda, Ganjam District, Orissa. *Height* 36″

One night as Sida was returning home from a neighbouring hamlet he fell ill with fever. The reason was that he had met Karnosum and his relatives going to a dance and had offended them unwittingly. The ikon shows Karnosum and his relatives wearing tufts of feathers for their dance.

III. IKONS MADE TO ASSIST CHILDBIRTH

There are various means of accelerating delivery and one of them, though it is not very common, is the painting of an ikon. Such pictures always contain a pregnancy or delivery motif, and are generally made in the name of Gadejangboi or one of the deities who are notorious for interfering at this time.

25. *In the house of Redga, Barasingi*
Height, 27″ (No. 25)

Redga's wife Sukiboi had a great deal of trouble at her first confinement and the shaman recommended sacrifice and an ikon for Darammaboi and Gadejangboi.

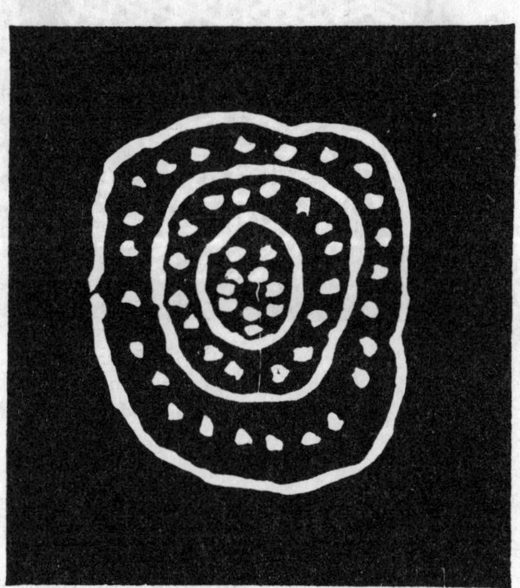

Fig. 21

The ikon is not very clear, but it was explained to me that the group in the lower right hand corner includes Sukiboi herself and that Gadejangboi is holding her. Darammaboi has her hand on the mother's belly, ready to remove the child from the womb. Darammaboi's daughters have come with pots of water to bathe mother and child after delivery.

26. *In the house of a shaman at Thodrangu*
Height, 21″ (No. 26)

This ikon, which was painted for Gadejangboi when the shaman's own wife was faced with a difficult delivery, shows the pregnant woman with her attendants, and Gadejangboi herself with pots of water for the bath.

IV. IKONS WHICH REPRESENT SHRINES AND HILLS

Most of the ikons are built up around some central figure which represents a house, shrine or hill, for (as we have seen) the ikon is the 'house' of the spirits. I found many pictures of this kind in the beautiful hill-village Arangulu; they were simple and effective, and in a style which I had not seen elsewhere. Shrine-ikons are often made when spirits demand some sort of place to rest on their visits to a village; they are much more economical than actual shrines. Hill-ikons may be painted if one has inadvertently offended a hill-god by cutting a clearing on his hill or by picking herbs or leaves without his permission.

FIG. 22. Saora symbol of the sun, under the name of Yuyungboi. *Width* 27″

27. *In Singraju's house at Arangulu Height*, 24″ (No. 27)

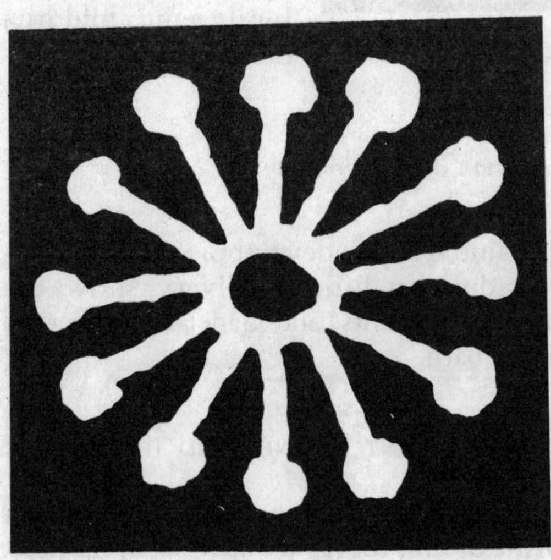

FIG. 23

Long ago Singraju's father made a shrine for Karnosum. After his death, the shrine fell into disrepair and Singraju forgot all about it. But one night towards the end of 1943, his father's ghost visited him in a dream and said, 'I made this shrine for Karnosum and offered sacrifices there while I was alive. Repair it at once and make an ikon for him inside the house.' Singraju

Fig. 24

repaired the shrine, but considered that in demanding an ikon as well the ghost was asking too much. But shortly afterwards Singraju's wife fell ill, and when the shaman was consulted he declared that the trouble was due to this misguided attempt at economy. That night Singraju had another dream: Karnosum came to him, insisted on an ikon and himself designed it, tracing the outline on the ground with a stick. The next day Singraju had the drawing made and his wife recovered. The picture shows Karnosum's shrine, with the characteristic peacock watchman on the top.

Fig. 25

28. *In Singraju's house at Arangulu*
Height, 23″ (No. 28)

Just before the Harvest Festival of the red gram Singraju had a dream about his ancestors. They said to him, 'Make a shrine for us where we can rest when we come to feast with you, and we will see that your next harvest is the best you have ever had.'

29. *In Hargu's house at Arangulu*
Height, 20″ (No. 29)

One of Singraju's neighbours, an elderly and rather drunken Saora called Hargu, had a regular picture gallery in his house, which might be taken as illustrating the influence of the hangover on tribal art. For whenever Hargu returned home from a drinking-bout, he woke up the next morning convinced that some singularly unpleasant god was persecuting him and had an ikon made to put things right. We have had one example of this in No. 19; three others represent various hills on which the drunken Hargu got into trouble, his own interpretation being that he was accosted and followed home by the gods living there. A hill-god's house is, of course, a hill, and these pictures give an interesting idea of the Saora's symbolization of a hill-house. This ikon was made for the god Barongsum—*barongan* is an old Saora word for a mountain; it shows the hill with the god standing below.

Fig. 26

30. *In Hargu's house at Arangulu Height*, 27″ (No. 30)

FIG. 27

After another orgy Hargu made an ikon for Kurtisum of Deogiri, the great mountain of the Saoras, and in a dream he promised to keep all other gods away. Hargu, who was an Ittalmaran, drew these pictures and those in Singraju's house himself; in this ikon he portrayed Kurtisum standing on the summit of the hill with his umbrella and his son to one side with a tuft of feathers in his hair.

31. *In Hargu's house at Arangulu*

FIG. 28

One day in 1943 Hargu went to the forest on a hill called Ladiolenga to get some wild spinach. Directly he got home he went down with a sharp attack of fever and vomiting. The shaman declared that Gunjusum, a local god living on the hill, had been annoyed at the theft of the spinach from his home and had followed Hargu back to the village. 'There will be no end to the trouble I am going to give this fellow,' declared the god. The alarmed Hargu immediately made an ikon of the hill with Ganjusum standing below it, sacrificed a pig and in due course recovered.

32. *In the shaman's house at Gundripadar*
Height, 42" (No. 31)

The people of this village go to make their clearings on a hill, not far from their homes, called Surjibudi. When they first went there many of them fell ill, for Labosum was angry at being disturbed. At about the same time Uyungboi gave a number of people fever, and a composite and rather elaborate ikon was made to satisfy both gods.

Fig. 30

Fig. 29

In the upper right hand corner of the ikon there is a design of concentric circles and above it a shrine out of which grows a banyan tree. This is the house of Uyungsum the Sun. In the centre is Surjubudi Hill and Labosum and his wife riding on an elephant. All round are the various animals and birds which live on the hill. To the top at the left, the ghost of Uyungsum's son (see p. 307)[3] riding on a dog is about to swallow the sun.

While the artist was painting this picture, Tangorbasum

[3] Refer to original edition, *The Religion of an Indian Tribe* (OUP, 1955).

came upon the shaman and insisted that he should have a share in it. So in the lower left hand corner we find Tangorbasum's house—this god's shrine was actually on a path leading to the hill—and there are monkeys climbing over it, and a potter with his load of pots stands near by.

FIG. 32

The man on the bicycle is a Forest Guard who has come to see what was going on. At this time there was a good deal of friction between the Saoras and the Forest Department, which was trying to stop axe-cultivation, and the Guard was included in the ikon in the hope that he would henceforth leave them alone.

33. *In the Chief's house at Liabo*
Height, 22″

This is another ikon for Labosum who was offended because the people of this village cut clearings on his hill without permission. It gives a rough outline of the hill with Labosum's house inside it, and various poorly drawn figures including a gigantic lizard.

V. IKONS MADE IN HONOUR OF TUTELARIES

Ikons are always painted at the time of a marriage between a shaman and his tutelary, or a shamanin and hers; they may also be made at any other time when a tutelary feels that he or his relations are not receiving sufficient attention.

6

Folk-Songs of the Maikal Hills

by Verrier Elwin and Shamrao Hivale (1944)

Introduction

This second volume of *Specimens of the Oral Literature of Mahakoshal* contains a selection of the folk-songs of the aboriginal population of the Maikal Hills. These lovely mountains at the extreme eastern end of the Satpura Range, traditionally the home of some of the most famous Hindu Rishis, run from Amarkantak, source of the sacred Narbada river, through south-east Mandla into the Saletekri forests of Balaghat. Still wild, remote and lonely, the hills are inhabited by a largely aboriginal population, Baiga and Gond, Agaria and Dhoba, Pardhan and Bharia. We have confined ourselves for the present to the aboriginal poetry of the area, for this forms a clearly defined block of literature still little influenced from outside, still preserving much of its freshness and beauty.

It is possible to speak of this poetry as a whole. In the Maikal Hills all the different tribes mix together and share each other's recreations. The remotest Baiga villages do indeed have their own special movements in their dances and their own emphasis in their songs. The Agaria have their own technical songs about their craft. The Baiga still wistfully sing, as the Gond do not, about their traditional axe-cultivation. The Pardhan have their own long narrative poems of almost epic character which are not shared by the other tribes. But the bulk of the song is common to all and the variations arise only as one moves from place to place. The songs printed here can all, with a few exceptions noted in the text, be called Gond songs; but they could equally well be called Pardhan. We have included a few Baiga songs which are known also to the Gond. Probably the simplest way of reference would be to call them 'Gond songs' unless we have indicated otherwise.

It is generally said that anyone born in the Maikal Hills will never be content to die elsewhere, that those who have once slipped in the mud of Mandla will want to live there always. The beauty of the countryside, the charm of the climate, the friendliness of the people is reflected in the songs. Their poetry is often very beautiful both in form and content, in image and symbol. It is impossible to reproduce in a foreign tongue the often delicate artistry of the originals. But some attempt must be made to do so before this remarkable oral literature passes from the world in face of the spread of education and the decay of the tribes.

Sometimes, of course, to foreign ears the songs appear unpoetic enough. There are many songs about the prices of things, many work tediously through the whole Table of Affinity. References to betel, bidi, turmeric sendur, to dhoti and sari and the intimacies of underwear are not very romantic for the Occidental reader but they are full of poetic and often tender associations to the people themselves. To aboriginals who are always engrossed in matters of kinship and relationship the Table of Affinity is a thing of excitement and beauty. To very poor people living on the borderline of starvation the price of things and references to food and drink, to little presents and their few cheap luxuries, are fit subjects of poetry.

Many of the songs are, of course, very difficult. Some of them seem to have developed out of the riddle, a popular form of entertainment among these people. Riddles are actually sung as dance songs during the Saila competitions. Other riddles are asked and must be answered before a bride is allowed to leave her parents' house. Many of the songs have the severely condensed form, the obscure reference and the unusual symbolism that is normally characteristic of a riddle. The task of translating is thus difficult enough; that of interpretation is impossible without a wide knowledge of the social background.

Take, for example, this Doha song—

Are are bhai re
Gaye daihān aur lāne kharsi
Ek dauki aur banāle
Tela khohābe ghursi
Hai re.

Such a song cannot be translated into English. Consider the three key-words on which in the ears of the singers its poetic merit depends. The first is *daihān*, the cows' resting-place where the cattle gather at noon beneath shady trees in a clearing far out in the forest, and the Ahir sits by playing on his flute. You may see this scene again and again in the old Pahari paintings, and the very thought of it arouses emotion and delight in the mind of any Indian. But we have no word for this in English and practically nothing in Western life to correspond with the idea. The second important word in the poem is *kharsi*, the dry scraps of dung which are collected by girls from the cows' resting-place and brought home for banking the fire. The sweet-smelling, clean and charming cow-dung so dear to the heart of every Indian villager is not only unfamiliar to the Western reader, but may be positively repulsive to him. When Pope wished to emphasize the miserable death of Villiers he described the scene of his suffering as being

In the worst inn's worst room, with mat half hung,
The floor of plaster and the walls of dung.

Aldous Huxley describes how profoundly impressed he had been with those walls of dung. Indeed, 'they still disturb my imagination. They express, for me, the Essential Horror.'

The third word is *ghursi*. This is an earthen bowl made, not by a potter, but by the women of the house themselves, which is filled with cow-dung scraps and lit. It smoulders slowly giving out a very fair heat and generally lasts all night. To prepare the *ghursi* is one of the most intimate services that a woman can render her husband. She puts it under the bed to keep them warm as they sleep together, and people who are too poor to afford mattresses and blankets depend greatly on their fires. The thought of the *ghursi* corresponds emotionally to ideas of firelight glowing on a loved face or flickering flames illuminating a dark cosy room in Europe.

The song, therefore, may be translated,

> You go to the cow's resting-place
> And bring the scraps of dung
> Get a new wife
> And she will prepare your *ghursi*.

Not a very satisfactory version, and certainly not one that would arouse poetic feeling in any Western reader, yet in the original the suggestion that the new wife will prepare the *ghursi* is itself an intimate and romantic thought, for to prepare the fire for the lover is to arouse the fire of love.

This example—and we might easily give scores of such songs—will serve to illustrate the difficulty of translating verses that are so intimately connected with the life of the people and the countryside. A whole commentary is needed to understand them properly.

This book therefore must be taken as a supplement. Two of the tribes whose songs we have recorded have been exhaustively described in *The Baiga* and *The Agaria*. Our *Songs of the Forest* gives 290 songs, *The Baiga* 340 and *The Agaria* 14. These represent the cream of our collection of several thousands. In this volume we attempt to supplement the songs already published elsewhere, to discuss in more detail than hitherto their technical form and to relate them as fully as space will permit to their ethnographic background. We will not, however, repeat too much of what has already been written elsewhere.

The neglect, both by scientists and artists, of the Indian folk-song is astonishing. For a long time only religious and didactic verses were recorded. Gover admits that he dared not translate erotica, and speaks of 'a learned and estimable missionary who has been publicly condemned because he would faithfully translate a noble poem without a really impure thought in it, and was therefore compelled to commit the awful crime of likening a woman's bosom to a pomegranate.' In *The Poetry of the Orient* not a single folk-song has been anthologized. We have turned over thousands of pages of the great volumes of the Ethnographic Survey—Thurston, Risley, Enthoven, Anantakrishna Iyer, Russell and Hiralal—these are books of the dark half of the month: the light of the moon of verse does not shine through them.

Yet the songs are important, not only because the music, form and content of verse is itself part of a people's life but even more because in songs, in charms, in actually fixed and established documents we have the most authentic and unshakable witnesses to ethnographic fact. Anthropology has passed the stage when a report had only to appear in print to be accepted. Today we want to know whether the report is true. The anthropologist must not only be a detective, he must be a magistrate. In making up his mind he can have no better evidence than songs.

> If you want to know the story of my life
> Then listen to my Karma.

The songs are not all the evidence, but they are an important part of it. They round off and complete the picture. They are much nearer real life than are the folk-tales, for these seem to represent an escape from life rather than a reproduction of it.

Let us take one example: the tradition of domestic fidelity and the duration of marriage. Among the Muria of Bastar State there is a very high degree of marital fidelity and out of 2000 marriages examined only 49 had ended in divorce. The songs of the Muria reflect this situation. Although they are not wanting in love interest the theme of the deserted lover and the faithless wife and husband is almost unknown. But in Mandla where in a single village examined the divorce rate was no less than 56 per cent, the songs abound with descriptions of maidens betrayed, of broken hearts and of the faithlessness of man. Indeed in Mandla the song is often used as itself an instrument of seduction, and elopements are arranged and assignations made by what we may call code messages sung in the form of Karma or Dadaria.

Again the great variety of the Bastar songs witnesses to the fullness of its undisturbed tribal life. There are songs for festivals of every kind, scores of songs to accompany children's games, songs for dancing expeditions. In Mandla, where tribal life has largely decayed, there is little variety in the types of song. Half a dozen different kinds of dance, the Jawara festival, the marriage songs, craft and children's songs compose such variety as we have.

In most of these songs, of course, verse is wedded to the dance and to some extent depends on it. But we have today the curious situation that in these hills, though the songs remain, the dance is dying out. There is now a good deal of confusion about what song should be sung to what dance, and the dance songs are already being sung by the fireside or by lover to lover in bed rather than on the public dancing-ground. There will be a melancholy interest in watching during the next twenty years how far the disappearance of the dance will alter the style and rhythm of the songs that used to be wedded to it.

For one of the most tragic things about the contact of the aboriginal with civilization is the destruction of art and culture that so frequently follows. William Morris once spoke of the danger 'that the present course of civilization would destroy the beauty of life'. Among Indian aboriginals that is not only a danger but a fact. S. C. Roy has spoken of a 'loss of interest in life' among the Birhor and Korwa, J. H. Hutton of psychical apathy and physical decline in the Andamans, J. P. Mills of the 'awful monotony of village life' and its 'unspeakable drabness' in Christianized Assam. Sometimes this destruction is caused by outsiders, by well-meaning but rather unintelligent 'uplifters' and social reformers; sometimes the evil comes from within.

India is all too full of people like Mr Pumblechook who, it will be remembered, could not see a small boy without trying to benefit him by setting him problems in mental arithmetic. The Pumblechooks of India try very hard to make the aboriginal good: they only succeed in making him dull. It is hard to convince the missionary and reformer of whatever religion that the romance and gaiety of tribal life is necessary for its preservation. An Orissa Committee has urged the abolition of the village dormitory. The American Baptist Mission in Assam has stopped the great Feasts of Merit and with them the very few occasions on which the monotony of village life is broken. Any policy of Prohibition will ultimately destroy the dancing and many of the religious festivals of the people.

More commonly, movements for 'reform' appear to arise almost spontaneously. Seligman has described such mass obsessional neuroses which often take the form of new religions. In Papua five new faiths came into being 'under the stress of conflict due to white influence'. The apocalyptic message of Tokerna ordered the abolition of European utensils, luxuries and the killing of hundreds of pigs. Seligman compares this with the commands of Nongquase, the South African diviner, at whose command the Amaxosa in 1856 killed many thousands of their cattle and foretold that, when the cattle were killed, old chiefs would rise from the dead and there would be a miraculous supply of grain.

It would take a whole book to study similar mass neuroses in India, but we may illustrate their general tendency by a few examples. They are often marked by delusions of grandeur—the desire to recapture a former dignity—and by destructiveness. The Maria throw away their dancing dress, the Muria cut down thousands of trees, many tribes kill pigs and chickens. In 1924, the Ho of the Kolhan (Bihar) met at Lumpunguto and decided to stop their ancient songs and dances because 'they were looked down on by their cultured neighbours as very low and degrading', because their boys' health was damaged by late hours spent in dancing and their morals injured, and because they involved unnecessary waste of time and energy.

The destruction of beauty is always evil but never more so than when it means robbing the poorest of the poor of the few treasures that they have. The great Karma dance of the Gond is a precious and lovely thing: the Dadaria songs alone are enough to redeem their culture from mediocrity. The Saila dance is splendid recreation and exercise. Yet all this is rapidly being destroyed by so-called reformers who leave nothing in its place except the filth of Holi and the obscenity of the marriage abuse.

But it must be remembered that this passion for the destruction of beautiful things is not confined to India. In his speech at the Sexual Reform Congress in 1929 Bernard Shaw reminded his hearers that they were not to expect that democracy would mean real freedom. Modern democracy, he said, 'has become associated with ideas of liberty because it has abolished certain methods of political oppression, and we are apt to think that what makes for liberty in one thing will make for liberty in all things'. But this is not so. The more the people at large have to do with Government the more will the intellectuals and artists have to fight for their ideas and perhaps for their lives. Bernard Shaw illustrated his point by an anecdote which is relevant to the Indian situation. Cecil Sharp was a collector of many peasant songs especially in Somerset. He began there in the rectory of the Rev C. L. Marson.

One day they were walking in the rectory grounds near an enclosed fruit garden. Cecil Sharp heard a man on the other side of the wall singing a song, to what seemed to him to be a beautiful tune. He immediately noted in down, and said to Marson, 'Who is that singing?' 'He is my gardener', was the reply, Sharp insisted on finding out whether he had any more songs. He went in, full of the enthusiasm of the artist who had discovered something beautiful; and they told the man that they had heard him singing. He instantly threw down his spade, and called God to witness that he was an honest and decent man who had never sung a song in his life, and was not going to be accused of such debauchery and wickedness by any gentleman.

'They were amazed, because as members of our cultivated classes they did not understand that to the mass of the people art and beauty are nothing but forms of debauchery. They had the greatest trouble in persuading the gardener that they were both of them just as great blackguards as he was; and then he told them where they would find other songs, and undertook to introduce them to the singers.'

The moral drawn by Bernard Shaw from this story illuminates the situation in the Maikal Hills today. Slowly there is creeping over that lovely countryside the horrible belief that poetry and art are wrong and that if the aboriginal communities are to win respect and rise in the social scale they must rob their lips of beauty and their limbs of ordered movement.

Of course, the decline of the Indian folk-song is not only due to organized propaganda. There are many other causes. Alfred Williams has carefully studied the causes for the decay of the folk-song in England, and his analysis is so valuable and has so much bearing on conditions that either have come into being or will shortly come into being in India, that we make no apology for quoting him at length.

What, now, is the reason of the discontinuance and disappearance of the folk-song? Of course, there are many reasons. The dearth, or, at any rate, the restricting of the fairs, and, consequently, of the opportunities of disseminating the ballad-sheets is one cause of its decline. The closing of many of the old village inns, the discontinuance of the harvest-home and other farm feasts, the suspension and decay of May games, morris dancing, church festivals, wassailing, and mumming are other obvious reasons. Another factor was the advent of the church organ and the breaking up of the old village bands of musicians. That dealt a smashing blow at music in the villages. Previous to the arrival of the church organ, every little village and hamlet had its band, composed of the fiddle, bass viol, piccolo, clarinet, cornet, the 'horse's leg', and the trumpet, or 'serpent'. They were played every Sunday in church. But they did not solely belong to the church. All the week they were free to be used for the entertainment of the people. The musicians had to be continually practising, and much of it was done in public. As a matter of fact, the villages were never without music. And the need of the band kept the wits of the performers fully alive. They laboured to make and keep themselves proficient, and the training they took both educated them and exerted an unmistakable influence upon the everyday life of their fellows. But when the organ came, the village band was dismissed from the church; they were not wanted any more. Their music was despised. There was no further need of them, and the bands broke up. For a while the fiddle sounded at the inns and at the farm feast, and was soon heard no more.

Another reason for the disappearance of the folk-song is that the life and condition of things in the villages, and throughout the whole countryside, have vastly changed of late. Education has played its part. The instruction given to the children at village schools proved antagonistic to the old minstrelsy. Dialect and homely language were discountenanced. Teachers were imported from the towns, and they had little sympathy with village life and customs. The words and spirit of the songs were misunderstood, and the tunes were counted too simple. The construction of railways, the linking up of villages with other districts, and contact with large towns and cities had an immediate and permanent effect upon the minstrelsy of the countryside. Many of the village labourers migrated to the towns, or to the colonies, and most of them no longer cared for the old ballads, or were too busily occupied to remember them. Before the middle of the nineteenth century the writing of even moderately good folk-songs had ceased; all that have been produced since then belong to another and an inferior order, approaching to what is commonly known as the popular song of today. At the same time, the singing of the old songs went on as long as the fairs and harvest-homes were held, and even after they were discontinued, till they began to be rigidly discountenanced, or altogether forbidden at the inns. This was the most unkind and fatal repulse of all. It was chiefly brought about, I am told, not by any desire of the landlord, but by the harsh and strict supervision of the police. They practically forbade singing. The houses at which it was held, those at which the poor labourers commonly gathered, were marked as disorderly places; the police looked upon song-singing as a species of rowdyism. Their frequent complaints and threats to the landlords filled them with misgivings;

the result was that they were forced, as a means of self-protection, to request their customers not to sing on the premises, or, at any rate, not to allow themselves to be heard. The crestfallen and disappointed labourers accordingly held their peace. The songs, since they could no longer be sung in public, were relegated to oblivion; hundreds have completely died out, and will be heard no more. The gramophone and the cinema have about completed the work of destruction, and finally sealed the doom of the folk-song and ballad as they were commonly known.[1]

Devendra Satyarthi has pointed out that 'India's national movement does not seem to have recognized the importance of India's folk-songs as yet', and he quotes Freda Bedi as saying that

> Many things go towards making a national movement a living entity: the spirit of common effort, adequate organization, leaders, and very important, a common tradition. In forming a nation this national literature plays a big role. The Abbey Theatre movement, the work of Yeats and A.E. with their band of workers, nurtured the Irish fight for independence. The songs of Plunkett, himself a martyr for the Irish cause, were enshrined in the hearts of Irishmen after the successful wartime rebellion. . . . It is significant that the growth of interest in the 'songs of the people' is a factor in post-war development and that it coincides with the 'new nationalism' and radical trends in the world today. Love of folk-lore is . . . inherent in the cultural background of the Russian Soviet Socialist Republics, because of the emphasis on everything that comes spontaneously from the people. All efforts to create a rich tradition of national culture, not a culture grafted on to the old stock by a civilization that is strange in ideas and expression, but an indigenous one that springs from the very heart of the people, must be welcomed.

Devendra Satyarthi concludes that 'it is high time for nationalist India to arouse the imagination of our people to look upon their folk-songs as synonymous with national literature, and to call for an All-India Folk-Songs Revival Movement.

> Let us hope that the national movement of 'India reborn' will soon recognize the real value of India's folk-songs, and will give impetus to writers all over the country to make an enormous collection, from the living lips of the people, of almost all the songs, ballads and all other types of folklore—the legends, folk-tales, proverbs and riddles.

[1] A. Williams. *Folk-Songs of the Upper Thames* (London, 1923), 23f.

Folk-songs should also be sought out by our new writers and poets for the unparalleled fund of inspiration they have as the heartbeats of Mother India, as did Pushkin in Russia.

In translating the songs we have tried to keep as near as possible to the originals in meaning, though we have frankly abandoned any attempt to reproduce the form. Eunice Tietjens, in the Introduction to her anthology *The Poetry of the Orient*, divides the translators of Oriental poetry into four principal classes. There are those who reproduce as closely as possible the rhythmic and rhyme scheme of the original, sticking as close to the sense as possible. There are then those who feel that to reproduce a form exactly is to distort it, since the ear which must receive this form is not the same ear as that for which it was written. These translate the rhythm into one native to them, hoping thus to give the impression that the original gives to its own readers. The third type of translator is he who finding that it is very seldom possible to do justice to both form and content sticks to the content and lets the form take care of itself. He translates into free verse whatever the original form may have been. The fourth translator is he who despairing of doing justice to the original in any form whatever sets down in prose of scrupulous exactitude the precise shade of meaning as the sees it.

In India there have been few attempts like those of Louise Hammond for Chinese poetry to reproduce the exact rhyme and rhythm of the originals. Macdonell did something, but the majority of scholars belong to the second class; Powys Mathers' astonishing version of the *Chaurapanchasika* is indeed rather an interpretation than a translation. Dr and Mrs Seligman translated their Vedda songs into prose, and N. E. Parry did the same for his often beautiful Lakher songs.

A. G. Shirreff is a representative of the second type of translator. Indeed he says expressly in his introduction to *Hindi Folk-Songs* that 'in the translations which follow my aim has been to give as accurate a rendering as possible in a form which may remind English readers of folk-poetry with which they are very familiar'. He finds many resemblances between the Hindi songs of the United Provinces and English songs and ballads. Devendra Satyarthi considers that this idea of rendering songs in verse with the aim of reminding English people of their own ballads is dangerous, and he points out how Shirreff translates the word *sāri* as 'gown', and *ta yahi ran ban men* as 'under the greenwood tree'. This was probably also the method of such workers as Griffith, R. C. Dutt and Sir Edwin Arnold, who have produced poems that are often beautiful in themselves, but which cannot be regarded as satisfactory translations.

W. G. Archer has laid down some admirable principles for the translation of Indian folk-poetry into English. A poem, he says,

> is a combination of certain images, certain rhythms and certain effects of music, and only if a translation could provide an exact parallel for each of these elements could it be perfect. In actual fact, a translation from a tribal language into English can parallel only one of these elements. Differences of verbal structure are so great that if parallel images are retained, the rhythms will be different. If the rhythms are maintained, the images will suffer, while no form of English can reproduce the musical effects of Hindi, Uraon, Gondi, or Mundari. 'Certain things', said Ezra Pound, 'are translatable from one language to another, a tale or an image will translate; music will practically never translate.' A translation becomes possible, therefore, only when there is no attempt at all at complete correspondence.
>
> We believe that the best solution so far reached is that of Arthur Waley. In translating from the Chinese Arthur Waley was faced with problems which are identical with those of Indian languages. His solution has been a series of versions in which the literal meaning of the translation corresponds with the literal meaning of the original. In particular, the images are never added to and never subtracted from. The poem as a system of images remains in translation what it is in the original. Instead, however, of attempting a duplication of rhyme, rhythm, or music, his versions use the rhythms and sound effects which come most naturally to the English. The original form is abandoned and instead the effort is to create a new form which is valid for a contemporary sensibility.

This principle of not adding any new images is of very great importance. Arthur Waley himself says, 'Above all, considering images to be the soul of poetry, I have avoided either adding images of my own or suppressing those of the original.'[2] A vivid example of the danger of adding new images to a translation is seen in the works of Dryden whose translations are really

[2] A. Waley, *170 Chinese Poems* (London, 1928), 19.

remarkable original poems which have been suggested by classic models. In his famous stanza on Fortune occur the lines,

I can enjoy her while she's kind;
But when she dances in the wind,
And shakes the wings and will not stay,
I puff the prostitute away.

This is supposed to be a translation of the twenty-ninth Ode of the Third Book of Horace. But the excellent line which was so much admired by Thackeray—'I puff the prostitute away'—is represented in the original simply by the words *resigno quae dedit.* Here an entirely new image is added to the poem, for which there is no warrant in the original. Caution in this matter is all the more important when we consider the essential place that symbolism holds in village poetry.

We have, therefore, followed as far as possible the example of Arthur Waley and have worked on the principles laid down by W. G. Archer, that is to say, we have avoided rhyme and have made no attempt to reproduce the form of the original. We have tried to represent the original meaning as literally as possible, within the limits of the demands of poetry, and we have been scrupulous in introducing no word or image that is unrepresented in the original.

To illustrate the different methods of translation it may be of interest to compare here versions made by Laurence Housman of songs in two of our previous collections. In *Songs of the Forest* appears the following song:

The wind and the rain are beating down.
Take shelter or your clothes will be drenched.
The rain is falling, falling.
    In all my dreams I searched for you,
    But I did not find even the echo of your steps.

I have built a fence by the roadside.
I have made a fence for my garden.
Where have you hidden, thief of my heart?
    In all my dreams I searched for you,
    But I did not find even the echo of your steps.

I have cut tall bamboos; I have cut short bamboos.
Large are the hollows of the dwarf bamboos.
The thief who crouched behind my fence has hidden in
        those hollows.

In all my dreams I searched for you,
But I did not find even the echo of your steps.

This is Laurence Housman's version:

The wind and rain are beating down,
Come in, don't drown! Take shelter, do!
The rain, the rain: O, hear it beat!
In all my dreams I searched for you
But could not find one trace again,
Or hear the echo of your feet.

Between my garden and the track
I built a wall, I fenced it round,
I made it safe as holy ground.

O loved, O lost, come back, come back!
Thief of my Heart! I search for you,
I search, and still no footprint meet,
Nor hear the echo of your feet.

I built my wall of tall bamboo,
Of tall, and short, with hollow stem:
And in the hollow where they grew
The hidden thief lay crouched in them.
Now all my dreams I search for you,
And up and down the world I beat:
Rain beating on the tall bamboo
Has drowned the echo of your feet.

Again, in *The Baiga* appears the following:

In the midst of the river, the tree is full of leaves.
Among the leaves, monkeys are hiding—
They are eating the fruit that grows there.
O when will I meet my true love
Who will put aside the leaves,
And pluck the oranges that grow
So round and firm upon my tree?

Laurence Housman versified this as:

On an island in the river is a tree full of leaves;
And deep in among them, the monkeys, little thieves,
Come stealing the fruit which is hiding there below—
The fruit that hangs waiting there for thee.

Oh, when will my love come, and drive away the thieves,
And climb into the branches, and push aside the leaves,

And pluck from their shadows the oranges that grow
So full, and firm, and round upon my tree?

One of the greatest problems facing a collector of folk-songs is what to do with the originals. The ideal thing is of course to print the original side by side with the translation. But this has many practical disadvantages. It is difficult enough for a publisher to undertake a book of this kind in any case. If it is burdened with a large quantity of matter which not one in a hundred readers will understand, the task of publication becomes almost impossible. Then again Hindi is a language with a phonetic script very different from our own and there is no really satisfactory way of reproducing Hindi originals, especially in their obscure dialect forms, in roman characters. Even if that were done, there cannot be more than a few dozen Occidental readers sufficiently acquainted with the dialects in which these songs are composed to read them with any pleasure, while few indeed are the Indian readers who can bear to read any Indian language printed in roman script. We have decided therefore at some personal sacrifice (for the inclusion of originals so familiar to ourselves would have given us much pleasure) to omit them in the present volume and to publish them separately in the Devanagari script for the benefit of Indian readers and of such philologists as may desire to study them. This is the method that has been adopted by W. G. Archer in his important collection of the songs and riddles of Chota Nagpur and it has the double advantage of not only guaranteeing the authenticity of the poems, but of enabling such villagers as are literate to read them for themselves.

This collection is offered as a collection of songs rather than of poems. In the first place the description is more accurate, for every verse in the book has been sung and has been neither written nor recited; and secondly we have deliberately cast our net rather widely so as to illustrate as many aspects of village life as possible. The great majority of village songs have little poetry in them, and the more primitive we get the less poetry we seem to find; Gondi, for example, does not seem to lend itself well to poetic inspiration; the Juang, whose songs are full of poetry, do not sing (though they still talk) in their ancient tongue, but use Oriya. Take one of W. V. Grigson's songs, for example, in his *Maria Gonds of Bastar*:

Aleya reloya relo
Kokoreng koreng
Why are we not singing?
Kokoreng koreng
Come, lads, come!
Kokoreng koreng
This kind of song is no song,

and so on. How is any one to make a poem out of that?

Take another example, one of the first Indian folk-songs to be put into English, by Dalton who undoubtedly had the spirit and the tongue of a true poet. This is a 'close imitation' of a song sung 'by a rockbroken stream with wooded banks, the girls on one side, the lads on the other, singing to the accompaniment of the babbling brook in true bucolic style'.

BOYS

A kanchan flower bring to us
We'll listen whilst you sing to us.

GIRLS

We'll gather greens for dinner, dear!
But cannot think of singing here.

BOYS

A handful that of chaff and straw,
Us boys you surely beat at jaw!

GIRLS (*pouting*)

Ah! birds that chirp and fly away!
With us you care not then to stay?

BOYS (*amorous*)

Yes, yes, we've caught some pretty fish,
To part, dear girls, is not our wish.

GIRLS (*pleased*)

The clouds disperse, the day looks fair,
Come back then lads our homes to share.

BOYS

No! by the bar tree blossom! But
You come with us and share our hut.

GIRLS

The birds sing merrily, we agree
To leave pa ma and go with thee.

This is not really, as it sounds at first, something for *The Stuffed Owl*; it is an attempt to reproduce the way the boys and girls improvise songs at one another. Most of the Dadaria in Mandla are of very poor quality; they are improvisations and they are usually rhymed—and rhyme quickly introduces a cheapness and vulgarity into village song. But the scientist must preserve the cheap and vulgar as well as the high and beautiful.

The music of the songs was recorded by Walter Kaufmann in 1940 and an account of them was published by him in *The Musical Quarterly* for the following year, to which a valuable note was added by Curt Sachs, author of *The World History of Dance*.

Sachs refers to these Gond melodies as an 'important collection' and describes their 'music as simple and primitive as any tribal songs in the six continents. The typical Dadaria is opened by a stereotyped phrase (as in Breton bagpipe tunes), which begins just below the final of the scale and ascends, without halftones, the distance of a fifth; the melody remains at this level for a while—sometimes as a mere psalmodic repercussion—and descends stepwise the distance of a fourth to the final; a closing episode alternates the final with its upper neighbour. The range of a Dadaria is from four to six degrees, and its skeleton is the interval of a fourth. Several Dadaria are without halftones, while others are diatonic, mostly in the Lydian mode. Thus they represent an alloy of anhemitonic and diatonic, of chant and actual melody, both ascending and descending, in modal tetrachords.

The Karma songs are more archaic; one of them has only two tones, which lie a second apart, as have the melodies of certain Patagonian tribes and of the Vedda in the interior of Ceylon. This two-tone style is retained as a nucleus even when some other notes are introduced, and it is a fascinating experience to study the biological evolution from No. 17, through No. 17a, to No. 20, an evolution that presents us with a growth in two directions by introducing both halftones and tetrachordal structure. Moreover, these melodies, so strikingly similar to each other that we are tempted to take them for variants only, make clear how the high civilizations, drawing from the songs of the tribes that they had absorbed, came to the conception of melodic patterns, of ragas and maqamat, of Dorian, Phrygian, and Lydian.[3]

When we approach the pleasant task of acknowledging our obligations to our friends, before all others we must admit our debt to W. G. Archer. Of his beautiful and important book, *The Blue Grove*, he once wrote to us that 'but for *Songs of the Forest* it is certain that *The Blue Grove* would never have been written'. It is equally certain that but for *The Blue Grove* and its successor, *The Wedding of the Writers*, the present volume would not have been written either. The perfection of his technique, the beauty of his translations, the subtlety of his interpretation, the range of his knowledge, his devotion to Indian art and culture has been a continual inspiration and challenge to us in our task.

We must also acknowledge the devotion and inspiration of Devendra Satyarthi to Indian folk-literature. This writer, who has declared that the opinion of Andrew Fletcher, that a nation's ballads are more important than its laws, has touched his dreams, has wandered all over India and made a vast collection of village-songs. 'I have not been able', he says, 'to express my love for my country in political activity, nor could any form of social service suit me. I simply took to the songs of my people. The colour, fire, and sparkle of the peasants' poetry made an interesting story for me. A nation reborn must be inspired by its folk-songs.'

In the long labour of collection, translation and interpretation, which has now continued for ten years, we have had many helpers. Sunderlal Baghel and Sunderlal Narbada Prasad have helped us to collect songs from the beginning. Sounu Pardhan and his wife Phula, both of them poets, have been invaluable in interpretation. Baigin Gondin, Kachari Pardhanin and Ahaliya Pankin have thrown light on obscure references which only a woman's mind could explain and have themselves given many songs. Haricharan Syam, a Pardhan youth, Chandu,

[3] Walter Kaufmann, 'Folk Songs of the Gond and Baiga'. *The Musical Quarterly* (New York, 1941), xxvii, 280–88. In this book, Kaufmann's No. 17 is No. 11 and his No. 20 is No. 14. No. 17a is not printed here.

Jantri, Ram Pratap Baghel, Kartik Parteti and others have also helped. To Kosi Elwin a special debt is due for the singing of many beautiful songs.

Mr Rambharose Agarwal has been indefatigable in his assistance. He has collected many songs for us, and his advice and his unrivalled knowledge of Mandla District has always been at our disposal.

Part of the expenses of the preparation of this book were covered by a research grant from Merton College. Its publication was assisted by the Government of the Central Provinces and Berar. Little, however, would have been possible without the support and friendship of Mr. J. R. D. Tata and Mr J. P. Patel and of our friends (who must remain anonymous) on the staff of the Oxford University Press. To the Diocesan Press, Madras, belongs the credit of printing this and its companion volume with speed and precision at a time of unparalleled difficulty in the history of book-production.

From the day we first settled in aboriginal company, we have been impressed with the fact that the Indian 'primitive'—for all his material poverty and lack of conventional learning—is not to be pitied and 'uplifted', but rather to be respected and admired. Nothing in his life is more admirable than his flair for poetry, his sense of rhythm, his love of art. We believe that if he would be rightly guided, he would not be ashamed of these great things and that if he would employ them more enthusiastically he would soon win an honoured place in the social structure of modern India.

PATANGARH VILLAGE — VERRIER ELWIN
MANDLA DISTRICT — SHAMRAO HIVALE
INDIA
1 *May* 1944

NOTE

To make this collection as representative as possible, twenty-two songs have been reprinted from *The Baiga* (John Murray, 1939), nine from *Songs of the Forest* (Allen and Unwin, 1936), three from *The Agaria* (Oxford University Press, 1942), and one from *Phulmat of the Hills* (John Murray, 1937). Twenty of the Pardhan songs were printed in *Man in India*, Vol. xxii, and twelve of the Dadaria now appearing in this volume in *Man in India*, Vol. xxiii. The rest of the six hundred and nineteen songs have not been printed before.

7

India's North-East Frontier in the Nineteenth Century (1959)

Introduction

I

Very little has been written on the tribal peoples of the north-east frontier of India. In J. P. Mill's ethnographic bibliography of Assam only about one in ten of the items listed has anything to say about them. And these items are mostly articles or notes in periodicals now impossible to obtain and difficult to consult, or they are official publications which have been indifferently preserved. The few books of the early period, such as those by Robinson, Butler and Dalton, are today collector's pieces. Yet these elusive records contain much that is of absorbing interest.

In this book, therefore, I present a selection of passages from the older literature, down to 1900, which has a bearing on the history, people and problems of what is now known as the North-East Frontier Agency. These passages are of unusual value, for they give us a picture of the country as it was before it had suffered any external influence, and although the reader may sometimes regret that the writers did not use their opportunities for exact observation more fully, he must be thankful for what he has. He should remember that the administrators, soldiers, missionaries and explorers represented in these pages were not anthropologists. Even Dalton was not an anthropologist in the modern sense. Their information is not always correct; it is sometimes heavily marked by personal bias; some of it is obviously guess-work. But they were fresh to the country and their eyes were open; from them a general idea of what the tribal people were like sixty, eighty, a hundred or even a hundred and twenty years ago, does emerge, and despite all the faults both of fact and of taste their work is of value to scholars and administrators alike.

In contrast to both an earlier and a later age, the European travellers of the nineteenth century were under no illusions about the Noble Savage; in the main their opinion of the tribes was a low one and their attitude was all too often patronizing or scornful. In 1865, declared a leading article in the *Pioneer* of the day, 'the only idea which most men had, with reference to the hills and forests [of Assam], was that they were the habitat of savage tribes, whose bloody raids and thieving forays threatened serious danger to the cause of tea'.

The people were not even interesting: Lord Dalhousie pronounced the Assam frontier to be a bore, and even as late as 1911 we find the wife of an officer attached to the Abor Expedition of that year expressing herself in a series of puns: 'It is such a bore that my husband has to go off on that silly Abor Expedition to fight those stupid aborigines with their queer arboreal habits.'[1]

Even the serious writers took the same view. Butler declares that the troops of his command 'wish for nothing better than an opportunity of contending with the Singphos, or indeed with any of their treacherous neighbours (whom they hold in the utmost contempt) in a fair battle in the open country'. He speaks of the 'general degeneracy' of the Assamese people who are emaciated by their predilection for the 'pernicious opiate', opium, even though under British rule 'we may yet regard Assam as a rising country'. He calls the Khamptis 'a discontented, restless, intriguing tribe'; the Singphos are 'a rude treacherous people'; the Abors are 'as void of delicacy as they are of cleanliness'; the Nagas are 'a very uncivilized race, with dark complexions, athletic sinewy frames, hideously wild and ugly visages, reckless of human life'. Among such, says Butler in 1847, we might reasonably expect missionary zeal would be most successful. For the last eight years, however, two or three American Baptist missionaries had in vain endeavoured to awake in them a sense of the saving virtue of Christianity.

[1] Millington, *On the Track of the Abor* (1912), p. v.

Rowlatt, who explored the Mishmi hills in 1844, describes the Mishmis as 'disgustingly dirty: with the exception of a few of the Chiefs, they are seldom washed from one year's end to another. . . . They seem to have but a very faint idea of any religion'. M'Cosh, who included a chapter on the hill tribes in his *Topography of Assam* (1837), says of the Miris that their manners and habits are 'wild and barbarous and their persons filthy and squalid'. Robinson, though he speaks well of the Abors, describes the Daflas as having ugly countenances and a 'somewhat ferocious' appearance. The Mishmis are 'in general excessively filthy'. Beresford speaks of the Abors as 'truculent and aggressive . . . like all savages, the only law they know or recognize is that of force and in the ability of awarding prompt and speedy punishments'.

Even J. F. Needham, who was once criticized by authority for allowing himself to be 'cheeked by the men and pulled about by the young women', spoke on occasion in the most uncomplimentary terms of his people. 'Notwithstanding that they [the Abors] are most hospitable,' he writes in 1886,

> their manner is so rough and they are so provokingly impertinent (unmeaningly, I admit, for it is nothing but ignorance, coupled with self-conceitedness, that makes them so) and familiar, as likewise possessed of such monkey-like inquisitiveness, that their society very soon palls upon one, especially after the first novelty of being amongst them has worn off. They are so excessively suspicious too, that one shirks even asking them questions about their manners and customs, except in the most casual manner.

He also calls the Mishmis 'treacherous and cowardly curs'; they are 'blustering' and leniency is as little understood by this tribe 'as by any other similarly uncivilized and savage'.

Dalton's attitude, however, is very different, and he foreshadows the new attitude of respect, interest and affection that in the main governs the relations of literates and pre-literates in the modern world. Not only does he never speak of the tribal people with contempt or scorn, but he never misses an opportunity of recording instances in their favour. Even the Chulikata Mishmis, to whom he gives a bad character (adding, however, that 'I would not venture to have done so on any authority but their own'), have many virtues and are the 'most ingenious of the family'. He is impressed by the 'practical utility' of the Abor dormitory and by 'the ready alacrity and good feeling and discipline' of its members. Of Miri women he says that they make faithful and obedient wives and cheerfully bear the hard burden imposed upon them. The Tanaes (Apa Tanis) make war both effectually and honourably, fighting only men and inflicting no injury whatever on non-combatants. 'If this be true,' adds Dalton, 'the Tanae may claim a hearing as the most humane of belligerents at the next International Congress.'

Unhappily, such an attitude was rare and a lack of sympathy with the people accounts for many mistakes of the earlier writers. In no field are our old records more imperfect than in that of religion. We must remember that it was not easy, at that date, for the majority of European officers to take seriously any religion other than their own. The outlook of Sir James Johnstone, as expressed in his book *My Experiences in Manipur and the Naga Hills* (1896), is typical:

> I strongly urged the advisability of establishing a regular system of education, including religious instruction, under a competent clergyman of the Church of England. I pointed out that the Nagas had no religion; that they were highly intelligent and capable of receiving civilization; that with it they would want a religion, and that we might as well give them our own, and make them in this way a source of strength, by thus mutually attaching them to us.

Dalton also did his utmost to aid Christian missions among the Kols, when he was Commissioner of Chota Nagpur, his argument being, so Johnstone says, 'that they wanted a religion, and that were they Christians, they would be a valuable counterpoise in time of trouble to the vast non-Christian population of Bihar. In the same way it cannot be doubted that a large population of Christian hillmen between Assam and Burma would be a valuable prop to the State.'

This belief that the tribal people of Assam had 'no religion', or alternatively that what religion they had was (as Butler said of the Singphos) 'a mixture of all the various idolatries and superstitions' ever invented, did not encourage unbiased and scientific inquiry. Thus even Dalton says that 'the religion of the Mishmis is confined to the propitiation of demons', and of the Chulikatas he observes, 'I have met with no people so entirely devoid of religious feeling as are the Chulikatas. I had long conversations on the subject with several of the Chiefs, and they utterly rejected all notions of a future state or of immortality of any kind'. Of the Miris he declares that 'the religious observances of the Miris are confined to the slaughter of animals in the name of the sylvan spirits and vaticination by the examination of the entrails of birds'. Of the Nagas he says, 'they have no temples and no priests, and I never heard of any form of worship amongst them, but I do not doubt that they sacrifice and observe omens like other tribes'.

Yet this was not the last word of the older writers and a fine passage by T. H. Lewin, written in 1869, anticipates the attitude and policy of modern India:

> This I say, let us not govern these hills for ourselves, but administer the country for the well-being and happiness of the people dwelling therein. What is wanted here is not measures, but a man. Place over them an officer gifted with the power of rule, not a mere cog in the great wheel of government, but one tolerant of the failings of his fellow-creatures and yet prompt to see and recognize in them the touch of nature that makes the whole world kin, apt to enter into new trains of thought and to modify and adopt ideas, but cautious in offending national prejudice. Under a guidance like this, let the people by slow degree civilize themselves. With education open to them and yet moving under their own laws and customs, they will turn out not debased and miniature epitomes of Englishmen, but a new and noble type of God's creatures.

II

On the whole, very little is known about the men whose writings are reproduced in this book: only two of them find a place in the *Dictionary of National Biography*, and I have had to collect what information there is from chance references in journals and occasional autobiographical passages. The following notes, scanty as they are, will however give some idea of who our authors were and what they did.

John Butler

John Butler, author of *A Sketch of Assam* (1847) and *Travels and Adventures in the Province of Assam during a Residence of Fourteen Years* (1855), first visited Assam in 1837, when he spent three months at Goalpara. He was a soldier, belonging to the 55th

Regiment of the Bengal Native Infantry, and in November 1840 he was appointed second-in-command of the Assam Light Infantry. His journey from Calcutta to the 'desolate and remote' station of Saikwa took no less than sixty-five days, of which thirty-seven were spent travelling upstream to Gauhati, 'the metropolis of Assam'. On this second visit, Butler found that Gauhati had been greatly improved; roads had been made, many brick bungalows had been erected, the jungle had been cleared, while 'the view of the river, the islands, temples, and verdant foliage of the trees' made the place 'one of the most picturesque scenes to be met with in India'. From Gauhati he travelled in a canoe (formed of a single tree hollowed out and propelled by eighteen 'merry paddlers') up the Brahmaputra to Saikwa, 'the north-eastern frontier military post in Upper Assam'. Saikwa had been established in 1839 after the station of Sadiya on the opposite bank had been surprised and burnt in a tribal attack. Here at Saikwa the Light Infantry was posted 'to afford protection to the Tea Gardens from the sudden aggressions of the numerous wild, fierce, border tribes'.

Here Butler settled down in a mat-and-grass cottage plastered with mud 'in comfort and solitariness'. He had many adventures; one night his house was invaded by a great python, and he was constantly in trouble with the Brahmaputra.

His stay did not, however, last very long, for in the following year he was appointed to the civil branch of the service as an Assistant to the Agent to the Governor-General, North-East Frontier; and after a residence of about three years in Lower Assam, in the month of February 1844 he was placed in charge of the hill tribes subject to the Political Agent of Upper Assam. Now again he had to go to Saikwa, this time with his family, and in June of that year his house was washed away by the 'merciless river'. But Butler was never left in one place for long; indeed, as he says, 'during a period of twenty-seven years' service it has seldom been my lot to enjoy, at one place, an undisturbed residence of more than a few months', and the 'perpetual motion' in which he lived now took him to Nowgong in charge of the Cachar Levy. In 1846–7 he visited the Naga Hills and received tribute of ivory and hand-woven cloth from the Angamis who took solemn oaths to stop their raids on the villages of the plains, and in 1848 he again visited Khonoma.

He founded a small Levy Post and a market at Samaguting and opened cart-tracks to Dimapur. He came to the opinion, however, that Government should abandon any attempt to administer the hills, considering that official intervention in internal disputes had been a failure, and for a time his advice was followed, though a different policy was, of course, adopted after a few years.

Butler, in the fashion of the day, describes Assam as 'a wild, uncivilized, foreign land' and he suggests that 'to those accustomed only to the comforts of civilized life, or to the traveller who is indifferent to the beauties of scenery, the monotony, silence and loneliness of the vast forests of Assam will present few features of attraction'. But Butler clearly was attracted by this wild country, especially by its people, and he wrote his first book 'to make Assam better known, to remove some prejudices against it, and preserve the memory of many remarkable scenes'.

Butler was evidently what we would now call a 'character'. Wherever he went he carried with him two glass windows, one for a sitting-room and another for a bedroom, which he used to insert in the reed walls of the thatched houses which were usually allotted to him. Once, finding himself being carried down the Brahmaputra in the middle of the night with only one servant to attend him, he was not dismayed but hastily donned his red woollen nightcap and a pea-coat, seized a paddle and rowed most heartily until the skin peeled off his hands. Many other adventures make entertaining reading.

Major Butler retired in 1865. His son, also a John Butler, became Deputy Commissioner of the Naga Hills and was killed in a Lhota Naga ambuscade in 1875.

T. T. Cooper

Thomas Thornvill Cooper, from whose book, *New Routes for Commerce: The Mishmee Hills*, a number of extracts are given in Chapters XI and XII, has been described as 'one of the most adventurous of modern English travellers'. He was born in 1839, the son of a coalfitter and shipowner, and from his boyhood showed a desire for travel. While still in his teens he was sent on a sea-voyage to Australia for the good of his health, and on the way the crew mutinied; young Thomas, pistol in hand, mounted guard over the captain's cabin. In Australia he made several journeys into the interior and thought of settling down permanently there. But in 1859 he came to India and was employed by the mercantile firm of Arbuthnot and Company in Madras. This, however, was far too tame for his adventurous spirit, and after two years he resigned from his position, visited Sind and Bombay, and finally found himself in Rangoon.

He learnt Burmese, but even now could not settle down and in 1863 went to Shanghai to join a brother who was in business there. He was almost immediately involved in a rebellion and had to help in the protection of the city against the Taiping insurgents. The problem of expanding trade now became an urgent one, and at the age of only twenty-nine Cooper was invited by the Shanghai Chamber of Commerce to attempt to travel through Tibet to India. At the beginning of 1868, therefore, he left Hankow for Batang, whence he hoped to reach the first point on the Lohit Brahmaputra in eight days. The Chinese authorities, however, refused to let him proceed, and he went instead south to Bhamo, reaching Tse-ku, a splendid achievement for that period. Here he was less than a hundred miles from Manchi on the Upper Irrawaddy, which had been visited by Wilcox in 1826.

He now ran into serious trouble, for on passing Weisi-Fu, he was prevented from going further by a tribal Chief, and had to return to the city, where he was imprisoned for five weeks by the local authorities on suspicion of being involved in a rebellion at that time in progress in Yunnan. For a while he lay under the threat of death, but in August was permitted to depart. He had now been eight months on his journey, but it was not until the middle of November that he finally came back to Hankow. He returned to England and wrote an account of his adventures in his excellent book *A Pioneer of Commerce*.

In 1869, Cooper decided to try again. He had failed to reach India from China; he would now try to reach China from India. In October 1869, accordingly, he set out from Sadiya and worked up the Brahmaputra to a village called Prun, some twenty miles from Rima. But here again he was greeted with determined opposition and was compelled to return. It is this journey which he describes in his *New Routes for Commerce*, which contains a number of shrewd observations on Mishmi and Khampti life.

Later, he went again to Rangoon and was appointed Political Agent at Bhamo. But he was soon compelled by ill health to return to England, where he was attached to the India Office. In 1876 he was sent to India with dispatches for the Viceroy and was soon afterwards re-appointed Political Agent at Bhamo. Captain Gill, who was received here by Cooper after his remarkable expedition through China, describes their meeting in his book *The River of Golden Sand*. Only a year later, while still under forty years of age, Cooper was murdered at Bhamo in August 1878 by a sepoy in revenge for some minor punishment.

Cooper, says the *Dictionary of National Biography*, from which many of the above facts are taken, was a 'man of great physical powers, and was endowed with the calm courage essential for a successful traveller. Under a somewhat reserved demeanour he possessed a warm and generous nature, and won the regard and affection of all who knew him by his singleness of heart and his unaffected modesty'.

E. T. Dalton

Of all the works on the North-East Frontier written during the last century, there can be no doubt that pride of place must be given to the thirty-five pages on the subject in Dalton's great *Descriptive Ethnology of Bengal*, and to the remarkable 'lithograph portraits copied from photographs' with which the book is adorned.

Edward Tuite Dalton was born in 1815 and in due course joined the Bengal Staff Corps, of which he was a colonel in 1872 and a major-general three years before his death on the 30th of December 1880. His name appears but seldom in the histories, but we know that in 1845 he visited the hills in the neighbourhood of the Subansiri River, that he went to Membu in the Abor country in 1855, and that about the same time he was having official dealings with the Singphos. In 1851 he was Political Assistant Commissioner in charge of Kamrup and wrote in that year for the Asiatic Society on the 'Mahapurushyas, a sect of Assamese Vaishnavas', in which he praises the 'general respectability and intelligence of the disciples', and gives an interesting and sympathetic account of Sri Sankardeo. A little later he wrote on the ruined temples of Assam.

In 1855 Dalton was Principal Assistant to the Governor-

General's Agent in Assam. Three years later he was transferred to Chota Nagpur as Commissioner of the area and took part in an expedition to put down a rising in Palamau. He also accompanied the Field Force against the Singhbhum rebels in 1858–9. His period of duty in this part of India was as fruitful as his years in Assam, for some of the best passages in his book deal with the Juangs, Hos and Santals.

The *Descriptive Ethnology* was a direct sequel to the Ethnological Congress which was proposed early in 1866 to be held in Calcutta. The Congress, which was to have been an adjunct to a general industrial exhibition, was dropped on account of the practical difficulties of bringing the 'strange shy creatures', the tribesmen of the hills, to a great city. The Commissioner of Assam stated his conviction that even twenty typical 'specimens of the hill tribes of his province' could not be conveyed to Calcutta and back at any time of the year 'without casualties that the greatest enthusiast for anthropological research would shrink from encountering'. If any of the more independent tribes were to die on the way, 'it might lead to inconvenient political consequences'.

Before the scheme had been dropped, however, the Government of Bengal and the Supreme Government had called on all local authorities to furnish complete lists of the various races to be found within their jurisdictions, and Dalton was asked to edit this information and to draw up a 'descriptive catalogue' which would serve as a guide to the ethnological exhibition. Dalton, however, found that there was insufficient material even for a catalogue and it was then suggested that he should write an account of all the tribal peoples of what was then 'Bengal' and which included Assam and Chota Nagpur, 'the most interesting fields of research in all Bengal'. Many persons assisted Dalton in this project, and in particular he was able to collect a few photographs taken for the London Exhibition of 1862. A Dr B. Simpson, 'one of the most successful of Indian photographers', was deputed to the valley of the Brahmaputra, 'that most prolific of ethnographical fields', o take photographs, while the skill of Dr Brown, Political Agent at Manipur, was also utilized for illustrations of Manipuris and the neighbouring tribes.

For the publication of the work, the Government of Bengal

contributed a sum of Rs 10,000—an enormous sum for those days —and the book was printed under the direction of the Council of the Asiatic Society of Bengal, which from the first had done everything possible to encourage the project.

Dalton claims that he was himself responsible for the accuracy of a large proportion of the descriptions given. Unhappily a number of his manuscript tour diaries perished 'during the mutinies', and it is doubly unfortunate that these were the earlier diaries, referring to his travels in Assam, as a result of which his notices of some of the Assam tribes 'were not as full as he should like to have made them'.

Dalton's work did not escape criticism. It is curious, moreover, that it was not reviewed by any of the journals of the day, not even by the *Indian Antiquary* or the *Journal of the Asiatic Society of Bengal*. Captain John Butler, son of the author of *A Sketch of Assam*, was particularly critical and in a diary of March 1873 he writes:

> Amused myself by reading some of Dalton's work on the Ethnology of Bengal and was much surprised to find that the letterpress, at all events as far as the Naga Tribes are concerned, is not in my humble opinion worth very much and yet this is the very portion of the book for the accuracy of which he states in his preface that he himself is alone responsible. It seems strange that he should not apparently ever have considered it worth his while to refer to any of the Frontier Officers in Assam, for I notice that although he concludes his preface with a long list of officers to whom he is indebted for their contributions, there is not a single Assam Officer among the list.

Captain Butler also questioned the identification of some of the illustrations, though these were not those reproduced in this book. It is a pity that Butler did not elaborate his criticisms, for to say that a book is not 'worth very much' does not lead us anywhere. It is true that Dalton borrowed freely from his predecessors; that in some cases, he was writing up material gathered a quarter of a century earlier; and that in his day there were few anthropological precedents to follow and no anthropological training to be had. But his sympathy, his observation, and above all the elegance and purity of his style render his book one of the outstanding achievements of the anthropology of India.

J. Errol Gray

J. Errol Gray was a tea planter who was interested in extending the trade of Assam beyond the frontier. In 1891 he was invited by the Government of India to explore the Bor Khampti country in a semi-official capacity on their behalf, and on 24 November 1892 he left Saikwa in an attempt to cross into western China through the mountains first explored by Wilcox in 1827, and later by Woodthorpe and MacGregor in 1884–5. But Gray went further than any of his predecessors, crossing the Nam-Kiu and entering the valley of the Tisang, an important affluent of the Irrawaddy.

Gray travelled unarmed and with a comparatively small party of thirty-eight Khasi and eight Khampti porters, two military surveyors and one private servant. His diary is one of the most interesting of the early travel documents, and is enlivened by a controversy between himself and J. F. Needham about the behaviour of a Singpho Chieftain named Ningro who, annoyed at not receiving a political present, seems to have done all he could to hamper Gray's progress. Gray returned to Sadiya on 23 April 1893.

Although part of Gray's journey was beyond the frontier of what is now the North-East Frontier Agency, some of his most interesting observations were made within the Indian border, and his account of the Singphos is of special value.

Gray travelled hard and his relations with the people were friendly, though his journey was overshadowed by the behaviour of Ningro which led him to exclaim: 'There is no getting to the bottom of a Singpho.'

William Griffith

Dr William Griffith, M.D., F.L.S., was born in 1810 and died at an early age in 1845. He came to India in 1832 as an Assistant Surgeon on the Madras establishment of the East India Company. But he was essentially a botanist and a few years later he went with Dr MacClelland, the geologist, to explore Assam with the special aim of developing the cultivation of tea. This gave him the opportunity to make the expeditions for which his name became rightly famous. In 1836 he went into the Mishmi Hills 'from the debouching of the Lohit to about ten miles east of the Ghalums'. He explored the tracts between Sadiya and Ava and once marched right through from Assam to Ava and Rangoon. He fell ill and was given an opportunity to recuperate as surgeon to the Bhutan Embassy. On his way to Bhutan he visited the Khasi Hills. He also travelled to Khorassan and Afghanistan. In 1842 he took charge of the Botanic Gardens at Calcutta. He was a great collector, a daring traveller, bravely endured many hardships and illnesses, but he had a very bad temper. He has been called 'the acutest botanist who ever visited India'. His diary of the visit to the Mishmi Hills, from which we quote, first appeared in the *Journal of the Asiatic Society of Bengal* for 1837. After his death, there was published in Calcutta a large book of some 550 pages in which his friend MacClelland edited the many journals he had kept of his travels in Assam, Burma, Bhutan and Afghanistan. Although the interest of this work is largely botanical, it contains references to the Khasis, Singphos, Mishmis and Konyaks.

Father Krick

Father Nicholas Michael Krick, who, with his friend Father Bourri, was murdered in October 1854 in the Mishmi Hills, was born in 1819 at Lixheim in France, so that he was only thirty-five at the time of his death. After entering the priesthood and becoming a member of the *Société des Missions Etrangères*, he came to India in 1850 as Superior of the South Tibetan Mission, and proceeded to Gauhati on the banks of the Brahmaputra with the intention of making his way into Tibet through the Mishmi Hills. He was not the first, even at this early date, to think of doing so, though the reports he must have heard at Gauhati can hardly have been encouraging. Thirty years earlier, a soldier, Lieutenant Burton, had reported that the Mishmis 'were very averse to receive strangers'. In 1827, Wilcox made his way into the Miju country, as far as the point 'where the Brahmaputra after flowing nearly due south from Tibet suddenly changes its course and flows in a westerly direction', but the notorious Chief Jingsha forced him to retreat. Ten years later, Griffith succeeded in penetrating as far as the village of Ghalum on the Lohit, but was unable to enter the Miju hills. In 1845 Rowlatt went up the Du river as far as Tuppang, where he met a number of Tibetans. Early in 1848, a Hindu ascetic, Parmanand Acharya, whose name may be remembered with the Christian ascetics who suffered after him, was killed by Miju followers of Jingsha.

Father Krick, however, was undismayed, and alone and on foot, with his cross, his flute, sextant and medicine-chest, worked his way up the Brahmaputra and part of the Lohit. At Saikwa he obtained the services of a Khampti Chief as guide and pressed on through the 'rugged, grand but uncultured' mountains of the Mijus. After passing through the freindly villages, so Dalton tells us, he appears to have been guided so as to avoid the hostile clans, but on passing near the home of the formidable Jingsha, a young girl significantly pointed out to him the spot where the pilgrim from India had not long before been massacred, and intimated that a like fate awaited him if he were caught.

However, Father Krick succeeded in reaching the Tibetan settlement of Oualong, and was well received there, and was able to go forward to Sommeu or Samar, in a well-watered and well-cultivated valley not far from Rima, a small Tibetan administrative centre. All went well at first, but presently the Father's resources were exhausted and the people, once the novelty of his arrival was over, were not inclined to support him gratuitously and he was asked to leave the country. On the way back, he stopped at Jingsha's village, where he was roughly treated, but was fortunately able to cure a sick member of the family and was allowed to leave without injury.

After returning to the plains, Father Krick paid a visit to Membu, an important village of the Padam Abors, and then in January 1854 he set out again for Tibet, this time accompanied by Father Bourri, and, escorted by a friendly Mishmi Chief, reached Samar within seven months. The travellers successfully crossed the pass at the head of the valley to Zayul, but had to turn back from Makonglang as the weather was against them and their Mishmi guides refused to go further. They returned down the Du river and went up the Tellu instead.

Unhappily, the Fathers managed to offend a powerful Digaru Mishmi Chief, whose name is spelt variously in the records as Kaisa, Kahesha and Kai-ee-sha. This was not, apparently, their fault. They had invited Kaisa to take them over the Tho Chu Pass and had promised him money and guns as reward. But another Chief double-crossed Kaisa and got the reward instead, at the same time ensuring that the Fathers did not pay the expected friendly visit to Kaisa's house. The angry Chief followed the Fathers into Tibet and killed them as they came up the Tellu path by the mouth of the Tho Chu. He carried off their property and took their Singpho servant as a slave.

The following year, under orders from Lord Dalhousie, a small party of the Assam Light Infantry, with Khampti volunteers and porters, led by Lieutenant F. G. Eden, set out from Sadiya. 'For eight days', says Mackenzie, 'this little band pressed on by forced marches, swinging across dangerous torrents on bridges of single canes, climbing for hours at a time without water and in bitter cold, till in the grey dawn of a misty morning Kaisa was surprised and captured in his village on the Du, his elder sons slain in open fight, his people dispersed and the murdered Frenchmen to the full avenged.' Kaisa was tried and hanged at Dibrugarh (Dalton says it was Calcutta, but appears to be mistaken), but not before he had killed two of the guards who were watching him in the jail.

Father Krick's own account of his first Tibetan journey and his visit to the Abor Hills was published in Paris with the title *Relation d'un Voyage au Tibet* in 1854. The parts of it relating to the Abors were translated into English and published in the *Journal of the Asiatic Society of Bengal* for 1913, and selections from this are reproduced later in this book.[2]

In this relation Father Krick reveals himself as a witty, kindly person, a keen observer, a vivid and entertaining writer, and a man of unusual devotion and courage.

Father Krick claims that he was the first person to penetrate into the Abor country, although several agents of the East India Company had tried to do so. For the Padams were not anxious to receive visitors, especially English visitors. If once we allow Englishmen to enter our country, they said, they are sure to have an army at their heels. Father Krick entertains himself over his efforts to prove that he is a perfectly good Frenchman, a priest with no territorial ambitions, who has nothing to do with the English. But in tribal opinion, he observes, 'any white

[2] Please refer to original edition, *India's North-East Frontier in the Nineteenth Century* (O.U.P., 1959).

skin, any nose somewhat protruding, is of English make'.

Father Krick was not correct in supposing himself to be the first foreigner to visit the Abor area. Bedford and Wilcox were there in 1825–6, and in 1847 there had been a friendly conference of Padams and British Officers. But he was correct in stressing the tension between the Abors and Government, for from 1850 onwards there were a number of outrages and punitive expeditions. It is curious that in 1855, only two years after Father Krick, Colonel Dalton should have visited Membu in the company of Lieutenant Eden. He has left an account of it which differs in several particulars from that of the priest.

Father Krick was evidently a very human as well as a very courageous person. When we read his summary of the character of his hosts (and his impressions are far more sympathetic than those of many of his contemporaries) we cannot help suspecting that he himself had the same sort of virtues. 'The Padam,' he says, 'is very active, jolly, a lover of freedom and independence, generous, noble-hearted, plain-spoken, more honest than the average Oriental, not over-moderate in eating and drinking, at least as far as quantity is concerned. . . . He seems to possess much of the child's simplicity, and Membu is undoubtedly less corrupt than Paris.'

J. F. Needham

J. F. Needham had the unique distinction of serving for no less than twenty-three years in Sadiya. Belonging originally to the Bengal Police, he was posted to Assam as Assistant Political Officer in Sadiya in 1882 and did not leave the place until the end of 1905. In time he came to be regarded as the earliest of the advisers to Government on tribal affairs. He made many expeditions, though not so many as he desired, for he was considered rather too adventurous—'he had a dash', it was said—and a little too free with the people. In 1885–6 he visited the Mishmi Hills and nearly reached Rima, travelling without escort and following the route of Fathers Krick and Bourri who had been murdered in the Zayul Valley thirty years before. The following year he visited the Hukong Valley. In 1891 he crossed the Patkoi Range to Burma. In 1893 he went as Political Officer with the military expedition into the Abor Hills, and was blamed for a lack of foresight and a spirit of over-confidence which led to the disastrous massacre at Bordak. In 1899, he again accompanied an expedition (the Bebejiya Mishmi Expedition) which came in for severe criticism, this time from Lord Curzon himself, though he himself was praised.

Needham was a voluminous, lively and careless writer. The reports on his various expeditions are always worth reading. He was interested in linguistics and wrote outline grammars of the languages spoken by the Sadiya Miris, the Singphos, the Khamptis of the Sadiya area, and he made brief studies of the Digaru and Moshang Naga vocabularies.

William Robinson

William Robinson, an educationalist of the Gauhati Government Seminary, published his first work on Assam in 1841. In the fashion of the day it had a long and sonorous title: *Descriptive Account of Asam: with a sketch of the Local Geography, and a concise History of The Tea-Plant of Asam: to which is added, a Short Account of the Neighbouring Tribes, exhibiting their History, Manners and Customs*. Robinson was very interested in philology, and during the next fifteen years he published, on each occasion in the *Journal of the Asiatic Society of Bengal*, a series of articles on the Abor, Khampti, Konyak, Singpho, Dafla and Mishmi languages.

The *Descriptive Account* is well written and its picture of the frontier tribes is lively and informative, though most of Robinson's contemporaries were probably more interested in his chapter on tea, that 'polyandrous plant of the natural order Ternstiomicae'. Indeed Robinson declares in his preface that the subject is one of acknowledged interest. 'The daily increasing importance of Assam, and the conspicuous position it begins to hold as the scene of great commercial advantages to British India' render an account of the province a 'great desideratum'.

But Robinson's literary objective was not merely to bring 'this highly valuable province into more general notice'. Should his book 'even in the most distant manner lead to an improvement in the moral, as well as the temporal condition of the people, he will consider the labour bestowed on it, more than repaid'. The *Descriptive Account* is, in fact, one of the first of the gazetteers; it devotes chapters to climate and to the effect of climate on man, to geology, botany and zoology, to historical and political geography, to productive industry and to the civil and social state of the Assamese. The hill tribes are discussed in a separate and final section.

Robinson's knowledge was fullest for the Mishmis and Nagas. Except for a brief account of the Khasis and Garos, he confines himself largely to the frontier tribes. He frankly admits his ignorance, however, and indeed the general ignorance, of such tribes as the Akas, and he has likewise little to tell us of the Daflas.

R. Wilcox

R. Wilcox carried out a number of surveys in Assam during the four years 1825 to 1828 and gave an account of them in a *Memoir* which was published in the seventeenth volume of *Asiatic Researches* (1832). This was reprinted in *Selections from the Records of the Bengal Secretariat*, No. 23, in 1855. Wilcox was an intrepid explorer and in his 1826 expedition succeeded in penetrating the Mishmi country three-quarters of the way to Rima; fifty years later Cooper did not get so far. Sir James Johnstone describes him thus:

> Wilcox was one of the giants of old, men who with limited resources did a vast amount of work among wild people and said little about it, being contented with doing their duty. In 1828, accompanied by Lieutenant Burton, and ten men belonging to the Sudya Khamptis (Shans), he penetrated to the Bor Khamptis' country, far beyond our borders, an exploit not repeated till after our annexation of Upper Burmah.

III

In editing these extracts I have preserved as far as possible the original spelling, even though this results in many inconsistencies, and punctuation in order to emphasize the fact that they come from another age, which looked on tribal people with a different eye to ours. Very few of our writers indulged in the luxury of footnotes, and I have not included any of the originals; all footnotes should, therefore, be regarded as my own contribution.

Some confusion may be caused by the indiscriminate use of tribal names by the earlier writers, who used words like 'Abor' or 'Naga' as if they meant 'hillman' or 'tribesman'. This is specially true of the word 'Naga', which they applied to a number of tribes which we do not classify as Naga today.

I must express my obligation to the *Bibliography of Ethnology of Assam*, compiled in 1952 by J. P. Mills, on which I have inevitably drawn in the compilation of the select book-list at the end of this volume. I received every possible assistance from my friend B. S. Kesavan, Librarian of the National Library, and his staff, and from L. N. Chakravarty. I am grateful to the Asiatic Society for permission to reprint the extract from Father Krick's writings, translated into English by Father Gille, which appeared in the *Journal of the Asiatic Society of Bengal* in 1913.

Shillong V.E
October 1955

THE CROP-HAIRED MISHMIS

(E. T. Dalton, *Descriptive Ethnology of Bengal*, 1872, pp. 18ff.)

The hill country bordering on Asam, between the Digaru and Dibong, and on both banks of the hill course of the latter river, is occupied by a tribe nearly allied to the people last described as Mishmis, called Chalikata Mishmis by the Asamese in consequence of their habit of cropping the front hair on the forehead. Their country lies to the north of Sadiya, and their villages extend across the Sub-Himalayan range to the borders of Tibet. The hills being loftier, it is more rugged and difficult of access even than the country of the Tain Mishmis. So difficult indeed, that though we have had aggravation enough, an expedition into the interior of their country has never been attempted. I have been informed by the Khamtis that one route to the plains traversed by the Chalikatas is along the cliffs of the Dibong river. The path is generally a narrow ledge winding round a precipice, but in one place there is no ledge! *only holes in the face of the rock for the hands and feet.* The proper name for the Chalikata clan is, if I recollect right, Midhi. They are greatly detested and mistrusted by their neighbours, the Abors and Tain, and they are much dreaded by the Sadiya population in consequence of the prowling expeditions to kidnap women and children. They are full of deceit. They come down in innocent-looking parties of men and women to the plains, apparently groaning under the weight of the baskets of merchandise they are importing for barter. They proceed thus till they find an unprotected village, then throwing aside their fictitious loads, they pounce on the women and children, and carry them off to the hills. They thus attack villages of Tains and Digaru Mishmis, as well as Asamese villages, but they are afraid of the Abors, who are always on the alert.

The Midhi have some villages situated in low hills, about 16 miles to the west of the Dibong gorge, which are accessible, and which I have visited. I much regret that I have lost my journal of this expedition undertaken in company with Captain Comber in 1856, as we have no published account of the Midhi, and I have now nothing but my memory to trust to.

The inhabitants of the villages I visited were, in those days, in habits of intercourse with the plains, and frequented the Saikwah market. Wilcox tells us that they opposed Captain Bedford in his attempt to ascend the Dibong river in 1826. The attempt to visit their villages had been made by that officer, but the people came down in large numbers to the river, and showed themselves so unfriendly, that Captain Bedford deemed it expedient to retire.

The villages belonging to the people then so hostile are those we visited, and we found them very friendly. I recollect being much struck with a considerate act of delicate attention on the part of the women of the first village we came to, Anandia I think. The march from the river to this village was a long one, and there was no source of water on the road. When we got rather more than half way, and our people were suffering greatly from thirst, we came upon a group of girls with delicious spring water in new vessels made of the great hollow bamboo, called the *kaku bans* who had come thus far to meet, welcome, and refresh us.

The villages contained from 10 to 30 houses, each very lightly framed; they were long and narrow, about 60 feet by 12. One side was a narrow passage from end to end, the remainder was divided into small apartments in some of which were seats,—a sign of civilization not often met with in Indian huts.

The Gams rejoice in very sonorous names as Alundi, Alunga. They are hereditary Chiefs, and have considerable influence over their clansmen, but no power over their persons or property, and no authority to punish crime or even to take notice of it. The notions of the Midhi on this subject are truly savage. If an injury is inflicted on one of them by a member of another tribe, it is incumbent on the tribe of the injured party to avenge it; if one of his own tribe offend, it is the business of the person offended only. He has no law except that which he can take in his own hands, and between people in the same village feuds are thus perpetuated for ages.

I was told of some very large villages in interior, and I have heard from released captives of Chiefs of great wealth in cattle and slaves. One or two of these great men occasionally visited us, but generally there was cause of quarrel between us that kept them in their hills. The number of wives a man possesses is with them, as with the Tain, an indication of wealth, some Chiefs having as many as sixteen. Marriage ceremony there is, I believe, none; it is simply an affair of purchase, and the women thus obtained, if they can be called wives, are not much bound by the tie. The husbands do not expect them to be chaste; they take no cognizance of their temporary liaisons so long as they are not deprived of their services.[3] If a man is dispossessed of one of his wives, he has a private injury to avenge, and takes the earliest opportunity of retaliating, but he cannot see that the woman is a bit the worse for a little incontinency.

The Midhi, like the Mishmis previously described, are a trading people. Large parties are continually on the move trading with Tibet. On such occasions, men send their wives if they cannot go themselves, and to anyone who has seen how the men and women promiscuously bivouac at night, the exceeding complaisance of the husband will not appear wonderful.

The colour of the Midhi varies from dark brown to the fairness equalling that of a European brunette. Some amongst them have rich red lips and ruddy complexions, and I have seen Midhi girls that were decidedly good-looking, but their beauty is terribly marred by their peculiar method of cropping the hair. The front hair is combed down on the brow, then cut straight across from ear to ear, giving them foreheads 'villainous low' and they are generally begrimed with dirt. The back hair is collected in a knot behind, and secured with long bodkins of

[3] This is certainly not true today.

bone or porcupine quills. The men wear wicker helmets that come down in front right to the eyebrow, and unlike modern bonnets are large enough to cover the chignon behind. This gives them the appearance of having very large heads (they have not got small ones) and very scowling countenances. Their features are in fact of a coarse Mongolian type. The faces flat and broad, the nostrils wide and round, and the eyes small and oblique, but these characteristics, though stronger in the Midhi than in the Tain Mishmi, are less marked in the former than they are in the faces of their neighbours—the Abors. It has always struck me that the Midhi women are comparatively taller and finer creatures than the men.

Notwithstanding the bad character that I have given them (and I would not venture to have done so on any authority but their own), they are the most ingenious of the family; they have learnt to utilize for clothing many of the fibrous plants that grow wild in their hills, as well as cotton and wool.

They were probably the first people on this side of the Himalayas to discover the valuable properties of the *Rhea nivea*, and many others of the nettle tribe; with the fibre of one of these nettles they weave a cloth so strong and stiff that, made into jackets, it is used by themselves and by the Abors as a sort of armour. They supply themselves and the Abors with clothing, and their textile fabrics of all kinds always sold well at the Saikwah market. It was very interesting to watch the barter that took place there between these suspicious, excitable savages and the cool, wily traders of the plains. The former took salt chiefly in exchange for the commodities they brought down, and they would not submit to its being measured or weighed to them by any known process. Seated in front of the trader's stall, they cautiously take from a well-guarded basket one of the articles they wish to exchange. Of this they still retain a hold with their toe or their knee as they plunge two dirty paws into the bright white salt. They make an attempt to transfer all they can grasp to their own basket, but the trader, with a sweep of his hand, knocks off half the quantity, and then there is a fiery altercation, which is generally terminated by a concession on the part of the trader of a few additional pinches. In addition to the clothes, the Chalikatas bring to market large quantities of beeswax, ginger, and chillies.

The costume, with the exception of the head-dress, is very similar to that of the Tains, but the jackets worn by the women are larger and are sometimes tastefully embroidered. This garment is generally worn open, exposing an ample bust heaving under a ponderous weight of agate and glass beads. Their favourite weapons are straight Tibetan swords, daggers, bows and cross-bows, and they are the only tribe who always carry poisoned arrows. They have neatly-made oblong shields of buffalo hide, attached to which, inside, is a quiver full of finely-made poisoned *pangis*; with these they invariably garnish the path by which they retreat with their prey.

By an exchange of weapons, warriors become sworn comrades, and if one falls, it is the duty of the other to avenge his fate and recover his skull.

For the entertainment of their guests, the people of one village that we visited got up a very characteristic dramatical entertainment. The first scene represented a peaceful villager with his children hoeing the ground, and singing and conversing with them as if utterly unconscious of danger. A villainous-looking crop-head glides in like a snake scarce seen in the long grass, takes note of the group, and glides away again. Presently armed savages are seen in the distance. They come gradually and stealthily on, till within a convenient distance they stop and watch their prey like so many cats, then there is a rush in, the man is supposed to be killed, and the children caried screeching away.

This was followed by a dance. The Gam dressed himself in robes similar to those worn by the Mĭshmi priests, described by Monsignor Krick, and danced a stately measure with a young woman also similarly robed. I recollect being much struck with the imposing appearance of the dresses worn on this occasion, but I am unable to describe them accurately.

The robe of the female was ampler than usual, and had a fringe of more than a foot in breadth. She bore aloft, as she moved, a small drum which gave forth its sound at every motion. The male performer had a head-dress with horns, a broad belt round his waist with an enormous brass buckle, according with the popular notion of a bandit's girdle, and across the body was worn the singular embroidered shoulder-belt with its peal of small bells. This was a religious dance, used at funerals and other ceremonies. They bury their dead in the wood away from the village: a place is cleared in the forest in which the grave is made, and the remains of the deceased and his arms and clothes are deposited in it. They then dance over it.

I have met with no people so entirely devoid of religious feeling as are the Chalikatas. I had long conversations on the subject with several of the Chiefs, and they utterly rejected all notions of a future state, or of immortality of any kind. The spirits they propitiated were, they declared, mortal like themselves, and though they admitted there must have been a creator, they flatly denied that the being who called into existence their hills, rocks, rivers, forests, and ancestors could still be alive. Men die and worms eat them, is their creed, but when I suggested that their custom of placing in the grave, with the dead, weapons, food, and clothes must have originated in some idea that the spirit would regain such things, they said, it was nothing of the kind; it was done as a mark of affection to their departed relative—a feeling that indisposed them from using what he had used, and thus benefiting by his death.

8

The Nagas in the Nineteenth Century (1969)

Introduction

A few years ago I made an anthology of extracts from the nineteenth century books and articles, now rare and only available in the larger libraries, about the North-East Frontier of India. This book, which was published by the Oxford University Press in 1959, was unexpectedly successful and a new impression was issued in 1962.

At the time when I made this anthology I thought that I might do similar books for other tribal areas in India and the present work represents the first fruit of this idea. Here I have extracted passages about the Naga people on a broad geographical basis from printed books and articles covering the period 1827 to 1896. As in the earlier book I have concentrated on passages which illustrate the history, ethnography and problems of the people. My main interest, as it always has been, was in people, but inter-village feuds and punitive expeditions are inextricably mixed up with the story of Naga life.

This record is not presented as a correct picture but to illustrate how outsiders looked at the Nagas at the time. There are certainly many mistakes of fact, misunderstanding of customs and institutions; almost everything is very different now; some passages reveal a condescending and a hostile or resentful attitude on the part of the writers. I have left most of these in, for they are part of history and the Nagas themselves, who have a great sense of humour, are not likely to resent them.

The men who wrote these extracts found it difficult to get information. The Naga languages in those days, before English or even Assamese had become popular, were some of the most complex and difficult in the world. Visitors to the Naga Hills nearly always had to go under escort and Dr. J. H. Hutton points out how difficult this made inquiries even in his own case as late as 1923. He and his party could go nowhere, he says, during a tour in what is now called Tuensang 'without armed sentries standing over us like warders guarding a recaptured convict'. Captain W. B. Shakespear, he notes, who commanded his escort and who should at least have had a sort of 'family feeling for ethnology',[1] was sympathetic but took no risks. In addition to this supervision in what was then very wild territory, much time was inevitably taken up with 'transitory matters of politics, supplies or transport arrangements' and on the top of it there was constant bad weather. 'A succession of very rainy days not only dilutes enthusiasm, but very much limits opportunities' for obtaining information.

Moreover, none of the writers represented here were professional anthropologists, though some of them wrote better anthropology than many of the supposedly 'trained' young men of the present day. Most of them were soldiers. Dalton belonged to the Bengal Staff Corps. Johnstone began his career in the 'Bengal Army'. Woodthorpe was commissioned in the Royal Engineers. Godwin-Austen was educated at Sandhurst and commissioned in the old 24th Foot, afterwards the South Wales Borderers, and the same may be said of several others. Mackenzie and Damant were members of the Indian Civil Service and some of the officers of the Topographical Survey were civilians, but the soldiers predominated.

A last and unexpected problem arose in the fact that in those turbulent days precious notes and documents were lost. Many of Dalton's manuscripts were 'lost to him during the mutinies' with the result that his notes on some of the Assam tribes were 'not as full as he should have liked to have made them'. Damant's invaluable Manipur Dictionary and a paper on the Angami Nagas were destroyed by the Nagas in the Kohima stockade. In fact, far from criticizing the nineteenth century men for their defects we should be astonished that, under the circumstan-

[1] For his father, Colonel Shakespear, see Bibliography, original edition, *The Nagas in the Nineteenth Century* (O.U.P., 1969).

ces, they collected so much information and wrote as well as they did.

It has been impossible to avoid references to head-hunting and war for, as H. G. Wells said of the Europe of 1918, war was 'an atmosphere, a habit of life, a social order'. Some of the comments on Naga methods of war by these writers are very severe. But we should remember that in the nineteenth century, when they wrote, war was still comparatively a gentlemanly affair. I doubt whether officers who had had experience of the methods of Commandos or of Resistance Movements in modern Europe would have found anything very astonishing in what some of the Nagas used to do.

I found work on this book fascinating and it would have been possible to spend another two years editing it with appropriate footnotes and comments. It is, I think, the small details which are particularly delightful—General Johnstone's cat carrying off his breakfast at Samagudting; the bathing-drawers presented by Mrs Grimwood to her nine *malis*; Lieutenant Browne-Wood digging up surface coal with a Naga spear, the only implement he had with him. Then there is the delightful incident on Christmas Day, 1844, when Major Butler's surveyor came into camp completely exhausted after a long march. He was, Butler tell us, 'a very abstemious man and was always boasting of the inexpressible delight he experienced in satisfying his thirst from every limpid stream and eating sweet biscuits'. But in view of his condition that day Butler gave him a pint of warm porter whereon he rallied instantly, and with a dish of 'hermetically sealed soup' and a slice of ham soon got over his fatigue, and in later years found a glass of brandy more refreshing than the waters of a stream. Another day we see a party of surveyors buying a large basket of rice for one rupee paid in four-anna pieces, with which the Nagas immediately bought a worn spike of a spear, iron being more valuable to them than silver.

And there was the old lady with a very large goitre whose house Dr Brown approached when he visited her village. 'Standing at her hut-door she seemed enraged at our appearance and kept muttering as we passed. Occasionally she clutched her throat and made a motion of throwing her goitre at us, doubtless cursing volubly the while. We smiled benignly on the hag and passed on.'

The death of Captain Butler's Madrassi cook on tour was a serious loss for, says the narrator, 'a good cook is required to vary the monotony of camp diet by ingenious little culinary arts'. Perhaps the most sensational event in all John Butler's camps was the arrival in the evening of January the 5th, 1873, of a dak runner, staggering under the weight of Dalton's great book on the *Ethnology of Bengal* and the young Captain reading far into the night and eagerly spotting its few mistakes.

I am greatly indebted to Mr N. K. Rustomji for reading the manuscript of this book with his customary thoroughness and care and for his many suggestions, as well as to Dr J. H. Hutton who directed me to many documents about the Nagas which escaped the attention even of the late Mr J. P. Mills in his Bibliography. I owe much to Mr B. S. Kesavan, Mr Sourindranath Roy, Mr J. M. Choudhury, the Librarian of the State Library of Assam and the Librarian of the Anthropological Survey of India. Mr Kesavan and his staff in the National Library in Calcutta gave me every possible assistance while I was preparing this book and their courtesy and friendliness will always remain with me as a very happy incident in my literary endeavours. Mr Chowdhury, most obliging of men, did much to discover for me the books available in Shillong.

Although at no time did I hold an official position in the Naga areas, my knowledge of the Nagas is not confined to books. My first long tour in the Ao and Konyak areas (with a visit to Kohima thrown in) was in June and July 1947, when I had to walk from Nakachari to Mokokchang. At the beginning of 1954 I did a seven weeks' tour on foot in what is now the Tuensang District, and later I paid a number of visits to Nagaland.

Shillong V. E.
2 October 1962

7
COLONEL DALTON CRITICIZED

(a)

(John Butler, *Tour Diary of the Deputy Commissioner, Naga Hills, for the Year 1870–2*, p. 25)

5th January (1873).—We moved Camp today to a spot on the left bank of the Zullo near its source and close below the village of Phunama (one of the group called 'Sopvomah' by the Angamies and 'Mao' by the Manipuries) *en route* we passed through the villages of Jakamah, Viswemah and Khuzamah all the villagers of which thronged out to see us pass by.

In the evening Colonel Thomson's dak brought in Colonel Dalton's work on the Ethnology of Bengal[2] in which I was not a little amused to recognize my old friend 'Aja' Chief of Phusamah (one of the villages belonging to the Sopvomah or Mao group already referred to), figuring as an 'Angami Naga' and I am the more surprised that Dr Brown should have made such a mistake as, if I remember right, he laid considerable stress upon the differences existing between these two Tribes (the Angami and Mao) and in a measure very rightly so for even their languages are very dissimilar; however it appears this is not the only error he seems to have fallen into for Colonel Thomson informs me that the 'Manipuri' represented in the same plate (XIX) is he believes a Sylhetia one Jadub Sing, whose only claim to being a Manipuri rests upon the fact that he has served the Rajah of that State for the last 12 or 13 years, and if this is the case it only shows how particular one ought to be in compiling a work of this kind and I wonder it never struck Colonel Dalton to apply directly to the several officers in charge of Frontier Districts to assist him in the very difficult work he was undertaking.

9 March 1873—Amused myself by reading some of Dalton's work on the Ethnology of Bengal and was much surprised to

[2] Mildred Archer, writing in *Man in India*, Vol. XXVIII, p. 170, says, 'Its arrival must obviously have caused great excitement and like most men when confronted by evidence of excellence in a colleague, Butler was highly critical of its contents.'

find that the letterpress, at all events as far as the Naga Tribes are concerned, is not in my humble opinion worth very much and yet this is the very portion of the book for the accuracy of which he states in his preface that he himself is alone responsible. It seems strange that he should not apparently ever have considered it worth his while to refer to any of the Frontier Officers in Assam, for I notice that although he concludes his preface with a long list of officers to whom he is indebted for their contributions, there is not a single Assam Officer among the list. I should very much like to have Williamson's opinion on the Garo portion of this work, and Bivar's on the Khasiah, with Shadwell's on the Jaintias. Whilst talking of this I must not, however, forget to mention here that Thomson told me this morning that on further inquiry regarding the parentage of the Manipuri figuring on plate XIX he finds that the man really is a Manipuri. On the other hand I must also not omit to say that the two copper figures in plate XXXII are, I think, either Chirus or certainly Komo (Kukies) and not 'representations of the Koch nation' as Colonel Dalton would have us believe—indeed I think I have got a photograph of the man in the upper left hand corner, anyhow I feel pretty confident, I am not mistaken in pronouncing them not to belong to the Koch lot.

(b)

(H. H. Godwin-Austen, 'On the Rude Stone Monuments of Certain Naga Tribes', *J.A.I.*, 1875, Vol. IV, pp. 146–7)

The many Naga tribes vary greatly one with the other, although evidently of one common origin, and the Kutcha Naga is in dress and customs very different from even the Anghami, who adjoins him on the east.

Colonel Dalton, in his beautiful book, *Descriptive Ethnology of Bengal*, in Section 7, page 42, has fallen into error by adopting an artificial separation of the Nagas east and west of the Doyang River, and I trust he will forgive my criticism. This has led to a terrible mixing together of such very different ingredients as the Naga of Asalu, the Arung, and the Anghami, by quoting Major Stewart's (not Steward) really good account in the J.A.S. *Bengal* of the former tribes as the type of all living in his assumed geographical sub-province, while a well marked section of the Naga race, those in the Mikir Hills, the Rengmah Naga, are not alluded to at all. These last are undoubtedly emigrants from Lotha Nagas, east of the Doyang. Summing up at the end of this section—which, it is to be regretted, is all misleading—Colonel Dalton, still taking the Doyang as his boundary, decides that the Naga on the west is allied to the Munipuri (a decidedly mixed race—in truth, no race at all), and the Kukis and Nagas to the east to be 'allied to the Singpho and other pagan tribes further east'.

Now, no Kuki tribe—not even one single village, is to be found to the east of the Doyang, or even so far north as its head waters—i.e. north of the main watershed of the Irrawaddy and Brahmaputra, nor have they any connexion with the far distant Singphos in either language, manners, or customs. The last paragraph of this section is to a certain extent contradictory to the preceding, where the Munipuri and Kuki are supposed to be nearly allied. To a certain extent the population of Munipuri has mixed its blood with members of tribes to the south, but I should say—and I am supported by Colonel McCulloch—was of Naga origin.

The true Kukis have only very recently—about 1840—come up from the southward, and they have only within the memory of the present generation become neighbours of the Naga race on the Burrail range and in North West Munipur. Both sections referring to the Nagas and Kukis have been written without sufficient personal knowledge of the people. One great point of dissimilarity between the Anghami and Arung is in their songs and dances. The really pretty active dances of the Arung village maidens is never seen when in Anghami and Naga villages, and in the latter, singing is little heard, and when so is quite of a different kind. Other distinctions are observable in the form of their houses, in the arms they carry, and dress, particularly of the women, and mode of wearing the hair adopted by the unmarried girls. The Kutcha Naga carries the shortest and lightest of spears of any of the hill people I have seen, and seldom, if ever, a shield.

9

A Philosophy of Nefa (1960)

The Fundamental Problem

Separation and isolation are dangerous theories and strike at the root of national solidarity. Safety lies in union and not in isolation.

—A. V. Thakkar

The problem of the best way of administering so-called 'primitive', 'aboriginal' or 'tribal' populations has been debated for hundreds of years, and those people who even today so unfailingly remind us, whenever there is a proposal for a scientific approach to the subject, that we must not keep them as 'museum specimens', are in fact only intervening in a very old controversy.

It is an interesting controversy, for it is linked up with several allied questions. Is mankind really progressing? Is civilization any good? Is the country better than the town? Is Man better in a state of Nature or of Art? Is the untutored 'savage' happier, more moral, in a word better than the sophisticated and urban product of the modern world? Mahatma Gandhi, inspired to some extent by Ruskin and Tolstoy, set thousands of people thinking about these questions, and it may be worth while taking a brief glance back through history to see what replies have been given in the past.

The Classical Indian Tradition

In the classical Indian literature, the tribes get a very mixed press. The first Aryan settlers in India regarded them with antipathy, characterizing them as devils, man-eaters, black as crows, sprung from the sweat or dung of cows. The *Vishnu Purana* describes them as dwarfish, with flat noses and a skin the colour of a charred stake. The *Mahabharata* classes them with the 'sinful creatures of the earth', akin to Chandalas, ravens and vultures. The poet Bana opens his account of the Sabara army in his *Kadambari* with a procession of fifteen unflattering similes. The Sabaras were like 'all the nights of the dark fortnight rolled into one', 'a crowd of evil deeds come together', 'a caravan of curses of the many hermits dwelling in the Dandaka Forest'. Their leader was 'wet with the blood of buffaloes'. 'Ah!' says Bana,

> the life of these men is full of folly, and their career is blamed by the good. For their one religion is offering human flesh to Durga; their meat is a meal loathed by the good; their *shastra* is the cry of the jackal; their teachers of good and evil are owls; their bosom friends are dogs; their kingdom is in deserted woods; their feast is a drinking-bout; their friends are the bows that work cruel deeds; and arrows, with their heads smeared, like snakes, with poison, are their helpers; their wives are the wives of others taken captive; their dwelling is with savage tigers; their worship of the gods is with the blood of beasts, their sacrifice with flesh, their livelihood by theft; and the very wood wherein they dwell is utterly destroyed root and branch.

On the other hand, there are many passages which refer to the tribal people in friendly terms. A late passage in the *Mahabharata* describes how a Brahmin visits a village of Dasyus and finds them wealthy, truthful and hospitable. Even Bana cannot altogether withhold his admiration for the Sabara Chief. 'Horrible as he was, he yet inspired awe by reason of his natural greatness and his form could not be surpassed.' And he was certainly good to look at. He filled the woods with beauty sombre as dark lotuses, like the waters of Yamuna; he had thick locks curled at the end and hanging on his shoulders. To ward off the heat he had a swarm of bees which flew above him like a peacock-feather parasol. He was surrounded by hounds whose throats were covered with strings of cowries.'

In the *Katha Sarit Sagara*, the great anthology of tales current in India in the eleventh century, we find a still kindlier and almost romantic approach. It is true that some of the Sabaras, Bhillas and Pulindas are described as brigands and cattle-lifters, practising human sacrifice. Yet they are attractive in their simplicity and have many virtues. Adorned with peacock's feathers and elephant's teeth, clothed in tiger-skins and living on the flesh of deer, they are famous for their dances and have sufficient social sense to recognize the institution of kingship. There is a Saora king who is merciful and intelligent; he goes to find pearls on the heads of elephants and on the way meets an exquisite maiden riding on a lion. Since she is 'like the digit of the moon resting in the lap of an autumn cloud', he at once thinks of his friend, Vasudatta, goes to fetch him, takes him to the Himalayas, and arranges his marriage with her. Here we have an important Hindu of good family, son of a rich merchant, cherishing the friendship of a tribal Chief. Indeed he considers that he has attained all that his heart could wish 'in having Manovati for a wife and the Sabara prince for a friend.'

The King of Vatsa also owes much to a Sabara who came from the mountains of the sunrise and guides him to find his wife. Vishnudatta describes another tribesman as performing an act of 'surprising courage, characteristic of men of mighty mind'.

And Mrigankadatta says to the tribal King Mayavatu, 'When the Creator made you here, he infused into your composition qualities borrowed from your surroundings, the firmness of the Vindhya hills, the courage of the tigers, and the warm attachment to friends of the forest lotuses.'

The most famous reference to the tribes in Indian antiquity is in Valmiki's *Ramayana*, which describes how Rama and Lakshmana, in the course of their search for Sita, came to the banks of a lake or river, Pampa, lying to the west of 'Rishyamukha's wood-crowned height', where an aged ascetic Sabari, belonging to the famous tribe of eastern India, had made her home. Knowing that her visitors were on the way, Sabari collected the fruits for which the place was famous and offered them to Rama for his comfort. She showed him the hermitage saying, 'See the charming great forest abounding in flowers and fruit, resembling a bank of clouds, filled with all sorts of deer and birds; this is famed on earth as Matanga's forest.' Rama then gave her permission to depart from this world, and in the presence of the two brothers, she went into a fire and ascended into the heavens, while all the sky was lighted by her glory.

There is, of course, no idea as yet of 'doing anything' for the forest people—rather it is they who are doing things for their rulers—but it is most significant to find, even so long ago, an attitude towards them which anticipates the friendliness and respect which has come to fruition in modern times. And in the figure of Sabari there is a symbol of the contribution that the tribes can and will make to the life of India.

The Pastoral Tradition

Turning now to the Western world, we must first note what is called the pastoral tradition, which has always idealized the peasant and his simple life. It derived its ideas from the classical poets., Horace, Virgil and Hesiod, and even from such Latin prose writers as Cato and Columella, who wrote enthusiastically in praise of agriculture and farming. The life admired by these authors was not altogether 'primitive'; it had its elements of comfort and decorum; but it was simple, obscure and self-contained, in sharp contrast to the mercenary and unhealthy life of the towns. Many English poets extolled it in some such terms as those used by Cowley in a translation of one of the Horatian Odes:

> Happy the Man whom bounteous Gods allow
> With his own hands Paternal grounds to plough!
> Like the first Golden Mortals happy he
> From Business and the cares of Money free!
> From all the cheats of law he lives secure,
> Nor does th' affronts of Palaces endure.

You will, of course, always find an enthusiasm for agriculture among people who have never handled a spade.

In the Middle Ages, at least in Europe, there was no problem of what to do for the peasant, still less for the tribesman. This came later with the discovery of the New World, with its exciting populations of primitive people, which brought the problem before the whole of Europe. Opinion, then as now, was divided. Some, of whom Montaigne is an example, were in favour of leaving them alone. He considered that the inhabitants of the 'unpolluted and harmless world' of the hills and forests were naturally virtuous as compared to civilized man. In his essay, *Of Cannibals*, he declares that the American Indians are only wild in the sense that wild flowers are wild, but that in them are 'the true and most profitable virtues and natural properties most lively and vigorous.' Civilization has 'bastardized' these virtues, 'applying them to the pleasures of our corrupted taste'. He regrets that Plato did not live to see the discovery of primitive America, for he might then have given a better picture of the Golden Age.

Many other writers took the same view. Spenser has a gentle noble tribesman in *The Faerie Queene*; Drayton enthuses over the reports from America; Beaumont and Fletcher write of 'Sunburnt Indians, that know no other wealth but Peace and Pleasure'. And many deplored the corrupting influence of the first colonists and planters; Fuller spoke of Christian savages who went to convert heathen savages.

Other reporters, however, took a less optimistic view. We find the Indians spoken of as 'human beasts'; they are 'perfidious, inhuman, all savage'; Sandys says that the Indians, like the Cyclops, are 'unsociable amongst themselves and inhuman to strangers'.

Shakespeare on the Tribes

It may surprise many readers to find Shakespeare quoted as having views on tribal affairs, yet in *The Tempest* he does make a serious contribution to what was then an urgent problem, the relations of the contemporary colonist with the aboriginal peoples of the countries in which he settled.

In his play, Caliban (whose name has been derived from Carib, an aboriginal of the New World, and cannibal) stands for the Indian, and Prospero for the colonist or planter, and the conflict between them reflects the current controversies about the character and status of primitive man.

Caliban, who is of a 'vile race', the product of witchcraft, 'a freckled whelp hag-born', scarcely human in appearance, 'as disproportioned in his manners as in his shape', is the original owner of the island on which Prospero and his daughter have been marooned. His own description of the process by which he loses his rights makes rather uncomfortable reading.

> This island's mine, by Sycorax my mother,
> Which thou tak'st from me. When thou cam'st first,
> Thou strok'st me, and made much of me; would'st give me
> Water with berries in it; and teach me how
> To name the bigger light and how the less,

That burn by day and night: and then I loved thee,
And showed thee all the qualities o' the isle,
The fresh springs, brine-pits, barren place and fertile:
Cursed be I that did so!

Rebecca West has suggested that Prospero's 'treatment of the indigenous population, even though it numbered only one, would be hard to justify, according to the theory of natural law, for one whose grievance against fate lay in the infringement of a title recognized by that theory. His excuse for introducing the colour bar and peonage is not congruous with his special wisdom.' Yet in taking over tribal territory, he does not neglect some measures of social uplift and education, and in this his daughter Miranda is a keen and efficient assistant. Even though they reduce Caliban to a mere slave and woodcutter, she 'pities' him, takes pains to make him speak, teaches him each hour one thing or another.

This is not altogether successful. As Frank Kermode has recently pointed out, 'Caliban's education was not only useless, but harmful. He can only abuse the gift of speech; and by cultivating him Prospero brings forth in him 'the briers and darnell of appetites'—lust for Miranda, discontent at his inferior position, ambition, intemperance of all kinds, including a disposition to enslave himself to the bottle of Stephano.' Such is, of course, the very common result, even today, of a too rapid acculturation.

Not only has Caliban been wronged, but he himself is not wholly without virtue; he has an ear for music and, like tribal people elsewhere, he has poetry at command, and for a moment speaks words of sublime beauty. And the representatives of civilization who follow Prospero to the island do him nothing but harm. Stephano and Trinculo are drunken buffoons; Antonio is a malicious degenerate; the life of Alonso is deeply stained with guilt. It is under the inspiration of these representatives of the modern world that Caliban takes to drink and turns treacherously upon his master. It is surely not without significance that Shakespeare shows us this primitive man becoming a 'footlicker' of a drunken butler.

Shakespeare's view, then, seems to be that, although primitive man is not much good, contact with civilization can only make him worse.

Adam and Eve

Throughout the seventeenth century, however, this realistic attitude was obscured by a widespread sentiment in favour of the innocent shepherd, the happy husbandman, the Hortulan Saint. Under the stress of the Civil War and the prevailing Puritanism of the Roundhead movement, 'Nature' and the country life became more and more idealized; it was here alone that man could commune with God; it was here that the purest virtues could be practised. The most famous of the writers who infused the classical ideal of the Golden Age with a mystical enthusiasm was the Polish poet Sarbiewski, to whom the Biblical motif of the *hortus conclusus* or Earthly Paradise was a living reality. He seems to have influenced the Welsh Vaughan and the English Marvell, especially in the latter's garden-poems.

Along with this belief in the innocent beauty of the uncorrupt life of Nature went the theological problem of Adam and Eve. Today it may be a little difficult for us to take this famous couple seriously, but in the seventeenth century they were quite as real as any contemporary and far more cultured than Cromwell's Roundheads. The modern world, somewhat confused by the conflicting theories of the evolutionists, is clear on at least one point; that the first men were not nearly as good as we are. They were either tarsioid dwarfs, with big wondering eyes, or uncouth shaggy anthropoids; comic strips depict primitive man dragging his Eve about by the hair and knocking her over the head with a club for failing to clean the cave out properly. Milton saw things very differently. The first couple were 'of noble shape, erect and tall, godlike erect'. With 'native honour clad, in naked majesty', they seemed lords of all:

> For contemplation he and valour formed,
> For softness she and sweet attractive grace.

It is true that, like the Boris and Daflas, they had plenty of hair: Adam's 'hyacinthine locks' hung clustering to his shoulders, and as for Eve—

> She as a veil down to the slender waist
> Her unadorned golden tresses wore
> Dishevelled, but in wanton ringlets waved
> As the vine curls her tendrils.

They were a lovely pair; 'truth, wisdom, sanctitude' inspired them; 'simplicity and spotless innocence' was their's,

> Adam the goodliest man of men since born
> His sons, the fairest of her daughters Eve.

Adam and Eve in fact were created perfect—Aristotle is but the ruins of an Adam. The course of history was commonly supposed to have been steadily downhill, and civilization was a long corruption of what had originally been faultless. This led logically to Rousseau's back-to-nature movement in the following century.

Primitivism

The result of this was the emergence of an attitude to life which has been called primitivism and has been studied in great detail by a number of American scholars. Lovejoy, Boas and Margaret Fitzgerald. This has been divided into cultural primitivism, which regards modern 'uncivilized' societies as being, in all the fundamental values of life, better than civilized populations, and chronological primitivism, which holds that the earlier, pre-civilized periods of human life were the happiest and best. Adam and Eve were better and happier, partly because they were earlier in time, partly because they lived beyond the Inner Line that circled Eden.

Seventeenth century primitivism led to an increased interest in primitive peoples, and R. W. Frantz, in an important study of the travellers of the period, has pointed out that 'certain voyagers discovered, or thought they discovered, traces of a universal and fixed morality and the prevalence of three cardinal virtues—piety, benevolence and self-control—which seemed to be fundamental to all peoples, whether semi-civilized or totally savage.' The idealist was easily able to persuade himself that 'the good and noble life was to be lived not in towns and cities, but in the solitude of the American forests or the South Sea Isles'.

An interesting result of this was that, unlike later Imperialists who justified themselves as having to bear the white man's burden of native superstition and ignorance, the first colonists tried to encourage immigration to the tribal areas by painting their inhabitants in glowing colours. Thus when Walter Hammond wrote his pamphlets on Madagascar, he called the first of them (published in 1640) 'A Paradox, proving that the Inhabitants of the Isle called Madagascar, or St Laurence, are the Happiest People in the World'. Who then would not jump at the chance of going to live among them?

Primitives were further divided into 'hard' and 'soft'. In antiquity, says A. O. Lovejoy in his *Documentary History of Primitivism*, 'the men of the Golden Age under the Saturnian dispensation were soft primitives, and the imaginary Hyperboreans were usually soft savages; on the other hand, the noble savages par excellence, the Scythians, and the Getae, and later on the Germans, were rude, hardy fellows to whom "Nature" was no gentle or indulgent mother; they were extolled for the fewness of their desires and their consequent indifference to the luxuries and even the comforts of civilized life.' In more recent times, the soft, sensuous and elegant primitives of Tahiti or Bali have excited the admiration of artists and poets, while the virile hardy primitives of, let us say, the North-East Frontier of India have won the respect of soldiers.

Even at this comparatively early period, there is evident, in the attraction felt for the 'soft' primitives, a delight in the erotic freedom, the lack of inhibitions and the sexual innocence supposed to have been enjoyed by man before he was corrupted by modern society and its rules. It is significant that the expression 'the Noble Savage' did not originate, as is so often thought, with Rousseau, but with the astonishing Mrs Aphra Behn, that ardent missionary of free love, whose poems, plays and stories constantly compare the advantages of the simple rural life with the frustrations of sophistication, and look back to fulfilment,

> In that blest Golden Age, when Man was young,
> When the whole Race was vigorous and strong;
> When Nature did her wondrous dictates give,
> And taught the Noble Savage how to live . . .
> When every sense to innocent delight
> Th' agreeing elements unforced invite.

The hero of Mrs Behn's *Oroonoko*, though a 'native' of Surinam, is a great gentleman who found happiness by refusing to be 'civilized'. Mrs Behn was no anthropologist and she assumed, of course quite wrongly, that primitive man had no need for external government (which only exists to curb the greed and ambition of educated persons) and enjoyed all the raptures of free love.

Other poets of this century who exalted the primitive were Thomas Heyrick, whose poem, *The Submarine Voyage*, describes the people of the South Sea Islands as 'happy in ignorance' and 'strangers to care', and Waller who, in his *Battle of the Summer Islands*, draws an idyllic picture of the inhabitants of plantain-shaded atolls of sensuous beauty and ease. And the great Dryden himself, in a famous couplet, spoke of the happy days,

> Ere the base laws of servitude began,
> When wild in woods the noble savage ran.

The last thing that the poets and travellers of this period wanted was to 'improve' or 'uplift' these aboriginals; what they desired was to go and share their lot. There was no question of keeping them in a museum; they wanted to enjoy their earthly paradise.

In the following century, the voyages of Captain Cook and other explorers provided factual support for these sentiments. According to Captain Cook, the 'savages' of Australia may indeed appear to be the most wretched people upon earth, but in reality 'they are far more happy than we Europeans, being wholly unacquainted not only with the superfluous but with the necessary conveniences so much sought after in Europe; they are happy in not knowing the use of them.' And visits to Tahiti and the Friendly Islands confirmed this picture of the Noble Savage.

This fitted very conveniently into the more advanced thinking of certain philosophers and revolutionaries, especially in France. The doctrine of original sin, it was supposed, was discredited by what Bougainville found in the Pacific. The child is happier and better than the man. The existing state of modern society appears decadent before the peaceful and truthful civilization of the islanders; it must therefore be overthrown. Christopher Lloyd epitomizes the views of Diderot, whose article on 'Savages' was so subversive that it was omitted from the Paris edition of the French Encyclopedia. In a remarkable dialogue, which he pretended was a supplement to Bougainville's Tahiti journal, Diderot 'accused his countrymen of acting the part of the serpent in this new Eden. He makes an old islander beg him to go away and leave the natives in peace. Otherwise such men as he will return with a cross in one hand and a gun in the other to enslave their bodies and poison their minds. For civilization, according to Diderot, was indeed a kind of poison injected into the mind of natural man, thereby creating a sort of war within ourselves which lasts all our lives. Natural man is at odds with artificial man, and the best description of the unhappy product was, in the words of his friend Buffon, *Homo Duplex*.'

A similar view was expressed by the fur-merchant, D. W. Harmon, who spent sixteen years among the Canadian Indians in the early years of the nineteenth century.

I very much question,' he said, 'whether they have improved in their character or condition, by their acquaintance with civilized people. In their savage state, they were contented with the mere necessaries of life, which they could procure with considerable ease; but now they have many artificial wants, created by the luxuries which we have introduced among them; and as they find it difficult to obtain these luxuries, they have become, to a degree, discontented with their condition, and practise fraud in their dealings. A half-civilized Indian is more savage than one in his original state. The latter has some sense of honour, while the former has none. I have always experienced the greatest hospitality and kindness among those Indians, who have had the least intercourse with white people. They readily discover and adopt our evil practices; but they are not as quick to discern, and as ready to follow the few good examples, which we set before them.

This attitude was not shared by everyone. Already in the eighteenth century Dr Samuel Johnson had declared it nonsense. Boswell, who after all had personally visited Rousseau, was all for the Noble Savage. Johnson was not. 'Don't cant in defence of savages,' he exclaimed, and when Boswell attempted to argue for the superior happiness of the simple life, he retorted, 'Sir, there can be nothing more false. The savages have no bodily advantages beyond those of civilized men. They have not better health; and as to care or mental uneasiness, they are not above it, but below it, like bears.' He thought that the American Indians had no affection; had he been born one, he must have died early, for his eyes would not have served him to get food. One evening he poured scorn on those who preferred living among savages. 'Now what a wretch that must be, who is content with such conversation as can be had among savages!'

And now came the new European Imperialism and with it a great expansion of the missionary movement. Colonists and missionaries alike had to justify their existence by showing how necessary they were to the heathen world. Henceforth primitive man was painted in the darkest terms. Even in Java, as Bishop Heber suggested, though every prospect pleased, man was vile, blind, benighted.

Can we whose souls are lighted
With wisdom from on high,
Can we to men benighted
The lamp of life deny?

Darwin, who visited Tierra del Fuego in the course of the epoch-making voyage of H.M.S. *Beagle*, said that the difference between the Fuegian 'barbarian' and civilized man was greater than that between a wild and a domesticated animal, and he found it hard to see a 'fellow creature' in him.

We have come a long way from Cook and Hawkeworth, from Boswell, Rousseau and Diderot. To them primitive man was not fallen, he was *better* than modern man; we had much to learn from him; and the best thing we could do for him was to leave him alone. To the missionary and the colonist, however, primitive man seemed to exemplify the ancient doctrine of original sin, and it was above all necessary that he should be saved.

The Policy of Charles Dickens

Charles Dickens, who strongly disapproved of the missionary movement, considering it more important to reform society in unregenerate England than to send preachers to foreign parts, had a policy of his own. In a little-known 'reprinted piece', he declares that he has not the least belief in the Noble Savage, but considers him a prodigious nuisance. 'Howling, whistling, clucking, stamping, jumping, tearing', he is something 'highly desirable to be civilized off the face of the earth'.

Dickens draws on his enormous vocabulary and all his powers of invention to heap scorn on the unfortunate savage. He is 'cruel, false, thievish, murderous; addicted more or less to grease, entrails, and beastly customs'; he is a 'conceited, tiresome, blood-thirsty, monotonous humbug'. He makes fun of the Zulu Kaffirs who were then being exhibited in London; they are, he admits, rather picturesque, but he cannot resist making fun of their methods of war, their marriage customs, their attitude to disease, their system of Chiefs. He parodies everything recorded about them in a manner that is itself far more savage than the inoffensive Zulus who were the objects of his contempt.

Another tribe which excited Dickens' scorn was the Ojibbeway Indian. Catlin had written 'a picturesque and glowing book' about them, which the great man considered nonsense. 'With his party of Indians squatting and spitting on the table before him, or dancing their miserable jigs after their own dreary manner, he called, in all good faith, upon his civilized audience to take notice of their symmetry and grace, their perfect limbs, and the exquisite expression of their pantomime; and his civilized audience, in all good faith, complied and admired.' Yet as mere animals, they were 'wretched creatures, very low in the scale and very poorly formed.'

What irritated Dickens was not so much the savage himself, but the sentimentalizing over him—the 'whimpering over him with maudlin admiration, and the affecting to regret him, and the drawing of any comparison of advantage between the blemishes of civilization and the tenor of his swinish life'. It is extraordinary, he says again, 'how some people will talk about him, as they talk about the good old times; how they will regret his disappearance'.

Dickens concludes:

> My position is, that if we have anything to learn from the Noble Savage, it is what to avoid. His virtues are a fable; his happiness is a delusion; his nobility, nonsense. We have no greater justification for being cruel to the miserable object than for being cruel to a William Shakespeare or an Isaac Newton; but he passes away before an immeasurably better and higher power than ever ran wild in any earthly woods, and the world will be all the better when his place knows him no more.

The result of this sort of propaganda, which was fairly common right up to modern times, was to give the peoples of the West a thoroughly low opinion not only of the tribes but even of Indian and African culture in general. When Swami Vivekananda visited America at the end of the last century he was amazed to find the misconceptions about Indian civilization that were current in spite of the labours of such European Orientalists as Max Müller and Sir William Jones. Later, the work of Miss Mayo encouraged those who wanted to believe that subject nations were not, and could never be, fit to govern themselves.

The Pendulum Swings Back

Yet the pendulum swung back again, and the poets and artists regained the influence that they had for a time lost to the Church. Picasso discovered African sculpture. Gauguin went to Tahiti. A score of poets exalted the simple life of nature. Ruskin and William Morris stressed the value of manual labour and praised the art of unsophisticated people. The enormous authority of Tolstoy provided an atmosphere in which respect for the 'primitive' world could flourish. Matthew Arnold expressed what many felt even in the Victorian Age and what many probably still feel, about the impact of civilization on simple, primitive folk.

O born in days when wits were fresh and clear,
  And life ran gaily as the sparkling Thames;
    Before this strange disease of modern life,
  With its sick hurry, its divided aims,
    Its heads o'ertax'd, its palsied hearts, was rife—
      Fly hence, our contact fear!
  Still fly, plunge deeper in the bowering wood!
    Averse, as Dido did with gesture stern
    From her false friend's approach in Hades turn,
  Wave us away, and keep thy solitude!

But fly our paths, our feverish contact fly!
  For strong the infection of our mental strife,
    Which, though it gives no bliss, yet spoils for rest;
  And we should win thee from thy own fair life,
    Like us distracted, and like us unblest.
      Soon, soon thy cheer would die,
  Thy hopes grow timorous, and unfix'd thy powers,
    And thy clear aims be cross and shifting made;
    And then thy glad perennial youth would fade,
  Fade, and grow old at last, and die like ours.

Yet this escapist attitude could not be a real solution. The general attitude to primitive populations continued to be confused and inspired by largely sentimental motives. And then at the turn of the century, scientific anthropology began to come into its own. During the past five decades, the anthropologists have done a great deal to interpret what had at first seemed esoteric or merely curious; they showed that 'primitive' life had a meaning, that its various aspects were co-ordinated and each was important for the whole picture: there was a sort of architectural design in it. They did a great deal to change the attitudes, alike of sentiment or scorn, taken towards the 'savage'; even missionaries, of the more intellectually respectable communions, took up the study of anthropology, with profit to themselves and their people.

Applied anthropology is of comparatively recent growth, but today there are few tribal areas in the world where professional anthropologists are not employed to advise their governments. They have stressed the importance of tribal systems of jurisprudence, the respect due to social and religious institutions, the need of combining sociological with agronomic studies in any attempt to improve tribal methods of cultivation. They have helped us to understand the difficulties of social change expressed, for example, in the extraordinary movements that from time to time sweep across tribal society, such as the Hauhau cult of the Maoris, the Pa Chin Hap of the Burmese Chins, the Cargo cults of New Guinea and even the Mau Mau, and to realize, as Dr Raymond Firth says, that these must not be regarded as

> mere delusion, or as the product of 'political' agitation, or as a simple reversion to savagery and atavistic thinking, but as phenomena manifesting strain in adaptation. They are attempts at a solution, albeit an ineffective and misjudged one, to the grave difficulties of making old and new institutions, claims and values meet in a harmonious way.

The new anthropology, based on observation and recorded fact, has helped the world to take a more balanced view of the entire problem.

And yet, especially since the Second World War, changed circumstances have raised new problems and made them more difficult to solve. In the popular Science Fiction of the last two decades, the value of a highly mechanized, and over-administered, civilization has often been questioned. In *Brave New World*, which is in effect an important anthropological study of the conflict between civilization and primitivism, Aldous Huxley examines the reactions of the 'Savage' taken from his Reservation into the world of tomorrow. He is 'poisoned' by it and ends by committing suicide.

To George Orwell, the 'proles' of 1984 were at least happier, because they were more independent than the privileged members of the Party. In *The Bright Phoenix*, Harold Mead finds the 'barbarians' living in the jungles better and happier than the regimented but well-provided citizens of the State of the Human Spirit.

The invention of the hydrogen bomb, the establishment over a large part of the earth of totalitarian governments, the ever-increasing power of the bureaucracy in the most democratic nations has made people of today rethink their whole attitude to civilization and progress.

It is impossible to consider the fundamental problem of the tribal people without bearing in mind the context of contemporary society. Is it worthwhile making them part of a way of life whose standards we ourselves are beginning to doubt?

But after all perhaps our doubts are wrong. For the bombs, the secret police, the tortures in hidden prison cells, the taxation, the corruptions, the intrigues are not the last word about the modern world. There is a great fund of goodness; there are executions, but there is also mercy; there are countries curtained off with iron, but there are other lands where the winds of thought blow freely and men can speak their minds. There is art, beauty, comfort, health, and the ideal of freedom from want and fear.

The difference in our outlook on the future of the tribal people today is this. Formerly, the artists and poets said: 'Because these people are noble and good, there is no need to do anything for them.' The reformers, the uplifters, the clergy said: 'Because these people are ignoble, superstitious and miserable, we must do something for them.'

We say:

It is just because we believe them to be noble and good that we want to do all we can for them. We do not do this because we pity them, we do it because we respect them. We do it because we believe that we can bring them the best things of our world without destroying the nobility and the goodness of their's, and that one day in their turn they will help us.

The Problem in Modern India

When we turn to modern India we find the same fundamental problem and people, according to their temperament and upbringing, still asking much the same questions.

Is there not a case for the view that by and large the tribal people will probably be happier if they are left alone, or at least very largely alone, in the grandeur and freedom of their hills? They lack many of the amenities of life, but on the other hand they are free: no one interferes with them; they are able to live according to their own religion and traditions. Voltaire's Candide, after exploring all the civilizations of his contemporary world, came to the final conclusion that there was no greater happiness than in cultivating one's own garden. Why not let them do so?

On the other hand, it is argued, would it not be better to 'civilize' them as rapidly as possible? Their life is nasty, brutish and short; their art is crude, their religion a medley of superstitions; they are dirty and diseased. The early explorers and administrators tumbled over one another in their use of uncomplimentary adjectives to describe the people of NEFA. The Singphos are described as 'a rude treacherous people', the Khamptis as 'a discontented, restless, intriguing tribe', the Nagas as 'a very uncivilized race with dark complexions and hideously wild and ugly visages'; the Abors are 'as void of delicacy as they are of cleanliness'. As Dickens urged, surely the only thing to do is to civilize them off the face of the earth.

Few of us today would adopt either of these view in their entirety, certainly not if they are expressed in so crude a form. Yet the two policies have both been advocated, and followed, in India during the past fifty years.

The Policy of 'Leave Them Alone'

The British Government inclined, on the whole, to leave the tribesmen alone, partly because the task of administration, especially in the wild border areas, was difficult and unrewarding, partly from a desire to quarantine the tribes from possible political infection, and partly because a number of officers sincerely held the view that the people were better and happier as they were.

This policy is commonly attributed to the influence of the anthropologists who are invariably accused, whenever the subject is discussed, of wanting to keep the tribal people in zoos or museums for their own purposes. In the Legislative Assembly, during a debate on the Excluded Areas in February 1936, a number of speakers attacked anthropologists as wishing to keep the primitive people of India 'uncivilized' and 'in a state of barbarism' in order to add 'to their blessed stock of scientific knowledge'. It has always puzzled me how this curious idea arose. It is true that I myself, writing many years ago when India was under British rule, advocated a policy of *temporary* isolation for certain small tribes, but this was not to keep them as they were, but because at that time the only contacts they had with the outside world were debasing contacts, leading to economic exploitation and cultural destruction. Nothing positive was being done for their welfare; national workers were not admitted into their hills; but merchants, money-lenders, landlords and liquor-vendors were working havoc with their economy and missionaries were destroying their art, their dances, their weaving and their whole culture.

But a policy advocated to meet a set of special circumstances does not hold when those circumstances have changed, and neither I nor any other anthropologist would dream of suggesting such a policy since Independence. I agree entirely with Dr B. S. Guha who wrote in 1951:

> Complete isolation has never led to progress and advancement, but always to stagnation and death whether we look to lower animals or human beings.
>
> On the other hand, the history of human society shows that civilization everywhere has been built by the contact and intercourse of peoples, which has been the chief motivating power behind progress. There are innumerable instances of the borrowing of cultural traits by peoples of different countries, such as articles of food, use of metals, domesticated animals, methods of agriculture, spread of the alphabet. So long as the borrowing has been natural and in harmony with the cultural setting and the psychological make-up of the people, it has been entirely beneficial and even added to the richness of their culture.

As I have shown in the preceding pages, it is the literary men, the artists, the poets, the philosophers who have wanted to keep the tribal people as they were: the artist Gauguin has probably had more influence on the modern attitude to the 'primitive' than all the anthropologists put together. In any case, the scientists are just not interested in that sort of thing. They are more concerned with developing than with static societies, with culture-change rather than with culture 'as it is', and the blessed stock of scientific knowledge is thus more likely to be augmented when the doors of the zoo are thrown open than when they are kept closed. But since this appears to worry people, let us briefly consider what is wrong with the policy of isolation.

It is exposed to at least three important criticisms. In the first place it has rarely been implemented in practice. There are some twenty million tribal people in India, and before Independence little was done for them. At the same time, they were not in actual fact left alone. As I have said, they were exploited by landlords and zamindars, robbed by money-lenders, cheated by merchants, and their culture was largely destroyed by foreign missionaries.

Secondly, the belief in the happy care-free Noble Savage is a myth, except perhaps in the South Seas long ago. In NEFA at least the people had not enough food; they suffered from abominable diseases; they died young; they were heavily burdened with anxiety; their life was distracted by war, kidnapping, slavery and cruel punishments. They were not even free; weaker tribes had to pay tribute to the strong; rich and powerful Chiefs grew richer on the labour of hundreds of serfs; freedom of movement was severely restricted by inter-village conflict.

And thirdly, while isolation was possible in the last century, it is impossible today. Modern industry is transforming the whole world; the humanitarian ideals of a welfare state no longer permit the neglect of any section of the population; political necessities forbid the existence of any administrative vacuum on the international frontier; tribal leaders themselves demand greater opportunities. And no one (least of all the scientist) wants to keep the tribal people as museum specimens for the benefit of science.

The NEFA Administration has been accused of isolating the

hill people from the people of the plains, the most curious charge being that they are doing this by stressing the national language in schools.

This, of course, is nonsense. The Administration is not isolating the tribal people at all. Indeed, if it is to be criticised, it might rather be on the ground that it is brining them a little too quickly into the main stream of modern life. It is pressing forward everywhere with roads which will make the plains easier of access; it is encouraging both the national language and Assamese to help the tribesmen to communicate more readily with the outside world; it takes schoolboys on tours round India and sends parties regularly to New Delhi on great occasions; it is awarding stipends to its outstanding boys and girls to study in various parts of India; its officers are penetrating into the wildest regions with the message that beyond the hills there is a friendly world with a desire to help and serve.

But the NEFA Administration believes that advance in these long-neglected areas must be on scientific lines. When a man breaks a long fast, he is not immediately given a full meal; he takes a sip of orange-juice. Otherwise he may fall seriously ill. To learn from history, to follow the universally accepted principles of sociological science, to dig firm foundations is not to delay progress; it ensures that *real* progress will be made.

The Policy of Detribalization

In sharp contrast to the first policy is a second one of assimilation or detribalization. This has now become popular and Christian missionaries, social reformers and village uplifters are following it, sometimes on a large and enthusiastic scale. For this too there is something to be said. The Christian missionaries have produced a number of educated tribesmen who are proving of great value to the country, and not least to the NEFA administration. Assimilation into Hindu society has sometimes led to a better way of living and to economic advance.

In general, the supporters of this policy take a rather poor view of tribal life: 'animism' should be replaced by the purer ideals of Christianity or Hinduism; the social organization, the 'vices', the 'superstitions' should go; tribal dress is a mark of inferiority and should be replaced by shorts and shirts, blouses and frocks. You cannot make an omelette without breaking eggs, and the continued existence of the tribes as tribes is regarded as of less importance than the march of civilization.

Detribalization is a possible solution of the future of India's tribesmen. It is simple and easy, and it sometimes works. It has, however, serious disadvantages. Its type of progress is by a break with the past, not by an evolution from it. It tends to make the tribesman ashamed of his own culture and religion and so creates that inferiority complex which is a political as well as a social danger. Although it favours a few gifted individuals, who are able to assimilate the new way of life, it generally deprives the mass of the people of their standards and values without putting anything comparable in their place. All over the world it has been noted that the break-up of tribal society leads to a loss of the tribal virtues and a rapid acquisition of the vices of civilization.

The weakening of tribal solidarity and of the folk-legal sanctions deprives the younger generation of their moorings and sets them adrift in an unfamiliar world. All too often, the arts and crafts, the music and dancing, the former self-reliance and independence, the corporate discipline disappear. At the same time, throughout tribal India there is a tendency towards the transformation of tribes into castes, and these 'castes' are usually at the bottom of the social scale. In areas where free commercial penetration has been permitted, there has been much economic exploitation, inevitable among a people who but yesterday learnt the use of money and who are simple and trusting.

A detailed account of the dangers of this line of approach has been given in an anonymous memorandum on

'The Impact of Modern Civilization on the Tribal Peoples of Madhya Pradesh', with special reference to the situation in Bastar, a wild tract of country, largely inhabited by tribal populations, which presents many parallels to NEFA. From this I take the following extracts:

On contact with their more advanced neighbours, whether through educational institutions of a secular as well as religious character, such as those of the Missions, or through contact with them in work, such as in the mines, it is a generally observed fact that the result is that the virtues of truth and honesty are lost first. It would seem therefore that the break-up of tribal society inevitably leads to a loss of the tribal virtues and a rapid assimilation of the vices of civilization.

This is due to the weakening of tribal solidarity and of the folk-legal sanctions. The man who has gone away to the mines, or the youth taken from his community and put into a school, considers himself free of, and, indeed, superior to the laws, regulations and customs of his 'backward' parents and relations, and needs little inducement to adopt the vices he sees being practised in the urban civilization into which he has been introduced but which, had he remained with his own people, he would have scorned.

Not only has contact with a higher civilization this effect in the moral realm, but it is equally disastrous in that of craftsmanship. At a time when soil erosion and declining fertility of the soil is bound to become an ever-increasing cause of anxiety, the developing of cottage industries, as a secondary source of livelihood, becomes increasingly important.

But at this actual juncture, the very existence of the surviving folk-arts and industries is threatened. At Jagdalpur, one may see the tribal people in the bazaar buying metal and other articles, brought in large quantities by merchants, and which were made in Raipur or even further afield.

How great is this exploitation by commercial interests of the tribal people may be seen when it is realized that they will walk anything up to forty miles to Jagdalpur or Kondagaon[1] to sell in the bazaar a few eggs, mushrooms or other products for a total value of one or two rupees. When they have acquired this money, representing the whole stock of the profit of their husbandry, they will then spend it on some article which formerly they would have made for themselves.

Therefore commercial penetration of these regions, which is going forward at an ever-increasing rate as roads are developed, is threatening to extinguish, on the one hand, folk-crafts and, on the other hand, draining the region of what little money it may have.

In the immediate neighbourhood of Kondagaon there are villages occupied by tribal people who are now virtually in process of detribalization. One of the results of this process is that, while it is the declared policy of the Government to abolish casteism, casteism is here in the making. Such tribal people have worked out a caste relationship the one with the other, and all with the structure of the surrounding Hindu population, the result of which is that each one forms a caste below the other, and all below the lowest neighbouring Hindu castes.

To see this in active operation throws light upon how caste, in many cases, may have arisen in the past, as a result of similar clashes of culture and races, but, other than a matter of observation of great academic interest, it is an undesirable development. For it would mean

[1] Jagdalpur is the chief town of Bastar, and Kondagaon, in the heart of the Muria country, is a sub-divisional headquarters.

that as all these tribal peoples become absorbed by their neighbours, they would form lowly castes beneath them, thus perpetuating not only a system which the Government desires to abolish, but a form of helotism and exploitation of the tribal peoples which is contrary to universal ethical standards. This fact alone would suggest the desirability of avoiding the absorption of the tribal peoples and the destruction of their own distinctive civilization.

Under these circumstances the tribal peoples, whether as individuals drifting into the surrounding populations, or as deculturized tribes, are destined to be exploited by the more advanced populations if the tribal societies are broken up and if, in addition, an adequate measure of protection for them is not afforded by the Government.

Therefore cultural penetration, leading to deculturizing of the tribes, is a menace of a very serious order to the well-being of these peoples.

History is full of warnings of this kind and we will make a serious mistake if we lightly ignore the findings (which so far as I know are almost unanimous) of scientists who have approached the problem without bias and with the sole aim of achieving the best and happiest way of life for the people whom their studies have taught them to respect.

The fundamental point is that tribal society, and even the tribal physique, has been adapted through hundreds of years to a special kind of life in a special environment, and that there is grave danger in upsetting too rapidly the harmony between the two.

For example, Dr Buchi, the Swiss biologist, points out that the pygmy Onges of Little Andaman are perfectly adapted to the tropical sun and the dense forests of their environment. They do not represent an 'old and primitive form'; physically they are not at the beginning but at the end of a specialization. Moreover, their type is not the product of a planless evolution; it is one marvellously adjusted to the world they live in.

In this high specialization, however, lies also a great danger. The adaptation is not only physical, it is a complete biological adaptation to the given circumstances. Contact with civilization changes these circumstances and causes situations for which these people are not prepared, conditions for which they have no powers of resistance. Changes in their way of living, the introduction of diseases and luxuries previously unknown to them may have a catastrophic effect and may lead to their complete extinction in a short time.

It is consoling to know that attempts are being made to spare the Onges such a fate. Contact with civilization cannot be avoided today.

The authorities, however, are trying their best to keep the destructive influences away and to bring these survivors of a special branch of mankind under control without destroying their normal environment.

In an important paper on 'The Indian Aborigines and their Administration', which appeared in the Journal of the Asiatic Society in 1951, Dr B. S. Guha has pointed out that the history of civilized man's relation with primitive folk falls into two distinct phases, an initial period of conquest and spoliation, and a subsequent period when attempts are made to 'redeem to some extent the wrongs done to them and recognize their right of existence and own mode of living.' The first contacts of the aboriginal populations of the New World, Oceania, Africa or South-East Asia with the outside world were disastrous; 'the once proud and warlike Red Indian tribes of the U.S.A., living in tipis and hunting the bison on horseback, were reduced to one quarter of their estimated total strength.' In Australia many of the aborigines suffered the same fate, while the native Tasmanians were reduced from 7,000 to 120 by 1764, and in 1786 'the last representative of this ancient race passed away from this world, a sad commentary on civilized man's solicitude for the aboriginal' and indeed a curious commentary on the romantic attitude towards him described earlier in this chapter.

But even during the second period, when attempts were made to protect and help the tribal people, the trend of depopulation continued. In America measures for stopping exploitation were not very successful, and Dr Guha points out that between 1887 and 1923 the Red Indians were swindled out of ninety-one million acres of land and, with the exception of the Navahos, showed a rapid decline in population, for which the chief causes were exploitation, lack of adaptability and loss of a will to live. Similarly in Australia, Melanesia and Polynesia, official commissions and scientific investigations conducted on behalf of British scientific associations revealed that the very high rate of decline in the population was due to economic exploitation leading to the disappearance of original arts and crafts, psychological apathy and unwillingness to shoulder the burdens of life.

Of these, the latter was undoubtedly the most important and was the outcome of the disintegration of tribal culture and authority. When contact with a higher culture takes the form of a clash, and tribal patterns and values are too quickly replaced by others of a different order, primitive man is unable to adapt himself to changing conditions and an upsetting of the harmony and balance of his life takes place. This disquieting feature reveals itself in a significant change in the birth-rate with high masculinity. It was found among all the aboriginal tribes in Oceania and the U.S.A. that this was the danger-signal marking the onset of a decline in population.

It is thus essential to 'supply the machinery for enabling the tribesman to adjust himself to the changing conditions of his surrounding environment, and until this is done on the basis of his culture potentiality and cultural accessories, no amount of spoon-feeding or uplifting measures are likely to be effective'.

The Prime Minister's Policy

Is there any way out of this dilemma? We are agreed that the people of NEFA cannot be left in their age-long isolation. We are equally agreed that we can leave no political vacuum along the frontier; that we must bring to an end the destructive practices of inter-tribal war and head-hunting and the morally repugnant practices of slavery, kidnapping of children, cruel methods of sacrificing animals and opium-addiction, none of which are fundamental to tribal culture. We wish to see that the people are well-fed, that they are healthy and enjoy a longer span of life, that fewer babies die, that they have better houses, a higher yield for their labour in the fields, improved techniques for their home-industries. We would like them to be able to move freely about their own hills and have easy access to the greater India of which at present they know little. We want to bring them into contact with the best people and the finest products of modern India.

Above all, we hope to see as the result of our efforts a spirit of love and loyalty for India, without a trace of suspicion that Government has come into the tribal areas to colonize or exploit, a full integration of mind and heart with the great society of which the tribal people form a part, and to whose infinite variety they may make a unique contribution.

And at the same time, we want to avoid the dangers of assimilation and detribalization which have degraded tribal communities in other parts of the world.

Is this possible?

Mrs Indira Gandhi has asked the same question. After visiting the Kulu Valley, she was impressed by the need to help the villagers in their life of poverty and hardship. Yet she admits to a 'lurking fear' in the back of her mind.

How would this opening-up affect the valley and its attractive people? Would contact and competition with the 'clever' people of the plains not destroy their charming naivete? Cannot greater comfort and material gain be achieved without lessening the people's spiritual quality? Is there no way of improving the economy and bringing in better education, health and transport services without also introducing the restlessness of the plains, which might cause a weakening in their vital touch with nature?

There is a way. It is not an easy way, but I believe it may be found in the middle path between doing too little and doing too much, on which the genius of the Prime Minister, Mr Jawaharlal Nehru, has set our feet. His policy may be summarized as one which approaches the historical development of tribal life and culture with respect and the people themselves in a spirit of affection and identification that eliminates any possibility of superiority. It would not ignore the past, but would build upon it. It would bring the best things of the modern world to the tribes, but in such a way that they will not destroy the traditional way of life, but will activate and develop all that is good in it.

In a number of remarkable speeches, Mr Nehru has spoken of the strong attraction which he has for the tribal people and has described how he has always approached them 'in a spirit of comradeship and not like someone aloof who had come to look at them, examine them, weigh them, measure them and report about them or try and make them conform to another way of life.'

He has given serious warnings of the dangers of the 'assimilation' approach. Pointing out the disastrous effect of the 'so-called European civilization' on tribal peoples in other parts of the world, 'putting to an end their arts and crafts and their simple ways of living', he has declared that 'now to some extent, there is danger of the so-called Indian civilization having this disastrous effect, if we do not check and apply it in the proper way.' 'We may well succeed in uprooting them from their way of life with its standards and discipline, and give them nothing in its place. We may make them feel ashamed of themselves and their own people and thus they may become thoroughly frustrated and unhappy. They have not got the resilience of human beings accustomed to the shocks of the modern world and so they tend to succumb to them.' We must, therefore, be very careful to see that 'in our well-meant efforts to improve them, we do not do them grievous injury'. 'It is just possible that, in our enthusiasm for doing good, we may overshoot the mark and do evil instead.' 'It has often happened in other areas of the world that such contact has been disastrous to the primitive culture and gradually the primitive people thus affected die out.'

'I am alarmed,' he has said again, 'when I see—not only in this country, but in other great countries too—how anxious people are to shape others according to their own image or likeness, and to impose on them their particular way of living.' He has declared that he is not sure which, the modern or the tribal, is the better way of living. 'In some respects I am quite certain their's is better.' 'They possess a variety of cultures and are in many ways certainly not backward.'

> We must cease to think of ourselves as different from the so-called tribal people. This is a vicious idea. It is due to a superiority complex which has no basis in reality. I can say with complete honesty that some of the tribal people have reached a high degreee of development, in fact I have found that in some places they are highly educated and disciplined and lead a corporate communal life which, I think, is far better than the caste-ridden society from which we suffer.

The Prime Minister has further emphasized the importance of encouraging the tribal languages, so that they will not only prevail but flourish. He has insisted that a measure of protection must be given so that 'no outsider can take possession of tribal lands or forests or interfere with them in any way except with their consent and goodwill'. It is his desire that the high sense of discipline, the power to enjoy life, the love of dance and song will endure among them. 'I am anxious that they should advance, but I am even more anxious that they should not lose their artistry and joy in life and the culture that distinguishes them in many ways.'

Schemes for welfare, education, communications, medical relief are no doubt essential; 'one must always remember, however, that we do not mean to interfere with their way of life, but want to help them to live it.' 'The Government of India'—

and in this sentence Mr Nehru's entire policy is epitomized—'is determined to help the tribal people to grow according to their own genius and tradition; it is not the intention to impose anything on them.' Development, he has said again, 'must be according to their own genius and not something that they cannot absorb or imbibe and which merely uproots them. I would much rather go slow in our plans for development than risk the danger of this uprooting. I feel, therefore, that it is unwise to try to do too many things at the same time there which may result in disturbing the minds of the people or in upsetting their habits. I have no doubt that development and change and so-called progress will come to them, because it is becoming increasingly difficult for any people to live their isolated life cut off from the rest of the world. But let this development and change be natural and be in the nature of self-development with all the help one can give in the process.'

These ideas have been emphasized by a number of the country's leaders. The President of India, Dr Rajendra Prasad, has written:

There can be, and should be, no idea or intention of forcing anything on them either by way of religion, language or even mode of living and customs. Even where we feel that the religion or the life that is offered is better than their's, there is no justification for forcing it upon them against their will. My own idea is that facilities for education and for general improvement in their economic life should be provided for them and it should be left to them to choose whether they would like to be assimilated with, and absorbed by the surrounding society, or would like to maintain their own separate tribal existence. In India with its variety of life, there is enough room for the tribal people to carry on their separate social existence if they so desire. If they find however that from their own point of view it would be better for them to get assimilated, they will do it without any large-scale effort on the part of others. In other words, personally I am for service to them uninfluenced by any consideration of winning them over for particular groups, religious or other. It is only in that way that we can win their confidence, and even for raising their standard of living and improving them educationally, it is necessary to win their confidence first.

In a similar spirit Pandit G. B. Pant, Union Home Minister of India, has emphasized the contribution that the tribal people can make to the life of the country. He is reported as saying in a recent conference at Koraput that:

India is a vast country with a rich variety of culture and topography and in this scene of diversity our tribal brethren occupy a very important place. The tribal people have been truly described as an artistic creation of God passionately devoted to their own way of life. They express their joy of life through the colourful forms of their folk-dances and the rhythm of their music.

Their frankness, love of truth and unshakable loyalty to those who win their confidence are well known. They are literally sons of the soil, and the skill with which they create neat and clean habitations and meet the other requirements of life are a matter for admiration.

It is wrong, therefore, to consider these people less civilized or backward. They are our own kinsmen and non-tribals can learn many good lessons from their way of life.

Mr Jairamdas Doulatram, former Governor of Assam, has expressed the same idea in a striking simile.

Each section of our large population contributes to the making of the nation in the same manner as each flower helps to make a garden. Every flower has the right to grow according to its own laws of growth; has the right to enrich and develop its own colour and form and to spread its own fragrance to make up the cumulative beauty and splendour of the garden. I would not like to change my roses into lilies nor my lilies into roses. Nor do I want to sacrifice my lovely orchids and rhododendrons of the hills.

And Mr S. Fazl Ali, the present Governor, speaking of the 'human and sociological adventure' on which the NEFA Administration is engaged, has said:

Our approach to the tribal people must be conditioned by human understanding and must be free from any traces of superciliousness or condescension. The people of NEFA are sensitive and intelligent and though they might occasionally be bewildered by the advance of an unfamiliar world, yet I think they will be disposed to greet this advance with all the friendliness of their open-hearted and hospitable nature. They are observant and intelligent and are deeply conscious of the natural dignity of their simple ways of life.

We must, therefore, approach them not with any feeling of civilized superiority, but with a genuine spirit of service and seek to learn from them at least as much as we would like to teach them. They must be made to feel that it is their own prosperity and happiness which we are anxious to promote. If we try to change their traditional modes of living too rapidly or too rigidly in accordance with any pre-conception of what a civilized social order should be, they might be easily led to believe that we are seeking to disrupt their way of life or to uproot them.

We must follow the golden mean between leaving too much alone and interfering too obtrusively in their daily life. It is our duty to go ahead with the task of removing their pressing needs and doing everything which will really add to their happiness and prosperity and broaden their outlook. But they should not be overwhelmed by a multiplicity of projects in such a way as to undermine their self-reliance without evoking their enthusiasm. More important than the number or magnitude of such projects is the effectiveness with which we can demonstrate the usefulness and desirability of those that we find necessary to take up in their interest. Even a few schemes well and conscientiously executed will, I think, serve to arouse the enthusiasm and co-operation of the tribal people who will then be able to realize in their own way the advantages of more intimate association and contact with the rest of India.

This policy is not unique; very similar ideas have been expressed by John Collier in America, by Rattray in Africa, by Macdonald in Borneo. But I think it is unique to find so many of the great figures in the public life of a country so filled with concern and speaking with so unanimous a voice about its tribal population. And I am sure that there has seldom, or never, been so sincere and energetic an attempt to implement the policy as has been made in NEFA.

This attempt to steer a middle path between the two older ways of approach is hard and delicate: it demands imagination, sincerity and constant care. The assimilation or detribalization policy, which held, as we have seen, that there is not very much to be said for tribal life; that if it disappears, it will not matter greatly; that the 'backward' must be brought forward and the low 'uplifted', is simple and straightforward; it is logical and it brings certain benefits—at a price. So did the old British policy of leaving well alone, though at a different price.

But there can be no doubt that Mr Nehru's policy is the right one. It is supported by the findings of anthropological science and the warnings of history. It is a charter of religious, social, economic and cultural rights. It is the embodiment of the spirit of reverence. It is the gospel of friendliness and equality. It is the gate whereby the tribal people may enter into full union with the India of which they form so important and valuable a part.

Today we can see the tribal peoples without sentiment, but equally without prejudice. Isolation in the modern world is impossible; it would not be desirable even if it was possible. The old controversy about zoos and museums has long been dead. We do not want to preserve tribal culture in its colour and beauty to interest the scientists or attract the tourists. To try to preserve and develop the best elements in tribal art, religion and culture is something very different from wishing to keep the people in a zoo.

We do not want to preserve the tribesmen as museum specimens, but equally we do not want to turn them into clowns in a circus. We do not want to stop the clock of progress. but we do want to see that it keeps the right time. We do not accept the myth of the Noble Savage; but we do not want to create a class of Ignoble Serfs.

We see now that the tribal people will be of the greatest service to India if they are able to bring their own peculiar treasures into the common life, not by becoming second-rate copies of ourselves. Their moral virtues, their self-reliance, their courage, their artistic gifts, their cheerfulness are things we need. They also need the comradeship, the technical knowledge, the wider world-view of the plains. The great problem is how to develop the synthesis, how to bring the blessings and advantages of modern medicine, agriculture and education to them, without destroying the rare and precious values of tribal life.

We can solve this problem if we do not try to go too fast: if we allow the people a breathing-space in which to adjust themselves to the new world: if we do not overwhelm them with too many officials; if we aim at fundamentals and eliminate everything that is not vitally necessary; if we go to them in genuine love and true simplicity. In a word, if we follow Mr Nehru's policy, there is a chance we may succeed; if we do not, it is certain we will fail.

CONCLUSION

What I have written applies with special force to the North-East Frontier Agency, but it has its bearing on all the tribal areas of India, for many of the problems are the same everywhere, though their urgency varies from State to State. In one the people may be chiefly agitated about their land and forests or the commercial exploitation that brings them so much anxiety and loss. In another the central problem may be their emotional integration with their neighbours in the plains; a third may be disturbed by religious controversies; in a fourth the coming of large numbers of refugees may be gravely disturbing the entire tribal economy. Yet everywhere the great fundamental principles laid down by Mr Nehru and elaborated in this book, modified and adapted to the special circumstances of each area, will help towards a solution. Honestly applied, these principles may involve a lot of rethinking, even the reversal of conventional policies; they are disturbing principles, tiresome if you like, unpopular, easy to twist and misunderstand, and vulnerable to the thoughtless criticisms of the ill-informed. Yet if those concerned will take the trouble to understand them, and sincerely try to put them into practice, I believe they can bring about a transformation of the tribal situation throughout the country.

When I once asked Mr B. P. Chaliha, the great-hearted Chief Minister of Assam, what magic he had used for the solution of the many human and political problems in the Autonomous Districts of his State, he replied, 'A little understanding, a genuine respect, a lot of affection.' This is the real magic that works wonders in human hearts.

And it is with this magic that administrators and social workers everywhere must approach the tribal people and their problems. But they must translate their idealism into very practical realities. Under the programmes of the Five Year Plans they will be trying to bring greater prosperity, more food, better health, roads, clean water, education; all this we take for granted. But there is no point in growing rich if there is a thief lurking behind the hosue. They must guarantee the tribal folk their land, give them a generous freedom of their forests, eliminate the middleman by Co-operatives, banish the mondy-lender, build up the tribal councils. And they must never forget the imponderables, never forget that man does not live by bread alone, but that the greatest of all treasures is a quiet mind and inner happiness. They must adapt themselves and all their enterprises to the local scene; they must revive creativeness in those who have lost their arts, stimulate the old joy and zest in living, restore self-respect and a pride in their own religion and culture among those who have been infected by a feeling of inferiority, and above all give them a sense of freedom through a vision of what they can contibute to the great country which they have come to love, and the hope that they will soon play their full part in administering themselves.

But now let us return for a moment to NEFA before I close my meditation. The first important points is that an Administration of this kind works as a whole; everything fits together, everyone has a share in it, and it all affects in one way or another the life of the tribal people.

One of the great achievements of the NEFA leadership has been the creation of the Single-Line Administration which stresses the inter-relationship of the entire work and the importance of every aspect of it. Even those members of the staff who do not deal directly with the tribal people have it in their power to influence them, for good or evil. Thus the officers dealing with supply and transport have a vital part to play in maintaining supplies for building institutions and keeping the staff supplied with the necessities of life. But equally they have the opportunity of ensuring that the good imported into NEFA will not corrupt tribal taste or tempt the people to waste their money on unnecessary and unsuitable things, but will rather enrich their life with the best products (within, of course, a limited price-range) that India, traditionally an artistic and beauty-loving country, can supply.

The Assam Rifles can play a large part, not only in maintaining law and order, but in setting an example to the people of smartness, descipline self-help and the dignity of manual labour. By their friendliness and readiness to help in all emergencies, the jawans have always proved good ambassadors and their influence has been of great value in integrating the people with the rest of India. They are now being moee closely associated with the development programme, in the making of roads and bridges, and in the growing of food.

The work and influence of the office assistant, the accountant or the Sub-Treasury Officer is not confined to the keeping of accounts and dealing with files. The people of NEFA are remarkably sensitive to two things: the first is delay, the second is corruption. The prompt and courteous settlement of bills, whether for contracts, porterage, casual labour on roads, airstrips or buildings; a readiness to spare time to listen to a grievance, the elimination of long waits outside an office—have their social and political effect. And conversely, delay, neglect, irritability and impatience create the worst possible impression on the tribal mind and foster the sense of inferiolrity and alienness.

Integrity, fidelity in the keeping of accounts, a constant watch to see that Government money is put to the best possible use for the benefit of the people, the determination that the bulk of the money will be spent for their good and not for the staf fare of the utmost value in winning the sometimes suspicious and critical heart of the educated tribesman.

Even the motor-driver, the peon, the medical attendant in the hospital has his part to play in this great task. The tribal people look at the Administration as a whole, and however good a Political Officer may be himself, he will fail unless he can unspire his entire staff with his own ideals. One bad assistant, or corrupt chaprassi, or oppressive interpreter can undo much of the good done by the higher officers.

Success in the very delicate task of steering a middle way between leaving too much alone and interfering too officiously and imposing too l heavily on the life of the people will depend on an appreciation of the fundamental ideas set out by the Prime Minister. As an aid to this, administrators of all the tribal areas throughout India might well adopt the following touchstones of any scheme for development, welfare, relief and expansion: the sentences within quotation marks are from Mr Nehru's own speeches and notings.

1. Will the scheme help the tribesmen 'to grow according to their own genius and tradition'?
2. Or will its result be merely 'to shape them according to our own image or likeness and impose on them our particular way of living'?
3. Will it tend to make of the tribesmen 'a second-rate copy of ourselves'?
4. Will it 'uproot the tribal people from their surroundings' and 'make them grow soft and thus lose some of their fine qualities'?
5. It is open to the criticism that 'it is grossly presumptuous

on our part to approach the tribesmen with an air of superiority or to tell them what to do or not to do'.

6. Will it involve too rapid a process of acculturation or, in other words, are we trying to go too fast?
7. Is there any danger that we are overwhelming the tribes by too many projects, each good in itself, but in the aggregate imposing too heavy a burden?
8. Will it impair or destroy in any way the self-reliance of the people?
9. Is it really, on a long-term basis, for the ultimate good of the tribesmen, or is it simply something that will make a good show in the press or an official report?
10. Will it, in the case of NEFA, help to integrate the tribal people with Greater Assam and with India as a whole?

NEFA offers a unique opportunity to every member of the Administration, for it is attempting an exciting and unusual experiment which, if successful, will write a significant page in the history of civilization's dealings with primitive people. Elsewhere in the world, colonists have often gone into tribal areas for what they can get; the Government of India has gone into NEFA for what it can give. Whenever a new project is considered or policy proposed, the one criterion is whether it will be for the benefit of the tribal people.

The keynote of the Administration's policy indeed is this: the tribesmen first, the tribesmen last, the tribesmen all the time.

The fundamental policy and approach which I have tried to describe in this book was laid down as far back as 1953 by Mr N. K. Rustomji, during his first term as Adviser to the Governor. We have much, he says, to learn from the hillmen, as they have from us.

> Much of the beauty of living still survives in these remote and distant hills, where dance and song are a vital part of everyday living, where people speak and think freely, without fear or restraint. Our workers must ensure, therefore, that, in their enthusiasm and in their zeal, the good that is inherent in the institutions of the hill people is not tainted or substituted by practices that may be 'modern' and 'advanced', but are totally unsuited to the hillman's economy and way of thinking. The hillman has, essentially, a clean, direct and healthy outlook; he is free, happily, from the morbid complexes inhibited by the unnatural

life of the city folk, whose every activity is linked with the machines made by man, but divorced from the works of God—the beauty of nature, fresh sunlight, and free, spontaneous laughter.

The song and the dance of the hills are simple; they are the very expression of the spirit, as are the patterns of the cloth they weave. Their industry is, necessarily, a home-industry; for lack of communications has not permitted them, and will not, for some time to come, allow them to find a market for their produce in the outside world. But they sing and dance and weave their homely designs for their own pleasure, the pleaure of their family members and the pleasure of their fellow-villagers—in a sense, the truest of artistic pleasures.

The greatest disservice will be done, therefore, if in an excess of missionary zeal, our workers destroy the fresh creative urge that lives, strong and vital, within the denizens of the hills. For if we wish to serve, we must show that we have respect for the hillmen and their institutions, their language and their song; and, in showing such respect, we shall secure their confidence in the work that lies ahead. It is for this reason that it is enjoined upon every worker in the hills to make it his first task to familiarize himself with the language of the areas within which he serves, to take an interest and come to understand the customs and usages of the people amongst whom he finds himself and to share fully in their life, not as a stranger from without, but as one amongst the people themselves.

The tribal people of India offer us a very special challenge. Their simplicity, which is most lovable; their art, which often gives them the dignity of princes but is so easily destroyed; their courtesy and hospitality, discipline and self-reliance; their ability to work hard and co-operatively; their occasional bewilderment before the advance of an unfamiliar world, and yet their welcome and friendliness to that world; these things win the heart and call for the very best in those who try to serve them. Nothing can be too good for them, but with what care that good has to be shared!

10

Note on UNESCO Manual, Cultural Patterns and Technical Change (1963)

1. *The Governor asked me to try to put in more simple language, part of the UNESCO Manual* Cultural Patterns and Technical Change *edited by Margaret Mead.*
2. *I am sending herewith a draft of what I have tried to do. I am not very satisfied with it but there are parts of this Manual which are so technical that I do not think any human being could make very much of it. But I have been able to bring out a few points which might stimulate some members of our staff to think about these problems.*
3. *I have sent a copy to the Governor.*

—Verrier Elwin, 2.7.63

Some years ago the Administration distributed to a number of our senior officers an important book called *Cultural Patterns and Technical Change*, which was prepared by a team of doctors, psychiatrists and sociologists working under the auspices of UNESCO, in close connection with the World Federation for Mental Health. Although this book is not concerned with specifically tribal problems, it is a discussion of change among undeveloped peoples in many parts of the world, and it has been suggested that I should bring it again to your attention and set out in simpler language some of its fundamental points, especially those of the difficult last chapter. This is of great interest to us here for the essential problem raised by the UNESCO team is very similar to the problem that has faced the NEFA Administration during the last fifteen years and is epitomized by them as follows:

'If the abolition of hunger and want is to be brought about only by industrialization, by urbanization, by mechanization, by westernization, by secularization, by mass production, will not the cost be too great? Of what use to introduce a tractor which increases the yield of the grain fields, if in so doing the whole distinguishing fabric of life which had characterized a society will be ripped into shreds?'

This question has been asked frequently in recent years and we have had warnings from all parts of the world about how 'destructive contact has been in the past between highly developed and less developed cultures, how often the price of progress has been to turn proud, aristocratic tribals into pitifully limited factory workers, shorn of their own tradition and provided with no new values.'

The conflict of two points of view—between those whose imagination is caught by the possibility of releasing mankind from the spectre of famine and those who insist that man does not live by bread alone—finds its echo in the questions that are asked whenever technical assistance is mentioned. Eyes light up with the vision that is offered. For the first time in history there is a possibility that no man need be hungry.

But then faces fall, as people ask the second question: How is it to be done—in human terms? Granted that we know the technical answers: what will be the cost in terms of the human spirit? How much destruction of old values, disintegration of personality, alienation of parents from children, of husbands from wives, of students from teachers, of neighbour from neighbour, of the spirit of man from the faith and style of his traditional culture must there be? How slow must we go? How fast can we go?

But more urgently, we live in a world which is so haunted by the destructive powers which have been released in the twentieth century that it is of vital importance that we have reason for faith in our world, a reasoned belief in the future of human living. The speed with which the peoples of the world can learn the skills which will free them from their age-long fears is the measure of our right to hope. Upon our ability to hope will depend our willingness to act in the living present. Such reasoned belief must be based on knowledge. We must *think* about the question: *How can technical change be introduced with such regard for the culture pattern that human values are preserved?* We must think about these patterns, these changes, and these considered attempts to protect the mental health of a world population in transition.

There has sometimes been a feeling, I think, that our 'Philosophy for NEFA' is something rather extraordinary, unusual, even eccentric. Anyone who reads the UNESCO Manual will see that this is not so, but that very similar problems of change are being tackled, in a very similar way, throughout the world, although neither we nor the UNESCO team can dogmatize about their solution. The UNESCO team also stresses the importance of regarding people with respect, emphasizes the need to associate them in every proposal for change and, above all, urges, as we have urged, that we must *think* about the problems and not rush in with ready-made solutions which may do as much harm as good.

I hope that as a result of this note all our officers will read this book or re-read it and try to apply it to our circumstances in NEFA.

Along with this book I would like to recommend two others which deal with development and change and which everyone of our officers should study. One is what has been described as one of the greatest international bestsellers of today, *The Ugly American*, and the other is a fascinating study by Dr and Mrs Milne, *The Balance of Nature*, which describes the effect of induced change on the animal world.

Let us turn now to the UNESCO Manual.

CULTURE IS AN INTEGRATED WHOLE

The approach of the UNESCO Manual is based on the recognition that a culture is a systematic and integrated whole, and that a change in any one part of a culture will be accompanied by changes in other parts, and that 'only by relating any planned detail of change to the central values of the culture is it possible to provide for the repercussions which will occur in other aspects of life. This is what we mean by "cultural relativity"; that practices and beliefs can and must be evaluated in context, in relation to the cultural whole.'

As each culture is a whole, however sorely torn at the moment—whole in the sense that it is the system by which and through which its members live—in all relationships between cultures, each must be accorded dignity and value. Much of the present phrasing of technical-assistance planning is conducted with explicit or implicit denial of the dignity of members of those countries which, while often the inheritors of much older traditions, have not been in the vanguard of modern science. This is self-defeating, in that it arouses violent resistances and attempts at compensation and retaliation from those whose feelings of self-esteem have been violated; it is also contrary to the findings of modern psychiatric practice, which insist on the recognition of the patient's validity as a human being.

Phrases which divide the world into the 'haves' and the 'have-nots' overvalue bread and plumbing and devalue music and architecture. Those whose status is defined as a 'have not' may come to repudiate the possibility of learning anything at all, or of sharing anything at all except 'bread' with those who have so denigrated their cherished ways of life. Phrases like 'under-developed', 'backward', 'simple'—to the extent that they cover a whole culture—are equally defeating. If, instead, we draw on an image in which two adults—one experienced in one skill, another in a different skill—pool their knowledge so that each can use the skill of the other for a particular task, as when foreign explorer and local guide venture together into a forest, much more viable relationships can be set up. Leaders of the newest countries, only recently established by revolution or mandate or negotiation, are young adults, not children—less experienced but not less adult than those upon whose skills and resources they need to draw.

The earlier chapters in this manual are devoted to the consequences of change seen on the social level: which cultural attitudes must be taken into account, how the cultural practices of a people may be used to facilitate change, how a people who resist hospitalization may come to use it, how a people whose food-habits prevent them from obtaining adequate nourishment may be persuaded to alter those habits. Throughout the discussion, the major assumption is made that it is necessary to take into account the whole culture when a particular change is made and that unless this is done, various types of destructive changes may be set in motion in the society, in addition to the programme of change itself being resisted and sabotaged.

Principles Involved in Developing Mental Health during Technical Change

Let us now summarize certain general principles.

1. The culture of each people is a living unity in the sense that a change in any one aspect will have repercussions in other aspects. This is true even in those cultures which, while in the process of very rapid change, are torn by conflicts and contradictions.

2. An active concern for the mental health of the peoples of the world includes an active concern for the ways in which technical change is taking place. When the introduction of technical change is purposively initiated, such purposiveness

involves responsibility for the effects not only in improved living-conditions, but also upon the total way of life of the people, for reintegration as well as a defence against disintegration.

3. As each culture is unique, and as each particular situation within which a change occurs is unique, it is not possible to lay down prescriptions for what is to be done in any particular case. It is only possible so to describe the process which occurs that each individual or team concerned may be able to act in terms of this process. For example, it is possible to point out that in any programme involving popular education in public health, the problem of language is a serious one.

Whenever possible we should work through the familiar and the homely.

> It has been proved by experience that the mother-tongue is the most effective and the most emotionally satisfying medium of instruction. In this way literacy is not merely associated with the foreign, but becomes an instrument in familiar life. Learning to read and write can be experienced within the security of the known, and the hurdle of a new medium need not be surmounted. And in educating in areas of living, the use of the mother-tongue provides the greatest facilitation, as it can express immediately the meanings and specific concepts of the culture. What is true of the mother-tongue is true of all aspects of living. Working through the known patterns and the existing social groupings has proved to be the most effective procedure in fundamental education.

4. All changes should be introduced with the fullest possible consent and participation of those whose daily lives will be affected by the changes.

5. Every change, even such apparently conspicuous modifications of the external environment as building a dam or a railroad, occurs for the benefit of living individuals, their aspirations and hopes, and their limited capabilities.

6. At a time of change, the new things must be made attractive by every kind of encouragement.

> The learning of desired new behaviours and attitudes can be achieved by the learner's living through a long series of situations in which the new behaviour is made highly satisfying—without exception if possible—and the old not satisfying.

SUMMARY

As a rule, an individual's behaviour, beliefs and attitudes grow and change only to the minimum extent that is demanded by his immediate situation. All that is required is that his daily behaviour and perception has meaning and integration. So when a boy marries he must alter his behaviour to that of a married man; a married man must learn to be a father; a newly-elected official must alter his behaviour to suit his new role. But when an individual is confronted not by an expected change in role, but by a chaotic external environment to which he cannot adjust with emotional satisfaction, and which he cannot explain to himself, he is impelled to seek a new adjustment—which relieves his tension. He tends also to seek a new explanation of his changed environmental situation, and this new explanation also relieves his tension. A man thrown out of a job in an industrial society tries to adjust himself to living unemployed, and he may also for the first time feel a need to understand how the economic system works. Groups which have themselves felt and expressed a need for technical change are more likely to be aware of the crisis which develops in their lives as a result of the desired change, and so be able to make an effort to adapt to it constructively.

A technical change will be perceived by the affected individuals as a smaller change if the change can be incorporated into an unchanged larger pattern of relationships, thus taking advantage of the way in which human perception organizes objects or events together on the basis of proximity in time or space, or culturally determined similarity. Thus families may migrate a great distance but preserve their usual habits of family life. Or upon entering a new country an individual may begin to do new work, but of a type which has been defined as appropriate for anyone from his country, so that his sense of his national identity is strengthened even while the work itself is new and strange.

Even in very complicated situations, in which technical changes cannot be fitted into an existing community or family framework, it may be quite possible to find in operation institutions which have sufficient similarity to the new desired forms of behaviour to make the introduction of change easier.

In any attempt to use old ways of behaviour to facilitate change, it is, however, important to keep in mind that sometimes a change will be accepted more easily if it is new in a new context. So a new kind of organization may be perceived as more appropriate for a new kind of activity—so that people will accept a factory and a union together where either one alone might be rejected. Paper cups may be accepted more readily if an unfamiliar beverage is served in them. New foods may be accepted if they are introduced together with a new kind of stove or fuel. Thus, the tendency of the human mind to organize and simplify may be invoked by grafting new forms of behaviour onto old forms so that the new seems old and familiar, or by letting one break in traditional behaviour carry a number of other breaks.

An individual's ability to learn is a function of the way in which he perceives a situation. Failure to understand this leads to unwarranted discouragement about the learning capacities of other people. 'They can't learn from experience', we say. This often simply means that what the expert saw in a sequence of events differed sharply from what the people saw. Each person learns from the sequence as he perceives it.

A famous example of the operation of this principle was the unforeseen effect upon the American public of Upton Sinclair's novel *The Jungle*. Mr Sinclair was a crusading friend of the overworked and underpaid; he hated cruelty, exploitation, and the cheating of the innocent. He observed how people lived in the Chicago stock-yards and put his burning indignation down in vivid words. The fact which he was relating demonstrated to him the need for a co-operative commonwealth. The vast majority of his American readers, however, were not socialists, but they were meat-eaters. They perceived Mr Sinclair's facts in their own way. They read about the human beings and the rats who had fallen into the lard vats and were then sold as food. They concluded that a new pure-food law was required, and Upton Sinclair's novel led to a reform in the handling of meat rather than of men.

As memory is selective, just as perception is, great attention must be given, in all educational efforts, to allowing for sufficient time and enough repetition so that facts which are less easy to assimilate are not lightly forgotten.

Sometimes a perception will be so dependent upon an underlying set of fundamental beliefs that it will not be possible to change a practice without altering the whole structure of belief. Thus a desire to lower the infant death rate may not develop until there is a new conception of the importance of each human individual, or a desire to compete with other nations in the field of vital statistics.

The agents of change have a wide choice of methods: they can attempt to influence the perceiving individual directly; they can alter the environment so that it will in turn alter his perception; they can create situations within which he will continue to remain in contact with the new situations; they can attempt to satisfy the needs and emotions which lie at the root of the existing behaviours in a way which will include the proposed change; they may create social support for the individual who adopts the new behaviours. Taken together, these methods involve working through many or all of the personality-forming agencies in a society—institutions, individual people, objects. Any programme aimed at successful change needs to be multidimensional.

Any programme of change which has been shown to work on a small scale must be very carefully evaluated before any of its principles can be applied in a different setting. It is particularly important to allow for the extensive qualitative differences which quantitative changes may introduce. A village is not a model for a province or a nation.

From the standpoint of mental health, the hazards of change are actually not as great for those who are immediately involved as they are for their children. The peasant who comes to the city brings with him all the stability derived from a childhood spent within a traditional and coherent social order. His personality reflects that experience and he often withstands enormous pressures, and meets crisis after crisis with courage and imagination. It is not among the first-generation immigrants from country to city, from agricultural country to industrial country, from simple levels of life to complex levels, that we find the principal disturbances which accompany technical change. Rather, it is in the lives of their children, reared in conditions within which no stable patterns have been developed, by parents who, while they may be able to weather the storm themselves by drawing on a different childhood experience, have no charts to give their children. Juvenile delinquency, alcoholism, drug addiction, empty, defeated, meaningless lives, lives which are a series of drifting rudderless activities, adoption of oversimplified political programmes which promise relief from their feelings of inadequacy and lack of direction—these are the prices which are paid not so much by the first as by the disturbed members of the second generation. Here there is urgent need for agencies which will help parents to develop new ways of being parents, and children to develop new ways of growing up. Assuring mental health to the second generation, the children of the uprooted who have not yet themselves taken root, requires more than the observation of sound psychological principles such as those outlined in the chapter for adjusting adults to change; it requires new social inventions, most of which have not even been glimpsed in outline.

Among such inventions are new methods of child care, which substitute new flexibility for the rigid patterns appropriate to a stable, relatively unchanging society, so that the child learns to fit together his internal rhythms and the demands of his environment flexibly, safely—going to sleep not only at a fixed time in a familiar bed, but also able to sleep trustingly in new places, because he has learned to trust even in a world that is not fixed and predictable. We need new methods of education which will leave the child's mind open longer, leave his muscular adjustments freer, less stylized, methods which teach him that safety lies not in knowledge but in knowing what could be but is not known.

In all technical change, even when it seems to be concerned with tools, machines and other impersonal objects the individual person is both the recipient of change and the mediator or agent of change. His integrity as a person, his stability as a personality, must be kept ever in focus as the living concern of all purposive change.

CONCLUSION

To conclude, I would emphasize the fact that the UNESCO Manual points out the danger of change does not mean, for a moment, that it would delay change or oppose it, any more than the 'Philosophy of NEFA' would delay change or oppose it. It is true that it is not possible to lay down definite prescriptions, for this would be contrary to the very flexibility which the Manual emphasizes again and again; each culture, each situation must be examined afresh.

The main lesson, however, is that officials, social workers and all concerned in developing under-developed areas like NEFA must be mentally alert. The examples given in this note may stimulate some of them to note down the similar problems arising in NEFA and it would be good if these could be written out and sent to the Administration. The important thing is that we should not just go ahead pressing for change merely because it is change, still less that we should adopt stereotyped plans from the cities or other parts of India which may be entirely unsuitable. The approach of the UNESCO Manual is the same as that of the 'Philosophy of NEFA'. We must go to the tribal with the mind of the tribal and try to look at things from his point of view, associate him in all our plans and, wherever possible, leave it to him to do the actual implementation. If we do this we may be able to answer the fundamental question: 'How can technical change be introduced with such regard for the culture pattern that human values are preserved?'

11

The Art of the North-East Frontier (1959)

INTRODUCTION

On Tuesday, June the 15th 1784, Dr Samuel Johnson was shown the three recently published volumes of Captain Cook's account of his voyages to the South Seas. The great man did not approve. 'Who,' he demanded, 'will read them through? A man had better work his way before the mast than read them through; they will be eaten by rats and mice before they are read through. There can be little entertainment in such books; one set of savages is like another.' To this Boswell protested: 'I do not think the people of Otaheite can be reckoned savages.'

JOHNSON : Don't cant in defence of savages.
BOSWELL : They have the art of navigation.
JOHNSON : A dog or a cat can swim.
BOSWELL : They carve very ingeniously.
JOHNSON : A cat can scratch, and a child with a nail can scratch.

The word 'savage' has passed and with it the attitude of mind it expressed, yet although the primitive art of Africa, America and the South Seas is today admired and even fashionable, the tribal art of India has not hitherto attracted much attention, and some of that attention has been critical or even Johnsonian in its scorn. Thus Dunbar, in an otherwise appreciative paper on the Abors and Gallongs, speaks of 'the utter lack of an artistic sense in the tribes on this frontier': they could not even decorate their quivers and scabbards. He says again that the Adis' ideas of art 'are limited to elementary patterns on the loom and to the rough conventional designs of the smith in his clay and wax castings', which were generally imitations of imports from Tibet. Similarly Dalton says of the Subansiri tribes that 'there are no people on the face of the earth more ignorant of arts and manufactures.' The early explorers of the frontier vied with one another in their use of uncomplimentary adjectives, and even today the common use of the expression 'backward tribes' who are to be 'uplifted' hardly suggests an attitude of respect.

Yet an attitude of neglect or scorn is as mistaken as one which casts a romantic glamour over all things tribal. For, as Raymond Firth says,

> one aim of a clear aesthetic judgement is to recognize the worth of traditions of art different from our own, to perceive in an apparent distortion of reality the expression of a valid and interesting idea, of a formal and forceful design.

There is much beauty to be found in Indian tribal art, particularly in the art of the North-East Frontier, but to appreciate it requires sympathy, imagination and the ability to relate it to its human background. It is also necessary to understand the difficulties against which the artist has to struggle: lack of materials, the general psychological demoralization into which many of the people have fallen as a result of contact with the outside world, and the absence of official or private patronage and encouragement in the past.

On the North-East Frontier there are additional difficulties. Only the most primitive tools are available for wood-carving. In many areas the local clay is not suitable for pottery. The walls of houses are not plastered with mud and washed with cow-dung and red or white clay, and this means that there is none of the modelling on walls common in other parts of India and there are no wall-paintings, except in the Buddhist institutions of western Kameng, where the painting is on wood. Cotton is not extensively grown, for the people are hard put to it to provide themselves even with sufficient food, and although a number of natural dyes are known, their use is slowly being abandoned before the competition of coloured bazaar yarn and synthetic dyes, with the result that the old colours are inevitably changing.

Lack of materials and the uncertainty of frontier life combined to discourage the artist in the past. Even now the highly inflammable bamboo houses, thatched with grass or palm leaves, and huddled together on a hillside are subject to disastrous fires. In former days there was much burning of villages and houses in the course of kidnapping raids and inter-village feuds. Earthquake and flood still take their toll of buildings and all they contain. The graphic and plastic arts require a sense of security if they are to flourish, and we will never be able to estimate the artistic and cultural impoverishment caused by the great earthquake of 1950. The climate too, with its heavy rainfall, causes everything to decay. And there is nowhere to keep anything. There are few cupboards or boxes in which to store one's more precious possessions, which have to be tied up in bamboo baskets. The wood-smoke that fills every tribal home preserves wooden and bamboo objects, but the thick dust settles on everything and quickly robs the most beautiful cloth of its lustre.

In Tirap there is a further difficulty. It may be dangerous to make a striking or beautiful thing. Publicity can shorten life. It is risky to carve well, for people will ask who the artist was and such queries are unlucky. When a pillar is carved in a morung (village-dormitory or guard-house), a dog must be sacrificed and a period of taboo observed; the artist must restrict his diet and observe a rule of chastity for a number of days. If he breaks these rules he may fall sick; he may even die. A Konyak who made me a small wood-carving had to sacrifice a pig to avert these dangers before he gave it to me.

There are other restrictions. In some Wancho groups only the wife and daughters of a Chief can weave; among the Konyaks, Changs and others there are strict rules governing the kind of dress that can be made or used by certain people. The Sherdukpen, Hrusso and Monpa aristocracy, with its strong sense of protocol, controls the use of fine and beautiful things. There is a general tradition that a human figure can be carved in a morung only by someone who has himself taken a head, and a tiger by someone who has himself killed a tiger. With the passing of head-hunting and the extermination of wild life, the artist's opportunities have naturally been restricted.

The production of cloth is also hampered by an elaborate system of taboos. Their incidence varies considerably from place to place and there is room here for only two examples, but these will suffice to indicate the kind of restrictions that exist. For the Padams and Minyongs every festival involves a taboo on weaving as well as on other activities. There is no weaving for five days after the Ampi Dorung ceremonial hunt, for twenty days after the Aran Harvest Festival, for ten days after the Sollung Festival which celebrates the sowing and transplantation of paddy. If any special ceremony such as, for example, the Mime Rego Ipak, is performed for a woman to avert certain kinds of disease she must not weave or spin for six months and the other women in the household must not do so for ten days.

Even more rigorous are the taboos imposed by a death in the household. After a natural death the family must not weave for five days, but if anyone is killed by falling from a tree or is struck by lightning or if a pregnant woman dies in child-birth, the whole family is forbidden to spin or weave for a year. If anyone is killed by a snake or a wild animal, the taboo is less severe but lasts for a month. If a woman suffers an abortion she cannot weave for a whole year, her family must abstain for a month and the village for a day. Curiously, there is no ban on a woman weaving during her period.

There are similar but less stringent taboos among the Mishmis. Unlike the Adis, they forbid a woman to weave during her period, but the ordinary taboos do not last so long. Eleven days are observed after a man's death, nine days after a woman's; it is much the same when a child is born. Most sacrifices and festivals give a complete holiday from all kinds of work, including weaving and basketry, for a number of days, and among the Kamans there are special periods of taboo on weaving for any sacrifice offered to Mollo and Bronmai, the gods who introduced the art to the world.

Another tradition which is destructive of the traditional art throughout the entire area is the practice of burying the possessions of a dead man with his body or of hanging them on his tomb. In Tuensang and Tirap, and to some degree also in Siang, Lohit and elsewhere, the tombs have the appearance of miniature museums: decorated hats, colourful bits of cloth, ornaments, spears, guns and daos may be observed rotting in the wind and rain. For the deceased must have these things with him. In the Land of the Dead he will have to build a house, so he will need his dao; he will go head-hunting or to war, so he will need his gun; there will be festivals to attend, so he must have his best clothes. I have been told that if these things are not placed on the tomb, the ghost comes to the shaman and says: 'I have no clothes, I shiver with cold; I have no gun, how can I hunt? I have no dao, how can I clear my path?' And he threatens that, since his descendants will not help him, he will not help them and will spoil their crops.

The Idu Mishmis believe that when a man's soul reaches the other world, the older ghosts rob him of his clothes, and one of the penalties of death is that it sends you to a place where there are no weavers. There is, therefore, a special ceremony, the Iya, which is performed six months to a year after a death, at which many pieces of cloth are offered on the tomb; these clothes must be made by members of the household—not other relatives—who are thus kept busy preparing them. Many fine things are made but are never used or worn; they pass straight to the land of shadows and decay.

The result of this is that, although certain beads, charms, sacred bells and brass bowls are handed down as heirlooms in a family, it is very hard to find anything old; death destroys not only an individual, but a tradition.

This is one of the reasons why it is so difficult on the North-East Frontier to make any satisfactory collections of specimens for museum purposes. In a Wancho village I once saw a remarkable basket, decorated with wooden skulls and bear's fur. But when I tried to buy it—at a very high price—the owner, an old and poor man, refused to sell. 'In a few months,' he said, 'I shall be dead, and unless this bag hangs on my tomb, I shall be without credit in the other world.'

Another difficulty is that many of the people think it is dangerous to part with an object that has been used or worn. This may derive from a belief that the owner's vital essence permeates an article he has used, and that if he parts with it, his soul may fall into the power of the buyer. In a Bori village in northern Siang, the priests declared that if any one sold me one of his personal possessions he would die. I once bought a carved comb from a woman in Tirap, but before she gave it to me, she carefully removed every little hair from it; if she had not done so, I was told, she would have always felt a little anxious. When J. H. Hutton visited the Tuensang hills in 1923, he found that nothing he and his party had used, not even the bamboo mats they borrowed for screens, could be touched again after they had gone.

The Adis believe that there is an *aith* or 'soul' in material objects, in the grain stored in the bins or in a precious ornament like the *dudap* (page 123).[1] If anyone robs a granary and is caught, he has not only to pay a fine in compensation for what he has stolen, but has to provide the materials for a sacrifice which will persuade the *aith* to return to its proper home.

I once tried to buy a little bamboo holder for a Jew's-harp from a Tangam woman, but she explained that she was pregnant and that if she parted with anything used or worn by her, it would affect the 'soul' of her unborn child. A Shimong woman, a Miri or shaman of the Yang Sang Chu Valley, had a striking ear-ornament, which she would on no account part with, for some of the dirt from her neck, she said, had got onto it and with the dirt was her *aith*. If then she parted with the ornament, she might be separated from her 'soul' and this would offend her tutelary spirit.

Thirty years ago J. P. Mills wrote of trade between the Ao Naga weavers and the Tuensang tribes. 'Clothes of patterns specially admired by their trans-frontier neighbours, but no longer worn by the Aos, are made expressly for this trade, and on a fine day one may see the sitting-out platforms "dressed" with cloths to catch the eye of a passing Phom. An Ao usually wears cloths woven by his wife, and if he buys a decorated cloth he must be careful to brush it six times with a bunch of nettles before putting it on, while he utters a prayer that all ill luck that may be in it may depart. A man of the Mongsen group goes further. Besides brushing it with nettles he lays it on a dog before he wears it himself and prays that all misfortune attached to the cloth may pass to the dog and not to him. Ivory armlets, too, and crystal ear-ornaments are dangerous things to buy. The purchaser on his return home must sacrifice a fowl and pray that, since the ornaments have not been bought with stolen money but with wealth honestly come by, the wearer may live long to enjoy them, Aos scrape a shaving from a spear or pull a thread from a cloth before selling it.' Similarly, before putting on a new bead-necklace or collar of tushes, a Sema puts, or used to put, them on a dog, so that any evil in them may affect

[1] Please refer to original edition, *The Act of the North-East Frontier*, 1959, NEFA Administration.

the dog and not the wearer. In Subansiri today, if an Apa Tani sells a piece of cloth to a Dafla he pulls out a thread before parting with it; if he sells ornaments to anyone, he carefully washes them first.

Yet another factor hostile to the development of art is a sense of inferiority in face of the commercial products of 'civilization'. This is sometimes so strong that people will hide their own products from an outsider's view, and I have known girls at a dance attired in entrancing dress and ornaments drape them selves completely with white bed-sheets from the shops in order to look 'modern'. Shimong girls wear a pretty knee-length skirt with the *beyop* ornament, as illustrated on page 118.[2] But today they cover this with a dingy white skirt down to the ankles, concealing the bright colours and gleaming brass. Some Mishmi girls cover their own blouses with jackets of black mill-cloth, debasing the exquisitely-woven tribal garment into a kind of underwear. To the tribal mind it is the bazaar product which is the exotic, the fashionable, the unusual and people all too often take the beautifully-made traditional ornaments from their hair or ears and put cheap plastic hair-clips and ear-rings in their place.

A great deal of tribal art is associated with religious beliefs and practices and as these weaken the art weakens with them. Missionary influence has generally been highly destructive of folk art, whether it be dancing, song, carving or even weaving—for so many of these good things have been closely associated with 'pagan' ideas.

Yet in spite of this the hill people, who love colour and beauty, have succeeded, as the pictures in this book will show, in making many things that are original, striking and, in their own way, beautiful. They have an excellent taste in colour and in combining colours; some of them show remarkable skill in devising patterns and, if the old records are to be believed, they have developed many of today's designs during the past fifty years, and are still creating new patterns, partly under the stimulus of external example but largely as a result of their own natural zest for creation. The wood-carving often reveals vitality and

[2] Please refer to original edition, *The Act of the North-East Frontier*, 1959, NEFA Administration.

strength; the cane-work reaches a high standard of technical perfection. In the art of personal adornment, even the remotest tribes reveal a singular fertility of invention.

Today, as I show in my last Chapter, the Government of India is doing all it can to encourage the traditional creativeness of the frontier people and check the psychological factors and external influences that threaten it with destruction. This book suggests that such an enterprise is abundantly worthwhile and, despite every difficulty, may succeed.

A FRONTIER OF HOPE

At the beginning of this book I expressed my faith that it is not inevitable that the art of the frontier peoples must decline, but that properly guided and encouraged it may go forward to a far-reaching and exciting renaissance. For today there are many grounds for hope. There is a tradition on which to build. The people have found a new zest for living in the era of peace and security which a settled administration has brought them. Government is sympathetic and anxious to encourage and assist in practical ways.

But it would be unrealistic to suppose that the path will be easy. For the people's art has several enemies.

There is first the competition of bazaar goods. These come with the prestige of 'modernity', of novelty, and the fact that they are so largely used by the official staff. The tribesmen are earning a good deal of money, in road-making and building, in porterage and by selling their animal and vegetable produce. It is only natural that they should spend this money on manufactured goods instead of going to the trouble of making them themselves. Plastic ornaments easily take the place of the older, far more beautiful, ornaments of bone, seeds, and wings of birds. A singlet takes the place of the decorative coat; shorts supplant the finely woven and cowrie-decorated apron or the loin-cloth of leopard-skin.

Again the motif for much of the old art is disappearing. We have seen how the wood-carving, weaving, and personal ornamentation among certain tribes depended largely on head-hunting and the giving of Feasts of Merit. The Administration has stopped the one, the American Baptists have, in a number of places, stopped the other. Elsewhere, the splendid hats, decorated spears, war-coats were mainly associated with war; now that peace has come, why should they be made? There are taboos on the wearing of certain kinds of cloth, on the carving of certain kinds of figures. It is no longer possible to perform the deeds that permitted this, yet the taboos are still operative.

Even where the art still flourishes, the mere impact of 'civilization' has a deteriorating effect, as scholars have noted in other parts of the world. Raymond Firth, for example, describes how the art of New Guinea has gone down.

'Certain it is that, when the culture of these people has been disturbed by European influence, in nearly every case the quality of their art has begun to fall off. The removal of the ancient norms of their economic, ceremonial and religious life has not resulted in the release of the energies of the individual artist and inspired him to novel and better creative efforts, but has destroyed the most effective stimuli under which he worked. This is the case even though by European agencies the craftsmen are provided with much more efficient tools than before. Though new elements of design are introduced, in wood-carvings, for example, the work becomes flatter, less bold, the relief is lower, the execution is more careless and the more difficult types of design and of handicraft tend to disappear.' Boas too has written of the 'slurring' of Aztec pottery designs as a result of rapid mass production. And, nearer home, there is constantly before us the result of attempts to 'improve' the textiles of Manipur which have deteriorated as they have grown more popular.

What can be done to avoid these dangers? The first, most elementary, need is to ensure a plentiful supply of raw materials of the right kind. In other parts of tribal India, wood-carving has died out partly as a result of official restrictions on the extraction of wood and bamboo from the forests. In Orissa, misguided social workers at one time told the Gadabas and Bondos that it was contrary to the teachings of Mahatma Gandhi to weave with their traditional bark-fibre and they introduced spinning-wheels and the unfamiliar cotton. At the same time forest officials checked the free use of the shrubs from which the fibre had been taken. The result was that many Gadabas and Bondos stopped weaving altogether and began to buy mill-cloth instead.

In the areas under the North-East Frontier Agency administration the tribal people have large freedom over the raw materials of wood, bamboo and cane. Cotton and wool are more difficult to obtain. Sheep are kept only in a few places and cotton is grown only on a small scale. The people have in the past depended on yarn imported from the plains by merchants and sold in small quantities at a rather high price. The Administration is now importing large quantities of cotton yarn and wool for sale at cheaper rates, and this has undoubtedly already given great encouragement to the weaving industry.

The next step is a psychological one. The Government is doing all it can to create among the people a sense of pride in their own traditions—their music and dance, their weaving and carving their own dress, their own institutions. Every official is trained to approach tribal life with respect and humility and to ensure that nothing is imposed upon it.

Cultural centres, consisting of a museum, library and emporium, are being opened in each Division with the hope that as the tribal people see their own best products treated with honour and exhibited for the admiration of visitors, they will be encouraged to produce more and raise the standard of what they make. Many officials are now wearing elements of the hand-made tribal dress, especially Adi and Mishmi coats, and some of their wives wear the very beautiful skirts and shawls woven by different tribes. School uniforms, based on the traditional models, have been devised. Hand-woven tribal cloth is being increasingly used for curtains in offices, for cushion-covers and table-cloths. Carpets and mats woven in Tawang and Bomdi La are bought as soon as they can be made. There is a steady demand for the painted bowls of the Monpas, and the wood-carvings of the Konyaks and Wanchos, when available, have a ready sale as ornaments.

If, however, this is to be fruitful of genuine progress in art, a great responsibility lies on the purchasers: it is essential that they should refuse to buy inferior articles and those which show a falling-off from the high standards of tradition. The visitor or the official often needs education in aesthetics more than the tribesman, whose own taste is usually sound and true.

Much will depend on how far it proves possible to retain and develop the old designs and idioms for their decorative value, even though the former ritual associations may disappear.

As Leonhard Adam, speaking of the Central Australian tribes, many of whose ceremonial objects are 'undoubtedly aesthetically attractive', says:

> If these aborigines should ever be given the opportunity of developing their artistic talent in a changed world, where there is no room for primitive rituals, they should be encouraged to turn these ancient patterns into a modernized decorative style in connection with useful arts and crafts. That this is not impossible is proved by the development of American Indian art in the United States.

There is no reason in the world why even those tribes which have become Christian should lose their weaving and carving. In actual fact, there has been a revival of weaving among the Christian Lushais and Nagas, and the example of Achimota College in West Africa shows how a genius for wood-carving, formerly inspired by traditional ideas, can express itself with equal success in Christian themes.

Modern African art owes much of its progress on the right lines to the sympathetic research of artists and scholars. We need for the frontier areas of India, men of the calibre of Vernon Blake, whose work on 'The Aesthetic of Ashanti' threw a flood of light on the subject, or of Roger Fry who was one of the first to reveal to Europe the true values of Negro sculpture. Such an artist would first survey the whole field, studying technique and design, and then with caution, humility and patience help the tribal craftsmen to select the finest models of their own tradition for preservation and develop new techniques and styles out of their past heritage.

The value of research in the finest traditional designs is illustrated by the revival of pottery among the Hopis of North America. At the end of the last century Nampeyo, a woman of Hopi First Mesa, was inspired by the artifacts unearthed at the Sikyatki excavations; she imitated the technique, colour and design and an entire new school of pottery came into being. Similarly Ruth Bunzel describes how a well-known potter was employed at the Santa Fe Museum and in various archaeological diggings, and this revealed to him many new designs and techniques; he and others devised a new process of applying dull black paint to a polished black surface; the result was something which has become famous throughout the world. Dr

Bunzel points out the significant fact that the style grew simpler in response to the demands of the new technique.

To what degree we should 'interfere' in the course of primitive art, how far we should try to teach and instruct, and above all whether we should create, among people where art is the possession of the whole community, a class of artists and castes or guilds of craftsmen is a matter which has excited considerable controversy. The problem is not made easier by the very varied results that have been achieved in different places.

For example, in his study of African masks, Leon Underwood points out: 'so soon as a traditional carver is made art-conscious—by European notions of art as something specialized—apart from ordinary life—his powers of expression decline', and he goes on to refer to the cautionary example of the Government Experimental School at Omu in Nigeria. The Superintendent of Education there, J. D. Clarke, was concerned about the preservation under modern conditions of the Yoruba tradition of carving and he persuaded a brilliant African artist who, as a young man, 'when he did not know he was an artist', had produced many fine works, to come twice a week to the school to instruct the boys in wood-carving. 'But there was something lacking. The work done subsequently by both boys and their master suffered. It acquired an art-consciousness, parting from the ordinary position of art in African life, and soon became typical of the meritorious though lifeless work in European art-craftsmanship exhibitions.'

Clarke believed that the reason for this was threefold: an inferiority complex was created as a result of contact with the technologically advanced people of the west; in the African boys who went to school 'the link between the individual and the soil' was often severed; and the idea arose that an artist was something special, who worked mainly for profit and not, as formerly, to enrich his own life or decorate his religious and social institutions.

The strange and rather tragic story of the Carrolup School illustrates another point, the danger of turning tribal children into artists without making proper provision for their future. The Carrolup Native Settlement was established shortly after the First World War to accommodate some of the detribalized aborigines of the Great Southern District of Western Australia.

It quickly became a 'dumping-place for the human refuse' of the whole area: here came the incorrigibles and inebriates, the rogues and misfits, both full-bloods and near-whites. A school was started, which ran with difficulty, until in 1945 Mr and Mrs Noel White took charge. The Whites had previous experience of the children of self-respecting tribal parents who earned their living by trapping foxes and kangaroos or working as stockdrovers and shearers, and whose self-respect did not allow them to accept any assistance from Government for themselves or their children. These girls and boys used to carve pictures on emu eggs, and shaped twisted roots and branches into birds, animals and reptiles. The situation at Carrolup was very different: the people were pauperized by misguided official benevolence; the surroundings were corrupt; the school curriculum was uninspired.

Noel White found that the children had been taught a little drawing and painting, mostly of objects which they copied from textbooks and rarely or never saw in their daily life. He started them on 'scribble' patterns, encouraging them to scribble in their notebooks and fill in the spaces with different colours. He taught them to portray natural objects with which they were familiar and, as time went by, to sketch what they had learnt in their regular classes. He left the style alone, being content to encourage their interest and observation. They became fascinated by problems of light and shade; they discovered perspective for themselves.

At the same time the boys began to carve beautiful inlaid trays and platters, and the girls worked tapestries in startling colours. Above all, under White's guidance, they recovered their love of the bush and respect for their tribal ancestors, of whom they had seldom spoken hitherto except in disparagement. White told them of Namatjira, the Central Australian aborigine, whose paintings had become famous; he taught them to listen to folktales and take interest in their traditional way of life.

Hitherto the children had been half ashamed of their interest in the stories of the old people and had talked with them surreptitiously. Now they gathered happily round their camp-fires, learning the stories, almost forgotten, of the fine old tribes, following the words and movements of corroborees and ceremonial dances. They learned how the warriors of old had arrayed themselves for sacred occasions, of the weapons that had been used in the hunting-days, how the bush people had stalked and killed their prey.

From their own people they learned that which no white man could teach them—the deep, aboriginal feeling for country, a sense of mysticism and ancient magic, which they infused into many of their pictures.

As a result they were producing before long the remarkable paintings which amazed all Australia and caught the respectful attention of the art-critics when they were exhibited in London. The style was not 'tribal'; the materials used were 'modern', but the inspiration and subject-matter represented a true interpretation and revival of the ancient life.

And then—the whole thing broke up. A few boys were sent to the cities and given jobs, but they soon left them and went off to the vagabond existence in which they had grown up. The school was closed. The children scattered, some to farms and timber mills; others were put into a large Agricultural School, where there was no nonsense about art and which aimed at being a revenue-making institution. Nearly all the boys abandoned the art work which had brought them such happiness and fame.

In their leisure time they were drawn to the local cinemas or the gambling schools; their homes were again the squalid camps of their people.

When questioned now as to their painting the boys seem vaguely troubled. A shadow of bewilderment clouds their dark eyes, as there was once a vision of beauty, colour, and hope that filled the days with promise and excitement, but the vision faded and was lost.

The experience of the Carrolup School shows that tribal children may develop unexpected and singular gifts, but that these may easily be lost without constant fostering care and the creation of a psychological and social atmosphere in which they can thrive.

On the other hand, the success of G. A. Stevens at the Prince of Wales College, Achimota, suggests that attempts to revive traditional tribal art are by no means necessarily doomed to failure. Stevens went to Africa believing that 'primitive art is the most pure, most sincere form of art that can be, partly because it is deeply inspired by religious ideas and spiritual experience, and partly because it is entirely unselfconscious as art' and everything he saw confirmed him in this belief. Although it was obvious that it might be impossible to recapture the perfection of the older forms, Stevens was convinced that 'the peculiar characteristics of the African artistic genius' should certainly continue in whatever form was found most suitable.

There were, of course, plenty of new forms. Nearly every African boy who went to school was trained in 'Hand and Eye' or 'Brushwork', and he learnt something of light and shade, perspective, proportion and mixing of colours. 'There was widespread regard for the subject as an asset in examinations; a fairly widespread vulgar pleasure in imitative skill; very little power of selection between one kind of subject and another, and no attempt to represent living or moving forms.' Yet 'you can never quite destroy the artistic genius of a people', not even through your training institutions, and Stevens' first task was to discover whether there was any new and worthy inspiration that would set free the artistic impulse which he felt sure was there. He began by showing his students photographs of the superb masks, figures and stools of tradition; the result was ridicule and a suspicion among the sophisticated students that their teacher was a crank. 'Their ancestors had not been to school, had not received "Hand and Eye", and therefore could not draw. To hint that perspective was not a *sine qua non* of good drawing was almost blasphemy.'

Then one day Stevens discovered certain sketches with which the boys had decorated their dormitories. These had been done 'out of school' and were graphic, vigorous and exciting. Stevens decided to bring them into the classroom. He gradually weaned the boys from merely personal and scandalous cartoons to something which could be dignified by the name of imaginative composition.

> Drawing from observed objects was no longer called 'copying' but was confined either to objects, generally local in character which were interesting in themselves, or to exercises in the analysis of form and appearance of objects as closely related as possible to what they needed for their compositions.

Stevens remarks that to those who are not artists this may not seem a very big change, yet it was in fact a complete revolution of aims and values.

People who are not artists and yet who have to teach the subject almost invariably make the mistake of fastening on the mechanics of art, while neglecting or ignoring the psychological processes which go to make a work of art and the development of the artist.

It was not easy to bring about the change, but gradually the finished work bore

less and less resemblance to second-rate European drawing and more and more resemblance to the forms of the older indigenous art. The same love of clear design, rich pattern, rather precious surface quality, tremendous solidity, and appreciation of volumes; the same characteristics in the treatment of the human figure—large head and small bent legs—all came about, in these drawings, as if the race spirit, after lying dormant for so long, had found itself again.

In fact, so successful was the experiment that when Captain Rattray asked Stevens to illustrate a book of Ashanti folktales, he turned the task over to his students: 'thus was effected a linking-up with the past and a linking-up of two arts at the same time.' Before Stevens left Achimota, it was the Congo mask or Ashanti pottery that excited his boys and the last shreds of disrespect for 'bush art' were vanishing.

Wood-carving also was revived with great success at Achimota. This was partly achieved by changing the subjects; instead of carving motor-cars or aeroplanes, the boys were taught to make local and familiar things, State swords, Chief's stools, household implements and animals. The effect of 'injudicious teaching' and the result of following 'the worst European taste' was reversed; the boys were persuaded of 'the beauty and desirableness of their own native forms' and have since produced work of high quality.

All this has been mainly to do with painting and wood-carving, but it might apply equally well to weaving, for the people of India's frontier paint their pictures and write their poems on their looms. We have seen how, in Kaman Mishmi tradition, designs were evolved from familiar natural objects—the ripples on the surface of a stream, the interlacing of branches against the sky, the markings on snakes, fish and butterflies. The border designs on the wings of the Northern Jungle Queen or the Manipur Jungle Queen may have directly inspired some of the Mishmi patterns and it is possible that the Mishmis and other tribes got their idea of the triangle and even the diamond from butterflies, though the diamond may also have come from the cobra. More important, I suggest that the 'architecture' of the weaving designs may have been inspired by the lay-out of the patterns on butterflies' wings. The ability to build up an elaborate design in which every item plays its part, perfectly articulated into the whole, is one of the most remarkable achievements of the Mishmi weavers, especially when it is considered that the women make no kind of sketch and are constantly devising new arrangements of line and colour.

There is often talk of 'improving' the tribal patterns; it would be better to let them grow, naturally and inevitably, as they have done in the past.

> By viewing nature, nature's handmaid, art,
> Makes mighty things from small beginnings grow;
> Thus fishes first to shipping did impart
> Their tail the rudder, and their head the prow.

On the north-east frontier, painting is a traditional art only in western Kameng, and here it is largely Buddhist in style. Yet the possibility of developing drawing and painting is illustrated in this chapter. When Shri N. Sen Gupta first visited Along, he gave paper and crayons to various youths who had never had them in their hands before. One of these boys was a Minyong, the other a Bori. Their different interpretations of the human figure are of great interest. The Minyong shows the hair cut short in the fashion typical of his tribe; the traditional ornament (illustrated on page 123)[3] is round his neck: he has a dao in his hand, suggesting that he is the leader of a dance. Here are the chief interests of the Minyongs clearly portrayed.

The Bori figures are of a quite different shape, but equally characteristic. The Boris, unlike the Minyongs, wear a cloak supported by a string over the head. The leader of the dance also carries a dao. One of the girls has her breasts uncovered, for this is the custom in the remoter Bori villages. The dance is performed at night and an enveloping mantle of black surrounds the figures.

Inspired by this, a similar experiment was tried in the Bomdi

[3] Please refer to original edition, *The Act of the North-East Frontier*, 1959, NEFA Administration.

La school. The tidy samples of jugs, desks, tables and some remarkably symmetrical cocks that had been displayed there were removed from the walls and instructions were given to the teachers that they were not to interfere with the boys in any way. Then the boys were asked to make drawings illustrating certain familiar themes, such as religion, trade, cultivation, and so on. Some of the results are shown on pages 89 and 197.[4]

Sir William Rothenstein has observed that 'the African has preserved his strong sense of pattern; do not let us weaken it by putting before the young the dreary outlines of chairs, jugs and candlesticks, which are still found as examples to be copied in Indian elementary schools.' Let us too not introduce such models into the Cottage Industries centres and schools of India's frontier.

A number of these centres have been opened in NEFA and they will succeed provided that those responsible are able to approach the people's art in a spirit of humility and do not try to impose their own ideas on the craftsmen. All the guidance needed, says Adam in the course of a discussion on the possibility of developing handicrafts among the Australian and other aborigines, should be 'purely technical—how to handle the loom or the potter's wheel—whereas aesthetic arrangements of the designs and shades should be entirely left to the genius of the aborigines, without any interference by white artists whose vision is different and whose ideas would naturally spoil the originality of aboriginal work'.

Long ago, William Morris warned the world of the danger that the course of civilization would 'trample out all the beauty of life and make us less than men'. 'The aim of art,' he said again, 'is to increase the happiness of men, by giving them beauty and interest of incident to amuse their leisure, and prevent them wearying even of rest, and by giving them hope and bodily pleasure in their work; or shortly, to make man's work happy and his rest fruitful.' On the north-east frontier of India today we have the situation as it existed in the European Middle Ages, towards which Morris looked with nostalgic yearning, when there were few professional 'artists' but everyone was a creator.

[4] Please refer to original edition, *The Act of the North-East Frontier*, 1959, NEFA Administration.

The humblest peasant woman on the frontier makes her contribution to the colourful and varied beauty of the whole picture; every aspiring boy and maiden ripe for love adds to it by making delectable ornaments and decorating head and ear and limbs. Art belongs to the entire people; it has not yet become a monopoly of the few. And because it belongs to them, it brings them refreshment and happiness.

It is fortunate for the frontier people and indeed for India as a whole that the Government of India has recognized the importance of tribal art, and is doing everything in its power, not of course to freeze the cultural and artistic level as it is at present, but to develop, if need be to change, but always along the lines of the people's own genius and tradition. It hopes to bring more colour, more beauty, more variety into the hills, which in turn will inspire the world outside with some of its zest and freshness.

'Blessed are the innocent, for theirs is the Kingdom of Art.'

12

Nagaland (1961)

I

A Fine People

On the 1st of August 1960, Mr Jawaharlal Nehru told India's Lok Sabha (House of Commons) that his Government had decided to create a new, sixteenth State within the Indian Union to be known as Nagaland. Although this was hardly noticed by the world at large, it was the most momentous and exciting occasion in the extraordinary history of an extraordinary people. For years the Nagas had been clamouring and struggling for some sort of autonomy. Had they realized it, the essentials of this had been for years within their grasp. For, as the Prime Minister said in his speech at the time, 'Our policy has always been to give the fullest autonomy and opportunity of self-development to the Naga people without interfering in any way in their internal affairs or way of life.'

'India', he said again, 'achieved her independence thirteen years ago and the Nagas are as independent as other Indian citizens. We have not the slightest desire to interfere in the tribal customs and usage of the Nagas or in their distinctive way of life and in the new State they should be able to find the fullest opportunity for self-expression.'

Who are these Nagas, for whom India has offered so much sympathy, given such special privileges and felt such great concern? They are an Indo-Mongoloid folk living in the north-eastern hills of India, divided into over a dozen major tribes, speaking more than a dozen languages and dialects, formerly notorious for head-hunting, which is almost the only thing most people know about them, but today awake and stirring, anxious to progress. They are a fine people of whom their country is proud, strong and self-reliant, with the free and independent outlook characteristic of highlanders everywhere, good to look at, with an unerring instinct for colour and design, friendly and cheerful with a keen sense of humour, gifted with splendid dances and a love of song.

THE KIRATAS

The great authority of Dr S. K. Chatterji, supported by other scholars, considers that the classical word 'Kirata' is the equivalent of what today we call 'Indo-Mongoloid', a word which itself is useful as defining both the Indian connection of the people to whom it applies and their place within the cultural milieu in which they have established themselves, as well as their original racial affinities, and he includes among them

> all those Sino-Tibetan-speaking tribes, Mongoloids of various types in race, who entered into or touched the fringe of the cultural entity that is India—the Himalayan tribes (the Nepal tribes and the North-Assam tribes), the Bodos and the Nagas, the Kuki-Chins, the Ahoms, the Indian Tibetans, the Khasis, and the earlier tribes (of unknown affiliation within the Tibeto-Burman branch of the Sino-Tibetan family) who have now become absorbed in the populations of the plains of northern and north-eastern India.

There are four or five million Indo-Mongoloids, including the Nagas, and some of them have been in India for a very long time, their presence being first noted in the tenth century before Christ, at the time of the compilation of the Vedas. From this time onwards the word 'Kirata' was used for the non-Aryan tribes living in the mountains, particularly in the Himalayas and in the north-eastern areas of India, who were clearly distinguished from the tribes of Austric origin, the Sabaras, Pulindas, Nishadas and Bhillas, who were settled elsewhere.

The ancient Sanskrit literature describes them as hillmen living mostly on game, fruit and roots, dressing in skins, warlike and wielding formidable weapons. They were a good-looking folk and there is constant stress on their 'gold-like' colour in contrast to the dark skin of the other pre-Aryan people of the plains. These early Kiratas were rich with the natural wealth of minerals and forest produce of their mountains and were adepts in the art of weaving cloth, as the Nagas still are; in ancient as well as modern times the fabrics they made have been greatly in demand in the plains. An exhibition of Naga art held in Delhi at the beginning of 1960 came as a revelation to many who had no idea of their creative achievements.

Some Kiratas became Hindus, some Buddhists, recently a few have become Christians. Their importance in Hindu tradition is indicated by the fact that Siva Mahadeva, the great God, is described, as early as the *Mahabharata*, as taking the form of a Kirata, with Uma beside him as a Kirata woman, and going together to meet Arjuna. It is possible that Buddha himself was an Indo-Mongoloid or Kirata and through him India has a spiritual link with the whole Buddhist Mongoloid world.

In Assam other famous Indo-Mongoloid tribes are first the Bodos, linguistically connected with the Nagas, who spread all over the Brahmaputra Valley and occupied the Garo Hills, ultimately leaving their mark throughout the whole of Assam. Later Indo-Mongoloid immigrants were the Asams or Ahoms who established themselves in the east of the Brahmaputra Valley at the beginning of the thirteenth century and gave their name to Assam. By the middle of the sixteenth century they had conquered the powerful Bodo kingdom of the Kacharis and ruled over Assam until the British annexed the Province in 1824.

We need not detain ourselves with an account of the other Indo-Mongoloid elements in the general Indian population, except to note that they have always been significant and that the Licchavis, the Newars, the Koches and Kacharis along with others have contributed to the evolution of Indian culture for the last three thousand years and they have had an important place in Indian history, beginning with the battle of Kurukshetra. As a result of their long isolation and lack of cohesion as a single people, the Nagas have hitherto been denied this, but now there will be every opportunity for them to take their share in the Indian renaissance of today.

There has been a tendency to regard the Nagas as a lonely island isolated amidst an alien culture in which the rest of India took little interest. History, however, shows that they form part of an important branch of the great and varied Indian family.

THE NAGA COUNTRYSIDE

Nagaland, which is now divided into three Districts—Kohima, Mokokchung and Tuensang—with its administrative headquarters at Kohima town, is a long narrow strip of hills running more or less parallel to the south or left bank of the Brahmaputra. If we take Manipur as the southern base, then Nagaland will ascend across the map in a north-easterly direction, with Burma to the east, the Tirap Frontier Division of the North-East Frontier Agency (NEFA) to the north and the broad valley of the Assam plains all along the western foothills. The entire country is covered with ranges of hills, which sometimes break into a wild chaos of spurs and ridges, and sometimes, as round Kohima, descend with gentler slopes. Most villages stand at three to four thousand feet, though some hills rise above them to six thousand and the highest peak in Kohima District is Japvo, at 9,890 feet. The main concentrations of population, very typical of the Nagas, are on the tops of hills and at the higher elevations, and the unhealthy foothills towards the plains are only thinly populated. Rainfall is sufficient but not excessive, averaging 70″ to 100″ in the year, and there are many rivers and streams, but no lakes or tanks.

There is still a great deal of forest left, but much has fallen before the axe of the shifting cultivator and most of the wild game has been lost to the hunter's spear. Wild elephants and buffaloes, tigers and leopards, bears and various kinds of deer remain in only small numbers. Among birds, the Great Indian Hornbill is the most treasured, for use in decoration and magic.

THE WORD 'NAGA'

The derivation of the word 'Naga' is obscure. It has been explained as meaning 'hillman', from the Sanskrit *naga*, a mountain. It has been linked to the Kachari *naga*, a young man or warrior. Long ago, Ptolemy thought it meant 'naked'. It has nothing to do with snakes.

The most likely derivation—to my mind—is that which traces 'Naga' from the word *nok* or 'people', which is its meaning in a few Tibeto-Burman languages, as in Garo, Nocte and Ao. It is common throughout India for tribesmen to call themselves by words meaning 'man', an attractive habit which suggests that they look on themselves simply as *people*, free of communal or caste associations.

The name, however, was not in general use among the Nagas until recently. It was given them by the people of the plains and in the last century was used indiscriminately for the Abors and Daflas as well as for the Nagas themselves. Even as late as 1954 I found the people of Tuensang rarely speaking of themselves as Nagas but as Konyaks, Changs, Phoms and so on. In the same way the Mikirs usually speak of themselves as Arlengs, the Garos as Achikrangs (hill people), the Abors as Minyongs or Padams. Gradually, however, as the Nagas became more united they began to use the name for themselves, until today it has become widely popular.

The application of the name is equally confused. Dr J. H. Hutton, our greatest authority on these tribes and one of the truest British friends that they have ever had, says that:

> It is generally assumed in a vague sort of way that those tribes which are spoken of as Nagas have something in common with each other which distinguishes them from the many other tribes found in Assam and entitles them to be regarded as a racial unit in themselves.... The truth is that, if not impossible, it is exceedingly difficult to propound any test by which a Naga tribe can be distinguished from other Assam or Burma tribes which are not 'Nagas'.

THE NAGA GROUPS

At the same time, there is an atmosphere, a spirit, in a Naga which is unmistakable, and is shared by the following tribes inhabiting Nagaland. Until the Census of next year it is only possible to give a rough estimate of their population, but the following figures are, I believe, reasonably accurate.

Angamis	30,000	Mixed tribes	5,000
Aos	50,000	Phoms	13,000
Chakhesangs	31,000	Rengmas	5,000
Changs	17,000	Sangtams	20,700
Khienmungans	17,000	Semas	48,000
Konyaks	63,000	Yimchungrs	17,500
Lhotas	23,500	Zeliangs	5,250

There are also 2,400 Kukis in the hills and a mixed community of 8,600 at Dimapur, a small town in the foothills which gives

Nagaland rail communication with Assam, making a total population of a little over 3,57,000.

The tribal groups of Nagaland are forming new affiliations and using names hitherto unknown to anthropology. The Chakhesangs, for example, are a combination of Chakru, Khezha (both southern Angami) and Sangtam groups with two Rengma villages living to the east of Kohima and north of Manipur, who adopted the new name about 1946, and the Zeliangs are similarly a mixed group of Zemis, Liangmais and others. The great Konyak tribe consists of two rather sharply distinguished divisions, one ruled by powerful and autocratic chiefs, the other more democratic, which now calls itself Shamnyuyungmang.

NAGA LIFE AND CULTURE

It is very difficult to give a general account of the many tribes covered by the word Naga, for there are both differences and similarities among them just as there are many aspects of their life and culture which can be paralleled by tribes in other parts of India. For example, the Bondos of Orissa resemble in a quite remarkable way the Konyaks of Tuensang.

In physique and appearance the different Naga groups vary considerably, the Angamis, for example, being tall with regular features and the Semas shorter with more strongly pronounced Mongolian features. In colour too there are differences. Most are a beautiful light brown—the typical Kirata 'gold', but differing in shade from tribe to tribe and a light colour is generally admired, though it has been recorded that some Nagas, years ago, expressed their dislike of the 'English' colour, regarding it as unripe or 'undercooked'. There is wavy hair and straight hair and even the Negrito frizzly hair.

Some of the Nagas make great wooden drums or xylophones, splendid instruments which can send their message for several miles. Other groups, however, especially in the south, do not make them at all. Some of the tribes use a reaping-hook for harvesting, but the Semas traditionally only use their hands. The Angamis have excellent terraces and in this they are followed by a few other tribes who have come under their influence, while others do not practise terracing at all, though this type of cultivation has been, to some extent, introduced by Government.

Even in methods of sowing there are distinctions. The Angamis, Lhotas, Rengmas and Semas are very careful with their grain, making little holes in the ground and dropping in the seed. The Aos, Changs and Konyaks, however, scatter the seed broadcast. Monoliths used to be set up by the tribes, such as the Angamis, practising terrace cultivation (it is interesting to note that the Saoras of Orissa, who make even better terraces than the Angamis, also put up megalithic monuments for their dead) and by the Lhotas and Rengmas. To the north and east, however, the tribes rarely do this until we reach the Konyaks who erect monoliths for a number of purposes. In traditional funerary practice the Nagas vary greatly, some burning or burying their dead; others, such as the Konyaks, exposing corpses on platforms; while the Khienmungans used to have a practice of desiccation.

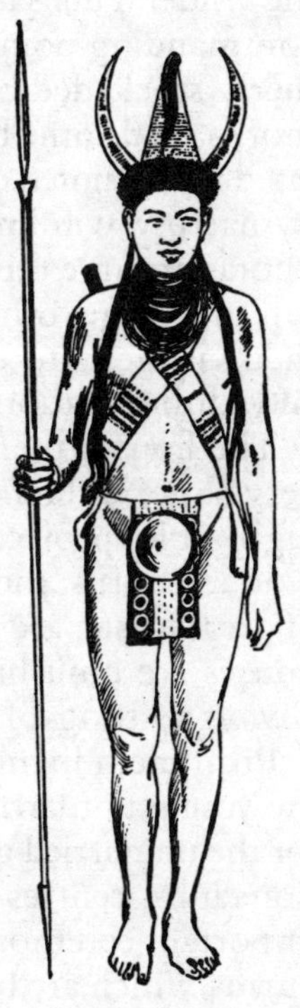

Eastern Rengma (after Mills)

Naga society presents a varied pattern of near-dictatorship and extreme democracy. There is a system of hereditary chieftainship among the Semas and Changs. The Konyaks have very powerful Chiefs or Angs who are regarded as sacred and whose word is law: before the greatest of them no commoner may stand upright. The Aos, however, have bodies of elders who represent the main family groups in the village and the Angamis, Lhotas, Rengmas and others are so democratic that Hutton remarks that in the case of the Angamis it is difficult to comprehend how, in view of their peculiar independence of character, their villages held together at all before the coming of the British Government.

THE NAGA VILLAGES AND HOMES

As long ago as 1873 Captain Butler spoke of the Angamis as occupying 'a most charming country, enjoying a beautiful climate and most fertile soil, well cultivated, drained, and manured, the hillsides being covered with a succession of terraces of rich rice, with numerous villages in every direction, some of them so large that they might justly be called towns'. The size of the villages and their dignity is very striking even in the wilder Tuensang border ranges; they are built on the most commanding points along the ridges of the hills and were formerly stockaded by stone walls, palisades, dykes or fences of thorns, and some had village gates, great wooden doors decorated with painted carvings in bas-relief, which were approached by narrow winding paths sunk in the ground. The Aos and Lhotas arrange their houses in regular streets, often along the top of a ridge; other tribes build as they please; but all divide their villages into *khels* or quarters, each with its own headmen and administration.

The houses themselves are usually fairly large, sometimes very large, and reflect the importance of the owner. Some have high gables projecting in front; others are crowned by crossed wooden horns; the trophies of the chase, and equally the relics of great feasts, are proudly displayed in the front porch. Many houses are built high above the ground on stilts and there is always a sitting-platform at the back.

Prominent in many villages is the Morung or dormitory for the young unmarried men—some tribes also have small houses for the unmarried girls. The Morungs are guard-hosues, recreation clubs, centres of education, art and discipline and have an important ceremonial purpose. Many house the great wooden durms which are beaten to summon for war or to announce a festival. Formerly skulls and other trophies of war were hung in the Morungs and the pillars are still carved with striking representations of tigers, hornbills, human figures, monkeys, lizards and elephants.

The staple food of the Nagas is rice supplemented by meat and, except occasionally for individual or clan taboos, they cast their net widely, though they prefer beef and pork. They are now drinking tea and even taking to milk, on which until recently they had a taboo. But their favourite drink is rice-beer, which may be described as a nourishing and palatable soup with a kick in it. For while its alcoholic content is small, it contains most of the essential nutrients and is an important source of Naga energy and strength.

It is impossible to describe Naga dress here, for it varies from tribe to tribe and is changing all the time. We will be content to note that the Nagas are very protocol-minded about dress, and in the old days the finest cloth could be worn only by the head-hunter or the donor of Feasts of Merit. I have given here a number of drawings, based on photographs in the older books, which illustrate various types of traditional attire. It would be hard to beat a Naga in his ceremonial finery, and he makes full use of his natural skill and taste in the use of cowries, feathers, goat's-hair dyed red, shells, bone and ivory. Naga textiles, of great variety, are woven by the women on small loin-looms of an Indonesian pattern.

A Naga morung (after Shakespear)

In the past the Nagas made almost everything for themselves, and some tribes developed a singular competence in the creation of both useful and artistic objects. Their iron work is still expert, and they have a little pottery. They have extraordinary dexterity in the use of bamboo, and with wood some of the tribes, especially perhaps the Konyaks, can produce strong and graceful carvings. The universal implement is the dao, a bill or hatchet, which is used in cultivation, as an effective weapon of war, and as a general tool of all work. Other weapons are spears and guns—the Konyak forges have turned out simple muzzle-loaders for generations.

The basic interest of every Naga is in his family, the clan, the *khel*, the village. This is what he regards as his culture which must not be interfered with. He is passionately attached to his land, his system of land-tenure, the arrangements for the government of his village, the organization of cultivation, the administration of tribal justice through the village and tribal courts.

RELIGION

Naga religion is of a type common throughout tribal India. There is a vaguely imagined supreme creator and arbiter of mankind, and many minor deities, ghosts and spirits of trees, rivers, hills: all nature is alive with unseen forces. There are priests and medicine-men who placate these spirits, banish those who give disease, attract those who help and guard, and who take the lead in the rites and festivals which stimulate the processes of agriculture, bless the marriage bed and protect the craftsman at his work.

Naga ideas of the after-life are confused and vary from tribe to tribe, but there is universal agreement that the soul does not perish at death. Some say it goes onward by a narrow path guarded by a spirit with whom it must struggle; some think it finds its final home below the ground, many believe that it takes the form of various insects, especially butterflies; some say that the good soul goes to a Village of the Dead towards the sunrise, the bad to a less pleasant place towards the sunset.

FEASTS OF MERIT

A central feature of traditional Naga life is the giving of what have come to be known as Feasts of Merit, in which the splendour, colour and extravagance of Naga life is concentrated. These Feasts consist, broadly speaking, of a series of ceremonies, in a rising scale of importance, leading finally to the sacrifice of the mithun—that great creature (the *bos frontalis*) which is the chief domestic animal and used almost as currency, to settle a marriage or pay a fine. The Feasts bring the donor honour

A Naga dao: there are many other types

both now and after death and he can henceforth wear special clothes and ornaments and decorate his house in a special way. Only a married man can give one of these Feasts, for his wife must take a conspicuous and honoured place in the proceedings.

A mithun

The Nagas have never shown much interest in Hinduism, but it is interesting to find some agreement between the ceremonial of these Feasts and that of the old Vedic religion. In the elaborate sacrifices of the later Vedic age, sheep, goats, cows or oxen and horses were killed. The ceremonies lasted for days and the householder and his wife had to take part. The bull-killing sacrifice and the killing of the mithun in the Naga Feasts are done almost in the Vedic manner, in each case the animal being killed by a sharp stake of wood which pierces its heart, and the important place given to the wife of a man performing these sacrifices is another point of contact.

HEAD-HUNTING

The practice of head-hunting is found all over the world and has attracted great attention. So-called civilized countries, which can destroy whole populations with a single atom bomb, can hardly afford to look down on a method of ritual warfare which, at the most, involved the loss of a few hundreds of lives every year. The Nagas say that originally they did not know how to make war but one day a bird dropped a berry from a tree, and a lizard and a red ant fought for it. Someone saw the ant cut off the lizard's head and thus men learnt to take heads.

The reasons for head-hunting are complicated and interesting. The practice is probably based on a belief in a soul-matter or vital essence of great power which resides in the human head. By taking a head from another village, therefore, it was believed that a new injection of vital and creative energy would come to the aggressor's village when he brought the head home. This was valuable for human and animal fertility. It stimulated the crops to grow better, especially when the head was that of a woman with long hair. Moreover the Nagas have always been a warlike race and the warrior, especially the young warrior, who had taken a head held a great advantage over his fellows in attracting the most beautiful girl of his village for marriage. Indeed, it is said that a youth who had not taken a head found considerable difficulty in obtaining a wife at all.

Head-hunting was something more than war. It inspired wonderful dances. It stimulated artistic production, for the most elaborate textiles could only be worn by a successful head-hunter or his relations. Small replicas of heads were carved to be worn almost like medals. Wooden pipes, with their bowls fashioned as heads, were made. Strong and vigorous human figures were carved and attached to baskets and the warrior's grave was the most splendid of all.

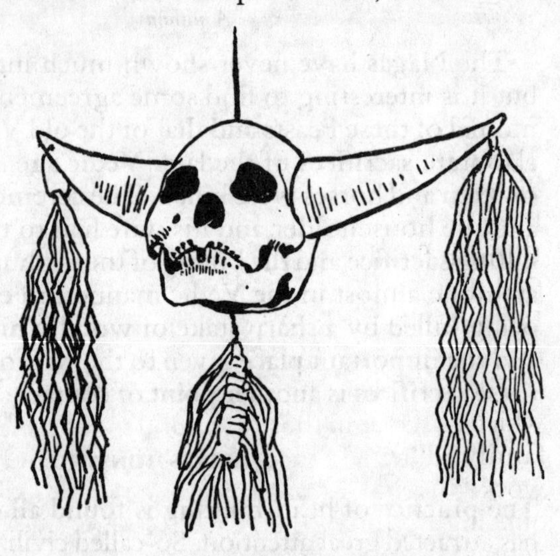

Decorated skull of a head-hunter's victim

Head-hunting virtually ceased soon after the British began to exercise effective control over the Naga Hills area, though it continued in Tuensang until recently. Here also it would probably have died out altogether if it had not been revived as a result of rebel action in the more distant villages. The last recorded case was in 1958.

THE NAGA LANGUAGES

The linguistic topography of Nagaland is remarkable for very complicated and numerous dialectical variations. In some areas the dialect differs from village to village, and in earlier days men and women in the same household sometimes had to use different forms of speech. To this confusion the former division of the people by inter-village feuds undoubtedly contributed.

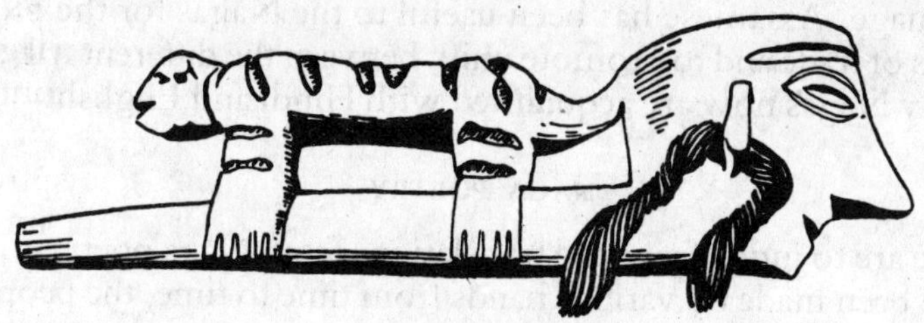

A Konyak tobacco pipe

There is, however, a general similarity in the languages and dialects spoken by the Nagas which belong, according to the Linguistic Survey of India, to the Naga group of the Tibeto-Burman family. An American philologist has recently re-classified them, placing the majority of them in what he calls the Burmic division, and a small minority in the Baric division, of the Sino-Tibetan tongues.

The Naga languages, however, possess a number of features which differ from those common to the general Tibeto-Burman family. They are, as Mr Das Shastri, a philologist who has worked in north-eastern India for a number of years, points out, highly tonal; the vowels do not conform to any known definite category and appear to be indistinct; the consonants, specially when they occur at the end of words, are glottalized; aspiration characterizes liquids and nasals; locative variety predominates in the case system and the conjugational pattern presents an extremely rich variety of moods and well classified tenses; negatives are mainly prefixed or suffixed, infixation occurring in a few instances; classificatory terms, both numerical and nominal, are in use,

Within the group lexical resemblances between Angami, Sema, Lhota, Ao and Meitei (Manipuri) have been noted. Morphological resemblances between Ao and Meitei; Angami and Kachari; Ao, Angami and Mikir; and Ao, Angami and Kachari, are very striking.

For a long time past, Nagas of different groups have talked to one other either in broken Assamese or in English, and the Nagas themselves observed with some amusement that at a conference at which they demanded separation from Assam, many of the speakers made their speeches in the Assamese language. Assamese has been useful to the Nagas for the purposes of trade and to promote unity between the different tribes. Many Nagas now are acquainted with Hindi and English.

NAGA POETRY

If we are to judge from the translations from Naga poetry that have been made by various hands from time to time, the people have a high capacity for the purest romantic love and a rich vein of poetic thought which should surely be better known. The Naga passion for beauty and colour, which inspired them to decorate almost everything they used or wore, appears too in their songs which, like all tribal poetry, is not written down but is treasured in the memory and brought out to music. I have seldom heard such beautiful singing as once when at night in a Konyak village high up on the Burmese border, girls sang as they husked rice together in a great mortar. Or again when a group of Chakhesang youths sang a love-song, gradually lowering their voices until it was as if each was whispering into the very ear of his beloved. Girls and boys in fact constantly make love to each other in poetry. 'You are beautiful,' says a Rengma poet, 'as a rhododendron bud and a red berry.' Says an Angami boy:

From youth on let there be no parting
I will wait by the path to watch;
I gaze at that fairest one from afar.
When her hair is long and bound up,
Then will I wait for her at dawn,
I will take her beyond the others.

And in an Ao Naga song (translated by J. P. Mills), a flying squirrel falls in love with a bird and the boy sings to his girl, the bird.

THE SQUIRREL SINGS

From far Lungkungchang
All the long road to Chongliyimti
Have I come to where my beloved sleeps.
I am handsome as a flower, and when I am with my beloved
May dawn linger long below the world's edge.

THE BIRD REPLIES

Countless suitors come to the house where I sleep,
But in this lover only, handsome as a flower,
Do mine eyes behold the ideal of my heart.
Many came to the house where I sleep,
But the joy of my eyes was not among them.
My lover is like the finest bead
On the necks of all the men of all the world.
When my lover comes not to where I sleep,
Ugly and hateful to my eyes is my chamber.

I will also quote a Konyak poem, recorded and translated by C. von Fürer-Haimendorf, about two lovers who were in a forbidden relation to each other, and who had to die. The poet does not condemn their love, but idealizes it in the image of the smoke of the separate fires uniting and mingling in death.

Yinglong and Liwang
They loved each other,
Loving, they lay together,
Red as the leaf of the ou-bou tree,
Flamed love and desire.
On the paths to the village,
The two lit fires,
Skywards, upwards curling,
The smoke of the fires united,
And mingled, never to part.

Submerging these cultural specialities (on which I have only had time to touch with extreme brevity) is the great tide of daily life. The ways in which men resemble each other are far more important than those in which they differ. The Nagas, like other people, are concerned first with their daily bread; they are interested in cultivation and trade; they are interested in knowledge, achievement, progress. They are born, they grow up, they love and marry and discover the joys and anxieties of parenthood, the rewards of age, the comfort of religion, they grow old and die. Naturally, you will say, we all do that—and that is just my point: we all do the same things, feel in much the same way, experience pleasure and suffer pain together. In essentials, the Naga is just like everyone else in the world.

A TIME OF CHANGE

And, like everyone else, the Naga is changing rapidly. This is nothing new: contact with the plains through trade has been continuing for much more than a hundred years: a new religion, an ordered administration, two World Wars, the recent disturbances have had their varied impact, and it does, in fact, say much for the vitality of Naga culture that it has not disappeared altogether.

New accessibility of markets and improved communications have led to the import of many novelties—there are blouses, brassieres, falsies, lipsitck for girls: plastic ornaments and celluloid combs usurp the old decorations of shell and bead, bird's-wing and flowers. School-boys have a uniform of shirt and shorts, with gay coloured bush-coats in American style. Brass or aluminium pots take the place of the old bamboo vessels for cooking and drawing water, enamel mugs replace the old bamboo vessels which were something skilfully carved or decorated with poker-work; there are electric torches, petromaxes, chairs and tables, smart walking-shoes, fashionable hats of every kind.

But the real changes go much deeper. The fundamental difference has come in shifting the gear of life from war to peace, the cessation of head-hunting and the gradual disappearance of the Feasts of Merit. This has led to all sorts of unexpected consequences. It is no longer possible to wear some of the finest products of Naga textile art, for these depended on success in war or generosity in feasting. Wood-carving has suffered for the same reason. The architecture of houses has changed, for certain features could only be added by families who had earned the right to do so. The maintenance of the morungs is no longer urgent, now that there is no need to keep a guard always on duty.

Conversion to Christianity has made other changes: the stress on personal salvation has introduced a new individualism in place of the former community spirit. Hymns have taken the place of the old songs; many dances, which celebrated head-hunting raids, cannot now be danced or simply linger on for exhibition to important visitors. Among the newly educated there is, as all over the world in similar circumstances, a turning away from the land, a reluctance to work with one's own hands, a desire for white-collar jobs.

In some ways, however, the last few years have witnessed a revival of Naga culture. Except for a few 'modern' girls, nearly all the women retain much of their hand-woven dress. Even the Christian Nagas are showing a new interest in their traditional dances: they want to build up their own literature in their own languages, to record their old epics and stories; they are developing a sense of history.

They are, in fact, beginning to feel that there is less conflict between yesterday and tomorrow than they had once feared. Their innate sense of beauty, their good taste, their own self-reliance will probably maintain the tradition of weaving and other arts. And the old life on the hillside, in the forest or by the mountain stream, which was a good life, will continue, and the stories and ideas of the countryside will survive, but with new motives and a new direction.

Myths of the North-East Frontier (1958)

PREFACE

This is the first of what I hope will be two or more volumes dealing with mythology and folklore of the North-East Frontier Agency of India (NEFA). The Philological Section of the NEFA Research Department will produce other volumes containing the original versions of these and similar stories. Dr B. S. Guha, formerly Director of the Department of Anthropology, is engaged in recording and translating the great Adi (Abor) myths, the *abhangs*, especially those known in the Pasighat area, and these will form the subject of yet another volume. I have, therefore, not attempted to reproduce any of the *abhangs* as such here, though I have included certain episodes from those chanted in the northern Siang villages, and I have left the task of printing the originals of the stories to our philologists, who are far more qualified to do so than myself.

This book, therefore, has the modest and restricted purpose of making available English versions of nearly 400 tales, many of which are of exceptional and some of unique interest, and all of which throw a great deal of light on the thought and poetic imagination of tribes about whom little has hitherto been written.

In all tribal areas, there is a great divergence of ideas, especially in the realm of folklore, mythology and religion; stories and the names of gods and heroes vary from place to place; the same informant may even pronounce a word, or use a name differently on two successive days. This is inevitable in a region where there is no fixed deposit of doctrine, no sacred books to carry traditions from one generation to another, and where the repositories of knowledge are human beings exposed to the inspirations of their dreams and fancies.

In northern Subansiri, for example, I found the name of a great tribal ancestor pronounced in several different ways. The Tagins said something between Abo-Tani and Abo-Teni; the Miris said Abo-Teni or Ab-Teni; and the Apa-Tanis and Gallongs said Abo-Tani. It was equally difficult to decide the proper transliteration of the Wancho name of the Supreme Being; informants would say Rang, Jang and Zang almost in the same breath.

In translating I have followed the principle described in my *Tribal Myths of Orissa*.

> My custom was to translate the stories on the spot, as they were narrated or interpreted to me. I have translated them literally, as if I was translating poetry: that is to say, I have inserted no new symbol or image, and I have tried to avoid words which, though neutral in themselves, carry associations alien to the tribal consciousness. I have never, of course, tried to make the stories intelligible or attractive to my readers.

In making a collection of this kind a scholar is bound to incur many debts of gratitude. My chief debt is to the tribal interpreters who travelled with me and went to enormous pains not only to make the meaning of the stories clear but to persuade informants to tell stories at all. For, although the Sherdukpens and some of the Adis were forthcoming and even eager to explain their traditions, others, especially in Tirap and Tuensang, were reluctant to do so. NEFA is not an easy place for research; it does not give up its secrets readily. A common attitude was summed up by one of my assistants: 'he doesn't know and if he did know, he wouldn't tell'. In the Khamlang Valley only the priests can tell stories, and for nearly the whole of my visit there, no priest was to be found—until, at the very end, one was proudly produced, and he proved deaf and dumb!

In an area where a fantastic variety of dialects is spoken it was inevitable that I should have had to depend on interpreters, except in a few cases where informants told stories directly in Hindi. But I was fortunate in obtaining the services of exceptionally good official interpreters, among whom I must make special mention of Shri Wangdun of Tirap, Shri Tapang Taki of Siang, Shri Ita Pulu of Lohit and Shri Bini Jaipur of Subansiri. To them, and many others, I tender my grateful thanks.

The stories were collected mainly on long tours in the frontier mountains during the four years 1954 to 1957. Others were recorded for me by my indefatigable assistant, Shri Sundarlal Narmada, who has now worked with me for nearly a quarter of a century. He is responsible for collecting the Singpho, Bugun, Hrusso and Dhammai myths (most of which I personally verified later) and he went with me on most of my tours. A few other stories were collected by the Assistant Research Officers of the NEFA Administration and in particular by Shri T. K. Barua, who has spent a number of years among the Mishmis, and who accompanied me on arduous tours along the Patkoi Range and in the Khamlang Valley, and by Shri B. K. Shukla who has been working for the past year in Subansiri. I must also express my appreciation of the loyal and tireless work of my stenographer, Shri S. Lahiri, and typists, Shri P. Banerji and Shri Higher Land Syiem, in the preparation of the manuscript.

I am grateful to the Asiatic Society for permission to reproduce a number of stories from G. D. S. Dunbar's 'Abors and Galongs', which appeared in the *Memoires of the Asiatic Society of Bengal*, Vol. V (1913–17).

In the second volume I hope to give much more introductory material, and in particular a full account of the various tribes. But in view of the keen interest that the tribal people are themselves taking in the preservation of their own oral literature, it seemed desirable to produce this preliminary collection as soon as possible, and I hope that its publication will encourage others also to record the NEFA mythology before its clear and original outlines become dimmed by the external influences which inevitably accompany the march of material progress and development. A Motif-Index to cover both books will be included in Volume Two.

SHILLONG
29TH DECEMBER 1957

VERRIER ELWIN

INTRODUCTION

The North-East Frontier Agency is a wild and mountainous tract in the Assam Himalayas which covers some 27,000 square miles bounded by Bhutan to the west, Tibet to the north and Burma to the south-east, and into which the Valley of the Brahmaputra projects like a great spur. It is now divided into five Frontier Divisions, Kameng, Subansiri, Siang, Lohit and Tirap and accommodates about four hundred thousand people. Some parts, such as central Siang, are heavily populated; others, like northern Subansiri and Lohit, are sparsely inhabited in isolated villages along the river valleys. The rainfall is heavy, as much as 200 inches in Subansiri. The countryside offers almost every possible type of mountain scenery. On the 14,000-foot Se-La Pass on the way to Tawang, with its masses of rhododendrons and other multi-coloured flowers, the traveller is reminded of Kashmir; in the lovely valleys of Siang with their background of snow-capped mountains, you are at one moment in Austria, at another in Wordsworth's Lakes. Nor are the formidable slopes of the Patkoi, the wide and open glories of Tirap, the dark jungles of Lohit, easily forgotten. An early traveller described this country as 'back-breaking': I would rather call it 'heart-warming', for though the marches are long and difficult, the people's welcome and hospitality quickly wipes away the memory of fatigue.

This area, which was almost completely isolated until very recently, is populated by a large number of tribes speaking different languages and dialects of the Tibeto-Burman family and exhibiting a great diversity of culture, dress and custom. It may be divided into three main cultural areas. The first is largely inspired by Buddhist ideas and includes the people of Western Kameng, small tribal groups living all along the northern frontier through Subansiri, Siang and Lohit, and the Buddhist Khamptis and Singphos in the foothills near Tezu and Margherita. The second cultural province consists of the great central block of territory—eastern Kameng, Subansiri, Siang and Lohit and the third to the south-east, is a small but important area, now consisting only of part of the Tirap Frontier Division which is populated by the Wanchos and Noctes. Although each of these provinces has much in common with the others, there are a number of definite cultural traits which distinguish them.

The Buddhist or near-Buddhist tribes have a developed civilization which has been considerably influenced by Tibet and Burma. In western Kameng live the Monpas and Sherdukpens, gentle, courteous people who cultivate on terraces, maintain large numbers of cattle, sheep and horses and are to a great extent under the influence of the lamasery of Tawang. Both tribes combine in their religion and mythology traditional tribal ideas with the Buddhist theology. In fairly close geographical proximity live the Buguns (Khowas), Hrussos (Akas) and Dhammais (Mijis) who, although not Buddhists, share some aspects of their neighbour's culture. The Membas and other tribes living along the northern frontier may be conveniently grouped with them and so may be the Buddhist Khamptis and Singphos who migrated in historical times from the Irrawaddy Valley and have lived for some generations in close proximity to the Assam plains.

The great central area is populated by a large number of tribal groups who have been divided from one another by the difficulty of communications and by the state of war in which they lived for centuries before they were brought under regular administration. In the east of the Kameng Division is a fairly large population of Daflas, who are here known as Bangnis; the same tribe extends into the west of the Subansiri Frontier Division. The wild and desolate hills of Subansiri are also inhabited by the Tagins and Gallongs in the north, by a tribe which for want of a better name is usually called the Hill Miri and by the Apa Tanis whose system of cultivation would be remarkable even in a fully settled area. The life of the people in the northern and western mountains, where puny man fights an arduous battle against the giant forces of nature, is in striking contrast to that of the Apa Tanis on their beautiful plateau where nature has been largely dominated and controlled by tribal genius.

Siang, the happiest of the NEFA Divisions, is the home of bright colours, lovely weaving, dancing, singing and an enchanting people formerly known collectively by the Assamese word 'Abor', which means 'independent', but who now call themselves Adi or hillmen. Here too are striking contrasts. On one side is Pasighat, now a prosperous little township, with a

High School, a fine Hospital and various training establishments. On the other, are the remote valleys to the north inhabited by Ashings, Pailibos, Ramos, Bokars, Boris and other tribes of whom we still know comparatively little.

Also included in the central area the Mishmis of Lohit who are divided into three main groups—the Idus (Chulikattas), the Taraons (Digarus) and the Kamans (Mijus). The Taraons and Kamans differ only in dialect and are not easily distinguished. The 'crop-haired' Idus, however, who represent an earlier wave of migration from Burma, differ in many ways and resemble in appearance (though not in culture) the Padams who are their neighbours. All Mishmis, however, live in very small villages, some of which consist of a single great house in which as many as forty to sixty persons may be accommodated. They have few social virtues and are the most individualistic of the NEFA tribes. On the other hand, their weaving is probably the finest in the whole area and the Taraon and Kaman women are distinguished by their attractive hand-woven cloth and the coiffure and silver ornaments which give them an unusual and striking appearance.

In Tirap are the virile and picturesque Wanchos, who are organized under influential and wealthy Chiefs; the Noctes, who have adopted a very elementary form of Vaishnavism and have been more in contact with the outside world than any others, with a resultant loss of much of their traditional culture; the many small groups collectively known as Tangsa, a charming friendly people who have migrated from Burma, and still have many links across the border; and small populations of Singphos and Khamptis.

Throughout NEFA the unit of social organization is the patrilineal family; polygamy is fairly common, a fact which is often emphasized in the tales, and there are traces of polyandry among the Gallongs. Each tribe is divided into a number of exogamous clans and, as a general rule, the tribes do not intermarry, although there are many examples of this rule being ignored. The people all live in villages, but the Mishmis and Daflas tend to make the house rather than the village the centre of their social interests. Village government varies from the autocracy of the great Wancho and Nocte Chiefs to the highly democratic system of the Adi tribes, which are governed by a

Kebang or Council of the leading members of the village clans. The people are generally well organized, at least within the clan or village, a state of affairs which is encouraged by the existence of communal dormitories among the Wancho, Nocte and Adi groups.

All the tribes live by what is known in Assam as *jhuming*, or shifting cultivation, the harvests of which they supplement by a wide variety of forest produce. Many of them are also skilled hunters and fishermen. Few of them drink distilled spirit, but everywhere they make a light and nourishing rice-beer which is used on all ceremonial and social occasions. Many of them grow their own tobacco and some grow opium for their own consumption and for trade. Although formerly suspicious and hostile to strangers, they have, under the present policy of the Government of India, become friendly and co-operative. They are in the main hospitable and well-disciplined, hard-working, truthful and honest. Former customs of inter-village wars, head-hunting, kidnapping and slavery have largely disappeared and in the new era of peace there is an increased inter-mingling of the tribes, a fact which will undoubtedly have its influence on their mythology and folktales in time to come.

Until Independence such contacts as the people of NEFA had were with soldiers, the merchants to whom they sold their goods, a few explorers and members of the Topographical Survey and, in the later years of the British period, with a few Political Officers who visited their villages and settled some of their disputes.

There is no space here to recall the long and distressing story of tribal raids on the inoffensive plains or of the punitive expeditions that went into the hills to rescue captives or avenge the dead. In the thirties of the last century, for example, Tagi Raja, the Chief of the Kapaschor Akas or Hrussos, led his followers to murder and pillage and in 1835 wiped out a British outpost at Balipara. The Adis made frequent attacks on the plains villages throughout the century, and their hostility culminated in the murder of Williamson and Gregorson with forty-two of their followers in 1911. The first official record of the Mishmis, in 1825, declares that they were 'very averse to receive strangers' and in 1854 the intrepid Father Krick with a fellow-priest who had successfully crossed the pass at the head of the Zayul Valley was murdered on their way home. Forays by the Daflas and Apa Tanis were less serious, but the Khamptis and Singphos proved worthy antagonists of British arms in their early raids on Sadiya, though they later settled down to the pacific life to which their Buddhist faith naturally inclined them. The tribes of the Tirap hills have always had more friendly relations with the plains people, and except for an occasional kidnapping of individuals for slavery or sacrifice, the only outstanding tragedy was the massacre of Holcombe's Survey party by the Wanchos in 1875. The people of Tuensang further south lived in almost complete isolation; they were visited by Dr J. H. Hutton in 1922, and in 1936 Mr J. P. Mills led an expedition to punish a village called Pangsha, which had taken 400 heads in a few months.

The policy of Government in the pre-Independence period was to attempt no more than a skeleton administration in the foothills; to send out punitive expeditions in reaction to the more serious raids; to impose blockades and establish fortified posts at strategic points; and in certain cases to pay what is called *posa* to the Chiefs on condition that they kept their people under control.

Another form of external contact was through the explorers who from the earliest times pressed into the interior.

In 1826, for example, Wilcox reached the Upper Irrawaddy from Assam and the following year went into the Kaman Mishmi country as far as the point where the Brahmaputra, 'after flowing nearly south from Tibet suddenly changes its course and flows in a westerly direction'. Ten years later the botanist Griffith succeeded in travelling as far as the village of Ghalum on the Lohit, but was unable to enter the Kaman hills. In 1845, Rowlatt went up the Du river as far as Tuppang where he met a number of Tibetans. E. T. Dalton, later to become famous as the author of one of the classics of Indian anthropology, the *Descriptive Ethnology of Bengal*, made a trip up the Subansiri River in 1845 and visited the Adi country, though not very far in, ten years later. Perhaps the most remarkable of these early travellers was T. T. Cooper, a British businessman who, in 1868, was invited by the Shanghai Chamber of Commerce to attempt to reach India from China through Tibet. In this he failed and the following year attempted the journey in reverse, starting out from Sadiya. He came to within twenty miles of Rima, but was then compelled to return.

The first person to visit the Apa Tanis was an adventurous Tea Planter, H. M. Crowe, who went into their hills in 1889 and got on very well with them, an experience which was not shared by the German explorer von Ehlers who followed him a few years later but was robbed and driven out of the country. Another Tea Planter, who made extensive explorations with the idea of extending the trade of Assam beyond the frontier, was J. Errol Gray who left Saikwa at the end of 1892 in an attempt to cross into western China. He travelled unarmed with a comparatively small party and succeeded in crossing the Nam-Kiu and entering the valley of the Tisang, an important affluent of the Irrawaddy.

When the Topographical Survey of India directed its attention to this area a number of survey parties went far into the interior and the leaders of some of them such as R. G. Woodthorpe, H. J. Harman, and C. R. Macgregor established friendly relations with the tribes.

Another way in which the hill people came in touch with the outside world was through trade. The Mishmis have always been keen traders and they brought down musk, *Mishmi teeta* which was at one time widely used as a febrifuge, ivory and skins. At one time, the Apa Tanis brought large quantities of rubber for sale. The Adis bartered skins, cane and wool for salt. The Mishmis and some of the tribesmen in Tirap also used to smuggle opium into the plains areas. The Hrussos and Sherdukpens have had trade contacts with Assam for generations.

From the middle of the last century annual fairs were held at Udalgiri, Doimera, Sadiya and elsewhere, and were visited by large numbers of hillmen.

Finally, there was the impact on the people of Government officials. It was not until 1894 that a Political Officer, J. F. Needham, was appointed to study the languages and politics of the tribal people and try to win their goodwill by sympathy and contact. He made many promenades (as they were then called) to within a few miles of Rima, to the Hukong Valley, to Burma across the Patkoi Range, and accompanied two disastrous military expeditions, one in the Abor Hills and another in the last year of the century to the Idu Mishmi country. There is no doubt that he, as well as his successor Williamson, made many friends on the frontier and contributed to the more hospitable reception which visitors received in later years. During the present century the number of visitors as well as the gradual expansion of some sort of administration naturally increased and we may mention the work of the Miri Mission in northern Subansiri in 1911 and the still more adventurous expedition of Dr C. von Fürer-Haimendorf in 1944 to the Upper Kamla Valley and beyond.

These varied contacts had remarkably little effect on the life and culture of the people. They were probably too transient and occasional to have a deep effect, but they did succeed in slowly bringing the inhabitants to realize that the greater world outside their hills was not hostile to them but only wished them well. At least the isolation of NEFA was not complete.

This may account for the fact that, although many of the NEFA stories are original and most of the common motifs of Indian folklore are absent, there are some traces of external influence. A very few myths show traces of missionary teaching, heard on visits to the plains; there is an occasional echo of the Ramayana; one Singpho myth is based on a Jataka tale; a fable from a school primer finds its way, greatly altered, into the body of the mythology.

Among the motifs common in other parts of tribal India which will be found in NEFA are those of an original primeval ocean out of which the world was formed, of earthquake as caused by the great animal on whose back the world rests, of lightning as the pursuit of a girl by an unwanted lover, traditions of a Land of Women, of opium as the reincarnation of a girl whom nobody loved in her lifetime, the taboo on opening something during a journey, the Fox Woman, the Trickster cycle and the widespread idea that monkeys were originally human beings who lost their status through idleness or breach of a taboo.

But on the whole the tales are remarkably original and seem to be genuine products of tribal creativity and imagination. There are no moral tales, though a few suggest the possibility of divine punishment for sin. There are very few formulistic or cumulative tales; there is little stress on sacred numbers; not a hint of astrology; and only one reference to the 'soul index' motif so popular in Indian folklore.

The myths are told on a variety of occasions: some are chanted during the dance, as for example the Adi *abhangs*, and the Sherdukpen tales; some are repeated at ceremonies, at a funeral or harvest thanksgiving or to save the life of a child; others are told round the fire in the Naga *morung* or Adi *moshup*, yet others are perhaps not told publicly at all, but are passed down from shaman to shaman as a kind of traditional wisdom or history.

Long ago Tylor suggested that myth was primitive history and ethnology expressed in poetic form. The poet contemplates the same natural world as the man of science, but he expresses his discovery in a different way. And the primitive poet who puts his inspiration in the form of myth shapes in out of 'those endless analogies between man and nature which are the soul of all poetry'. The truth of a myth is thus in a way irrelevant. 'Myth is the history of its authors, not of its subjects; it records the lives, not of superhuman heroes, but of poetic nations.'

Many tribal people have a deep vein of poetic imagination, and only the difficulty of interpretation prevents us from enjoying it as we should. Many of the NEFA myths are rich in 'poetic' ideas, an expression which can hardly be defined, but which most readers will appreciate.

The NEFA stories of the origin or creation of the world, the sky, and the heavenly bodies have an almost Miltonic grandeur of conception. Earth and Sky are lovers and when the Sky makes love to the Earth every kind of tree and grass and all living creatures come into being. But the lovers must be separated, for so long as they cling together there is nowhere for their children to live. In a Minyong tradition, after their separation, the Earth always longed to return to her husband to be one with him again. But as she was raising herself to the Sky, the Sun and Moon appeared, and she was ashamed and could go no further. That part of her which was reaching towards her lord became fixed for ever, as the great mountains. In a Singpho story the rainbow is a ladder by which a god climbs from earth to meet his wife in the land of the Moon, high in the sky, and in Tagin stories the rainbow is a bridge by which a bride goes to her husband's house.

There is poetic inspiration in the Sherdukpen story about rainbows which tells how there are four water-spirits, white, black, yellow and red, who live in springs among the hills and from time to time wander across the heavens for ever seeking wives as lovely as themselves. The rainbow is the path of blended colours that they make across the sky.

The people of NEFA have a strong sense of beauty and love bright colours and flowers. There is a Nocte tale of two brothers, one of whom lives on earth and the other, the younger, in the sky. 'From time to time the younger brother dances and throws showers of rain-drops down to earth. Then he asks the lovely fair-coloured girls of earth whether they have such beads on their necks. Sometimes too he throws the lightning down and asks the earth-people if they have such wondrous magic as this. Sometimes he beats his drum and when it thunders across the sky, he asks the earth-people if they have any music to match it.' Lightning always delights the tribal poets and myth-makers; it is, say the Minyongs, the flashing of a divine mother's eyelids; to the Mishmis it is the beauty of a star-girl running across the sky; to the Buguns, it is the long hair-pin with which a girl threatens an undesired lover.

The tribesmen are realists and there are plenty of ugly people in their stories, women with, for example, only one eye, one ear, one breast and one leg, but there are also many lovely creatures whose memory has come down from generation to generation. The Singphos, for example, speak of Raja Sitte-Charka whose queen shone like the light. 'When he went anywhere at night he used to take her with him so that her beauty could lighten the path by which he had to go. Not only light but a delicate scent came from her body.' Even after her death her body lay for months with its scented beauty unimpaired.

Such ideas, and others similar to them which will be found in this book, are the material of true poetry. It is consoling to reflect that Imagination, which is the light of the finest and most cultured minds, illuminates also the hard lives of the people of the hills.

Very common is the idea that the world arose from a primeval ocean or was formed upon its surface. Also common is the notion of the world as a macrocosm, transformed from some great personage or even a tree. A few stories speak of a direct creation by heavenly beings; there are Hill Miri, Hrusso and Khampti tales of a cosmic egg; and there are traditions of earth and sky being 'born' of a universal Mother.

It is remarkable that people who have never seen the sea nor even, so far as we can tell, large sheets of water of any kind, should have devised the idea of a primeval ocean from which all things have emerged. This tradition, of course, is as old as the Upanishads, several of which declare that the original material of the world was water. The Ramayana maintains the tradition, saying that all was water at first and that the earth was formed beneath it. Then Brahma arose and, becoming a boar, raised up the earth.

Throughout central India, Orissa and Bihar, tribal creation myths echo this belief. In some of these the world develops from the primal sea directly; in others there is an original world which is destroyed by flood for fire and is then created afresh. The NEFA stories are usually of the first pattern, although one Kaman Mishmi tale describes a great flood succeeded by fire which destroys the original world as a punishment for sin, and a Singpho tale tells how the Supreme Being rebukes man's iniquities by fire and flood. Bori, Gallong, Hill Miri, Nocte, Sherdukpen, Minyong and Taraon Mishmi stories describe how at first everything was water. The Gallongs attribute the emergence of the earth to the prawn and the crab: the prawn collected a great pile of rubbish on the surface, the crab dug a pit below to drain off the water. The Hill Miris say that an enormous tree grew out of the sea and worms ate the wood until, by the constant falling of the dust into the water, the world was formed. In Minyong tradition, a great mithun dug a pit into which the waters poured and allowed the dry earth to appear. In two Nocte stories, the water subsided of its own accord, allowing the earth to rise above it. Among the Sherdukpens, it is believed that two heavenly brothers threw a lotus down onto the surface of the ocean, whereupon it was covered with flowers, over which the four winds blew clouds of dust until the earth was formed. A Taraon Mishmi tale describes how there was a lot of mud below the waters and a god erected in it a pillar, up which a swarm of white ants climbed with their mouths filled with earth. This idea of animals bringing earth from the bottom of the primal ocean to make the world is common in central India.

A more remarkable idea found in some of the NEFA stories is that of creation by sacrifice or the transformation of some great personage into the world, an idea which echoes the famous Purusha-Sukta in the Rigveda. 'Far, far back out of the recesses of the Vedic cultus the figure of Maha-Purusha emerges as the symbol of creation by sacrifice. A vast cosmic Man, human in person but divine in nature, submits to be offered up by the gods. . . . The Purusha has a thousand heads, a thousand eyes, a thousand feet, expressive of omniscience and omnipresence. He envelops the earth and transcends it; he is identical with the whole universe; he is the sum of all existence: he includes all that is and all that shall be. From this exalted Person spring all the objects and beings of the world.[1]

This was the beginning, and the macrocosmic idea of the world as a vast personage transformed is frequently repeated. The Atharva-Veda (10.7.32–34) describes the earth as the base of the highest Brahma, the air is his belly, the sky his head, the Sun and Moon his eyes, the fire his mouth, the wind his breathing. In the Brihad-Aranyaka Upanishad (1.2) the demiurge Death dismembers himself. 'The eastern direction is his head. Yonder one and yonder one are the fore-quarters. Likewise the western direction is his tail. Yonder one and yonder one are the hind-quarters. South and north are the flanks. The sky is the back. The atmosphere is the belly. This earth is the chest. He stands firm in the waters.' The magnificent and mysterious opening of the Aitareya Upanishad (1.1) describes how fire comes from the mouth of the world person, 'from his nostrils the wind, from his eyes the sun, from his heart the moon, from his navel death, from his male generative organ water'. A later Upanishad—the Mundaka—describes

> the issue of all kinds of beings from the Imperishable, like sparks from a fire. From him, as he became personalized in creation, were born breath, and all organs of sense, ether, air, light, water, earth. Fire is

[1] J. E. Carpenter, *Theism in Mediaeval India* (London, 1921), p. 43.

his head; the Sun and Moon his eyes; the wind his breath; his heart the universe. From him come the devas, men, cattle, birds, the up and down breathings.

In central India the Bhuiyas, Juangs, Gonds, as well as the Madigas of southern India, repeat this tradition, but more commonly with the motif that the world is made from a human sacrifice rather than from a divine transformation. In NEFA, however, the stress is rather on the sacrifice of some great creature for the sake of the world or on the formation of the world out of some person or animal who has died. Thus the Apa Tanis tell how the original human beings lived on the surface of the belly of the giantess Kujum-Chantu (a primitive version of Mother Earth) until one day she realized that if she got up and walked about, they would fall off and be killed, and so she died of her own accord. Every part of her body became part of the world and her eyes turned into the Sun and Moon. In a Bori story the only creatures in the early world were two spirits, one of whom had the form of a mithun and the other the form of an elephant. They fought and killed each other and from their flesh and bones the world was formed. In the Hill Miri story of the tree, to which I have already referred, the tree itself finally falls to the ground and its bark becomes the skin of the world, the trunk turns into rocks and the branches into hills. In another Apa Tani story there is a great Wiyu in the form of an earthen ball. When she dies, her thighs turn into the earth and her eyes into the Sun and Moon.

Other stories attribute the origin of the world to some kind of direct creation. The Buguns describe how the two sons of the Supreme Zongma made the earth and sky. The Sherdukpens similarly describe how two brothers, neither of whom is the Supreme Being, created the world by throwing a lotus onto the primal ocean. The Kaman Mishmis tell of two powerful spirits who do not actually create the world, but come down from the sky and make the hills and mountains. The Taraon Mishmis have a similar tradition and, in their case, the god Techimdun, who lived at first below the great waters, plays an important part in creation by setting up the pillars which support the earth laid by white ants on the surface.

In many cases the tribal story-tellers are concerned to explain how it is that part of the world is flat and part mountainous, and in general, whatever may have been the origin of the world itself, the piling up of part of it in the form of mountains and hills is attributed to certain gods or spirits.

It is interesting to note that the creation of the world is not usually attributed to a Supreme Being, but to lesser gods who often act in pairs.

Two Hill Miri stories speak of a cosmic egg—in one the earth and the mountains come from it, in the other the first rivers flow when it is broken. Hrusso tradition tells of two great eggs, forever revolving in space. They collide and break open: from one comes the Earth, from the other the Sky, her husband. This idea is echoed in a Khampti myth. Here we have an interesting parallel with the Gond tradition that the first human beings were born from the eggs of great birds who lived on the face of the ocean, an idea which appears again in Santal and Saora mythology.[2]

Finally, there is a tradition that earth and sky have descended from a sort of universal Mother. For example, in an interesting Singpho story, a woman in the form of a cloud is born out of the primeval fog and mist. She has a son and a daughter, who are like snow, and from them the earth and sky are born. At first the earth is only mud and the sky lies upon it as a thick cloud, but when the wind is born, it dries the mud, thus making the earth solid and drives the sky far away. Similarly, in a Dhammai story, earth and sky are born of parents whose nature is not revealed. A worm swallows them, but is caught by the father and split open. The children are still in the worm's belly, the upper part of which becomes the sky and the lower the earth. Earth and sky then come together and produce the mountains; from their next encounter are born frogs, and from the frogs are born beings who, though human, are entirely covered with hair.

Stories about the beginning of the world are rarely consistent. In a Bugun story, we find an elderly man living with a young wife who deserts him for an attractive water-god. The husband then goes to Lhasa and on the way meets the hideous Nikauma-Madongma. From their union the first rock is born and from it flow the first rivers. Then she bears a son who goes into the

[2] See my *Myths of Middle India*, pp. 16 ff.

sky and makes the thunder and lightning and another who goes below the earth to cause the earthquake. A fourth son is a rain-maker, the fifth originates the four winds and the sixth causes the rainbow. Other children are snakes, poisonous insects and demons of disease. Last born is the pathetic child of death who unknowingly kills his own parents and then, in searching for them, kills everyone he meets.

Some of these Creation stories have an almost Biblical dignity and are inspired by the very spirit of poetry.

14

A New Book of Tribal Fiction (1976)

PREFACE

This book is a successor or supplement to my earlier *Myths of the North-East Frontier of India* as well as, in a sense, to the three other collections of folk-tales which I have recorded *Folk-Tales of Mahakoshal*, *Myths of Middle India* and *Tribal Myths of Orissa*.[1] I have never been a folklorist in the technical or exclusive sense but I have been impressed by the light thrown by stories, legends and myths on the customs and thinking of tribal people. I have thus not gone into their territory with the specific aim of collecting folk-tales but have always been engaged primarily on other work, sometimes on the study of religion, sometimes busy with social organization, art or crime, sometimes working in the field of applied anthropology. During the past ten years I have spent a great deal of time on long tours in the remotest hills of NEFA and during these I have collected stories wherever that was possible and time permitted.

In *Myths of the North-East Frontier of India* I published stories which were mainly concerned with the origins of things; most of them were myths in the technical sense of the word. I reserved others, most of which were more properly classified as fairy stories, for a second volume. This book does, in fact, contain a number of myths of origin which I recorded after the first book was published, but the longer and more interesting stories are of a general kind.

[1] These have been fully indexed in Stith Thompson and Jonas Balys, *The Oral Tales of India* (Bloomington, 1958).

Since most of these stories, except the Singpho collection which was recorded mainly by my assistant, Mr Sundarlal Narmada, were taken down by me on tour, I have prefaced each chapter with a brief Tour Diary to give, in a natural and unforced manner, brief glimpses of the people and countryside which I saw as I went slowly along. I had to rely on interpreters, inevitable when I was covering such a large area where many different languages and dialects are spoken, but my interpreters were very good and in each village where we recorded stories, the work was almost that of a committee, with one or often two interpreters, several village elders, Sundarlal and myself, and we were able to check and re-check the stories in the very place where they were told. During my Khampti tour, in the course of which I also obtained a few Singpho stories, I had the efficient and knowledgeable help of Mr T. K. M. Barua who has been with me on a number of expeditions.

One of the difficulties that face the investigator in all the tribal areas of India is that there is no standard, no canon of doctrine, titles or names, and the result is that it is possible to record stories in different villages where the plot is mainly the same but the characters have very different names. Sometimes even in the same village the people will not agree on the names of the hero or heroine and other characters.

I must express my obligation to Mr B. Das Shastri for generous help, given freely to me as to many others, and to Mr Someswar Lahiri, my stenographer, who did the first English renderings of many of the stories recorded in this book.

SHILLONG VERRIER ELWIN
31ST OCTOBER 1963

1
INTRODUCTION

The NEFA Background

In this book we visit three Divisions of the North-East Frontier Agency—Kameng for the Sherdukpens, Siang for the Ashings, Shimongs, Ramo-Pailibos and Khambas, and Lohit for the

Khamptis and Singphos. To those who know these areas the stories will have a special appeal, indeed parts of them cannot be understood without some background knowledge of the tribes. For example, we have references to people looking up from underneath a house or creeping below a house in order to listen to what is being said inside. This is intelligible only when we realize that the majority of houses in this part of the world are built high above the ground on piles and that the space thus formed is left open; during the day pigs, dogs and fowls search for food which, since the floors of the houses are generally very badly made with many gaps, often falls down for their benefit. The houses also have verandas and in more than one story the development of the plot turns on the use of what I have called a drying-rack, a bamboo-frame which is hung above a central hearth and on which meat and fish is spread to dry. There is also generally a loft above the main room where things can be stored.

In these stories we get brief glimpses of the former institution of slavery, which has now almost disappeared from NEFA. In an Ashing tale (2.13)[1] it is proposed that a girl, who is a thief, should be made into a slave, though the Village Council decides in the end that if she pays compensation this need not be done. Similarly, a Wiyu girl of low morals, who is also a thief, is declared a Mipak (outsider) and a slave. As such she is not allowed to go into the girls' dormitory (2.27). In former days it was common for a man, who was unable to pay a fine imposed on him by the Village Council, to be made a slave. In a Ramo-Pailibo story (4.5) Abo-Tani, who is unable to pay the bride-price for his wife, promises that he will give any children he has as slaves to his father-in-law and other relations in settlement of his debt. In another Ramo-Pailibo tale (4.8) Pollo the Moon unable to find a husband, seduces one of her father's slaves and this is why she only appears at night because she is so ashamed of what she has done, for any intimacy with a slave is regarded as a very serious matter by the Adis. There is also a Bori story[2] which attributes the eclipse to the institution of slavery: a great Wiyu (spirit) in the form of a bear kidnaps the Sun and Moon

[1] This and other such references are to the original edition, *A New Book of Tribal Fiction*, 1976.

[2] Verrier Elwin, *Myths of the North-East Frontier* (Shillong, 1958), p. 39.

and keeps them to work in his fields as slaves. Men, animals and Wiyus redeem them in part, but they are unable to pay the whole price and from time to time the Wiyu comes to claim his debt and this causes an eclipse.

The Village Council (Kebang) is frequently mentioned in the Adi stories. In the Ashing tale of 'The Woodpecker and the Bees' (2.13) there is an account of a Kebang held to settle what is to be done to a girl who steals, and the story tells us that two of the men present are great drinkers and they drag on the discussion as long as possible so that they can go on drinking other people's rice-beer. It is a common charge against the old men on the Council that they lengthen the meetings out so that they will be able to drink more at the general expense. In another Ashing story (2.18), a Council is held to decide what should be done to the snakes who bite and kill people. This is a Council of Wiyus and they resolve that the fangs of the snakes should be.removed as a punishment and their heads cut off in compensation. In a Shimong story (3.11), also about snakes, a Kebang decides that a snake who has bitten a man without any reason, should have its fangs broken and it must pay beads which in those days snakes wore as necklaces, in compensation.

The Rasheng is an institution which organizes and disciplines the unmarried girls of an Adi village. The girls use this little hut, which is what it usually is, only at night and there they spin and weave and dance until they go to bed. It is under the leadership of an elder girl and as Roy says, 'it is a training institution for the girls in discipline, comradeship, responsibility and leadership'.[3] The Rashengs are organized on a clan basis and are visited by boys who are seeking girls to marry. Roy quotes B. S. Guha as saying that: 'It also helps... the growth of a spirit and comradeship among men and women and a life of healthy relaxation which provides the outlet for the release of tensions and repressed forces which otherwise would have developed into factionalism and marred the development of a healthy tribal life'.[4] This institution plays its part in the stories, some of which cannot really be understood without knowing what it is.

Many stories have references to trade. The Khampti Choupet and his friend take ivory, the horns of deer and rhino to barter

[3] S. C. Roy, *Aspects of Padam-Minyong Culture* (Shillong, 1960), p. 201.
[4] Ibid., p. 202.

in distant villages (6.16). It is when Motik Gyelbo goes to trade that he is betrayed by his wife (5.1). Tsowa Tsongpon comes from Tibet to India with loads of beads, iron and salt and we have a vivid picture of the rigours of the two months' journey: The horses die; there is no firewood to keep the travellers warm in the thick snow; and they nearly perish from cold and hunger (5.2). Ashing stories describe how a Wiyu's wife takes her crab-daughter to Tibet to trade skins for salt and wool (2.14) and how the fly takes a small party of a bee, a caterpillar and a locust also to Tibet to obtain wool and food-stuffs (2.21).

There is a remarkable difference in atmosphere between the Adi and the Buddhist stories and I have often been struck by the fact that although some of the Buddhist tribes have taken Adi or other tribal items of theology into their thinking, the Adis themselves have hardly been influenced at all by the Buddhist groups who live so near them. The Ramos and Pailibos have a great deal to do with the Buddhist Membas with whom they trade and from whom they have at least learnt to drink milk and make butter, but I find very little influence of the Buddhist theology in their stories. Similarly the Shimongs and the Tangams live in frequent contact with the Khambas of the Yang Sang Chu Valley but have borrowed little beyond a few ornaments and certain elements of dress.

Adi stories are dominated by the Wiyus, the unseen spirits who have so great an influence on human life and whom I describe at the beginning of Chapter 3.[5] They also have a large number of animal stories; sometimes all the characters are animals, sometimes animals and human beings marry each other. A frog takes a Wiyu wife; a girl marries a bear. It is interesting that Goswami observes that 'not many Assamese tales illustrating this motif group are available'.[6]

On the other hand, in the Buddhist stories, although there are plenty of animals, particularly among the Sherdukpens, they are not very prominent. Many of these stories have a moral, which other tribal stories rarely teach.

In general, the Buddhist stories are more sophisticated, perhaps because many of them have an ultimate literary origin.

[5] Please refer to original edition, *A New Book of Tribal Fiction*, 1976.

[6] P. Goswami, *Ballads and Tales of Assam* (Gauhati, 1960), p. 178.

One fact may immediately strike the reader: the Adi tales refer to village elders or headmen, the Buddhist tales to kings and queens. There is not really very much difference. Some of the Adi elders had the authority and power of minor kings; some of the Buddhist 'kings', ruling over their own small villages, are no more than landlords or headmen.

The Attitude to Women

In the Buddhist stories the attitude to women is often unfavourable. It is, of course, a common psychological device adopted by Buddhists to attain freedom from attachment to meditate on the unpleasant or transitory character of worldly things. Thus the devout Buddhist is enjoined to meditate on the filthy nature of the human body, to think about the graveyard and what happens to us there, to contemplate the dreadful speed with which human life passes away and the folly of attributing ultimate value or importance to it. To a monastic order one of the greatest temptations comes from women, and both in the traditional Buddhist literature and in these folk-tales we are shown that they are just not worth our attention. For example, the Mudu-pani Jataka[7] illustrates how impossible it is to keep women from going after their own desires. Even if a father holds a daughter by the hand it is impossible to guard her and the Jataka reminds us that though women are soft in speech they are insatiable and that a man should be free from them, for they will burn him like fuel in the fire. The Gulla-palobhana Jataka[8] points the same moral that women in the old days drive the most faithful souls to sin and the story emphasizes the idea that a woman's company can make even an ascetic fall into evil for she is full of seductive wiles, deceitful and tempts the most pure-hearted to his fall. Again and again the Jatakas return to the same theme. The Gahapati Jataka[9] insists that women can never be kept right; somehow or other they will sin and trick their husbands. The Radha Jataka[10] declares that it is impossible to keep guard over a woman ('No guard can keep a woman in

[7] *The Jataka*. Edited by E. B. Cowell (London, 1957), Vol. II, pp. 224ff.
[8] Ibid., Vol. II, p. 228.
[9] Ibid., Vol. II, p. 94.
[10] Ibid., Vol. I, p. 309.

the right path') and tells how a Brahmin entrusted his wife to the charge of a parrot when he had to go out on business whereupon she misconducted herself daily: there was no end to the stream of her lovers in and out of her house. And the Bodhisatta says that even though a man carries a woman about in his arms she will not be safe.

The Asatamanta Jataka[11] says that women 'are lustful, profligate, vile and degraded' and asks why any sensible person should allow himself to be 'tossed by passion' for them.

The Panchatantra and the Tibetan tales from the Kah-Gyur emphasize the ingratitude of women. A Tibetan story describes how a husband twice saves his wife's life, even cutting some flesh off his own thighs, giving it to her to eat and opening the veins of his arms and giving her his blood to drink. But in spite of this she conspires against him with a handless and footless cripple. The Panchatantra tale describes how a woman dies of thirst in a forest and the husband hears a voice saying that if he will give up half his own life she will be revived. Soon after her recovery her husband goes away somewhere and in a garden she hears a cripple singing so beautifully that she falls in love with him at once. She takes an early opportunity of pushing her husband into a well.

In our stories here there is an interesting contrast between the Adi and the Buddhist tales. On the whole, the Adi's attitude to women is more generous and more trustful. It is true that there are some bad girls. There is an Ashing story (2.13) of a girl who steals beads and gets into trouble for it. There are a number of faithless Wiyu girls—the lovely but wanton Wiyu Lodo (2.22), whose freedom results in an illegitimate child who is born dumb and ugly. There is another Wiyu girl who is hard to please and refuses to marry not only Wiyus in human form but animals as well. She steals and is condemned to slavery. In the end she conceives by the wind and gives birth to the cricket (2.27). Another girl, whose fault is not so much in the field of sexual morals as in cruelty, is at first human, but her husband dies and she becomes a Wiyu in the underworld. Her son goes to find her and she is so afraid that if the other Wiyus discover that she has a human husband and a human child they will laugh

[11] Ibid., Vol. I, p. 148.

at her and perhaps drive her away, that she kills her son in a singularly cruel manner (2.31). A curious Shimong story (3.3) shows Pollo the Moon, who is here regarded as a woman, falling in love with a cock. Her husband the Sun catches her with her arms around her lover and the Village Council orders the cock to be mutilated in compensation. The wife of the hero of another Shimong story, 'The Adventurous Frog', is not unfaithful but she eats the food which her husband thinks she should have given to him and behaves in a careless and vulgar manner (3.4).

On the other hand, the picture of women in the Adi stories is generally friendly. Jebo-Samir, a Wiyu girl, who lived in the underworld, used to go everywhere completely naked and animals, gods and even insects pursued her but she appears to have retained her chastity (3.7). It is possible that the institution of the Rasheng, where sex is disciplined and controlled, has contributed to this higher attitude towards women among the Adis.

In our Buddhist stories, however, as in the classic tales, the picture of women is less favourable. The story of the credulous merchant, Motik Gyelpo (5.1) describes how his wife professes to love him so much that she will not let him out of her sight. When he goes to visit a neighbouring Raja she forces him to make a clay image so that she will have him always with her, and he says: 'A woman who really loves her husband can never make love to others.' Yet within a few hours of his departure she has seduced a rather unwilling friend. A little later in the same story the Raja, who also believes in his wife's virtue, is betrayed by her with a mad man and when the merchant discovers it, he exclaims: 'How astonishing it is! But this is the nature of women. They only pretend to be loyal to their husbands while in actual fact they betray them.' The Raja and the merchant accordingly agree to live together as brothers and never to have anything to do with women, deciding that it is because women have more desire than men that they are never satisfied and have to go to others. But in the end desire is too strong and they remarry, sharing a wife between them. Yet she too betrays them with a young and handsome servant. After this the friends leave their home and now 'their aim in life is only to worship God and do good to other people'. The Khamptis have a very similar story (6.22) where a supposedly devoted wife insists on the Raja, her husband, making a golden image of himself to keep her company when he goes away. But he is not so simple as Motik Gyelpo and an hour or two after his departure he returns to his palace to see whether his wife is true to him or not. He hides himself inside the image and has the mortification of seeing his wife seduce a mahout. He goes away to visit another Raja and secretly observes his friend's wife also betraying him with a swineherd. This amuses him so much that he laughs and laughs until he dies.

We may note that in these stories there is a Gamekeeper motif, as we may call it, for the women are unfaithful with lovers of definitely lower social status—a mad man, a servant, a mahout and a swineherd.

In general, the Buddhist stories show women as ready to yield to anyone who approaches them. In the story of the Flying Vessel (5.6) the hero goes to visit five women in succession, each of whom insists that he should spend the night with her. Even though these relationships are ultimately regularized by marriage the moral is evident.

In the Khampti story (6.18) of the Five Wives there is a similar picture of girls who, immediately on seeing the hero, are filled with love and give themselves to him.

The Khampti story of Nang-Padungma (6.24) suggests that there are few women who are at once beautiful and faithful. Nurses, though often good dancers and singers, are particularly dangerous. They love many men and provide girls for their charges.

Singpho stories are equally severe on women. In the story of 'The Conversion of the Demons' (7.6) there is a very pretty princess who goes to seduce boys, though in the end she is converted to religion.

Women are also witches and there is a grim Khampti tale (6.20) of a well-known and widely-respected monk living in peace and virtue, who is enchanted by a witch and nearly destroyed. Another Khampti story (6.21) of witches describes how one of them turns into a vulture and devours the children of her village.

Women, even the wives of deities, suffer from jealousy and there are Singpho stories illustrating this unpleasant trait (7.7). The Khampti Choupet's wife quarrels with her husband who is a murderer and in her temper lets out the story of his crime and thus leads to his death (6.16).

In a Sherdukpen story (8.4) the three daughters of a demon Raja each promises her father that after his death she will do everything possible to trouble mankind. One turns into a rat and spoils the harvest; the second becomes a pretty girl and makes love to the young men and their desire for her drives them to quarrel and fight each other. The youngest becomes a mouse and spoils the religious books and other precious things in the monastery.

But women who do not behave themselves face an evil fate after death. The Singpho story of 'The Monk and the Bitch' (7.10) is about a woman who used to steal her husband's food and betray him with other men. After this she goes to hell and is turned into a bitch and the God, Mathum-Mathā, tells her son: 'Your mother is in hell where she has been turned into a bitch, for she used to go to other men and gave your father dirty food and the leavings from her own plate. Those who do such things become dogs in hell.' In spite of this, her virtuous son rescues her and sends her to heaven.

The Virtue of Generosity

Among the virtues praised in the Buddhist stories perhaps the most honoured is generosity, the practical expression of non-attachment. In this collection we have the Singpho tale of the Good Old Man (7.9) who almost ruins himself and the happiness of his home by giving away the chickens that he is supposed to sell. But the most important is the tale of Dime Kundan (5.5) in which the hero gives away everything he has, including his children, his wife and his own eyes after being driven into exile on account of his liberality. In time, of course, everything is restored to him but he passes through a period of great suffering first.

This theme is popular in Buddhist fiction everywhere. The most famous story, and that which most closely resembles the story in the text, is the Vessantara Jataka[12] which describes how the Bodhisatta, like our Dime Kundan, is miraculously born and begins to speak directly after his birth. He is named Vessan-

[12] Cowell, op. cit., Vol. VI, pp. 251ff.

tara and his highest quality is generosity. When he is eight years old, after he has given priceless necklaces to his nurses, he says to himself: 'If one should ask my heart, I would cut open my breast, and tear it out, and give it; if one ask my eyes, I would pluck out my eyes and give them; if one should ask my flesh, I would cut off all the flesh of my body and give it.' He marries the princess Maddi but this does not, as in our tale, turn him from the path of righteousness. He does not have a magic jewel or talisman but a glorious white elephant who brings rain wherever he goes. One day there is a great famine in Kalinga and the people there ask for the elephant and the prince gives it to them. This makes him very unpopular and his own people want to slay him but in the end his father persuades them to agree to his going into exile. After distributing princely gifts he goes with his wife into the forest, gives her to a Brahmin and even gives away his own children. This version of the story, however, does not include the incident of the giving of the eyes.

The same story is given by Spence Hardy[13] and von Schiefner, who refers to the Kah-Gyur, and tells the story of Vessantara in a rather shorter and clearer form than that given in Cowell's edition of the Jataka.[14] In von Schiefner's version the prince's name is Visvatara and the English editor, Ralston, writes sympathetically about the sorrows of Madri, the princely ascetic's wife, who is reduced, by her husband's passion for giving everything away, first to exile and poverty, then to bitter grief on account of the loss of her dearly loved little children, and finally to slavery, but submits to all her husband's commands.

Ralston refers to other stories of this kind. One of them is the Nidanakatha[15] which describes the great generosity of Mangala Buddha.

The story is that when he was performing the duties of a Bodhisatta, being in an existence corresponding to the Vessantara existence,[16] he dwelt with his wife and children on a mountain. One day a demon named 'Sharp-fang', hearing of his readiness to bestow gifts, 'approached him in the guise of a Brahmin, and asked the Bodhisatta for his two children. The Bodhisatta, exclaiming, 'I give my children to

[13] *Manual of Buddhism*, pp. 116–24.

[14] W. R. S. Ralston, *Tibetan Tales* (London), pp. 257ff.

[15] Translated in C. A. F. Rhys David's *Buddhist Birth-Stories*, p. 33.

[16] His last birth before attaining Buddhahood.

the Brahmin,' cheerfully and joyfully gave up both the children, thereby causing the ocean-girt earth to quake. The demon, standing by the bench at the end of the cloistered walk, while the Bodhisatta looked on, devoured the children like a bunch of roots.

Similar is the tale of Harischandra, which has been recorded in folk-tale form in Stokes's *Indian Fairy Tales* (No. 13). In this story Harischandra promises to give an ascetic two pounds and a half of gold but his wealth is turned into charcoal and in order to keep his word he is compelled to sell his wife and child for a pound-and-a-half of gold and himself for the remaining pound, with consequences tragic to himself and his family, although in the end everything is restored to him.

The *Katha-Sarit-Sagara*[17] contains a story of the generous demon, Namuchi, 'who was devoted to charity and very brave and did not refuse to give anything to anybody that asked, even if he were his enemy'. By his virtue he wins the magic horse at the time of the Churning of the Ocean and when his enemies, the gods, find themselves in despair they go and ask for it and he gives it to them, although he is their enemy, rather than mar the glory of open-handedness which he had been accumulating since his birth. When Indra goes to ask for the horse, Namuchi says to himself, 'If the glory of generosity, which I have long been acquiring in the worlds, were to wither, what would be the use to me of prosperity of life?'

Then we have the generous Induprabha, the son of the King of Kurukshetra.[18] There is a famine in his kingdom and his ministers do not want the King to give people relief but Induprabha tells his father that he is their 'wishing-tree' and should do so. This annoys the king and he taunts his son. When the boy hears this he makes a vow that he will attain by austerity the condition of a wishing-tree or die in the attempt. In the end he succeeds and makes his father's subjects as happy as if they were in paradise, for he grants them even the most difficult boons. Indra offers him entrance to heaven as a reward for his goodness but Induprabha refuses, asking how he can disappoint so many men by going to heaven for the sake of his own happiness.

[17] N. M. Penzer, *The Ocean of Story* (London, 1927), Vol: IV, p. 63.
[18] Penzer, op. cit., Vol. VI, p. 84.

Another story in the *Katha-Sarit-Sagara*, which resembles the Vessantara Jataka, is the story of Taravaloka.[19] His wife is Madri and their sons are called Rama and Lakshaman. He himself possesses an elephant and is famous for his generosity; he builds alms-houses for the distribution of food and other things. His enemies ask him for his elephant, for they think that once he has given it to them—and he cannot refuse—they will be able to take his kingdom from him. As in the other stories, the citizens are enraged at this and they send him with his wife and two children into exile in the forest and the remainder of the story follows the plot of the Vessantara Jataka, though this version also omits the gift of the hero's own eyes.

Yet another version of this story is given by Waddell which at the beginning broadly follows our text but includes the incident of the donation (often omitted) of the generous prince's own eyes. 'He meets a blind man, who asks him for his eyes, which he immediately plucks out and bestows on the applicant, who thus receives his sight. The prince, now blind, is led onwards by his wife, and on the way meets 'The Buddhas of the three Periods' who restore the prince's sight.[20]

Finally, among the Sherdukpen tales recorded by Mr Rinchin Norbu there is a story of a woman with a pious son who gives alms to Lamas and the poor and feeds the pilgrims who pass by their house. One day, while the mother is away, a very old woman comes to beg and the boy gives her all the food they have. The old woman blesses him and says that the Lord Buddha will reward him and that if he will go to a neighbouring hill he will find something of great value. When the boy's mother returns home, she is very angry that all the food has been given away.

The story goes on to say that the boy goes to the hill where he finds a tattered bag and a pair of old shoes and when he comes home these divine gifts make him so rich that he is able to spend all his time giving food and money to pilgrims and to the poor. The king of that place offers him his daughter in marriage in order to discover the secret of his wealth. From this point onward, however, the Sherdukpen story departs entirely from that in the text.

[19] Penzer, op. cit. Vol. VIII, pp. 126–9.

[20] L. A. Waddell. *The Buddhism of Tibet* (London, 1939), pp. 543–51.

The Magic of Laughter

Bloomfield has analysed the various kinds of laugh in Indian fiction. There are the laughs of joy, irony, malice, trickery and triumph. In some cases laughter and crying go together. Sometimes we have the sardonic laugh, the enigmatic laugh and the laugh of mystery.[21] Penzer's analysis is somewhat simpler. 'In Hindu fiction I would divide laughs into two distinct varieties: (1) those which clearly show their nature, but not the reason which prompted them; (2) curious and mysterious laughs which give no clue either to their real nature or their significance.

Both varieties are dramatic, the second more than the first. It is, of course, the dramatic laugh that becomes such a force in the hands of the story-teller. It has been observed that, with but very few exceptions, all Biblical laughs are dramatic—usually of scorn or derision. The innocent laugh of joy would nearly always pass unheeded by the chronicler or historian, as it would lack the interest necessary to produce a dramatic situation.[22]

Most of these types of laughter occur in our stories. In an Ashing story (2.3) a dead Otter gives a jeering laugh when he hears the Bat telling obvious lies, and in a Khampti story (6.12) we have another unusual laugh when a large fish, which has swallowed a Raja's son and is already dead laughs, when the fisherman prepares to cut him up. The reason, for this is apparently that the fish knows that the child is in his belly and is amused at the thought of the surprise which his captors will feel when they find it.

Neither of these mysterious laughs are as effective, for they are not quite so mysterious, as the laughs of the same kind in the *Katha-Sarit-Sagara*.

Then in an Ashing story (2.34) we have a ribald tale of a man who dies through laughing too much. In fact, there is often an element of cruelty in tribal laughter. Aimpet (6.15) chuckles to himself as he drowns the men of his own village by a clever trick. In another Khampti story (6.16), Choupet, who has murdered his friend after the latter has prayed to dark clouds overshadowing the sky, laughs while he is sitting with his wife and the sky is again darkened, thus reminding him of the dead that made

[21] M. Bloomfield, 'Psychic *Motifs* in Hindu Fiction', *Journal American Oriental Soc.*, Vol. XXXVI (1916), pp. 54ff.

[22] Penzer, op. cit., Vol. VII, p. 254.

him rich. This laugh leads to his destruction, for his wife insists on his telling her the reason for his amusement and finally blurts it out during a quarrel.

The fear of laughter occurs as a motif in a few stories. The Ashing tale (2.27) is of a Wiyu girl who conceives by the wind and through fear of being laughed at as the mother of an illegitimate child, goes away to the Land of the Moon and has her baby there. A very cruel Ashing story (2.31) describes how a widow murders her own son by crushing his head in a mortar because she is afraid that the Wiyus, among whom she is now living, will laugh at her if they find out that she has a human son from a human husband.

In two stories, one from the Khambas and one from the Khamptis, we have the motif of magic laughter combined with the theme of a wife's infidelity. In the first a man vomits when he laughs and brings up precious beads, so valuable that he grows very rich. But going one day to visit a Raja he is depressed by his wife's infidelity and cannot manage as much as a smile. It is only when he sees his friend's wife falling into the same error that he begins to laugh. The Khampti story is about two Rajas, both of whom have very profitable laughs. The first laughs when he is pleased and the sound of it brings rain. The second Raja laughs at anything surprising or unusual; he vomits and brings up gold and silver. As in the Khamba story he is depressed by his wife's infidelity and only laughs when he discovers that the first Raja is also deceived.

In these two stories are combined the motif of treasure falling from the mouth (D 1454.2)[23] which is known in Kashmir, the Punjab, Mysore and Madras, and the magic laugh, (D 2143.1.11) where a man laughs to bring rain. H 1194.1 is the motif of a man whose laughter brings rain but is unable to laugh until two people unknown to each other go to sleep in the same room and frighten one another.

The Power of Body-dirt

The motif of a deity or hero creating animals or human beings by rubbings from his skin is not as common as might be expected among people who do not often wash and who, therefore,

[23] These, and other, references are to Stith Thompson, *Motif Index of Folk Literature* (latest edition, Copenhagen, 1958.)

when they sweat, produce a fair amount of dirt when the skin is rubbed. The motif is classified in the Stith Thompson Motif Index A 1211.5, 'Man made from skin rubbed from Creator's (hero's) body'; A 1263, 'Man created from rubbings of the skin'; and under the headings A 1725.2 'Animals from body-dirt of deity (hero).' In the Khampti story (6.1) the Creator rubs many little bits of dirt off his body and they turn into honey-bees and ultimately create the world. In several Singpho stories we have the same motif. In one the Creator's back begins to itch; he scratches it and under his nails he gets a little dirt which turns into a spider (7.1). In another story (7.11) the Creator's wife rubs some dirt off her body and makes a beautiful young girl with whom she proposes to test the virtue of her husband. There is also a variant in a third Singpho tale (7.3) when the creator goes away to find food during a storm. His wife grows anxious and rubs her cheek until a little black pimple grows there. She scratches it off, it bleeds a little and she sends it to call her husband home. 'It spread its wings and flew away and the drop of blood became fire and lighted it through the darkness.'

In Orissa and Central India there are many examples of this motif which is known to the Kamars, Jhorias and Konds of Orissa.[24] It is also known to the Gonds, Kamars, Agarias, Kols, Murias and Bhuiyas of Central India.[25] A 1725.2 is found among the Konds, Kamars, Binjhwars and Parengas of Orissa.[26] Sometimes the dirt is rubbed from the Creator's body and is made directly into a human being or animal. Sometimes he makes little dolls and turns them into baby boys and girls. He creates man from the dirt of his forehead, from the dirt of his ear, the dirt under his toenails, or the dirt of the breast. Men are also created from sweat, blood, blood-clots, fingernails and spittle.

The variant, where the Creator's wife turns the body-dirt into an animal to frighten her husband home, is found in a Kamar story in which she creates a tiger, and a Parenga story where she makes little balls of dirt into mosquitoes. In my *Myths of the North-East Frontier* (p. 104), there is yet another variant where in a Bugun (Khowa) tale the first girl and the

[24] See my *Tribal Myths of Orissa*, pp. 4, 445, 480.

[25] See my *Myths of Middle India*, pp. 29, 47, 50, 125, 138, 177 etc. and my *The Agaria*, p. 90.

[26] See my *Tribal Myths of Orissa*, pp. 254, 338, 569 and 627.

first boy are separated by a great mountain. A bee settles on the girl's naked body, takes a little scrap of her dirt and, flying to the boy, puts it on his body. Then he takes a little of the boy's dirt to the girl. Both are filled with desire and, though there is no intercourse, the girl becomes pregnant and the first child is born.

In the same collection is a Digaru Mishmi story of a Khampti Raja who has the habit of rubbing his hands together. This causes a swelling which breaks open and a girl comes out.

Rare and Popular Motifs

It is interesting that some of the most popular and famous motifs known throughout the world are almost absent in this and the earlier book of NEFA tales. The stepmother does not figure in the stories, nor generally does the successful youngest son. The 'external soul' is found but seldom. The Hand of Glory is not known nor is the Act of Truth, and the theme of the Poison Damsel is rare.

There are no formulistic or cumulative tales, and there is little about sacred numbers.

On the other hand, very common motifs are those of the primeval ocean (A 810); the original sun or suns being too hot (A 720.2); earthquakes caused by a great animal or fish on whose back the world is supported (A 1145); the poppy flower growing from a dead body (A 2611); tobacco as a solace in time of mourning; the goat robbing the dog of its horns (A 2245); the rivalry between the pig and the dog (K 41.2); a few Trickster tales; the monkey as developed from human beings (D 118.2). There are a great many examples of magic charms, talismans and horns. The spider appears as teaching weaving to man (A 2091); there are flying elephants (A 2292.3); body-dirt turning into an animal messenger (D 444.2.3); disenchantment by the destruction of the hero's skin (D 721.3); many examples of magical aconception T 510-T 538) and many tests to which the hero is subjected (H 1010-H 1049). Surprisingly, in a very remote Ramo-Pailibo village I found a story (4.7) with the common theme of J 1191.1.1—where a clever dog arrives late at a trial with the excuse that he was delayed because the Siang River was on fire: he claims that this is no more absurd than to claim that a male mithun can have a calf.

There are a number of charming or significant motifs. The world, which grows out of a many-coloured lotus, is called 'honey-sweet'; it is so attractive that the gods who visit it will not return to the sky, they want to smell more and more of the sweet and beautiful earth (5.1). God looks down from heaven and sees its loveliness: the women of earth are more beautiful than those of heaven.

We have a number of beautiful girls in these stories. There is Lodo, the lovely but wanton young Wiyu girl (2.22); Pedong-Sune, the water-spirit, a girl with flowing hair (2.15); the very beautiful Jebo-Samir who goes about completely naked until she puts on a girdle (3.7); Nang Padungma who is born of a flower and cradled in a lotus—she is as gracious as a temple flower (6.24).

Some of the scenes in these stories are striking. We see a Wiyu girl in the Himalayas winnowing snow in her fan and sending it to fly through the air (2.7). Earth and sky lie in constant embrace until at last they have to separate: lightning is the lamp which the sky uses when he searches for his lover (3.2). I like the picture of the Tibetan girl and the future father of mankind who meet on a great rock among the high mountains and sing to each other and dance together till love comes to them (3.16). I like too the picture of the red, blue, yellow and black elephants following their King, the white elephant, in a great valley which is seen from above (5.19). And in another mood there is the contrast between the crabs, fish and frogs in a pond and enormous elephants who disturb their peace when they come to drink water (6.13).

We have a storm like a dark mountain, a snake as high as a hill and dark clouds which are the ill-omened witnesses of a treacherous murder.

There are too notable themes of another kind. In an Ashing story, after Kare the hero dies, his two wives turn themselves into birds and fly to the dangerous world of the dead to find and rescue him (2.20). In a Shimong story the frog's wife puts the heart of a pig, which has been killed for supper, on the top of a pole so that all can see it and realize 'her heart and her husband's are one as the heart is one' (3.3).

1

THE BATTLE FOR THE FISH

Long ago, before there were any fish in the world, Lopon Rimpoche[27] was walking along a river-bank. He saw that the water was dirty and full of weeds and said to himself, 'People will die if they drink the water from this river. What can I do to make it clean? If only there were some creatures that could eat the dirt, the water would be purified. I must do something about it.'

Thinking in this way he made some creatures in the shape of fish with the paper that the people manufactured in a village nearby, put life into them and threw them into the river saying, 'Eat all the dirt and weeds.'

Then he picked up some pine-fruits, gave life to them and threw them also into the river saying. 'Eat all the dirt and weeds and clean the water.'

From the paper came fish without scales and from the fruits came fish with scales.

Now the people did not know what to do with the fish. There were so many of them in the river that they found it difficult to go into it even to fetch water, and the animals could not drink the water as the fish used to bite their feet. But there was nothing they could do about it.

After a time Tsang Dande Rimpoche heard of it and came to look at the river but he could see nothing but fish and no water was visible. But since the fish had been created by Lopon Rimpoche he could not catch or kill them himself.

Presently he saw a stick floating down the river and picked it up. He put life into it and threw it into the water saying 'Go and eat the fish.' The stick turned into a water-rat and started to catch and eat the fish. In fact, he ate so many of them that soon there were very few left. Those who survived escaped by hiding under rocks and stones.

One day Lopon Rimpoche came to see how his fish were faring and was surprised to see so few of them. He called to

[27] Padma-Sambhava.

them and asked what the matter was. They began to weep and cried, 'Tsang Dande Rimpoche has made a creature which has eaten nearly all of us. Just a few of us escaped by hiding under rocks and stones but we ourselves are afraid that the rat will devour us also and not one of us will be left.'

'Don't worry,' said Lopon Rimpoche, 'So many fish will be born from you that it will be impossible for the water-rat to destroy you all.'

So saying the went away.

As the days went by, the number of the fish increased again and the water-rat got tired of eating them. Tsang Dande Rimpoche came again to see what had happened and asked the rat, 'Why are there so many fish in the river? Can't you eat all of them?'

'No,' replied the water-rat, 'the fish are increasing daily at such a rate that it is impossible for me alone to eat them.'

Tsang Dande Rimpoche said, 'From now onwards the bigger male fish will help you to eat the smaller fish.'

So saying he went away.

Now both the large male fish and the water-rat started eating the fish—the male fish ate the smaller ones and the water-rat the larger ones and again the number of fish decreased. Next time when Lopon Rimpoche came to see them and asked how they were the female wept before him and said, 'We are very unhappy. Formerly, only the water-rat used to eat us but now our husbands have joined him in destroying their own children.'

Lopon Rimpoche said, 'Hitherto you have given birth to your children directly but from now onwards you will lay your eggs and your children will be hatched out from them. Lay them near the river-bank and when your babies are hatched out you must hide them somewhere under the stones till they are strong enough to protect themselves from their enemies.'

So saying he went away. Since then fish have laid eggs.

Tsang Dande Rimpoche came yet again to look at the fish and again he asked the rat and the male fish, 'Why are there so many fish in the water? Aren't you eating anything nowadays?' They complained that the female fish were now laying eggs and hiding their children when they were born and that when they grew up it was impossible for the male fish to eat them. Tsang Dande Rimpoche said. 'From now onwards men, animals and birds will also eat fish.' Directly he said this, a desire for fish came to men, animals and birds and they began to catch and eat them. This is how men, animals and birds learnt to eat fish.

Now there was a girl of a poor Sherdukpen family whose name was Nyuphili. She used to pass a great deal of water, so much that her urine flowed like a river and many fish of a certain kind swam in it all the way down to the Assam plains. The Sherdukpens were very surprised at seeing so many of these fish and went about asking where they were coming from. The girl replied, 'It is my urine.'

They said, 'See how many fish are coming from your urine. Who is going to eat them? We certainly aren't going to.'

And ever since then those who catch and eat this particular kind of fish are regarded by the Sherdukpens as inferior people.[28]

2

THE TWO WIVES

There was a deer with his wife and a child. One day in a dream he saw a hunter coming towards them with a dog and a bitch. The dogs chased the deer and they all ran away but he himself was killed. In the morning he told his dream to his wife, and she said, 'Why should you die? If you die I will be a widow. It will be better that I myself should die.' The deer replied, 'If you die, who will give milk to our child?' She said, 'The child does not need milk any more. He is old enough to live on soft grass.' The deer said, 'No one in the world can bear to see his wife being killed. I will never permit it. It is I who will die.'

Soon afterwards they saw the dogs approaching. The deer said to his wife. 'Here they come. You run away with the child and let me die.'

The wife said, 'Very well, you die today and I will die tomorrow. After you are dead you will be reborn as a Raja's son and after I am dead I will be reborn as another Raja's daughter. When we have grown up we will marry and live together very happily.'

[28] Another Sherdukpen version of this story is given in my *Myths of the North-East Frontier*, pp. 315ff.

The bitch heard what they were saying and said to the hind, 'I will never let you be together.'

The hind ran away to the hills with her child and the dogs chased the deer to where the hunter was standing and he shot at him and killed him. He was very pleased and took the carcass home.

Next day the hunter came again with his dogs to the same place. When the hind heard the dogs barking she told her child, 'Yesterday your father went somewhere but he has not yet come back. I must go and see. Don't go anywhere but wait for me, for I will be back soon.' So saying she came out of the forest and the bitch chased her towards the hunter and he shot an arrow at her and it killed both her and the bitch. He was very sorry at having killed his bitch but at the same time he was happy at having killed the hind.

Now the deer, as she had foretold, was reborn as a Raja's son and the hind was born as another Raja's daughter. The bitch was born as a daughter in the house of a rich man.

When they grew up, the deer as the Raja's son and the hind as the other Raja's daughter were married and lived together very happily. One day the Raja's son was walking along the road and met the rich man's daughter. She was so beautiful that he fell in love with her and took her as his second wife.

Now everybody loves his younger wife more than his elder one and this also happened in the house of the Raja's son. Every day the younger used to quarrel with the older woman and tell her husband about it, with the result that the elder wife lost her peace of mind. She could not eat and gradually became very weak.

When she was on her death-bed she said to her husband, 'Now I am dying, But I remember those beautiful days in our previous life when we lived so happily as deer. You saw in your dream that you were going to be killed and told me about it the next morning. When I said that I should die instead, you were not willing to let me be killed before you. Then I said that after your death you should be born again as a Raja's son and after my death I should be born again as another Raja's daughter. While we were talking that bitch heard what we said and she told me that she would not let us be happy. The next day the bitch as well as I myself were killed and I was born in a Raja's house and the bitch was born in a rich man's house and now she has become your second wife. She made me so miserable that I could not bear it but I never told anybody, not even you, and now I am dying. I hope you will be happy with her. Let me die in peace.' She said to the bitch, 'After I die I will be reborn as a dog and after you die you will become a deer and then I will take my revenge.' Then she died and was reborn as a dog.

After the bitch-wife died she became a deer and this is why dogs chase the deer and kill them to this day.

If a man has two wives we know that the elder was a deer in her previous life and the younger was a bitch.

3
THE POWER OF INTELLIGENCE

Long ago, under a great rock lived a vulture. One day she gave birth to two puppies—one male and the other female. Presently a hunter passed by the place and saw the vulture feeding her children. He was surprised when he saw the difference between the mother and her children—the mother had feathers and two legs and was extremely ugly; and the children had no feathers but four legs and were very pretty.

He asked the vulture, 'How is that you have feathers and two legs and your children have no feathers and four legs? How is it that there is such a difference between you?'

The vulture replied, 'My children are not birds. They are very good hunting dogs. If you take them they will be of great help to you.'

'Would you really give them to me?' he asked.

'Yes', she replied, 'you may certainly have them.' And she gave her puppies to the hunter.

The hunter went on his way with the two puppies and after a time they met an elephant. The dogs, impressed by his size and strength, said to each other, 'Why shouldn't we go and live with this great animal?'

They said to the man, 'We are not going to stay with you any longer but we are going to live with the elephant.' So saying they went to the elephant to live with him.

That night the dogs barked and the elephant said to them, 'Don't make such a noise or the wild buffalo will come and kill me as well as you.'

The dogs asked, 'How will he kill us? Is he bigger than you?'

'No', the elephant replied, 'He is not big but he is strong and I am terrified of him.'

At that the dog said, 'We are not going to stay with you any longer. It is best to live with the strong animals. We will go to live with him.' And they left the elephant to live with the wild buffalo.

That night the dogs barked and the wild buffalo said to them, 'Don't make such a noise or the tiger will come and kill us.'

The dogs asked, 'How will he kill us? Is he bigger than you?'

'No', the buffalo replied, 'He is not bigger than me but he is a very strong and cruel animal.'

At that the dogs said, 'We are not going to stay with you any longer. It is best to live with the strong animals. We will go to live with the tiger.' And they left the buffalo to live with the tiger.

That night the dogs barked and the tiger said to them, 'Don't make such a noise, or the man will come and kill me as well as you.'

The dogs asked, 'How will he kill us? Is he bigger than you?'

The tiger replied, 'He is not bigger or stronger than me but he is very clever and he can kill not only me but all the animals.'

The dogs said, 'Then we are not going to stay with you. We will go and stay with the man and help him in hunting.' So saying they left the tiger to live with the man.

Ever since dogs have lived with men and have helped them in hunting.

4

THE DEMON'S DAUGHTER

Between the borders of Tibet and Gyakar Dorjeden (Buddha Gaya) there was a place called Peyur Chorten where Lopon Rimpoche was having a *mane* (shrine) made. But there was little water and the people had to work very hard. To encourage them Lopon Rimpoche said, 'When the *mane* is ready I will give you my blessings and whatever you want you will have.'

But there was a demon there who heard what Lopon Rimpoche said and he thought, 'I am a mighty giant, I should be able to do the work easily. I must go there to help but, if I go in my present form, Lopon Rimpoche will kill me.' So he turned himself into an animal which was rather like a yak and rather like a mithun but was actually neither a mithun nor a yak. When the people saw him they engaged him to draw water and he said to himself, 'When the work is finished I will ask Lopon Rimpoche to give me a boon so that I will be able to devour all mankind.'

He worked so hard that he gradually became completely exhausted.

When the *mane* was ready, Lopon Rimpoche called together all the people who had worked on it. They, not understanding that the animal was a demon, tied him to a pole and went to Lopon Rimpoche. Lopon Rimpoche blessed them and gave them what they desired and then departed. But when the animal learnt that the people had cheated him he untied himself and rushed to where Lopon Rimpoche had been living. When he found that Lopon Rimpoche was not there he was furious and said to the people, 'You used me to draw water and I worked so hard that I have become very weak. Without my help it would have been impossible for you to have built the *mane*. Now the shrine is ready but you didn't take me to Lopon Rimpoche. For this I shall take revenge. I shall become a Raja and when I rule over you I will give you every kind of trouble.'

After some time the demon died and was born again as the son of a Raja called Dui Langdar.[29] When he grew up the Raja arranged for his marriage and then in due time he died and the demon himself took the throne. Now that he was Raja he oppressed his subjects in every way: he used to drink the milk of the women and ordered that one human child should be brought to him to eat every month. Anyone who refused to obey was tortured. The people were very frightened and thought of running away but they were afraid that if they did the Raja would pursue and destroy them.

Then the Raja's wife gave birth to three daughters. When

they were old enough they went to school. The Raja used sometimes to inspect the school and one day he asked the children to examine his head and find out what there was in it. Nobody dared to do it except a very brave boy called Lalung-Peki Dorje who examined the Raja's head and found that there were two little horns there. This was such a great shock to him that he did not say anything about it then and ran away from school.

The boy could not forget what he had seen. 'How is it possible,' he thought, 'for a man to have horns? I must tell the people about this. But if the Raja hears that I have spoken of it he will devour me.'

So he dug a hole in the earth and went inside and made a trumpet through which he announced. 'The Raja has two horns, the Raja has two horns.'

When the people heard this they said to each other. 'This is a very extraordinary thing. The Raja cannot be a human being; he must be a demon. That is why he drinks human milk and eats human children. We must kill him at once.'

When the Raja heard that they were plotting to kill him he was so frightened that he hid and did not come out of his house.

The people looked for the Raja everywhere but could not find him. They said to one another, 'How can we kill the Raja if he never comes out? The best thing for us to do will be to dance in front of his house for seven days and there is a chance that he may come out to watch.' Then they discussed who should actually kill the Raja. Everybody was afraid to do so except Lalung-Peki Dorje and he went to join the dance with his bow and arrows in his hand.

The people danced for two days but the Raja did not come out. On the third day his eldest daughter said to him, 'There is a beautiful dance outside. You must go and see it.' But the Raja refused to go out.

On the fourth day his second daughter said to him, 'There is a beautiful dance outside. You must go and see it.' But he did not go out.

On the fifth day the youngest daughter said to him, 'They are doing a beautiful dance outside. You really ought to go and see it. But you needn't leave the house if you don't want to. I will open the window and you can look through that.'

The Raja was anxious, in spite of his fears, to see the dance, so he asked the girl to open the window and he looked out. When the people saw him they began to dance with great vigour to distract his attention. Among them Lalung-Peki Dorje was dancing with his bow and arrow and when he saw that the Raja was completely absorbed in watching, he realized his chance had come and he shot at the Raja and pierced his heart with an arrow.

As the Raja fell his soldiers began to shout and pointed at Lalung-Peki Dorje, who was the only person who had a bow and arrow with him. The boy ran for his life and the soldiers followed him.

Lalung-Peki Dorje reached a cave which had a cobweb across the door and he crept inside. One of the soldiers came to the cave but did not recognize the boy and asked him whether he had seeen anybody going along the path. The boy replied, 'Yes, I saw a boy running but by this time he must have gone far away.' This made the sepoy suspicious and he approached Lalung-Peki Dorje and felt his heart. As the boy was tired from running, his heart was still beating violently. The sepoy said to him, 'I know it is you who have killed the Raja but it is good that you have. He was a bad man and troubled us in every way. It is good that you have killed him and I won't tell anyone where you are.' So saying the soldier went home alone.

The Raja did not die of his wound but it was impossible to take the arrow from his heart. He said to himself, 'I am dying and what have I done? I was unable to give as much trouble to mankind as I desired, but in spite of that they have killed me.'

Then his eldest daughter said to him, 'Why are you worrying, father? You are in great pain and it is time for you to die. When I die I will become a rat and I shall go to the fields and spoil the harvest and in this way take revenge upon mankind.'

The second daughter said, 'Why are you worrying, father? You are in great pain and it is time for you to die. When I die I will become a pretty girl and I will make love to the young men and they will all desire me. This will make them quarrel and fight each other and many will be killed. In this way I shall take revenge upon mankind.'

The youngest daughter said, 'Why are you worrying, father? You are in great pain and it is time for you to die. My eldest sister will become a rat and ruin the harvest; the second sister will become a pretty girl and make the young men fight each other. I myself will become a mouse and live in the Gompas where I shall spoil the religious books and other precious things.'

When the Raja heard this he was relieved and said to his daughters, 'What you have said has made me happy. Now I can die. When I am dead, my body should not be buried but burnt.' And after some time the Raja died and they took his body to be burnt. When it was almost consumed by the fire a great wind came and blew away the ash and unburnt pieces of the body. From the larger pieces came all kinds of poisonous insects and from the smaller pieces came mosquitoes and dimdam flies. The intestines turned into every kind of snake.

In due course the three daughters died and as they had promised, the eldest became a rat, the second a pretty girl and the third a mouse.

And this is why even today the rats ruin the harvest, and mice spoil our religious books in the Gompas, and wherever there is a pretty girl our young men desire her and fight each other for her.[30]

[30] This story appears to be an imaginative version of something that actually happened as long ago as about A.D. 899. A man who has been called the Julian of Lamaism, Lang Darma, was a King of Lhasa who persecuted the Lamas and did everything he could to destroy the religion of Buddhism.

He desecrated the temples and monasteries, burnt their books, and treated the Lamas with the grossest indignity, forcing many to become butchers.

In the third year of his reign, however, he was assassinated by a Lama of Lhalun named Pal-dorje whose deed is commemorated in dances to the present day. 'This Lama, to effect his purpose, assumed the guise of a strolling blackhat devil-dancer, and hid in his ample sleeves a bow and arrow. His dancing below the king's palace, which stood near the north end of the present cathedral of Lhasa, attracted the attention of the King who summoned the dancer to his presence, where the disguised Lama seized an opportunity while near the king to shoot him with the arrow, which proved almost immediately fatal. In the resulting tumult the Lama sped away on a black horse, which was tethered near at hand, and riding on, plunged through the Keyi river on the outskirts of Lhasa, whence his horse emerged in its natural white colour as, it had been merely blackened by soot, and he himself turned outside the white lining of his coat, and by this stratagem escaped his pursuers.' L. A. Waddell, *The Buddhism of Tibet* (London 1934), pp. 34–5.

5

THE FIRST BEAR

There is a place called Khamjung[31] in Tibet. Long ago there lived a Khampa man and his wife with their children. But husband and wife were not on good terms with each other and used to quarrel every day. One day it went to such an extreme that the husband went away in a rage to the forest to live there. But he had no food to eat and got so hungry that he lost the power of distinguishing what was edible and what was not. In fact he ate anything he saw and one day ate some jungle charm which turned him into a bear. When he saw that the whole of his body was covered with long hair and that he was completely changed into an animal, he said to himself, 'I was a fool to quarrel with my wife and come to the forest. And now God has made me such a creature. Whatever was going to happen, has happened. Now I must go to my wife and ask her whether she will allow me to live in my house or not.'

In the evening he came to his house and called his wife. She came out of the room and when she saw him she was terrified. The bear said, 'Don't be afraid. I am your husband. I went away to the forest in a temper and there I had nothing to eat. So I started eating everything I saw. One day I ate some jungle charm and that has made me into a creature like this. Now I have come to you to apologize and want to know whether you will allow me to live with you. I promise I will never quarrel with you and whatever you want me to do I will do.' The wife said. 'God has made you a bear but how can I live with you? I am a human being and you an animal. Your home is the forest. Go there and live on jungle fruits. You should not stay here any more, or the people will kill you. So run away immediately.' The bear said, 'Very well, I will go but I must see my children before I do!' She said, 'Don't enter the room, for the children will be alarmed at seeing you.' So saying she came back to the room and closed the door. The bear was very angry and came to the door and made a hole in the plank and put his face through it. When he did this, the wife beat his face with a burning stick

31 Probably the Province of Kham.

from the hearth with the result that his face was burnt and he ran away.

After that he lived in the forest and was the first bear. And the black spot on the bear's face is due to the burn his wife made with a blazing stick long ago. Even today the bears remember the trouble a woman gave to their ancestor and take revenge when they can. This is why bears do not spare a woman when they catch one.

6

THE JEALOUS SISTER

In a little settlement in the valley leading from Shergaon to Rupa lived two girls. The elder was so lovely that it was as if the sun was shining through the hair hanging over her face. The younger was beautiful as the moon looking through clouds in a bright sky.

But both the girls had goitre on their necks and for this reason the young men did not come to marry them.

One day as the younger girl was walking by a river she met a Lama and asked him to heal her of her affliction.

'My daughter,' he said, 'you will be cured if you go on pilgrimage to Tawang.'

The girl accordingly bathed in the river, crossed it and began her journey through the hills. In the evening she lay down to sleep under a tree.

Now in this tree there lived two ogresses and as the girl was about to fall asleep she heard them talking to one another.

The first ogress said, 'Come, we must go and find something to eat.'

The second ogress replied, 'But look, here is something ready lying beneath our tree.'

The girl heard what they said, but she took the name of Konchosum and was not afraid. The next morning she got up and went to the river and was about to cross the stream. She looked down into the water and saw her reflection there. To her joy she saw that during the night the swelling of her goitre had disappeared.

What had happened was that the second ogress had stolen

the goitre for her supper. But when she put it in her pot to cook, although she kept it boiling all night long, it remained so hard that she could not cut it even with an axe.

The girl went back to her village and described how her goitre had been cured. But the elder sister, instead of rejoicing, was jealous and immediately set out on her way to Tawang. When she reached the tree where the other sister had slept, she too lay down there and fell asleep. But next morning, when she went to look in the river, she saw that she had two swellings instead of one.

What had happened was that the second ogress, angry at not being able to eat the younger sister's goitre, had fixed it on the neck of the elder one.

15

Democracy in NEFA (1965)

THE TRIBAL COUNCILS IN NEFA

The spirit of the tribal councils of NEFA is well illustrated in the traditional speech recorded by Roy, which is recited by the leaders of the *kebang* (Adi council) in Siang at the beginning of their meetings.

> Oh! villagers and brethren, let us strengthen our customs and our council, let us improve our regulations; let us make the laws straight and equal for all. Let the leaders who can speak best stand up and speak out for our betterment; let them speak out in a bold voice unabashed and undaunted like a cock crowing. Let our laws be uniform; let our customs be the same for all. Let us not decide differently for different persons; let us be guided by reason and see that justice is done and a compromise reached that is acceptable to both the parties. Let us keep nothing pending, let us decide while the dispute is fresh, lest small disputes grow big and continue for a long time. Let the fine be levied reasonably. Let it be commensurate with the guilt and be just. Poverty should have compassion and justice be tempered with mercy. We have met in this sacred place of justice; we have come together for a council-meeting and let us speak in one voice and decide on one verdict. Here are the iron pots and brass pots brought by the accuser and the accused; here stands the mithun. So let us decide and mete out justice so that all these go to him who is in the right.[1]

All the councils have certain features in common. They all derive their authority from ancient times and the fact that they are the expression of the will and power of the whole people. They are supported not only by social, but also by supernatural

[1] Sachin Roy, *Aspects of Padam-Minyong Culture* (Shillong, 1960), pp. 223f. (slightly modifed).

sanctions and to give false evidence, for example, may call down the vengeance of the gods as well as excite the scorn of men. Sacrifices are commonly offered to avert supernatural dangers, to implore the divine blessing on the councils' deliberations, and to bring peace between the contending parties.

All the councils are informal in character and except for the Monpa councils and the Adi *bangos*, which seem to be more highly organized, the conception of regular membership, committees, secretaries and so on has not yet come in. The people composing the councils are the accepted leaders of a village and always include the local priest, whose services are often required, and, of course, the officially appointed headmen who are issued with red coats.

Anyone, unless he is excommunicated, can attend and speak, though there are some tribes, such as the Daflas, who do not allow their women to do so.

Decisions are not taken by a formal vote but discussion continues until general unanimity is achieved.

The idea of 'electing' people is not yet familiar, though the Monpas are reported as having some sort of election.

Some tribes have what may be called a junior branch of the council. The *ajang buliangs* of the Apa Tanis, the *moshup* or *dere* boys of the Adis, the *morung* boys of the Wanchos and Noctes have always played an important part in looking after their villages, maintaining paths, helping in cultivation, providing a simple relief service: the northern Adis have a sort of fire-protection unit, staffed by these boys.

The functions of the village councils are threefold—judicial, administrative and developmental. On the judicial side the councils settle the disputes within the village boundaries and considerable powers have been given them under the Assam Frontier (Administration of Justice) Regulation of 1945. Even serious crimes against tribal society (but not against Government) have been and are being settled, generally to the satisfaction of all concerned, by these councils, Probably, to the tribal mind, this is the most important of the council's functions.

On the administrative side, the councils deal with the maintenance of paths and bridges; they see to the water-supply and sanitation of a village; they fix the dates of communal hunting and fishing and decide when the main agricultural operations should take place and when festivals should be held. Some of them make it their business to care for the poor and the disabled. There is no rule about this, and much depends upon the nature of the leading men of any particular council.

Similarly with regard to development, this depends largely on the extent to which the local officials have worked through the local councils in planning all the many-sided work of developing the country. There is endless scope for this and generally, when the council as such is approached by an official, the response is enthusiastic.

Throughout NEFA the tribal councils work within the general framework of the Assam Frontier (Administration of Justice) Regulation of 1945 which recognizes their importance and authority and gives them many powers. In the thirteen years since it was enacted, circumstances have greatly changed, but it has given an opportunity to the councils to prove themselves and show that they can, in the main, use their powers wisely and according to the new ideas of equality, humanity and order that have spread rapidly all over NEFA. Moreover, as I have already said, they have developed other than legal functions and, as they are strengthened, will in future play an increasing part in development activities.

Put very simply, the Regulation of 1945 provides that criminal justice shall be administered by the Political Officers, the Assistant Political Officers and the village authorities, all of whom are recognized as competent administrators of the law. It gives power to the councils to try a number of criminal offences such as theft, simple hurt, criminal or house trespass and assault, and to impose fines not exceeding Rs 50 for them, as well as to award payment in compensation to the extent of the injury sustained. The councils also have civil powers and can try all suits without limit of value in which both the parties are indigenous to the tract.

The Regulation provides for appeals in appropriate cases and lays down that the Political Officers shall be guided by the spirit, but shall not be bound by the letter of the Code of Civil Procedure. An important Section lays down that no pleader shall be allowed to appear in any case before the village authorities.

This Regulation does, in fact, give the councils very wide powers, for it is recognized that they will function and inflict punishment or order compensation according to their customary law. Since, according to custom and tradition, even crimes like murder, kidnapping and rape can be satisfied by payment of compensation, it is possible to bring almost every kind of offence (except those committed against the State) within their jurisdiction. This may also extend to non-tribesmen who are involved in disputes with, or offences against, the tribal people; if, for example, an official is accused of adultery with a tribal woman, he may have to appear before the local council and accept its decision, irrespective of any departmental action that may subsequently be taken against him. Where tribesmen are accused by non-tribesmen, their cases may be heard by the village councils, except in the immediate neighbourhood of the Divisional headquarters.

The 1945 Regulation has already limited the type of 'punishment' that can be inflicted, and in fact the heavy punishments of former days have already almost entirely disappeared. Girls may still have their hair cut for immorality, but they are no longer stripped naked and beaten. Offenders are no longer buried alive, rolled over cliffs, or pushed into rivers to drown; already, of their own accord, the people have adopted the system of compensation, which in practice is adjusted to the wealth and position of the accused.

The policy of the NEFA Administration is to accept this situation and to strengthen the councils and work through them. Where an autocratic system has previously existed, it has associated with the chief a number of elders and given them a stronger voice in village affairs. Where the council's authority is weak, it is teaching the people how to develop it and make it more effective.

Great care, however, has hitherto been taken not to over-administer the councils and make them conform to our own idea of what they, with regular membership, codified laws, resolutions, minutes and so on, should be. But in some areas, where funds are placed at their disposal, there has to be some sort of organization, though this is kept as simple as possible. For training the councils, and also to impress on the people the Administration's concern for law and order, whenever they have to try a case of heinous crime, an official arranges to be present, but only to help and not to control the proceedings.

The 1945 Regulation lays down that 'the proceedings of the village authority need not be recorded in writing', but that the Administration may require it to report its proceedings in any way which appears suitable. The decisions are nowadays reported to the nearest local official, who records them if he is satisfied that the compensation demanded is just. If he is not satisfied, he demits the case to the council for further consideration, and if he is even then dissatisfied he sends it to the Political Officer for a final decision.

Under the Regulation, the Political Officers have wide criminal and civil powers, though in civil cases they are required 'in every case in which both parties are indigenous to the tract to endeavour to persuade them to submit to arbitration' by the village council. In practice, therefore, the main task of the Political Officers is to settle those case, some of them fifteen to twenty years old, where the parties liable have refused to pay the compensation imposed on them by the councils. These, in an area where responsibility is so often corporate rather than individual, are usually highly complicated and demand in the official staff a profound knowledge of local custom and the utmost sympathy and patience.

In the sphere of development the value of the councils has frequently been proved. The people naturally take much greater interest in any project if it has been considered by themselves rather than imposed upon them, and in future, as they become more accustomed to the responsible use of money and to wise planning, more and more responsibility for development will be transferred from officialdom to the tribal bodies. There can be no doubt that this will do a great deal to give the people self-confidence, to make them feel that they are masters of their own destiny and that nothing is being imposed upon them, and to forward true progress throughout the hills.

This policy, in fact, holds an important place in the nation-wide programme of community development which aims at restoring to the village panchayat the authority and dignity it had in former days. 'The foundation of any democratic structure in India,' says Mr V. T. Krishnamachari, 'must be in the village, which is the oldest unit known in the country and has survived through many centuries'. He quotes Sir Charles Metcalfe, who wrote of the little republics having nearly everything they want within themselves, and almost independent of foreign relations: they seem to last where nothing else lasts. This union of the village communities, each one forming a separate little State in itself is in a high degree conducive to their happiness, and to the enjoyment of a great portion of freedom and independence.

Mr Krishnamachari goes on to say that in spite of the factions, caste tyranny and stagnation which undoubtedly existed, it was

owing to the life in the village communities and the measure of autonomy they enjoyed, that we achieved social cohesion and stability and succeeded in preserving our traditional cultural values over many centuries. This survival of our values during long periods of foreign dependence is certainly due to the continuity of the village organization. We must, therefore, recognize that modern democratic government can have a solid foundation only in village democracy.[2]

Note

A curious passage, written in the fashion of the day, in Mackenzie's *History*[3] illustrates the possible consequences of not following tribal custom in judicial matters. This happened about 1870.

The chief of one of our Duphla villages sought as a wife for his son the daughter of a neighbouring chief. The proposals were accepted, and to close the transaction presents were made in Duphla fashion to the lady's relatives. Probably some wealthier suitor appeared, for very shortly afterwards the intending bridegroom was told that his alliance was not desired. To this he might have become reconciled; but to the insult was superadded material injury—his presents were not returned. He was mulcted not only of his first betrothed, but of the means of procuring a second. He laid his wrongs before the deputy commissioner of Durrung, and was by that officer referred 'to the civil court'. The fatuity of thus treating the grievances of a Duphla savage will be evident to most minds, and drew forth eventually strong censure from Government. The deputy commissioner should, of course, have dealt with the case in his political capacity, summoning a Duphla panchayat and dispensing equal justice in a simple way.

The injured man failing to get redress in the plains (for to him 'the civil court' was a meaningless phrase), betook himself to the hills.

[2] Verrier Elwin, *A Philosophy for NEFA* (Shillong, 1960), pp. 171–4.

[3] Mackenzie, *History of the relations of Government with the Hill Tribes of the North-East Frontier of Bengal* (Calcutta, 1884), p. 29.

His brethren there took a more practical view of the case, descended one night with swift primitive retribution on the village of the dishonest marriage-mongers, and carried off as hostages all on whom they could lay hands. The mere fact of the raid was at first all that the Government came to know. The allowances of all supposed to be concerned in it were stopped, and a reward was offered for the capture of the ringleader.

The Duphlas in the course of a few months settled their private quarrel: the marriage presents were returned, and the hostages restored. But when they had so settled their feud, they were astonished to find that Government, or its local representatives, were still dissatisfied and not disposed to overlook the way in which the affair had been conducted. After waiting a time they threatened that, if the allowances were not restored, they would raid upon the plains. A foolish foray made by the deputy commissioner into the hills in search of the proclaimed chief still further irritated them, and at one time the political prospects were reported so doubtful that fresh stockades were established and the police guards increased.

Eventually, however, amicable relations were restored. The Duphlas were not apparently at that time prepared to violate the peace they had so long to their own advantage preserved; and though the ringleader in the raid escaped capture and punishment, the tribe as a whole gave no further trouble. Instructions were issued by Government which, it was hoped, would for the future lessen the chances of the occurrence of such raids.

16

When the World was Young (1961)

THE SUN AND MOON

For our next story we will go right across India to the great mountains of the north-east frontier. The Sun and Moon are regarded as deities by many of the hill people and, rather curiously, the Sun is often supposed to be feminine and the Moon is her husband, as in the following story told by the Minyoungs living on the left bank of the River Siang.

Earth is woman, Sky is man. They married, and when they came together, spirits, men and animals met in council to consider how they could save themselves from being crushed between them. Sedi-Diyor, one of the greatest of the spirits, caught hold of Sky and beat him so that he fled far up into the heavens leaving Earth behind. As he went away, Earth gave birth to two daughters. But she was so sad at losing her husband that she could not bear to look at them, and Sedi-Diyor had to find a woman to nurse them.

When the little girls were old enough to walk, light began to shine from them, and day by day the light grew brighter. After a while the nurse died and Sedi-Diyor buried her in the ground. The children wept for her as for their mother: they wept so much that they died, and the light they gave died with them.

Now it was dark again, and spirits, men and animals were afraid. The spirits thought that the nurse must have stolen something from the children and that it was this that had made them weep so much. So they dug up her body to see what it was. They found that it had rotted away, all except the eyes. They saw the eyes great and shining in the darkness, and their own reflection was mirrored in them, which made them think the dead children were living there. They took them to a stream and washed them in the water for five days and five nights, and made them shine more brightly. But they could not remove the images looking back at them from the eyes.

The spirits sent for a carpenter and he cut the eyes open with great care and removed the reflections, which turned into living children. They called one girl Sedi-Irkong-Bomong and the other Sedi-Irkong-Bong, and kept them very carefully inside their house.

But one day, when they were grown up, the elder girl, Bomong, dressed herself in gaily-coloured clothes and many ornaments, and went out in her beauty to wander through the world. As she came out of the house, there was light all round her, and it was day. She went across the hills and did not return.

After a long time, her sister Bong went to look for her, tracing the path by her fotsteps. But wherever she went, she shone so brightly that she caused the rocks to break, the trees to wither and men to faint in the heat.

Spirits, men and animals held yet another council. They were afraid to do such a thing and argued about it for a long time, but at last Frog went to sit by the path and waited bow in hand for the girl to come. When Bong came shining and lovely he shot her with an arrow in each side and she died. Then it was not so hot, the light was not so dazzling. The trees revived and men went again about their work.

But the girl's body lay where it had fallen. Then Rat came scampering along and found her: he dragged her corpse to Bomong on his back. On the way, he fell over and ever since the rat's legs have been crooked. But he got up and took the body to a river where Bomong was due to pass. When she saw her sister she wept for sorrow and fear that she herself would be killed. She took a path that no one knew and sat down, placing a big stone on her head. With the shadow of the stone the world became dark.

At this, spirits, men and animals were afraid and they went to search for light. For a long time they found nothing. Then they caught Rat, Wild Bird and Cock and sent them to find the missing girl.

Rat and Wild Bird went about their own business, but Cock searched patiently until at last he found Bomong and begged her to come back. 'No,' she said, 'they killed my sister and they'll kill me. Tell them that I will only come if they make my sister alive.' Cock returned and told the others what the girl had said. They found a carpenter who fashioned Bong's body, making it small, so that it would shine gently. He put life into it and when Bomong heard that her sister was alive again, she threw the stone down from her head and stood up. The day returned and as the light blazed out, Cock cried '*Kokoko-kokoko*'; Wild Bird sang '*Pengo-pengo*'; Rat squeaked '*Taktak-taktak*'. For they were glad at the light and heat.

The Brave Children

And finally here is a story about the strange, exciting days at the beginning of the world, when gods and men, animals and ogres lived and talked together. It is told by the Akas, who live in the hills to the west of the North-East Frontier Agency.

Long ago there was a man called Awa. His body was like a bear's, covered with thick hair, yet in spite of this he managed to marry Jusam, the Sun's beautiful daughter. At the wedding the Sun gave her a hen's feather and some pig's bristles. Awa took his bride home and in due time she gave birth to twins, a boy and a girl. They called the boy Sibji-Sao and the girl Sibjim-Sam.

When the children grew up a little, they both fell ill. The father sent for the priest who said that if Awa sacrificed a fowl and a pig the children would recover, but he insisted that the fowl and the pig must be house animals and not caught in the jungle.

Unfortunately Awa had no pigs or fowls in the house and did not know where to get any. When his wife saw him looking so distracted she asked him what was the matter and he told her what the priest had said. Jusam replied, 'Don't worry. Make a bamboo cage and a trough.'

Awa accordingly made a bamboo cage and put a wooden trough beside it. When everything was ready, Jusam sat down in front of the cage and, taking one of the feathers she had from her father's house, blew on it and a cock and hen immediately appeared inside the cage. Then she sat in front of the trough and, taking some of the bristles that she had from her father's house, blew on them, and a pig and a sow immediately appeared before the trough.

At once the pigs and the fowls began to weep. Jusam tried to console them by offering them milk from her own breast, but they would not take it and she said, 'Since you won't drink my milk, what are you crying about?'

The pigs and fowls replied, 'Because we're very hungry.'

Jusam said, 'I've got nothing else to give you; that's why I offered you my own milk.'

The fowls and pigs said, 'No, whatever we do, we're not going to drink your milk, for then you will never want to kill us—and we have been made to be killed.'

Jusam said, 'Well, that's all I've got to give you; if you don't want to have it, eat anything you can find.'

Soon afterwards the hen laid her eggs and hatched out chickens, and the sow had a litter. Awa took a chicken and a pig and sacrificed them for his children, who soon were well again.

In this way Awa and his wife got pigs and fowls in their house, but they had no seed. So Jusam said to her husband, 'Go to my father's house, for he has a great store of grain, and if you ask him nicely he will give you some of it.'

Awa replied, 'But I don't know the way to your father's house.'

Jusam, therefore, went with him part of the way as his guide. Then she said, 'Now you can follow the path, but presently you will come to a point where it divides in two. Be sure you take the right-hand path and not the left. If you go to the left, you will find yourself in all sorts of trouble.'

Jusam then returned home and Awa went on his way.

Presently Awa came to the point where the path divided in two and, remembering what his wife had said, went to the right, but there were so many thorns and pitfalls that he thought that she must have made a mistake, and turned back and went to the left.

He walked a long way until at last he came to a cave where a demon, black, with only one eye, one arm and one breast, was sitting beside a great fire. When the demon saw him, she threw a burning bit of wood at him and turned him into a dog.

Poor Awa slunk back to his house but did not dare go in; he just lay down in front of the door, placing his front paws together on the threshold. Presently the two children Sibji-Sao and Sibjim-Sam came out; they saw him lying there, and ran back to their mother and said, 'There is an extraordinary creature sitting at the door.'

Their mother came out hurriedly and, when she saw the dog, realized at once that it was her foolish husband who had taken the wrong path, and told her children, 'this is your father.'

But they replied, 'How can this be our father who is a great big man?'

Jusam said, 'If you don't believe me, spit on your hands and offer them to this creature. If he licks them, it will mean he is your father; if he doesn't, then he is something else.'

So the children spat on their hands and held them out to the dog who immediately licked them and Jusam said, 'There, don't you see? He really is your father.'

The children said, 'Yes, you are right, he is our father.'

Jusam explained things to them saying, 'What happened was that your father was going to my father's house to get seed but he took the wrong path and has been turned into a dog. Now how I am to feed you both I really do not know. The only thing for me to do is to go myself to my father. I'll send you some seed and you'll be able to make fields and cultivate them and in that way get some food to eat.' But the children began to cry and would not let their mother go and she had to wait till evening. After supper she put the children to sleep by the fire and then went secretly to her father.

When Jusam left the house, the evil spirits of the forest, seeing that the two children were alone, gathered round to devour them. But when the dog saw them coming he barked loudly and drove them away. In the morning when the children found their mother gone, they cried and said to each other, 'Come along, let's follow mother wherever she has gone.' The dog went ahead to guide them and the children followed him. He went as far as he knew the way, and then stood still. The children sat down to rest and the dog thought to himself, 'Let them sleep for a bit, while I go and try to find the right path.'

When the evil spirits of the forest saw the children alone, they gathered round to devour them and the children woke up and ran for their lives.

As they were running along they met a bear who asked them, 'What's the matter? Why are you running so fast?' They replied that the evil spirits of the forest were chasing them. The bear said, 'Don't be so frightened. I will save you.' He took them on his back and climbed up a high tree and, making them sit on a branch at the top, came down and scraped off the bark so that the spirits could not climb up. Having done this, the bear went away.

After the bear had gone, the evil spirits of the forest came to the tree and tried to climb up, but the trunk was too smooth for them. So they began to cut it down with their teeth.

When they saw what was happening, the children said to the tree, 'When you fall, fall towards the open country.'

But the spirits of the forest cried, 'Fall towards the mountains.'

At last when the tree did fall, it came down in the direction of the open country. It did this out of mercy for the children, for the evil spirits could not go towards the open country.

The children were safe for the moment but they were very lonely and said to one another, 'Somehow or other we must find our mother.' As they were wondering what to do, a vulture flew down and asked them what the matter was.

When they told him, he said, 'It is my duty to search every day for dead bodies and take their blood to the house of the Sun.'

The children said, 'But that's just where we want to go; our mother is the daughter of the Sun, so when you go take us with you.'

The vulture replied, 'You are too heavy for me to lift both of you at the same time. I can only take one of you.'

So he took Sibjim-Sam on his back and flew to the house of the Sun. When Jusam saw her daughter, she was very pleased and gave her a big basket of seed. She tied a rope to her hair and let her down to the earth, right in front of the house. When the girl reached home, she cooked some of the seed and made it into beer, and then sat outside watching the road until her brother should return.

Sibji-Sao remained standing where he was, for he did not know where to go, for a long time. But as he was wondering what he could do, his father who had been searching everywhere for the children found him. When he saw Sibji-Sao he jumped on him, licking his face, barking and wagging his tail and then led him back home. When they reached the house Sibjim-Sam made supper for them and gave them lots of beer, for they were all very happy at meeting again.

17

Poems (1955)

The Tribal Poet to His Love

O love, who met me by the well,
With water in your wind-tossed hair,
Which scattered in the evening light
Bright drops upon your shoulders bare,
Come to the shade of yonder trees,
Where fireflies wanton in the breeze.

Those fairy lights are all we have,
And the grave stars that watch above.
The village has long gone to rest,
And you and I alone can rove
Within our haunted wonderland
Like happy children hand in hand.

The cock has crowed, the cattle stir,
And now our enemy the dawn
In ambush on the distant hills
Will bring me to a day forlorn.
But ever in my heart I'll bear
A memory of wind-tossed hair.

The Drummer Dances with His Love

(AFTER A PARDHAN SONG)

Why will she not, lost in her song,
Join her dark eyes to mine?
I beat my drum enchantingly
As the dance moves in line.

She comes towards me in the dance
All delicate and fair.
I leap before her and my eyes
Are tangled in her hair.

I press my drum against her breasts,
I swing and leap and press,
But she will never meet my eyes,
Nor any love confess.

The thunder of the drums is harsh
As crows upon the tree,
Or croaking frogs before the rain
Unless she looks at me.

Why will she not, so lost in song,
Join her dark eyes to mine?
For I am the song she's singing,
The dance that moves in line.

Pity

O Pity, walk among our fields,
And touch the drooping ears of corn.
See how the scanty harvest yields
Its pittance from the tortured furrow,
And peasants fear to face the dawn.

And mingle, Pity, with the throng
That crowds the workshop and the mine,
Or in the jail where human wrong
Is punished with a world of sorrow,
Or where the broken-hearted pine.

And, Pity, come to visit homes
In villages remote, unblest,
Where death's sad step so quickly comes.
Regard that child with fever broken,
That mother with a cancered breast.

But first, make man's own spirit wise.
For only by the human hand,
And only through our human eyes,
Can Pity heal our desolation,
And spread compassion through the land.

To Any Young Child

Little drum in the dance of the years—
    They beat lightly as yet.
Will the sound be of laughter or tears
    When the pattern is set?

O tender young leaf of my tree,
    The dawn is here still.
But how will the green shadow be
    When the sun's on the hill?

Bright drop in the delicate stream
    That runs over the lea,
Will life be a cloud or a dream
    When you come to the sea?

18

Motley (1954)

Poets' Pets

The love of animals is almost universal in human beings, though perhaps a little more universal in some than in others. Authors, notoriously fond of collaring the conversation for themselves, have always liked to keep pets (in which they have sometimes been more successful than in keeping their wives) largely, I think, because the pets cannot answer back. 'Animals,' says George Eliot, 'are such agreeable friends—they ask no questions, they pass no criticisms,' and Walt Whitman in a famous passage declares that he could turn and live with animals, among whose many virtues he places first the fact that they cannot talk. They do not sweat and whine about their condition; they do not weep for their sins; they do not make one sick discussing their duty to God. They leave all that, and how rightly, to the poet.

Something of this kind was clearly in the mind of Samuel Butler's doctor in *The Way of all Flesh*.

> I have found [observed this sagacious physician] the Zoological Gardens of service to many of my patients. I should prescribe for Mr Pontifex a course of the larger mammals. Don't let him think he is taking them medicinally, but let him go to their house twice a week for a fortnight, and stay with the hippopotamus, the rhinoceros, and the elephants, till they begin to bore him. I find these beasts do my patients more good than any others. . . . With the elephants and the pig tribe generally he should mix just now as freely as possible.

And Butler knew a man who disliked parrots because they were too intelligent.

The most common pets are, of course, cats and dogs. There

have been many famous literary cats. There was Dr Johnson's cat Hodge, whom he treated with such great indulgence. 'He himself used to go out and buy him oysters, lest the servants having that trouble should take a dislike to the poor creature.' Boswell, however, had an antipathy to cats, and suffered a good deal from the presence of Hodge, when Johnson, smiling and half-whistling, rubbed down its back and pulled it by the tail.

Montaigne, we are told, used to relax with his cat. Isaak Walton and his cat would entertain each other with 'mutual apish tricks', such as playing with a garter. Gray wrote an ode to a favourite cat, the pensive Selima who was drowned in a tub of goldfishes. Keats writes of 'Hazlitt playing with Miss Edgeworth's cat'. Lear's cat, Old Foss, who lived to the respectable age of seventeen, is familiar to all lovers of the Books of Nonsense. How far Don Marquis's scandalous mehitabel was drawn from life I would not like to guess. T. S. Eliot wrote a whole book—*Old Possum's Book of Practical Cats*—in honour of these amiable creatures.

The Reynolds family, at whose house Keats was a frequent visitor, had an elderly cat on whom the poet wrote an excellent sonnet:

> How many mice and rats hast in thy days
> Destroy'd?—How many tit-bits stolen? Gaze
> With those bright languid segments green, and prick
> Those velvet ears—but pr'ythee do not stick
> Thy latent talons in me—and upraise
> Thy gentle mew—and tell me all thy frays
> Of fish and mice, and rats and tender chick.

But the best poem ever written to a cat is, in my opinion, Christopher Smart's ode to his cat Jeoffrey, that mixture of 'gravity and waggery', who could 'spraggle upon waggle at the word of command', so clean in the use of his fore-paws, so excellent an instrument for the children to learn benevolence upon.

Other writers have preferred dogs, who bark and frolic in and out of eighteenth century letters. Mrs Thrale had sixteen of them about the house; Horace Walpole had his Tonton, Beau Brummel his Vick, Campbell his Tray who saluted the smiling guests at his house. There is the famous story of Napoleon, Josephine and her dog Fortune, recently recalled by Mr T. H.

White. On their wedding night, the dog would not leave them.

'I had,' wrote Napoleon, 'to choose between sleeping beside the beast or not sleeping with my wife. A terrible dilemma, but I had to take it or leave it. I resigned myself. The dog was less accommodating. I have the marks on my leg to shew what he thought about the matter.'

John Gay wrote a pleasant elegy on a lap-dog:

He's dead. Oh! lay him gently in the ground!
And may his tomb be by this verse renowned;
Here Shock, the pride of all his kind is laid,
Who fawned like man, but ne'er like man betrayed.

The fidelity of the dog has constantly been celebrated. Crabbe wrote that 'a dog, though a flatterer, is still a friend', Byron considered the dog to be 'in life the firmest friend', the 'first to welcome, foremost to defend'. Pope was devoted to his Great Dane, Bounce, on whose grave he thought of putting 'O rare Bounce' but decided against it as possibly disrespectful to the memory of Ben Jonson. He once wrote that 'history was more full of the fidelity of dogs than of friends'. He presented a dog to the Prince of Wales and had the following couplet engraved on his collar:

I am His Highness' dog at Kew;
Pray tell me, Sir, whose dog are you?

And there is a famous French saying, which has been attributed to many people, among them Lamartine and Madame de Sévigné, to the effect that the more you see of men the more you admire dogs.

W. S. Landor was very fond of dogs, indeed of all animals, and Sydney Colvin has pointed out

the infinite affection and mutual confidence which subsisted between him and his pets of the dumb creation, both dogs and others, with whom the serenity of his relations used to remain perfectly undisturbed throughout the most explosive demonstrations against the delinquents of his own species.

In his villa at Fiesole he had a large dog called Parigi, a cat Cincirille, a marten and a leveret. Later he got a yellow Pomeranian, whom he called Pomero, and who was the source of much consolation. They were always together, and when Landor uttered one of his mighty laughs, Pomero too would leap about barking. Landor used to talk to the dog in English and Italian, and regarded him as a model of sagacity. He did the same with another dog, Giallo, the companion of his later years, whom he used to quote as a critic. He wrote many verses to Giallo, and when death seemed not very far away he wrote:

Giallo! I shall not see thee dead,
Nor raise a stone above thy head,
For I shall go some years before,
Where thou wilt leap at me no more,
Nor bark, as now, to make me mind,
Asking me, am I deaf or blind;
No, Giallo, but I shall be soon,
And thou wilt scratch my turf and moan.

Mrs Browning had a dog named Flush, who had been given her by Miss Mitford. He was the companion of her sick-room and accompanied her to church for her secret marriage and shared the excitement of the elopement. The poetess addressed to him a long poem, calling him loving friend, gentle fellow-creature, pretty sportive friend, for unlike other dogs who have a grand time in the open air,

Of *thee* it shall be said,
This dog watched beside a bed
Day and night unweary,—
Watched within a curtained room,
Where no sunbeam brake the gloom,
Round the sick and dreary.

The true Pan, she says in another poem to Flush, leads us by low creatures to the heights of love.

Sydney Smith did not share these exalted views. 'I don't like dogs,' he once said. 'I always expect them to go mad. A lady once asked me for a motto for her dog Spot. I proposed "Out damned Spot", but strange to say she did not think it sentimental enough.'

Other authors have been more original. Byron, who had a tame bear at Cambridge which he said he was training for a Fellowship, later developed a regular zoo. It started in this way. Every year he resolved to have a roast goose for Michaelmas. He would buy one well ahead, but by the time he had been fattening it for a month, he would be so fond of it that to eat it was out of the question. At last he had four of the over-fed creatures waddling about the houses. Shelley says that Byron at one time had ten horses, eight enormous dogs, three monkeys, five cats, an eagle, a crow, and a falcon, 'and all of them, except the horses, walk about the house, which every now and then resounds with their unarbitrated quarrels as if they were the master of it'. One day he met on the grand staircase five peacocks, two guinea hens, and an Egyptian crane. 'I wonder,' he said, 'what all these animals were before they were changed into these shapes.'

The poet Herrick had a lamb, a dog, a goose, and a pig. He taught the pig to drink beer out of a tankard. Sir Thomas Browne and his family had a passion for miscellaneous animals; they had, among others, many birds, an ostrich and a hedgehog. Gilbert White dug a tortoise out of his 'winter dormitory', and grew very fond of the 'poor embarrassed reptile', so closely imprisoned in his suit of ponderous armour that he had 'no disposition for enterprise'. Saint Évremond, in his great old age an epicure and sloven, was always feeding his ducks, and the fowls that he kept in his chamber. According to Pope,

he had a great variety of these, and other sorts of animals, all over his house. He used always to say that when we grow old and our own spirits decay, it re-animates one to have a number of living creatures about and be much with them.

Cowper was famous for his leverets or hares, but he also kept birds, among them pigeons, linnets, a magpie, a jay, a starling, and any number of robins, goldfinches and canaries who were some consolation to him amid 'the jarrings of life that made his skull feel like a broken eggshell'. The three best known of the leverets were named Puss, Tiney and Bess; two of them lived for over ten years; to 'old Tiney, surliest of his kind', he addressed the often-quoted *Epitaph on a Hare*.

A Turkey carpet was his lawn,
Whereon he loved to bound,
To skip and gambol like a fawn,
And swing his rump around . . .
I kept him for his humour's sake,
For he would oft beguile
My heart of thoughts that made it ache,
And force me to a smile.

Wordsworth kept goldfish, which he liked for several reasons.

They were 'mute companions', they were not subject to the tyranny of sense—'Cold though your nature be', he tells them, 'tis pure;' they had no sullen humours; and they were very pretty. He kept them first in a vase, but later transferred them to a pool in the pleasure-ground of Rydal Mount. This incident gave rise to a rather heavy poem, addressed to a female friend who shortly afterwards went out to Bombay where she soon succumbed to cholera, which well illustrates the moral and political value of even such humble pets as fish. The transfer from their 'bauble prison' to the larger and more hospitable elfin pool reminds the poet of the blessings of civil liberty and the right of mankind to live under laws which it itself has made. 'No sea', exclaims Wordsworth, as he gazes into the placid pool,

> Swells like the bosom of a man set free;
> A wilderness is rich with liberty.
> Roll on, ye spouting whales, who die or keep
> Your independence in the fathomless deep!
> Spread, tiny nautilus, the living sail.

And then, abandoning his oceanic metaphors, he retreats to the shore in these remarkable lines:

> The beetle loves his unpretending track,
> The snail the house he carries on his back;
> The far-fetched worm with pleasure would disown
> The bed we give him, though of softest down;
> A noble instinct.

Whether Browning derived any moral benefit from his animals is doubtful, but both he and Rossetti probably gained some of their power over the grotesque from a study of the queer creatures with which they filled their gardens. Even as a child, Browning had kept efts and frogs, monkeys, a hedgehog, an eagle, and two large snakes. When he was old, he had in his garden at Warwick Crescent a pair of geese, an owl, toads and lizards, and he seems to have had a way with them, for they were all great friends.

Mr Humphrey Hare, in his life of Swinburne, has given an entertaining account of Rossetti's menagerie.

There were blue rabbits, dormice, hedgehogs, white mice, squirrels, chameleons, salamanders, an opossum, wombats, an armadillo, a racoon, a jackass, parrots, peacocks, a raven, owls and a Brahmini bull. This last he bought because it had eyes like his friend Janey Morris, but it committed the solecism of chasing its master round the garden. Once acquired, the animals were left very much to their own devices. Indeed the problem of preventing their eating each other was one that was never satisfactorily solved. They had a tendency, too, to disappear. A missing armadillo, much to the chagrin of the cook, returned through the floor of a neighbour's kitchen; while a much sought-for opossum was found dead in a cigar-box. A lion, which Rossetti coveted, was only not acquired by reason of the difficulty of installing suitable heating arrangements, and he often talked of purchasing an elephant, which might be trained to clean the windows.

Add to this, says Mr Hare, Swinburne's 'engaging habit' of wandering about the house stark naked, and we can see that here was the epitome of all that we mean when we talk about the poetic temperament.

[illegible] whose [illegible] [illegible] [illegible] [illegible] [illegible] [illegible] [illegible] [illegible] [illegible] [illegible] [illegible] [illegible] [illegible] [illegible] [illegible] [illegible] [illegible] [illegible] [illegible] the [illegible] [illegible] [illegible] [illegible] [illegible] [illegible] the animals [illegible]

Add to this [illegible] [illegible] [illegible] [illegible] [illegible] [illegible] wonderful [illegible] about the [illegible] [illegible] naked [illegible] [illegible] [illegible] [illegible] [illegible] [illegible] [illegible] [illegible] [illegible] [illegible] [illegible] [illegible]

Bibliography

1924 *The Praise of His Glory* (poems: privately printed).

1925 *Onward Bound* (Oxford University Church Union).

1926 *Desiderium* (London: The Challenge).

1929 *Studies in the Gospels* (Madras: Inter-Religious Student Fellowship).

N.D. *Christ and Satyagraha* (Bombay: Popular Book Depot, reprinted 1930).

1930a *Richard Rolle: A Christian Sannyasi* (Madras: Christian Literature Society).

1930b *Christian Dhyana: Or Prayer of Living Regard* (London: Society for Promoting Christian Knowledge).

1931 *The Dawn of Indian Freedom*, in collaboration with J.C. Winslow (London: Allen & Unwin).

1932a *Mahatma Gandhi: An Essay* by Verrier Elwin, in *Sketches in Pen, Pencil and Brush* by Kanu Desai (London: Golden Vista Press).

1932b *Truth About India: Can We Get It?* (London: Allen & Unwin).

1932c *Religious and Cultural Aspects of Khadi* (Madras: M.R. Seshan).

1933a *St Francis of Assisi* (Madras: Christian Literature Society).

1933b *Supremacy of the Spiritual* (Madras: Christian Literature Society).

1933c *Spiritual Reading* (Madras: Christian Literature Society).

1933d 'Mahatma Gandhi's Philosophy of Truth', *Modern Review*, August, September, October.

1934 'A Mission of Service in the Wilds: The Gond Seva Mandal,' *Hindustan Times*, 14 May.

1935 *Songs of the Forest: The Folk Poetry of the Gonds*, in collaboration with Shamrao Hivale (London: Allen & Unwin).

1936a *Leaves from the Jungle* (London: John Murray; second edition, Bombay: Oxford University Press, 1958).

1936b *Birth and Death* (poems: privately printed in England).

1937a *Phulmat of the Hills: A Tale of the Gonds* (London: John Murray).

1937b 'Myths and Dreams of the Baigas of Central India,' *Man,* vol. 37, no. 7, p. 13.

1938 *A Cloud That's Dragonish* (London: John Murray).

1939 *The Baiga* (London: John Murray).

1941a 'Western Styles and Contrasting Eastern Jungle Fashions,' *The Illustrated Weekly of India*, 12 October.

1941b 'Dreams of Indian Aboriginal Lepers', *Man*, vol. 41, no. 21, pp. 55–60.

N.D. *Loss of Nerve,* pamphlet of 56 pages printed at Wagle Press, Bombay.

1942a *The Agaria* (Bombay: Oxford University Press).

1942b 'The Sago Palm in Bastar State', *Journal of the Bombay Branch of the Royal Asiatic Society*, vol. 18.

1942c 'Primitive Folk of the Hills', *Asia*, vol. 42.

1942d 'The Hobby Horse and the Ecstatic Dances', *Folklore*, Calcutta, vol. 53.

1942e 'Folk Poems: 20 Pardhan Love Songs', *Man in India*, vol. 22, no. 3, in collaboration with Shamrao Hivale.

1942f 'Use of Iron in Medicine', *Hindustan Times Annual*.

1942g 'Loss of Nerve', *Sunday Statesman*, 5 April.

1942h 'Jungle Medicines—Psychoanalysis. Autosuggestion, and Magic All Help!', *The Illustrated Weekly of India*, 12 April.

1942i 'As I See It', *The Illustrated Weekly of India*, 19 July.

1942j 'What the Well-dressed Jungle Man Wears', *The Illustrated Weekly of India*, 2 August.

1942k 'Maria-Gond Fashions from the Bastar State', *The Illustrated Weekly of India*, 2 August.

1942l 'A pair of drums, with wooden figures, from Bastar State, India', *Man*, vol. 42, no. 58, p. 97.

1942m 'A Note on The Faithful Dog as Security for a Debt', *Journal of the American Oriental Society*, vol. 62, p. 339.

1942n 'The Duration of Marriage among the Aboriginals of the Maikal Hills', *Man in India*, vol. 22, no. 1.

1942o 'Ceremonial Cross-dressing among the Murias of

Bastar State', *Man in India*, vol. 22, nos. 2 and 3.

1942p 'Suicide among the Aboriginals of Bastar', *Man in India*, vol. 22, nos. 2 and 3.

1943a 'The Baiga Land', *The Modern Review*, vol. 4, no. 4, Whole No. 328.

1943b *Maria Murder and Suicide* (Bombay: Oxford University Press; second edition, 1950).

1943c *The Aboriginals* (Oxford Pamphlets on Indian Affairs, No. 14; second edition, 1944, Bombay: Oxford University Press).

1943d Epilogue to Folk-Song Number of *Man in India*, vol. 23, no. 1.

1943e 'Ten Gond Poems', *Man in India*, vol. 23, no. 1, in collaboration with Shamrao Hivale.

1943f 'Twelve Pardhan Dadaria', *Man in India*, vol. 23, no. 1, in collaboration with Shamrao Hivale.

1943g 'Five Bhattra Songs', *Man in India*, vol. 23, no. 1.

1943h 'Ten Baiga Poems', *Man in India*, vol. 23, no. 1.

1943i 'The Attitude of Indian Aboriginals towards Sexual Impotence', *Man in India*, vol. 23, no. 2.

1943j 'An Anthology of Marriage Sermons', in collaboration with W.G. Archer, W.V. Grigson and T.H. Lewin, *Man in India*, vol. 23, no. 2.

1943k 'One Hundred Maria Murders', *Man in India*, vol. 23, no. 3.

1943l 'Riddles of the Muria, Agaria, Gond (with Shamrao Hivale) and Juang in "An Indian Riddle Book"', *Man in India*, vol. 23, no. 4.

1943m 'Extracts from a Riddle Note-book', *Man in India*, vol. 23, no. 4, in collaboration with W.G. Archer.

1943n 'Folklore of the Bastar Clan-Gods', *Man*, vol. 43, no. 83.

N.D. *Brief Survey of the Aboriginal Tribes of Ganjam and Koraput* (Orissa Government Press).

1944a *Folk-Songs of the Maikal Hills*, in collaboration with Shamrao Hivale (Bombay: Oxford University Press).

1944b *Folk-Tales of Mahakoshal* (Bombay: Oxford University Press).

1944c 'Notes on a Kondh Tour', *Man in India*, vol. 24, no. 1.

1944d 'Folk-Songs of Chhattisgarh', *Man in India,* vol. 24, no. 1.

1944e 'A Honey Festival', *Man in India*, vol. 24, no. 2.

1944f 'The Legend of Rasalu Kuar', *Man in India*, vol. 24, no. 4.

1944g 'Mahadev', in *Gandhiji: His Life and Work*, ed. D.T. Tendulkar, M. Chalapathi Rau, Mridula Sarabhai and Vithalbhai K. Jhaveri (Bombay: Karnatak Publishing House).

1945a 'Two Bondo Murderers', *Man in India*, vol. 25, no. 1.

1945b 'Funerary Customs in Bastar State', *Man in India*, vol. 25, no. 2.

1945c 'Two Folk-Tales about Witches', *Man in India*, vol. 25, no. 3.

1945d 'Saora Fituris', [*sic*] *Man in India*, vol. 25, no. 4.

1946 *Folk-Songs of Chhattisgarh* (Bombay: Oxford University Press).

1947 *The Muria and their Ghotul* (Bombay: Oxford University Press).

1948a 'The Anthropological Survey of India: Part I. History and Recent Developments', *Man*, vol. 48.

1948b 'The Anthropological Survey of India: Part II. The Five Year Plan', *Man*, vol. 48.

1948c 'Riddles of the Indian Countryside', *The Indian Annual*.

1948d 'Notes on the Juang', *Man in India*, vol. 28, nos. 1 and 2.

1949a *Myths of Middle India* (Bombay: Oxford University Press).

1949b 'Dancers of the Golden Age', *Geographical Magazine*, vol. 22, November.

1950a 'The Aboriginals Under the Republic', *The Statesman*, 19 March.

1950b 'Tribal Religion and Magic in Middle India', *Geographical Magazine*, vol. 23, May.

1950c 'Tribal Life in Middle India', *Geographical Magazine*, vol. 22, February.

1950d 'The Baigas of Madhya Pradesh', *Illustrated Weekly of India*, 9 July.

1950e 'The Marias', *The Illustrated Weekly of India*, 16 July.

1950f 'The Saoras', *The Illustrated Weekly of India*, 23 July.
1950g 'The Gadabas', *The Illustrated Weekly of India*, 30 July.
1950h 'The Juangs', *The Illustrated Weekly of India*, 6 August.
1950i 'The Kuttia Konds', *The Illustrated Weekly of India*. 13 August.
1950j *Bondo Highlander* (Bombay: Oxford University Press).
1951a *The Tribal Art of Middle India* (Bombay: Oxford University Press).
1951b 'India to Africa', *The Times of India Annual*.
1951c 'Indian Anthropologist's Fine Work', *The Illustrated Weekly of India*, 29 November.
1952a 'The Acholi Dance', *The Illustrated Weekly of India*, 9 March.
1952b 'The Temples of Thailand', *The Statesman*, 23 March.
1952c 'The Cause of an Eclipse', *Tribal Folklore*, 18 May.
1952d 'Lungbara Market', *The Illustrated Weekly of India*, 25 May.
1952e 'The Rainbow', *Tribal Folklore*, 25 May.
1952f 'Thunder and Lightning', *Tribal Folklore*, 1 June.
1952g 'The Discovery of Alcohol', *Tribal Folklore*, 8 June.
1952h 'The Starved Man', *Tribal Folklore*, 13 June.
1952i 'The Bird Wisdom', *Tribal Folklore*, 15 June.
1952j 'Tree Tales', *Tribal Folklore*, 22 June.
1952k 'Comic Strips of Rural India: The Krishan Lila', *The Illustrated Weekly of India*, 15 June.
1952l 'Comic Strips of Rural India II: The Santal Legends', *The Illustrated Weekly of India*, 22 June.
1952m 'Comic Strips of Rural India III: The Punishment of Hell', *The Illustrated Weekly of India*, 29 June.
1952n 'Tribals through Ages of History', *The Bombay Chronicle Weekly*, 22 June.
1952o 'In Quest of Tribal Art', *The Statesman*, 15 August.
1952p 'Puritanism', *Thought*, 16 August.
1952q 'Puritanism Creeping into Tribal Life: Anthropologist's Warning against New Trends', *The Times of India*, 21 August.
1952r 'Twenty-One Years of Tribal India', *The Illustrated Weekly of India*, 21 September.

1952s 'Tribal Art Faces Extinction', *The Illustrated Weekly of India*, 14 September.

1952t 'The Land of Women', *The Statesman*, 28 September.

1952u 'Children of the Forest at Play', *The Illustrated Weekly of India*, 26 October.

1952v 'The Gond Poet to his Love', *The Illustrated Weekly of India*, 12 October.

1952w 'A Festival of Bees', *The Illustrated Weekly of India*, 7 December.

1952x 'The Saora Priestess', *Bulletin of the Department of Anthropology*, Government of India, vol. 1, no. 1.

1953a 'On Being Eaten by a Tiger', *The Illustrated Weekly of India*, 4 January.

1953b 'On Reviewing and Being Reviewed: (i) As the Author Sees It, (ii) As The Critic Sees It', *The Statesman*, 22 Febuary.

1953c 'Hell', *The Times of India*, 22 March.

1953d 'Tribal Medicine in India', *The Statesman*, 22 March.

1953e 'A Great Tribal Medicine-man', *The Statesman*, 29 March.

1953f 'Folklore of Disease: (i) The Demon of Cholera', *The Statesman*, 5 April.

1953g 'Folklore of Disease: (ii) Small-pox: The Old Mother', *The Statesman*, 12 April.

1953h 'Folklore of Disease: (iii) Leprosy: Scourge of the Sun-god', *The Statesman*, 19 April.

1953i 'Folklore of Disease: (iv) Rabies: The Inexplicable Sport of Fate', *The Statesman*, 26 April.

1953j 'Carved Totems of the Uraons', *The Illustrated Weekly of India*, 5 April.

1953k 'Going Native', *The Times of India*, 24 May.

1953l 'Spinning and Weaving in Tribal India', *The Illustrated Weekly of India*, 7 June.

1953m 'Sacred Chief's Daughter', *The Illustrated Weekly of India*, 14 March.

1953n 'On the First Sight of Leprosy Discovered in a Young Aboriginal Girl', *The Times of India*, 23 June.

1953o 'The Worst of All', *The Times of India*, 30 August.

1953p 'The Ramayana in Tribal Mythology', *The Illustrated Weekly of India*, 16 August.

1953q 'Toys of Tribal Children', *The Illustrated Weekly of India* 18 October.

1953r 'A Policy for India's Tribesmen', *The Statesman*, 3 October.

1953s 'Santal Wood-carving', *March of India*, vol. 6, no. 2.

1954a *Motley* (Calcutta: Orient Longmans).

1954b *Tribal Myths of Orissa* (Bombay: Oxford University Press).

1954c 'The Tribal Art', *The Assam Tribune*, 18 July.

1954d 'Do We Really Want to Keep Them in a Zoo—The Adivasis?', *The Statesman*, 3 October.

1955a 'The Dance in Tribal India (i)', *The Illustrated Weekly of India*, 22 May.

1955b 'The Dance in Tribal India (ii): Marriage Festival of the Marias', *The Illustrated Weekly of India*, 22 May; reprinted in *Marg*, vol. 13, no. 1 (1959–60).

1955c 'The Dance in Tribal India (iii): Sacred Ceremonies of the Konds', *The Illustrated Weekly of India*, 22 May, reprinted in *Marg*, vol 13, no. 1 (1959–60).

1955d 'The Dance in Tribal India (iv): The Animal Ballet of the Juangs', *The Illustrated Weekly of India*, 22 May; reprinted in *Marg*, vol. 13, no. 1 (1959–60).

1955e 'The Dance in Tribal India (v): Dormitory Performances of the Murias', *The Illustrated Weekly of India*, 22 May; reprinted in *Marg*, vol. 13, no. 1 (1959–60).

1955f 'The Dance in Tribal India (vi): Ritual Conduct of the Saoras', *The Illustrated Weekly of India*, 26 June; reprinted in *Marg*, vol. 13, no. 1 (1959–60).

1955g 'The Musical Instruments of Tribal India (i)', *The Illustrated Weekly of India*, 27 November.

1955h 'The Musical Instruments of Tribal India. (ii)', *The Illustrated Weekly of India*, 4 December.

1955i *28 Poems* (Bombay: India Printing Works).

1955j *The Religion of an Indian Tribe* (Bombay: Oxford University Press).

1956a 'Tribal Art', *The Assam Tribune*, 10 June.

1956b 'People of N.E.F.A. (i): A Pilgrimage to Tawang', *The Illustrated Weekly of India*, 30 September.

1956c 'People of N.E.F.A. (ii): In Subansiri', *The Illustrated Weekly of India*, 7 October.

1956d 'People of N.E.F.A. (iii): In Siang', *The Illustrated Weekly of India*, 14 October.

1956e 'People of N.E.F.A. (iv): In Lohit', *The Illustrated Weekly of India*, 21 October.

1956f 'People of N.E.F.A. (v): In Tuensang', *The Illustrated Weekly of India*, 28 October.

1956g 'People of N.E.F.A. (iv): In Tirap', *The Illustrated Weekly of India*, 4 November.

1956h *Gandhiji: Bapu of his People* (Assam Government Press), reprinted 1964.

1957a *A Philosophy for NEFA* (Director of Information, NEFA), second edition, 1959 (NEFA), reprinted 1960 (NEFA).

1957b 'The North-East Frontier Agency of India', *The West Bengal Tribal Weekly* (Tribal Welfare Supplement), 18 July.

1958a *Myths of the North-East Frontier of India* (Director of Information, NEFA).

1958b 'Tribal Art of Assam', *Akashvani*, 4 May.

1958c *India's North-East Frontier in the 19th Century* (Bombay: Oxford University Press; reprinted 1962).

1959a *The Art of the North-East Frontier of India* (Director of Information, NEFA), reprinted 1968.

1959b 'Tribal Life in Other Planets', *The Illustrated Weekly of India*, 19 July.

1959c 'Tribal Administration on Other Planets', *The Illustrated Weekly of India*, 28 July.

1959d *Maisons des Jeunes chez les Muria* (French adaptation of *The Muria and their Ghotul* by Dr Alfred Bigot, Paris: Gallimard).

1960a *The Hill People of North-East India* (London: Oxford University Press, People of the World Series).

1960b *Nagaland* (Shillong: Advisor's Secretariat).

1960c 'Beating a Dead Horse', *Seminar*, Delhi, No. 14.

1960d (ed.) *Report of the Committee on Special Multipurpose Tribal Blocks* (New Delhi: Ministry of Home Affairs).

1961a *When the World Was Young* (Delhi: National Book Trust).

1961b 'The Beauty of Tribal Assam', *Folklore*, Calcutta, vol. 2.

1962 *A Philosophy of Love: Patel Memorial Lectures* (New Delhi: Publication Division, Ministry of Information and Broadcasting).

1963a *I Costumi Sessuali dei Muria* (Italian version of *The Muria and their Ghotul*, Milano: Lerici editori).

1963b 'A New Deal for Tribal India', abridgement of the Tenth Report of the Commissioner for Scheduled Castes and Scheduled Tribes for the Years 1960–1961 (New Delhi: Ministry of Home Affairs).

1964 *The Tribal World of Verrier Elwin* (Bombay: Oxford University Press, and New York: Oxford University Press).

1965 'Fieldwork in Tribal World', *Folklore*, Calcutta, vol. 6, no. 2, November, pp. 480–1.

1966 *Democracy in NEFA* (Director of Information, NEFA).

1967a *Girijana Prapancha* (Kannada version of *The Tribal World of Verrier Elwin*, Mysore: Janapada Sahitya Academy).

1967b *Elwin Kanta Palangkudi Makkal* (Tamil version of *The Tribal World of Verrier Elwin*, Madras: Bookventure).

1968 *The Kingdom of the Young*, abridgement made by Elwin of *The Muria and their Ghotul* (Bombay: Oxford Univeristy Press).

1969 *The Nagas in the Nineteenth Century* (Bombay: Oxford University Press).

1976 *A New Book of Tribal Fiction*

Index